D0151980

Multicultural Detective Fiction

Garland Reference Library of the Humanities
Volume 2094

Multicultural Detective Fiction

Murder from the "Other" Side

Edited by
Adrienne Johnson Gosselin

Garland Publishing, Inc.
A member of the Taylor & Francis Group
New York and London
1999

Library of Congress Cataloging-in-Publication Data

Multicultural detective fiction : murder from the "other" side / edited by Adrienne Johnson Gosselin.
p. cm. — (Garland reference library of the humanities ; v. 2094)
Includes bibliographical references and index.
ISBN 0-8153-3153-3 (alk. paper)
1. Detective and mystery stories, American—History and criticism. 2. Pluralism (Social sciences) in literature. 3. Afro-Americans in literature. 4. Group identity in literature. 5. Ethnic groups in literature. 6. Lesbians in literature. 7. Gay men in literature. 8. Race in literature. I. Gosselin, Adrienne Johnson. II. Series: Garland reference library of the humanities ; vol. 2094.
PS374.D4M85 1999
813'.087209—dc21 98-40001
CIP

Cover illustration, *The Miracle Mile*, by Adrienne Johnson Gosselin.

Printed on acid-free, 250-year-life paper
Manufactured in the United States of America

to ET for being my mother (but mostly for being my friend)

Contents

Preface

> This disdainful perception of popular culture was brought home to me when I (naively) sang the praises of my favorite females sleuths to a number of colleagues and their partners, and then was taken aback when, after dutifully skimming the novels, they eyed me suspiciously and pronounced: "But, this is trash."
>
> Percy Walton

The reviewer in me would describe this anthology as the collective effort of a small but impressive group of scholars whose collective perspective addresses the genre of detective fiction in terms of the specific social, historical, and political conditions that inform the literary work. As editor, I can say that this work has had many beginnings. One could be a paper I delivered for a MELUS panel on Bakhtin at the Modern Language Association in December 1992. Another would be the special session I organized on multicultural detective fiction for the 1995 MLA. Still another is the moment of which Percy Walton speaks, since, as Walton notes, to "do" popular culture leaves one open to derision.

I have come to identify this moment of disdain as what Katherine Fishburn would call a moment of misunderstanding, a crystallization of cultural difference, moments recognized as important learning tools. It is to this moment this anthology is directed, not to promote understanding of detective fiction as a genre, but an understanding of genre in multicultural studies.

Multicultural detective fiction is the detective story in the hands of authors whose cultural communities are not those of the traditional Euro-American male hero, whose cultural experiences have been excluded from the traditional detective formula, and whose cultural aesthetic alters the formula itself. Its potential in cultural studies has generated not only continued scholarly interest, but also a need on the part of professors practicing multicultural curriculum for works which facilitate ethical discussion. To that end, the essays in this book provide a forum for academic discourse on issues of multiculturalism and include a range of contemporary critical theory familiar to academic discourse. At the same time—and this is important to multicultural studies—while the critical interrogations herein are intended primarily for scholars, it is the intention of each contributor that language be accessible to the tradition in which it speaks.

I am exceedingly grateful to the contributors to this anthology. Their encouragement and enthusiasm made possible not only what we all consider an important critical study, but, for me in particular, a most enjoyable time. I especially want to thank Susan Elizabeth Sweeney whose presence literally made the MLA panel possible, as well as Tim Libretti and Wayne Templeton, also members of the panel. I also need to thank Ricardo Teamor for Leslie Marmon Silko's *Yellow Woman and the Beauty of the Spirit;* Njeri Nuru-Holm, Vice President for Minority Affairs and Human Relations at Cleveland State University, for the much needed time; and Arlene (Amy) Elder for her humor and her wisdom and her tolerance of me in general.

Adrienne Johnson Gosselin

Contributors

Phyllis M. Betz received her Ph.D. from the University of Maryland and currently teaches at LaSalle University. Her research interests include gay and lesbian literature and nineteenth-century American writers and she has published in the *Harvard Gay and Lesbian Review.*

Adrienne Johnson Gosselin is assistant professor at Cleveland State University, where she teaches American and African American literature and creative writing. Her research interests include the Harlem renaissance, multicultural theory, and women writers of color. She has published in *Modern Language Studies* and *African American Review* and is a recipient of the Raymond Carver Award for Short Fiction. She is currently working to remount the stage adaptation of *The Conjur[e]-Man Dies*, performed by the Harlem Unit of the National Federal Theater in 1936.

John Cullen Gruesser is associate professor of English at Kean College, author of *White on Black: Contemporary Literature About Africa* and editor of *The Unruly Voice: Rediscovering Pauline Hopkins.* He is currently working on *Black on Black*, a companion volume to *White on Black* which explores twentieth-century African American literature about Africa.

Jeffrey Langham is a doctoral student in English at the University of Southern California. He is currently completing his dissertation on genre and gay male subjectivity.

Tim Libretti is assistant professor of English at Northeastern Illinois University and has published in MELUS, *Race, Gender, and Class,* and *Women's Studies Quarterly.* He has also contributed to *Reconstructing the U.S. Hispanic Literary Heritage, volume II* and the forthcoming *Other Sisterhoods: Women Writers of Color and Literary Theory.*

Patricia Linton is associate professor of English at the University of Alaska Anchorage, where she teaches contemporary literature and film, critical theory, and postcolonial literature. Her current research focuses on narrative theory and concepts of self in contemporary fiction. She has published on ethnic American fiction in a number of publications, including MELUS and *Studies in American Indian Literature*.

William R. Nash is assistant professor of American literature at Middlebury College where he teaches African American Literature. He has published articles on Charles Johnson and Gloria Naylor and is a contributor to the *Oxford Companion to African American Literature.* He is currently working on a book-length manuscript titled *To See Darkness Differently: Charles Johnson's Aesthetics, Races, and the American Philosophical Novel*

Caroline Reitz is a doctoral candidate at Brown University completing her dissertation, "The Necessary Detective: Crime, Empire, and Victorian National Identity." She is also a contributor to the *Carlyle Studies Annual* and *Feminist Literary Theory: A Dictionary* .

Laurence Roth is assistant professor of ethnic literature and Jewish studies at Susquehanna University. He has published articles on assimilation and American Jewish poets, and his poetry has appeared in *The Antioch Review* and *The Jacaranda Review*. He is currently working on a study of American Jewish detective stories.

David Schmid received his Ph.D. in modern thought from Stanford University and is an instructor in the Department of English at SUNY Buffalo. He is currently working on a book-length manuscript titled *Mad, Bad, and Dangerous to Know: Serial Murder and Contemporary American Culture.*

Stephen F. Soitos is the co-author of three mystery novels: *Salt Cat Bank, Death in the Colony,* and *The Dancer Disappears*. He is the author of *The Blues Detectives: A Study of African American Detective Fiction,* which was awarded the 1996 CHOICE Best Academic Book Award.

Michelle Pagni Stewart is a lecturer at California State University, San Bernadino, where she teaches courses in Native American literature. She has published articles on Native American literature and is the author of "Moynihan's 'Tangle of Pathology': Toni Morrison's Legacy of Motherhood," included in *Family Matters in the British and American Novel,* forthcoming from Popular Press.

Susan Elizabeth Sweeney is associate professor of English at the College of the Holy Cross and is the author of numerous articles on narratology, Nabokov, and nineteenth- and twentieth-century British and American fiction. She is the co-editor of *Anxious Power: Reading, Writing, and Ambivalence in Narrative by Women* and the forthcoming *Detecting Texts: The Metaphysical Detective Story from Poe to Postmodernism.*

Wayne Templeton is professor of English at Kwantlen University College in British Columbia. He has published extensively on D.H. Lawrence, and Lawrence's involvement with the American southwest, and is the author of *States of Estrangement: The Novels of D.H. Lawrence.*

Priscilla L. Walton is associate professor of English at Carleton University. She has published numerous articles on Henry James and is the author of *Patriarchal Desire and Victorian Discourse: A Lacanian Reading of Anth Palliser's Novels*, and of *The Disruption of the Feminine in Henry James*. She is co-author of the forthcoming *Detective Agency: Women and the Hardboiled Tradition.*

Multicultural Detective Fiction

CHAPTER ONE

Multicultural Detective Fiction: Murder with a Message

Adrienne Johnson Gosselin

In the 1971 reissue of Rudolph Fisher's *The Conjure-Man Dies* (1932), the first detective novel set in an all-black environment, Stanley Ellin claims that Fisher's treatment invests the text "with the qualities of a social document," so that the reader is "drawn through the book by its story, but emerges at last with much more than the story in mind" (Introduction). Ellin's observation is echoed by Peter Freese some twenty years later when, in his study of ethnic detective fiction, Freese claims that when the detective belongs "to a community whose history, values, and way of life differ from those of the so-called mainstream, his or her story inadvertently turns into . . . a comment on the challenges of everyday life in a 'multicultural' society" (9-10).[1] What is striking is that both statements refer to a particular type of learning available through the detective story, one which Freese identifies as "inadvertent" and Ellin characterizes as having the qualities of a social document. Of interest as well is that both critics note the role of "story" in such a learning process: while for Ellin, the reader is "drawn through the book by the story," for Freese, the figure of the detective assumes the role of cultural mediator who guides the reader through the story. Finally, as both agree, the effect of this learning process is "more than the story in mind."

Theorizing ways in which inadvertent learning occurs in multicultural detective fiction became the central idea in, first, a session on ideology and multicultural detective fiction for the 1995 Modern Language Association convention and, later, this anthology.[2] And while efforts to examine the ideology at the core of this seemingly impalpable instruction involves a trajectory into two disparate realms of theory—that of multiculturalism and that of detective fiction as genre—which, by themselves occupy separate paths, the paths do converge in a terrain characteristic of Gloria Anzaldúa's notion of "borderlands," a presence that occurs "whenever two or more cultures edge each other" (Preface). With acknowledgment to Arlene Elder, I would like to suggest that theorizing the nature of inadvertent learning in multicultural detective fiction—or even the nature of multicultural detective fiction itself—is something like "theorizing from the borderlands," but here less a matter of the erasure of borders than of "discerning the forces which generate the borders in the first place (Shohat and Stam 359).[3] As Elder, Anzaldúa, and others agree, such a process necessitates a multilingual dialogue involving a "language of borderlands," a dialogue that occurs at "junctures of culture [where] languages cross-pollinate and are revitalized" (Anzaldúa, Preface), thus opening texts to new ways of reading experiences other than our own. It is as part of this multilingual dialogue that the essays that follow are presented so that critics, educators—and, yes, just plain readers of detective fiction—can access the range of frequencies on which multicultural detective fiction sounds.

As Heta Pyrhönen points out, the development of detective fiction criticism begins in 1883 in the May 5 edition of *The Saturday Review* with a "brief assessment of a recently published work accompanied by a recognition of the genre's popularity" (4). While the turn of the century saw some discussion of the subject, it was not until the 1920s that a serious body of criticism began to emerge in what Pyrhönen sees as the "first wave" of detective fiction criticism. The first critics consisted of detective writers themselves (most notably G.K. Chesterton, Dorothy L. Sayers, and S.S. van Dine), who were later joined by detective fiction "aficionados" motivated by a need to explain the nature of the detective narrative, as well as a need to "to justify their writing and reading habits" (Pyrhönen 4). The second wave occurs from the 1960s to the mid-1970s, when structuralist critics (here most notably Tzvetan Todorov and Umberto Eco) introduced narratological analyses as a means of reading the form. However, as Pyrhönen points out, when the structuralists selected detective fiction as an example of a closed narrative system, they unwittingly opened the form to a range of readings, some of which had the effect of contradicting structuralist claims (6). Arguments against structuralist claims were initiated by (who else?) the post-structuralists, whose approaches demonstrated ways in which detective fiction's (closed) form shrouded more complex issues, including moral dimensions embedded in the literary formula. The 1980s and 1990s make up the third wave of criticism, in which the application of various academic discourses demonstrate the genre's legitimization through acceptance at the university level.

While Pyrhönen's examination is the first comprehensive study to analyze the framework within which detective fiction is situated as "literature," and while her paradigm usefully isolates two main approaches to detective fiction criticism,[4] the focus of Pyrhönen's inquiry on Anglo-American detective fiction—even with her inclusion of (white) feminist criticism—leaves one confronted with what I have come to recognize as the wall of the "not quite," or what Kipling might, if "other" wise, have labeled the "multicultural burden." One encounters the wall of the "not-quite" when presented with theoretical postures or paradigms that, while applicable in a general sense, elide issues of "difference" stemming from gender, class, culture, or race; as a result, such theories are "not quite" applicable to multicultural concerns. For example, while Pyrhönen's critical framework is applicable to essays in this collection that focus on white heterosexual and homosexual female detectives, those same principles are not quite applicable to detective fiction whose heroes are also women of color. And while Pyrhönen finds that, as a subgenre, feminist detective fiction pits a "female-centered worldview against patriarchal, capitalist ideology (111), her critique of that ideology is not quite applicable to nonmainstream or nonwhite male detectives who operate within that same patriarchal framework. Nor are the cultural codes Pyrhönen analyzes in mainstream detective fiction quite applicable to codes assumed in multicultural detective fiction, particularly by multicultural writers whose texts deliberately resist her notion of (Eurocentric) "empiriohistorical readings."

Interestingly, Pyrhönen concludes her examination with the observation that while semiotics and philosophy are a "fascinating feature of the detective narrative for academics," when the critical focus turns beyond "poetics and ratiocination, enthusiasm starts to wane" (115). Such apathy is most notable when the detective narrative is read in relation to cultural developments, even though, as Pyrhönen concedes, "learning to read from a position outside the text . . . helps [the reader] make sense of the relations of power at a given historical moment" (115). Listing a number of academic objections to criticism that approaches the genre in terms of cultural function, Pyrhönen nevertheless defends the viability of such inquiry to acknowledge that the relationship of detective fiction to culture "exhibits questions that remain as yet unexplored" (116). Her conclusions are, of course, appropriate to this anthology, for it is from such academic questions that the essays in this collection begin.

This anthology attempts to address what Bonnie TuSmith sees as a "lag time in the production and publication of viable theories in multicultural literature," a gap which discourages academics from teaching multicultural texts (Introduction 2). Each essay focuses on detective fiction shaped by multicultural, multiracial, and/or multiethnic worldviews, and each is grounded in critical theory. At the same time, it would be a misreading to interpret the overall effort as a "unity with plural names" (McDowell xiv). Some essays subject detective fiction to what TuSmith calls "Big-T" theories, academic theories based on a "monolithic 'it'" which have traditionally retained the "high ground of pure thought" and are usually practiced in terms of ironic distance ("Opening" 63);[5] others draw on interactive ethnic theories which underscore Anzaldúa's notion that "theory can be fluid, down-to-earth, and attuned to a lived experience" ("Opening" 65). As the essays in Part One demonstrate, while multicultural detective fiction can indeed mediate between the reader and the culture represented, the works should not be read as "showcase windows to exotic cultures" (*Relatives* 29). In fact, as Patricia Linton points out in her essay, "Alter-Ideology in Linda Hogan's *Mean Spirit*," while detective fiction participates in formulaic rules that accommodate a readerly competence, some texts intentionally resist this narrative expectation, operating instead on strategies designed to produce a readerly "incompetence" by denying access to readers outside the culture. Linton's discussion finds that, unlike detective narratives which echo a positivistic universe, Hogan's text make readers (uncomfortably) aware of an alternative epistemology, one which can not only not be accounted for through Western concepts of knowledge, but which renders such concepts irrelevant.

As Abdul JanMohamed and David Lloyd note, because we as multicultural critics and writers have been formed within the dominant culture's educational apparatus, we must constantly reevaluate our own language and methodologies in order to avoid reproducing the dominant ideology in our interpretations (8-9). Certainly language intersects with power, and, as Wenying Xu cautions, the language of the colonizer is "anything but a transparent lens" that enables readers to understand radically different cultures (51). While Xu's comment is addressed to Asian-Indian writers, the point is also taken by Wayne Templeton, whose essay, "Xojo· and Homicide," examines postcolonial discourse in novels by Tony Hillerman. Templeton eliminates the ironic distance often perceived in Big-T approaches to postcolonial theories by focusing on the connections between policy and everyday life on the Navajo reservation. In Hillerman, Templeton claims, homicide becomes a "postcolonial metaphor for cultural genocide" in that it is impossible for a Native American to assimilate into American society and still remain a Native American. As Templeton's analysis illustrates, crime on the reservation becomes a metaphor for hegemonic crime and its systematic erosion of cultural self-determination.

Like Sonia Saldívar-Hull's claim that "Chicanas ask different questions which in turn ask for the reconstruction of the very premises of theory" (Saldívar-Hull quoted. in "Opening" 64), Lucha Corpi's Chicana detective asks different questions of detective fiction in order to reconstruct theories about culture and society. In "Lucha Corpi and the Politics of Detective Fiction," Tim Libretti situates Corpi's interrogation in terms of capitalism and the privileging of capitalism by challenging the "truths" considered endemic to the detection formula. Libretti's examination demonstrates ways in which Corpi's two novels foreground the discursive social practices that produce the discourse of criminality. For Libretti, Corpi's detective fiction moves toward conclusions that reconstruct the formula's traditional sense of closure as her detective recognizes the need to recapture the political activism of the past and calls for political action in the present.

In their focus on gay and lesbian detective fiction, the essays in Part Two demonstrate multicultural detective fiction in terms of what Robert Shohat and Ella Stam identify as intercommunal coalitions, wherein men as well as women address issues of gender, and members of the heterosexual community speak against homophobia (346). Phyllis Betz's examination of lesbian police fiction demonstrates that, like multiethnic literature, multicultural literature demands a critical approach flexible enough to articulate what John Maitano and David Peck see as a dynamic of both assimilation and alienation (4). In "Playing the Boys' Game," Betz theorizes ways in which issues of lesbianism transform the boundaries of the police procedural by exploring the dynamic of assimilation and alienation that occurs when lesbians "infiltrate" a community whose authority is based on strict definitions of acceptable and deviant behavior. Like Betz, Stephen Soitos examines issues of transgression in lesbian crime fiction but, unlike Betz, the object of Soitos's examination is an ambitious, well-educated black lesbian CPA, who works as an investment broker for the reputable Chicago firm of Whytebread and Greese. Soitos examines novels by Nikki Baker, whose detective offers an "insider's look at the corporate world" while exploring alternative and marginalized lifestyles in the context of lesbian culture. Soitos approaches Baker's three novels as an ongoing series in order to demonstrate ways in which crime traditionally associated with detective fiction becomes a background for issues of unfolding identity. The result, Soitos argues, redefines the traditional use of the hard boiled first-person in terms of marginalized difference, becoming, as the title of his essay suggests, a matter of "Queering the 'I.'"

Identity is also at issue in Susan Elizabeth Sweeney's examination of Barbara Wilson's *Gaudí Afternoon,* where the dynamic of translation becomes a metaphor for interrogating the subjective definition of "social, sexual, and gendered selves." For Sweeney, lesbian crime fiction builds upon the implicit eroticism introduced to the mystery's principle structure by Wilkie Collins and Dorothy L. Sayers, and later made explicit in the hard boiled tradition. In "Gender-Blending/Genre-Bending," Sweeney argues that Wilson uses the device of mistaken identity to elide distinctions between language, gender, and genre in order to underscore the subjective dynamics of identity formation, a strategy consistent with queer theory and transgender studies. Jeffrey Langham's analysis of Michael Nava's *The Little Death* also examines eroticism, but here in terms of the hypermasculinity ingrained in the hard boiled tradition. Langham's essay, "Subject to Interrogation," compares Nava's text to Raymond Chandler's *The Long Goodbye* in order to theorize hetero/homosexual identification as an ideological value in the hard boiled formula. While Langham draws on Freudian theory as a base for his examination, he replaces traditional references to Oedipus with theories of mourning and melancholia to argue "masculinity" as a subjective construction of both ideology and identity.

In their focus on community and the multicultural detective, essays in Part Three illustrate TuSmith's observation that the definition of community "can be quite ambiguous" (*Relatives* 21). While traditional definitions assign meaning in terms of locality, TuSmith contends such definitions fail to account for the "experiential, feeling level" invoked by the term in works by multicultural writers and offers instead Thomas Bender's definition of community as "a network of social relations marked by mutuality and emotional bonds" (Bender quoted in *Relatives* 22). Like TuSmith, the essays in Part Three define community by experience rather than place, underscoring TuSmith's observation that "community" itself stems from a range of factors, including social, historical, cultural, and personal choice. Michelle Pagni Stewart's analysis of *The Sharpest Sight* by Louis Owens finds that emphasis on Native American community and cultural traditions not only creates a text that is both inside and outside the genre of detective fiction, but forces readers to rethink notions of what detective fiction is. Stewart's essay, "By Any Other Name," points out that, among other things, prioritizing community explains why Owens utilizes a number of characters to solve the crime of murder rather than the traditional single investigator. As Stewart notes, the communal nature of storytelling rejects the idea of a single author as alien to Native American culture, a strategy that enables the mystery to be unraveled from multiple points of view, thus redefining fixed notions of truth.

According to TuSmith, in the broad American culture, there is a myth of the individual that parallels the myth of community, a claim addressed by Laurence Roth's essay, "Unraveling Intermarriage in Faye Kellerman's Detective Fiction." Here Roth interrogates Kellerman's Jewish American male detective, a character who seems at first to embody the male individualism of the hard boiled tradition. Roth's analysis reveals that Kellerman's treatment actually plays against the "pulp detective stereotype" in order to undermine the cultural assimilation of the American Jewish male into the mythic American structure where the trope of the detective and the topos of manhood in American Jewish fiction meld into the stereotype of the "successful social loner." Roth argues that Kellerman avoids such cultural assimilation by having her protagonist marry an Orthodox woman, who in turn saves the male detective from the "biological merger" that Roth identifies as the final phase of cultural assimilation. As a result, the detective's wife becomes, not only the "spiritual hero" of the series, but demystifies the boundaries Orthodox Judaism erects around Jewish women.

Extending her argument on the mythologizing of individualism and community, TuSmith notes that while the myth of the individual is considered "romantic and heroic," the myth of the community has "the negative connotation associated with nostalgia." As a result, TuSmith continues, "individualism often represents the strength of male power, while community becomes equated with female weakness" (*Relatives* 22). The mythologized hero tradition becomes the frame within which Caroline Reitz examines issues of community and individualism in Barbara Neely's two "Blanche" novels. In "Do We Need Another Hero?", Reitz analyzes Neely's creation of a black domestic detective (whose copy line reads "keeping other people's houses clean can be murder") to ask "what difference does difference make?" Neely's solution, Reitz argues, is not just "another" hero, but rather an "Other" hero, whom Reitz explicates in terms of "difference" and the hero tradition. And while Rietz's examination of Blanche finds white female detectives to be, in the words of Eve Sedgwick, "kinda subversive/kinda hegemonic," Sedgwick's notion could also be extended to John Gruesser's analysis of Walter Mosley's *Devil in a Blue Dress*. In "Walter Mosley's Un-Easy Detective," Gruesser draws on Henry Louis Gates's theory of signifyin(g)—which Gruesser defines as a "counter discursive strategy" that combines the "purely discursive" with the "strictly political and/or essential"—to argue that while Mosley remains faithful to the hard boiled tradition in this first novel of the series, he uses the convention to explore conflicts between individual and racial freedom. The strategy, as Gruesser points out, offers no simple solution and complicates the black hard boiled detective's relationships with the black community in ways not seen when the detective is white and male.

That the literary quest for alternative visions of community must include an evaluation of the author's mediating function in terms of that author's position on issues of community (*Relatives* 23) becomes the consideration of Priscilla Walton's evaluation of hard boiled women's detective fiction, which, while lauded by some, is also viewed as problematic by other feminist and antiracist critics. Walton's essay, "Bubblegum Metaphysics," addresses charges that creators of female hard boiled detectives "simply replace a male sleuth with a female one" and suggests that such novels offer a theoretical relationship encompassing the dynamic between politics, fictive practice, and the reading public. Focusing on formula and mass consumption, Walton's analysis demonstrates ways in which the appropriation of hard boiled strategies not only push textual and cultural boundaries, but effect a self-reflexity with the community of female detective themselves.

The essays in Part Four also focus on the ramifications of mass consumption and popular culture but do so in order to (re)evaluate the position of detective fiction in terms of academic prestige. In "Chester Himes and the Canon Wars," David Schmid interrogates the neglect of Chester Himes by the canon of African American literature and concludes that any form of fiction seen as representing "mass" culture rather than "folk" culture is overlooked by those responsible for institutionalizing literature, including editors of the most recent—and most prestigious—*Norton Anthology of African American Literature*. Noting the failure to include Himes's detective literature in any black anthology, Schmid draws attention to Henry Louis Gates's *Loose Canons*, where Gates appropriates the language of detective fiction to discuss literary criticism. Why, Schmid asks, "if hard boiled conventions are good enough to use in writing about canonization . . . aren't hard boiled writers considered good for canonization?" The relationship of literature and institutionalized prestige is also subjected to interrogation in "Doppelgängers and the Death of Double Consciousness," William Nash's analysis of *A Little Yellow Dog*, the fifth novel in Walter Mosley's Easy Rawlings series. Here, Nash examines the institutionalized notion of double consciousness, the trope of racial/cultural duality theorized by W.E.B. Du Bois, to argue that Mosley "reformulates" the trope in the relationship between Easy and Raymond "Mouse" Alexander." As Nash demonstrates, the strategy frames an analogy between Mouse's apparent death and the assassination of John Kennedy which Mosley uses to examine double consciousness as opportunity and limitation, as well as a means of surviving the violence that will eventually follow.

The collection concludes with an analysis of Rudolph Fisher's *The Conjure-Man Dies*, the text that, as I argue, marks the formal beginning of multicultural detective fiction. As the first novel to remove the detective fiction from its original Eurocentric setting, Fisher's text is also the first to flesh out the "bare bones of the inquiry structure" (Cawelti 110) with the expressions, concerns, and experiences beyond the white middle-class audience for whom the genre was designed. The shift from a Eurocentric to an Afrocentric worldview parallels Bakhtin's identification of the shifts in apperceptive background that alter the nature of heteroglossia in novelistic discourse and launch what Bakhtin argues to be the second stylistic line of development in the European novel. As I argue, Fisher's shift in apperceptive background—the background against which a story is told—has the same result in detective fiction, launching multicultural detective fiction, not as a subgenre, but as a second line of development within the genre itself. Fisher's re-accentuation not only reformulates the content and structure of classical detective formula, but introduces elements into detective fiction that "continue to grow and develop even after the moment of their creation"; moreover, as this anthology collectively argues, elements that "are capable of being creatively transformed in different eras, far distant from the day and hour of their original birth" (Bakhtin 422).

As contributors to the first collection of criticism to examine the cultural function of detective fiction from a multicultural perspective, our works represent a range of voices within the academic community both heard and unheard until now. What we as critics have in common is an interest in the difference a multicultural perspective makes in the detective narrative, as well as a firm belief in the literary potential of a genre historically dismissed as that of "entertainment." I would argue that with our theoretical inquiries, we have become what Shohat and Stam refer to as "one-person coalitions" (346), identifying factors which merit academic consideration, not only for scholarly theory, but for ethnical interpretation of ethnical representation in multicultural literature.[6] In short, we have become our own versions of multicultural detectives, sleuthing ideology in the critical borderlands.

NOTES

1. While Freese applies the term multicultural to works by ethnic writers, multiculturalism as used in this anthology represents what Ella Shohat and Robert Stam describe as a "polycentric" multiculturalism, one whose emphasis "is not on spatial or primary points of origin but on fields of power, energy, and struggle" (48). Multiculturalism in this context views communities as cultures, and cultures in relation to social power; as such, so-called gay and lesbian "subcultures" are here included as cultural communities along with communities based on race and ethnicity. Although Shohat and Stam discuss polycentric multiculturalism in terms of film and visual language, their delineation of the concept offers important considerations for the theory and practice of multiculturalism in literary interpretation.

2. I also discuss theorizing as a pedagogical practice in a special issue of *Modern Language Studies* dedicated to "color" and literary theory. See "Beyond the Harlem Renaissance: The Case for Black Modernist Writers," *Modern Language Studies*, volume 26, number 4 (Fall 1996): 37-46.

3. See Arlene Elder's article, "Criticizing from the Borderlands," in *Modern Language Studies*, volume 26, number 4, (Fall 1996): 5-12.

4. Pyrhönen categorizes those approaches as "internally oriented" which analyze the genre (or author) in terms of specific objects of study, and "externally oriented" which view the genre as a means to delineate larger theoretical principles. Pyrhönen finds the boundaries of approach to be "flexible" and argues for both.

5. TuSmith explains this practice as one which follows the social science model of "'objectivity', elevating literary interpretation and evaluation to the level of science ("Opening" 63).

6. Such factors also offer important considerations for identifying factors which merit academic consideration for ethical interpretation of ethnical representation in mainstream detective fiction. For example, in the Spenser series by Robert Parker, Spenser's character is as defined by race (Hawk) and gender (Susan), as well as elements befitting the traditional, white, male detective (loner, ex-cop, ex-boxer).

WORKS CITED

Anzaldúa, Gloria. *Borderlands/La Frontera: The New Mestiza.* San Francisco: Aunt Lute Press. 1987.

Cawelti, John. *Adventure, Mystery, and Romance: Formula Stories as Art and Popular Culture.* Chicago: U of Chicago P, 1976.

Ellin, Stanley. "Introduction" to *The Conjure-Man Dies*, by Rudolph Fisher. New York: Arno Press and The New York Times, 1971.

Freese, Peter. *The Ethnic Detective: Chester Himes, Harry Kemelman, Tony Hillerman.* Essen: Die Blaue Eule, 1992.

JanMohamed, Abdul, and David Lloyd. "Toward a Theory of Minority Discourse: What Is To Be Done?" In *The Nature and Context of Minority Discourse*. Eds. Abdul JanMohamed and David Lloyd. New York: Oxford, 1990.

Maitano, John, and David Peck. "Introduction." In *Teaching Ethnic American Literature: Nineteen Essays*. Eds. John Maitano and David Peck. Albuquerque: U of New Mexico P, 1995.

Pyrhönen, Heta. *Murder from an Academic Angle.* Columbia, SC: Camden House, 1994.

Shohat, Ella, and Robert Stam. *Unthinking Eurocentrism: Multiculturalism and the Media.* New York: Routledge, 1994.

TuSmith, Bonnie. *All My Relatives: Community in Contemporary Ethnic American Literatures.* Ann Arbor: U of Michigan P, 1994.

———. "Introduction." *Modern Language Studies,* volume 26, number 4 (Fall 1996): 1-4

———. "Opening Up Theory." *Modern Language Studies*, volume 26, number 4 (Fall 1996): 59-70.

Xu, Wenying. "Making Use of European Theory in the Teaching of Multicultural Literatures." *Modern Language Studies*, volume 26, number 4 (Fall 1996): 47-58.

PART ONE

Discourse and the Multicultural Detective

CHAPTER TWO

The Detective Novel as a Resistant Text: Alter-Ideology in Linda Hogan's *Mean Spirit*

Patricia Linton

Experienced readers of detective fiction are accustomed to certain kinds of questions at the beginning of a novel and certain kinds of answers at the end. Peter Rabinowitz has observed that experiences with particular kinds of stories form "rules of configuration," familiar patterns like those associated with detective fiction which "map out the expectations that are likely to be activated by a text" (113). While a literary work may or may not fulfill the expectations we have for texts of its kind, genre patterns influence the way we read (what we pay attention to, for example) and the way we construct meanings. Thus, the template associated with a familiar genre, Rabinowitz argues, "can be just as important to the reading experience when the outcomes it predicts turn out not to take place as when they do" (111).

In prototypical detective fiction, mystery surrounds a crime at the beginning—otherwise there would be nothing to detect—and the detective's answer to the question "who done it" provides closure. Moreover, competent readers expect to understand the solution; in other words, while they tolerate—even crave—shadows and secrets and tangled webs at the beginning, they seek to solve the mystery along with the detective or, failing that, to have the meanings of clues and the detective's logic in piecing clues together explained at the end. Readers of detective fiction are figuratively in the detective's shoes or looking over his or her shoulder as the investigation progresses. Readers identify with the detective because the detective's task is analogous to the paradigmatic task of the reader: the sifting and weighing of motive, character, circumstance. The detective reads the clues, and via the detective, readers of the novel follow the thread out of the labyrinth. As Jeffrey Nealon comments, "The reader of the detective novel comes metafictionally to identify with the detective, as both the reader and the detective are bound up in the metaphysical or epistemological work of interpretation, the work of reading clues and writing a solution or end" (92).

Often, in detective fiction, the detective him or herself is ambiguously positioned as an insider/outsider figure. In this genre, it is commonplace for the successful investigator to be partially marginalized—a detective may be freelance or amateur rather than a professional (Conan Doyle's Holmes or Christie's Miss Marple), a used-to-be police officer who is no longer on the force (Hammett's Sam Spade), or a police officer with a difference (P.D. James' poet/policeman Dalgliesh). In contemporary examples of the genre, the difference that marks the detective may have sociocultural implications: for example, the detective may be female, or a member of an ethnic minority, or gay. But the detective's difference proves useful to readers, because via the detective, readers are led to the solution. The detective who can navigate the world of criminal intrigue or corporate espionage or horse racing or any other subculture supplies expertise that most readers lack. In the contemporary detective genre, novels often develop an intriguing complexity by drawing on culturally specific detail, lore that the detective already knows or is particularly competent to bring to light. Indeed, the reader's appetite for arcane information—for exotic settings, rare expertise, cultural difference—is part of the appeal of the genre. Some measure of the detective's insight (whether that insight is brought to the case or acquired as a result of it) becomes available to readers. Thus, part of the satisfaction detective fiction provides is the (sense of) entrée into another world.

As it begins, *Mean Spirit* by Linda Hogan seems to situate itself within this familiar narrative genre—arousing the kinds of expectations that detective fiction is likely to fulfill. The novel is set in Oklahoma, in 1922. In the first twenty-five pages, we learn that a beautiful, wealthy Osage woman (Grace Blanket) has been brutally murdered, and her newly wealthy daughter (Nola Blanket), heir to her mother's oil-rich land holdings, has been placed in mortal danger. The murder of Grace Blanket is not an isolated event; rather, it is part of a pattern of murders in which members of the Osage tribe who hold title to land near the town of Watona, Oklahoma, have met sudden, violent deaths. Several members of the tribe, including the diviner/sage Michael Horse, have written to the federal government asking for help.

One federal investigator finally becomes interested in the Oklahoma murders. Stacey (Stace) Red Hawk is a border figure, an insider/outsider, in multiple senses. As a federal agent based in Washington, DC, he is an outsider in the small western community of Watona to which he has been dispatched. Moreover, Red Hawk's ethnicity sets him apart both from other federal agents and from local law enforcement officers in Watona. Further, as a Lakota Sioux from Eagle Butte, South Dakota, Red Hawk is both insider and outsider with respect to the Osage people in Oklahoma. While important aspects of his heritage and his worldview coincide with those of other Native Americans, he lacks the intimacy of close kinship with the Osage community in Watona and is even further distanced from the Hill Indians, a reclusive group committed to traditional Osage culture, who have lived in the hills and bluffs above Watona for sixty years. Because he does not automatically have the confidence of the Osage community, it is clear from the beginning that Red Hawk will need to actively investigate all aspects of the situation in Watona; neither the Osage nor the white community will immediately accept him. Nevertheless, with standing (however provisional) in both worlds, Red Hawk seems uniquely suited to penetrate the mysteries with which the novel begins. Therefore, after the first fifty pages, "mainstream" readers familiar with detective fiction can expect the novel to conform with the genre's "rules of configuration." Such readers have three expectations: first, that the crimes will be solved and the mysteries surrounding them explained; second, that in the working out of the plot, readers will acquire an understanding of historical conflicts in the Oklahoma oilfields and of the Indian community around which those conflicts revolve; and third, that Stacey Red Hawk is the agent who will accomplish both of those tasks-that Red Hawk, as detective, will serve as mentor and guide.

RESISTING THE LOGIC OF THE GENRE

Mean Spirit frustrates these expectations or fulfills them in ways the "mainstream" reader cannot anticipate. Indeed, Hogan uses the genre expectations of the enculturated reader—particularly the reader's habitual identification with the detective—to challenge the assumptions in which the form itself is grounded. Although narratives of detection are based on the movement from ignorance to knowledge, *Mean Spirit* resists the "mainstream" reader's will to know. Doris Sommer sees such a refusal as part of the cultural negotiation that may occur whenever a "mainstream" reader takes up a "minority" text. Such negotiation, as Sommer conceives it, involves not an open-ended invitation from writer to reader, but rather the working out of boundaries between insider and outsider, in which certain kinds of access are offered, some aspects of intimacy can be earned, and other kinds of intimacy are denied: "Some books resist the competent reader, intentionally. By marking off an impassable distance between reader and text, and thereby raising questions of access or welcome, the strategy of these books is to produce a kind of readerly "incompetence" that more reading will not overcome" ("Resistant" 524). Thus, in Sommer's terms, Hogan offers her narrative in a form accessible and appealing to readers who are outsiders, but flouts the detective genre's rules of configuration in order to make a larger point: a reader who is an outsider is not competent to know and not entitled to know the most intimate truths of another culture.

The norms of detective fiction are particularly useful for addressing this vexed relationship between "minority" writers and "mainstream" readers because the genre (as it is familiar to Western readers) arises from a distinctly Euro-American epistemology. Detective fiction has traditionally demonstrated that however intricate the web of events, however strained the motivation, however fortuitous the discovery of pertinent information, enough can be known about the relationships between events to constitute a solution. As William V. Spanos points out in an early discussion of the relationship between the norms of the detective genre and the assumptions of Western epistemology, "the form of the detective story has its source in the comforting certainty that an acute 'eye,' private or otherwise, can solve the crime with resounding finality by inferring causal relationships between clues"; in this respect, the norms of the genre echo the "'form' of the well-made positivistic universe" (21).

In fact, as enculturated readers, our faith in the linear logic of cause and effect is not fundamentally shaken even if the solution the novel offers is the "wrong" one. It is not surprising to discover that bureaucracies get it wrong or that justice is not done. Such an outcome is politically, but not epistemologically, disturbing. So long as we achieve a satisfactory understanding of events, with enough factual and contextual information to comprehend the world of the novel, our ways of knowing are not radically altered by the conclusion that an innocent person has been punished, that a guilty person has escaped, or that an institution has failed or has been subverted. Indeed, even a recognition that we do not know the facts (a recognition that the real culprit remains at large, that a mistake or a cover-up has occurred, that the resolution of the plot is false) can be accommodated within paradigmatic *ways* of knowing. When we acknowledge that the apparent solution is the wrong one—or even that an alternative answer is possible—we can still be convinced that "in reality" there is a linear relationship between events, whether or not it is discovered by the investigator or revealed to readers.

Mean Spirit challenges such familiar epistemological assumptions in two ways: first, it does not allow the linear logic of clue added to clue to yield a satisfactory narrative solution; more importantly, it makes us aware of an alternative epistemology—one that is fundamentally "other" in the sense that it can be represented but cannot be accounted for within normative Western conceptions of knowledge. Hogan's achievement is a significant one that goes beyond social critique—the social institutions which should yield a just solution to the problem posed at the beginning of the novel do not just fail, they are rendered irrelevant. Hogan uses the genre expectations of enculturated readers—particularly such readers' habitual identification with the detective—to challenge the patterns of thought that underlie the form itself.

By appropriating a genre for which the audience's expectations are relatively well-defined, Hogan situates "mainstream" readers in (what appears to be) familiar territory, while at the same time positioning them as outsiders. Louis Owens, in analyzing the formal and ideological complexity of fiction by American Indian writers, makes the point that such fiction represents "richly hybridized dialogue" aimed at readers with different kinds of competency (14). The ideal reader for such fiction is one who claims two kinds of privilege: the privileged cultural knowledge of the traditionally educated Native American as well as the privileged discourse of the educated Eurocentric reader. In fact, however, a majority of readers claim one competency or the other, not both. Owens argues that while the American Indian novelist positions the Native American reader as the text's privileged insider, he or she must also make the narrative discourse "internally persuasive for the non-Indian reader unaccustomed to peripherality" (14-15). One of the principal ways in which this is accomplished, according to Owens, is the appropriation of the written prose form of the novel (and in the case of *Mean Spirit*, the even more conventional form of the detective novel). As Owens notes, "The result of this exquisite balancing act is a matrix of incredible heteroglossia and linguistic torsions and an intensely political situation" (15).

Hogan's strategies in *Mean Spirit* also support Ramón Saldívar's argument (posed with specific reference to Chicano texts but broadly applicable to other texts by ethnic American writers) that a narrative arising from a marginalized culture represents the discourse of an oppositional ideology, one that confronts and competes with the prevailing ideology of Euro-American culture. For Saldívar, such narratives carry out "a counterhegemonic resistance to the dominant ideology at the level of various symbolic languages, attempting to figure what we might call, echoing Göran Therborn, an 'alter-ideology'" (Saldívar 17). Reading these narratives critically, then, must encompass an effort to trace the oppositional ideology from which they arise. In calling for such a reading, Saldívar acknowledges that ideology is something like a black hole: we can trace its existence only indirectly, up to the point at which it swallows us up—and then we have verified it but can no longer escape to tell the tale. Ideology is a force so dense that it is invisible: "Like a planet revolving round an absent sun, an ideology is made of what it does not mention" (Macherey 131-32, quoted in Saldívar 18). Ideology has nothing to say about itself, although the organizing pull of its unspoken logic creates a horizon, a threshold, between what is and is not within its sphere of influence. What a careful critic may be able to do is to trace the event horizon which separates the black hole from the space beyond, to map the borders of "the abyss over which ideology is built" (Macherey, quoted in Saldívar 18). These cosmic metaphors are appropriate for the sense of risk that they convey. By appropriating well-established genres, writers like Hogan make their narratives sites of cultural negotiation, in which both writer and reader have much at stake. The ethnic writer risks assimilation by willful or complacent readers, while the Eurocentric reader risks both the destabilization of a coherent worldview and the morally ambiguous status of the cultural interloper. Ross Chambers describes the reading of oppositional texts in terms of a "thematics of snooping," figuring the reader as a potential eavesdropper/voyeur passionately interested in a degree of cultural intimacy which is either impossible or possible only through a process of seduction that culminates in identification with the "other." In short, readers may refuse to take up the issues with which the text confronts them, or they may seek to identify so completely that they wash out the barriers and differences with which the text seeks to restrain them. Neither of these possibilities is socially desirable or morally healthy.

Similarly, Doris Sommer sees in the "mainstream" reader's passionate attention to "minority" texts an extraordinarily high danger of presumption and intrusion. What readers themselves believe to be inclusive interest may be inextricably bound up with "a readerly will to knowledge" that is both a product of and a means to sustain social power ("Textual" 142). In other words, readers who have always been culturally privileged may not permit themselves to be marginalized: "Privileged readers have never been (res)trained to stop at signs of resistance" ("Textual" 147). Instead we meet refusal with an even more enthusiastic embrace—interpreting it as an invitation to search for requisite information, to earn an intimacy which is more exciting for having been at first refused and which we never imagine will ultimately be denied. As Sommer puts it: "The very markers of resistance are often disregarded or overlooked and thus cannot restrain the intimately possessive knowledge that passes for love" ("Textual" 151).

What Sommer suggests, in effect, is a need for readerly tact: that is, readers who are accustomed to having or achieving competence must cultivate a decorum that most Euro-American texts do not require of them, a modesty that keeps them from beating on or beating down closed doors—and keeps them from fantasizing what may be happening on the other side. She argues that "[uncooperative texts] locate traditionally privileged readers beyond an inviolable border. . . . From that border we can be 'ideal,' paradoxically, to the extent that we are excluded. We can be competent to the extent that we cannot conquer" ("Textual" 153). When "mainstream" readers approach "minority" texts, the knowledge and the strategies that normally lead to competent reading may or may not be adequate. Sommer would have us understand that there are times when a forthright recognition of difference is a stronger response than trying to resolve it.

Mean Spirit's challenge to the epistemological assumptions of the detective novel is subtle and culturally specific. The detective genre presumes that an astute investigator can make sense of the world by uncovering hidden or misunderstood causal relationships among events. *Mean Spirit* does not suggest that events are unpredictable. Hogan's novel differs in this respect from other works which use the framework of the traditional detective novel to challenge our assumptions about linear causality. Other fiction that invokes and subverts the conventions of the detective novel—for example Paul Auster's postmodern *New York Trilogy*—calls into question the apparent relationship between cause and effect by emphasizing the operation of chance. In *Mean Spirit*, on the other hand, causation is taken seriously and pivotal characters argue that such causation must be understood. Rather, the novel confronts us with an alter-ideology in which the substance of knowledge, the ways of knowing, and the point of knowing differ from our expectations.

THE DETECTIVE AS MENTOR AND GUIDE

The implicit invitation to the reader to identify with Stace Red Hawk is an important component of the novel's narrative strategy. Because he works for the "U.S. Bureau of Investigation," Red Hawk initially seems to understand and, to some extent, share the assumptions of the dominant culture regarding what counts as knowledge and how it is acquired. Red Hawk begins his investigation with conviction, believing that he already understands the general contours of the truth and that he has the power to bring its specific details to light:

> He knew exactly what was happening. He'd seen it before. Large number of murders in the Badlands. All Indians, all with something the settlers wanted, or with a lien filed against their property. But now, this time, he was an angel of the federal government and he was able to intervene in Indian affairs and he believed he could help the Indian people. (127)

Red Hawk begins his investigation confident of his capacity to solve the crime and recognized even by complete strangers as a person with special insight. He arrives in Oklahoma, dressed like a traveling medicine man, a Lakota traditional healer. This persona is not entirely a pose, as among the Lakota he is recognized as a "keeper of tradition," a carrier of the sacred pipe of his people. In Watona, he carries with him a buckskin bag that holds "his most special medicines" and even passers-by on the street sense in him the power to know: "His presence made them uneasy. They could see he had some depth, some dimension they had never entered, a way of knowing that made them feel he could see inside them" (147).

But in a reversal of the normal progress of the investigator from ignorance to knowledge, from uncertainty to certainty, Stace follows a tortuous route from assurance to paralyzing doubt and then to a parallel knowledge in which the original question—who is guilty of the murders—is no longer the most important one. As he investigates the murder of Grace Blanket, the case that has brought him to Watona, the pattern of murders and other violence against Osage landowners continues. Data about the crimes accumulates, but it becomes increasingly clear to Stace that neither the search for facts nor the resolution offered by Western law—a verdict in a criminal trial—represents a satisfactory solution. Indeed the division of the evil at large in Watona into discrete "cases," each with a named victim and a named perpetrator, represents the inadequacy of "white" law to deal with the situation. The novel emphasizes that the destructive force which has blighted the lives of the Osage is larger than one person, that the "Mean Spirit" of the title is not an individual but a worldview. Moreover, it is *mean* in multiple senses: malicious in its contempt for any other, selfish and grasping in its single-minded pursuit of economic gain, and yet impoverished by its own narrowness.

Stace's investigation of the murders in Watona becomes a personal crisis in which he has to confront the crucial distinction between what he knows and what he can prove: what he can prove is ultimately so inadequate that his job is hardly worth doing. In his progress toward this painful insight, Stace's personal dilemma comes to parallel the social dilemma faced by the Osage people of Watona. His investigation moves him simultaneously in two directions. First, in his involvement with the extended Greycloud family, neighbors of Grace Blanket who have taken in her daughter Nola, he is increasingly immersed in the *experience* of the terror and the hard necessity of making a decision about what to do—to fight violence with violence, to seek a (white) legal solution, to abandon the land altogether. Second, in his encounter with the sage Michael Horse, he confronts an alternative mode of investigation, one directed not toward redress in the courts, but toward a different kind of testimony, the making of a historical record.

The (white) law Red Hawk has tried to serve becomes increasingly irrelevant. As the murder trial culminating the official case winds toward its conclusion, Red Hawk recognizes that it solves nothing. He comments to Lettie Greycloud: "You know, when we came here, to

Oklahoma, I thought we were doing something right. I thought there would be witnesses, honest people, and I thought the picture would come clear, the killings stop. . . . I worked hard to get them to come here. I didn't know it would be like this" (347). Disillusionment with his role as investigator, as an agent charged with responsibility for gathering facts and marshalling them to yield a formal conclusion, causes him to lose faith and ultimately to withdraw—to stop attending the trial, to stop making reports to his superiors, ultimately to join the Osage in a physical exodus from Watona and from Oklahoma. Red Hawk's metamorphosis begins with solitary trips into the countryside and the hills around Watona. Initially he tries to justify his forays beyond the locus of the investigation as a way to gather usable data, but he knows that what he really needs is a different kind of distance, an alternative to the narrowness of the official worldview: "He tried to sound confident that he could collect information pertinent to the case. But it wasn't information he was seeking. He had a feeling that he should go up beyond the roads, up to the bluffs and ridges. He knew that the facts weren't always all they needed. He didn't know what he wanted; he just had a feeling" (223).

What Red Hawk finds most disturbing is the official (and artificial) pressure for closure that is cast into high relief during the murder trial. In the ideology—and therefore the institutions—of the dominant culture, knowledge is the endpoint of a process of fact-gathering and reasoning. Too often, however, the cultural need for a solution means that whatever provides a solution is accepted as knowledge. The dynamics of the murder trial force Stace to recognize the distortions following from such insistence on closure:

> But something about the whole transaction eluded Stace Red Hawk and he believed [the sheriff] might have been guilty of forcing the confession. He did not go back to court that day. When he left the courthouse he wanted only to cleanse himself. He walked all the way to the water of Cimarron River, and sat quietly for a while, then offered tobacco and prayed. He washed in the muddy water. He didn't know the truth. He doubted he would ever know it. (351)

The legal system's rush to closure sends most obvious villain, John Hale, to prison, but his conviction has become a detail, not a solution to the crime: "Hale, sent to prison, was lost to time. Yet his presence had changed the world. And Stace was not yet certain the crimes were over, or that all of the culprits were locked behind bars" (360).

Like the social institution of the trial, the form of the conventional detective novel requires closure. The genre is most satisfying when it produces conviction—when the outcome can be accepted *as* knowledge. Thus, to focus the epistemological issues with which Hogan is concerned, it is valuable both to invoke readers' expectations of the genre and ultimately to subvert them. As the wise man Michael Horse, a self-appointed Osage historian, sits in court listening to the murder trial, he recognizes how the "genre" of the trial and its canonical form shape the kind of story it can tell: "they have books filled with words, with rules about how the story can and cannot be spoken. There is not room enough, nor time, to search for the real story that lies beneath the rest" (341).

Horse is "the diviner and translator and the keeper of accounts" for the Osage community (63). In that role, he keeps a journal of all the events in Watona, with a page on each one of the people involved in what will eventually become the adjudicated murder case. But Horse's writing has no canonical form; his record of events becomes an open-ended account of the present, past, and future. As he listens to the trial, with its partial and inaccurate testimony, acceptable as long as it is delivered according to the rules of the court, Horse feels an increasing strong impulse to offer a corrective:

> . . . Horse felt an even more urgent need to write, as if he could write away the appearances of things and take them all the way back down to bare truth. Those who sat near him in court grew used to the scribbling sound of his words on the paper. It became part of the trial. He was writing for those who would come later, for the next generations and the next, as if the act of writing was itself part of divination and prophecy, an act of deliverance. (341)

Horse's written testimony does not confine itself to a narrow compass of events. Eventually he sees that what is needed is an addition to the Bible: *The Book of Horse.* When Father Dunne, the local priest who is himself undergoing a crisis of faith, objects that the Bible is the word of God, articulated by men who "copied down what God told them to say," Horse replies: "That's what I am doing. . . . I just want to know how to get it copyrighted, is all. . . . I think the Bible is full of mistakes.

I thought I would correct them. For instance, where does it say that all living things are equal?" (273).

Horse's challenge to the canonical text is not so much that it is wrong as that it is insufficient; he resists the false closure of definitive revelation. Horse's writing borrows the tools and the texts of the dominant culture: he composes on a typewriter; he means his addition to the Bible—which will be identified with his name and formally copyrighted—to supplement, not supplant, the Judeo-Christian version. What Horse models—for Red Hawk and for readers—is an effort to learn from received texts (written and unwritten) and to contribute to them:

> In addition to his writing, Horse was learning the languages of owls and bats. It didn't come easy for him. He was poor at languages, he thought, even though he'd learned Chinese during the Boxer Rebellion and some Spanish from horse dealers in the older days, but he thought if he could learn the few difficult words of Creek that he knew, he could learn anything, so at night he'd go out with some of the Hill men and listen to the darkness. (260)

Clearly, Horse is not poor at languages but extraordinarily skilled, and his concept of language conveys the Osage worldview: every being has a language and every language is part of one whole text. the fundamental flaw in Western logic is the illusion of "cases," each with its own "solution."

As Red Hawk retreats from the bureaucratic investigation, the focus of his search changes. He spends more time in the fields, in the hills, in the medicine cave, seeking to recover an Indian way of knowing. On one of these occasions, he encounters Na-pa-cria, called Cry, the "teller of events" among the reclusive Hill Indians, "the woman who carried the weight of history on her back." She offers Red Hawk the support of the community as he works through his personal crisis:

> "What are you doing?" she asked. . . .
>
> "I don't know what I'm doing," he told her. His face looked darker, as if he were confessing. "I'm trying to understand something."
>
> "At this she laughed. He felt foolish, but she quickly grew serious. "We are all trying to understand." She looked at him with

> warmth. "Why don't you come home with me? We will take care of you. (338)

Red Hawk's search for insight takes the form of listening and remembering. He visits the Hill people, visits the Greyclouds, talks with Michael Horse, gradually abandoning his search for facts, recovering himself—at first painfully, then joyfully—and recommitting himself to traditional ways of knowing: "He knew from the stories he grew up with that there were times when a person could do nothing but wait and be silent, that an answer would sometimes come out of nothing" (348). In the depth of his despair he performs a ceremonial act: sprinkling tobacco on the water of the Blue River. He watches the moon rise and sees the foxfire shining on the limbs of dead trees. His ritual gesture of sharing and respect for the natural world represents a turning point, the beginning of his spiritual renewal: "He thought hope was like that foxfire, alive and bright and growing out of decay" (371).

ALTERNATIVE LOGIC

While some aspects of the novel's alternative ideology are articulated for us, in other important respects, *Mean Spirit* is what Sommer terms a resistant text. The principles that are made explicit come to us primarily through *The Book of Horse*, Michael Horse's corrections to the Bible, and through the dark nights of the soul experienced by three characters who are, or should be, spiritual leaders: Stace himself, Father Dunne, and Joe Billy. Stace is a keeper of the sacred pipe who has wandered away from his tribe and become a figure of authority in an alien legal system. Father Dunne is a Catholic priest who is tormented by his knowledge of what his people, the oil-obsessed white community of Watona, have become. Joe Billy is a Christian minister who is also an Osage "road man," one who shows people the path of life. Each of these characters ultimately abandons the white community; the evil it represents is so pervasive that the only response each of these characters can finally make is to leave.

Certain insights that motivate spiritual change in these characters are made explicit, while others remain largely unarticulated. Because Father Dunne's altered worldview represents the "discoveries" of a newcomer and because *The Book of Horse* is intended for outsiders, those who "don't believe anything is true unless they see it in writing" (361), ideas that would normally be assumed are expressed in words. A fundamental element of the articulated ideology is the recognition that "all living things are equal" (273). Therefore, animals have souls (238) and are regarded as people. As Joe Billy comments: "One of the best things about bats is that they are a race of people that stand in two worlds like we do" (257). When Father Dunne experiences for himself the revelation that the snake is our sister, he announces it to the Hill People as though it were new knowledge: "It is wisdom to know this" (262). But to the people it is old knowledge, so much so that the children regard the insight as trivial:

> "The snake is our sister," he repeated.
>
> They waited. "Yes, so what new thing did you learn?" asked one of the children.
>
> "Don't be rude," said his mother. (262)

When Michael Horse composes his revisions to the Bible, he takes issue particularly with the notion that humans should have dominion over the earth and its other creatures. His Book corrects the narrow Christian misinterpretation of "brethren": "We are part of everything in our world, part of the roundness and cycles of life. The world does not belong to us. We belong to the world. And all life is sacred" (361-62). But Horse does not regard his Book as new revelation, commenting: "This is the core of all religion. It is the creator's history, the creator who spoke to a white man as clearly as he spoke to me, and said to him, 'As you do unto the least of these, my brothers, you do unto me.' The creator said this and we abide by it" (362).

Nevertheless, *Mean Spirit* also exemplifies Sommer's argument that a "minority" text may display a "strategic refusal to accommodate the reader" (149). The implied reader, the "mainstream" reader likely to make up much of the audience, is "marked precisely as [a] stranger, incapable of—or undesirable for—conspiratorial intimacy" (150). This kind of reticence surrounds the nature and role of medicine in the Osage worldview (an ideology shared by other Native American tribes, including the Lakota). The concept first assumes strategic importance in the narrative as Joe Billy becomes increasing uncomfortable with his dual role as "minister" in two faiths, the Christian and the Osage. As his confidence in Western society and Western religion is dying, Joe Billy spends many nights pacing and praying:

> Joe Billy prayed in his study, holding his father's bat medicine bundle in his hands. He felt it speaking to him. It was urgent, he knew, even though he didn't understand what was being said from inside the leather bag. Something was stirring in there. (137)

At first, the medicine bundle's "speaking and stirring" poses a relatively modest challenge to Euro-American ideology because those terms can be taken on more than one level. The bundle contains a private (and therefore unidentified) collection of objects which have both cultural and personal significance; its "speaking" can be interpreted as the emotional and intellectual pull of Joe Billy's heritage. But as the narrative continues, Billy's white wife, who is alien to the community and to Indian modes of thinking, observes its movement as well:

> She saw her husband asleep in the wooden chair. He head dropped forward, and in his hands he held a leather pouch. Inside it, Martha could see that something was moving. The sight of it bumping and turning in Joe Billy's hands startled her and she drew in such a frightened breath that Joe Billy woke and looked from her blue eyes to the moving bundle that he held.
>
> "What's in there?" Martha asked.
>
> He blinked at her and all he could really say was, "It's the older world, wanting out." (138)

The fact that this phenomenon is witnessed and questioned by Martha Billy—who, like the implied reader, is marked as a stranger—suggests that we are avoiding the novel's alter-ideology if we read it as purely metaphorical: Martha actually sees the leather pouch bumping and turning in her husband's hands. Metaphor is not the Osage explanation for such an event. Metaphor offers a comfortable "literary" account of an otherwise unaccountable event: it permits perplexed readers to acknowledge and deny at the same time. In other words, if Native American spiritual concepts are alien, it may be easier for readers enculturated in a different worldview to read "as if" when the text says "is."

Such events in the narrative mark a boundary beyond which many, perhaps most, "mainstream" readers cannot proceed. As Sommer comments, resistant texts "neither assume nor welcome comprehension by the reader who would . . . assimilate them" (150). They remind us of important differences that cannot finally be accommodated within a Euro-American worldview. Another similar incident occurs later in a bat cave where Michael Horse finds a painted and quilted medicine bag. When he picks it up he finds it is moving: "It bulged and struggled. He opened a corner of it to see what was moving inside the bag when a bat flew out" (241). While a skeptic could devise a "rational" explanation for this incident (a bat managed to crawl into the closed bag just prior to the moment when Horse discovered it?), Michael Horse interprets it with a different logic: "[T]he bats had come out of the medicine. The medicines were coming alive" (241). To read this as symbolism or as magical realism may be to miss the point: what counts as "fact," what counts as "logic," is culturally determined.

A more subtle element of the novel's alter-ideology is the social process by which the Osage community (the Greyclouds, Michael Horse, their neighbors and tribespeople) decide how to deal with the unrelenting attacks upon them. As the novel draws to its close, most of the significant characters on whom the narrative has focused are leaving the town of Watona. Michael Horse has withdrawn first to Sorrow Cave and then to the village of the Hill People. Belle Greycloud has taken temporary refuge with the Hill tribe, then rejoined her family shortly before they all depart. Stace Red Hawk has similarly withdrawn and returned several times before finally leaving for good with the Greyclouds. Michael Horse has recorded in his Book the historical pattern of expulsion and withdrawal by a succession of Indian peoples, "the people who were bent under their losses, no longer a part of their land, no longer in their own lives" (341-42). As he reads passages from his Book, Horse makes a general prediction:

> The people will go out of their land. They, like the land, are wounded and hurt. They will go into the rocks and bluffs, the cities, and into the caves of the torn apart land. There will be fires. Some of them will be restored to the earth. Others will journey to another land and merge with other people. Some will learn a new way to live, the good way of the red path. But a time will come again when all the people return and revere the earth and sing its praises. (362)

Even though the pattern of departure is clear, however, there is no moment in the narrative of the Osage people of Watona when a definitive plan is made or a decision taken. Red Hawk keeps saying that he must leave and not doing it; the Greyclouds leave individually but don't leave together—or for good—until the final attack by landgrabbers in which their house is blown up. The Osage people's lack of faith in white justice, their refusal to provide clues to the official investigators or to testify at trial, is easy for outsiders to understand, but their apparent passivity and indecision in the face of imminent threat may be more perplexing, particularly since it violates not only conventional notions of likely behavior in a crisis but the conventional narrative's impulse toward resolution.

Anthropologist Hugh Brody, writing about a different group of Native Americans, describes the way a similar mode of decision-making confuses an outsider. Brody focuses on the apparent failure of members of an Athapaskan tribe to plan an extended hunting trip: "the floating conversation will have alighted on several irreconcilable possibilities, or have given rise to quasi-predictions. It is as if the predictions are about other people—or are not quite serious" (36). By the end of the day, a "strong feeling" has arisen that the group will depart the next morning, but no one has made practical, formal plans. In the morning, however, something different has "drifted into conversations," other possibilities are floated, an altered consensus seems to be forming. As Brody explains,

> The way to understand this kind of decision making, as also to live by and even share it, is to recognize that some of the most important variables are subtle, elusive, and extremely hard or impossible to assess with finality. . . . [The hunter] considers variables as a composite, in parallel, and with the help of a blending of the metaphysical and the obviously pragmatic . . . [avoiding] the mistake of seeking rationally to focus on any one consideration that is held as primary. What is more, the decision is taken in the doing: there is no step or pause between theory and practice. As a consequence, the decision—like the action from which it is inseparable—is always alterable. . . . (37)

Like the hunters described by Brody, the Osage people in *Mean Spirit* have had "floating conversations" and evolved a shared sense that it may be necessary to leave. In the end each person's decision to do so is "taken in the doing." But as Brody points out, it is difficult for outsiders to recognize this kind of alert, thoughtful, but fluid response as anything other than inaction. Brody comments: "Planning, as other cultures understand the notion, is at odds with this kind of sensitivity and would confound such flexibility" (37). In fact, in the logic of this Native American worldview, a plan is the endpoint of thinking and therefore cuts off rational response to developing possibilities by predetermining a course of action before it is necessary or desirable, before the moment of doing.

Hogan's narrative, particularly its ending, is commensurate with the worldview it represents:

> They looked back once and saw it all rising up in the reddened sky, the house, the barn, the broken string of lights, the life they had lived, nothing more than a distant burning. No one spoke. But they were alive. They carried generations along with them, into the prairie and through it, to places where no road had been cut before them. The traveled past houses that were like caves of light in the black world. The night was on fire with their pasts and they were alive. (375)

The Greyclouds and their tribespeople act to preserve themselves, and Stace himself accompanies them toward a future that is both certain and uncertain. If an ideology is made of what it does not mention, if the most fundamental elements of a worldview are so deeply held that they are only lived—not argued, defended, or even discussed—then moving on, carrying generations, to places where no road has been cut, represents an ideology grounded in both continuity and change. Horse has prophesied that the people will go out of their land, wounded and hurt: "Some of them will be restored to the earth. Others will journey to another land and merge with other people. Some will learn a new way to live, the good way of the red path" (362). Thus, the emphasis at the end of the novel is on living, not justification, a conclusion entirely at odds with the expectations of traditional detective fiction. The compulsion to explain everything is resisted both *in* the text and *by* the text. Belle Greycloud doesn't insist that Nola Blanket understand all that the family knows about the death of Nola's husband, Will. Stace Red Hawk never knows whether the confessions introduced in the murder trial were forced; he acknowledges to the Greyclouds: "I don't know. . . . I hope not" (367). The fates of the characters who survive are shaped by necessity and shared values; their decisions are local and contextual. Hogan's narrative, like Horse's, avoids "thou shalts."

For many readers, this is unfamiliar terrain. The ideological reticence of the text is especially striking in light of the genre expectations invoked at the novel's beginning: expectations of clarity, of social order, of control restored. Indeed, the knowledge and experience which seem to define the competent reader at the beginning of the novel are considerably different from the competencies called into play at the end. Like Red Hawk, the reader must follow an indirect path to an unforeseen destination.

Patricia Linton
University of Alaska Anchorage

WORKS CITED

Brody, Hugh. *Maps and Dreams*. New York: Pantheon, 1982.

Chambers, Ross. *Room for Maneuver: Reading (the) Oppositional (in) Narrative*. Chicago: U of Chicago P, 1991.

Hogan, Linda. *Mean Spirit*. 1990. New York: Ivy/Ballantine, 1992.

Macherey, Pierre. *A Theory of Literary Production*. Trans. Geoffrey Wall. London: Routledge, 1978.

Nealon, Jeffrey T. "Work of the Detective, Work of the Writer: Paul Auster's *City of Glass*. *Modern Fiction Studies* 42.1 (1996): 91-110.

Owens, Louis. *Other Destinies: Understanding the American Indian Novel*. Norman: U of Oklahoma P, 1992.

Rabinowitz, Peter J. *Before Reading: Narrative Conventions and the Politics of Interpretation*. Ithaca: Cornell UP, 1987.

Saldívar, Ramón. "Narrative, Ideology, and the Reconstruction of American Literary History." *Criticism in the Borderlands: Studies in Chicano Literature, Culture, and Ideology*. Ed. Héctor Calderón and José David Saldívar. Durham: Duke UP, 1991. 11-20.

Sommer, Doris. "Resistant Texts and Incompetent Readers." *Poetics Today* 15 (1994): 523-551.

———. "Textual Conquests: On Readerly Competence and 'Minority' Literature." *Modern Language Quarterly* 54.1 (1993): 141-154.

Spanos, William V. "The Detective and the Boundary: Some Notes on the Postmodern Literary Imagination." *boundary 2* 1.1 (1972): 147-168. Report in *Early Postmodernism: Foundational Essays*. Ed. Paul A. Bové. Durham: Duke UP, 1995. 17-39.

CHAPTER THREE

Xojo· and Homicide: The Postcolonial Murder Mysteries of Tony Hillerman

Wayne Templeton

Tony Hillerman, a longtime resident of Albuquerque, New Mexico, has written eleven murder mysteries, all of which take place on the Navajo Reservation, a 25,000-square-mile tract (larger than New England, we discover in *The Blessing Way*) covering parts of Arizona, New Mexico, Colorado, and Utah. Hillerman's detectives, who appear alone in some, and together in other of his works, are Lieutenant Joe Leaphorn and Officer Jim Chee of the Navajo Tribal Police. These detectives offer a variety of characteristics and perspectives not usually found in this genre. Joe Leaphorn, the elder of the two, intellectual, skeptical, and shrewd, is often arbitrator in conflicts between the FBI and his colleagues, Navajo elders and archaeologists, Navajos and people of other tribes, his people and the bureaucrats who would order their lives. Jim Chee, exuberant, romantic, idealistic, is a novice *xata· li* (singer, religious practitioner) who attempts to encourage in his people a continuing process of integration rather than assimilation by embracing and propagating the concept of *xojo·* [1] (harmony), the foundation of the Navajo religious and social ideology described in their *diné bahanè* (creation narrative). In novels which have received critical acclaim from, most importantly, the Navajos themselves, Hillerman extends the genre in ways which allow them to become part of a larger literary canon, and of particular interest to those involved with both postcolonial literature—which Hillerman's work is—and cultural studies.

CRIME AS METAPHOR

Most critics of detective fiction focus on the admitted majority of works within the genre which propagate hegemonic interests, and even those critics who don't do this—Stephen Knight, for example—are often concerned with idealistic works, such as the novels of Raymond Chandler, whose protagonist Philip Marlowe stands for rugged individualism and a moral clarity which at times borders on the utopic. Certainly Chandler criticizes society, but he is somewhat of a romantic realist compared to, say, Dashiell Hammett, whose various protagonists are quite starkly realistic, and whose principles are invariably ambiguous, to say the least. (Sam Spade, for example, does not resist Brigid O'Shaughnessy's plea for clemency from a moral desire to see justice done, but from a baser desire for revenge.) Hammett also conveys the shortcomings of society *and* of those who oppose society. Hillerman does the same (although not to the same degree). Leaphorn and Chee may not be tempted to cross a moral or judicial line, but they have doubts, they make mistakes; their personalities—especially Chee's—occasionally interfere with their work.

William Stowe believes that while most detective fiction "tends to affirm rather than question social structures and moral codes" (570), the genre is not inherently aligned with sociopolitical hegemony. "On the contrary, the detective fiction formula lends itself admirably to a critique" of hegemony (570). So, too, is it able to address moral issues both social and individual. Stowe cites W.H. Auden, who in his essay "The Guilty Vicarage" describes the detective novel as a "ritual exercise in the localization and expulsion of guilt" (573). Typically, wrote Auden, "'a murder occurs, many are suspected, all but one suspect, who is the murderer, are eliminated; the murderer is arrested or dies.' In the most effective detective novel, he continues, an ideally innocent society is violated by a symbolically heinous deed. 'The job of the detective is to restore the state of grace'" (573-74).

Hillerman's novels proceed somewhat further than Auden's model, however, by functioning as metafiction. In them there are two societies—Navajo and Euro-American—two possible states of grace and two levels of crime: the immediate—the murder, for example—and the larger, more pervasive, injustices against the Navajo people. [2] The detection and the solution are as complex, for when Leaphorn or Chee brings a murderer to justice, he is doing the FBI's work for them, and bringing the criminal to Euro-American justice. And yet this hardly returns the non-Reservation society to a state of grace, for unless the crime involved a native person killing a non-native, that society is untroubled by the crime in the first place. At the same time, the Navajo society is also not returned to a state of grace, and will not be so until the larger crimes, which Hillerman is always also careful to describe in some detail, are "solved"—that is, cease to be. So, like Dashiell Hammett, whose existential protagonists realize that they are solving lesser crimes such as murder in a corrupt society in which there exist unsolved far more affective crimes involving crooked politicians, cops, and business people, Hillerman uses crimes as a metaphor for crime—small for large—and has created detectives whose main purpose is not solving the lesser crimes but, constantly pointing out the larger ones and revealing how they continue to victimize.

This involves recurring references to and descriptions or explanations of the Navajo culture, religion, traditions, and the history of their colonization. Knowledge and understanding, in other words, are what Hillerman offers in his attempts to play a part in ending the crimes against the Navajos. Such a role for an author of murder mysteries is historically and generically unique. From writers such as Dostoevsky, Collins, and Dickens, whose detectives' personal lives are mostly unknown, to later writers such as Doyle and Christie, whose detectives begin to be known (Holmes, the neurotic, violin-playing occasional user of cocaine; Poirot, the fastidious, self-aggrandizing eccentric) we eventually are granted an extensive sense of personality, and then, in Hammett and Chandler, we are given something of the sleuth's moral philosophy as well. Hillerman extends this knowledge to include religion combined with a keen sense of ethical responsibility. He has produced as a result two unique characters: Joe Leaphorn, at least the moral equivalent of Philip Marlowe or Sam Spade, albeit in a less strident way, and Jim Chee, the slightly naive if exuberant cop, lover in conflict, and aspiring *xata· li*, and as such one of the most well-rounded of fictional detectives.

Chee, then, is not simply a detective, nor is Hillerman only a creator of well-rounded characters. A point I shall elaborate upon throughout is that the United States is an empire, and the Navajos, like other natives, have been a colonized people, and are now, as Hillerman makes clear, a postcolonial people. [3] The definition of postcolonialism I am using is fairly literal and straightforward. As Said and others define it, postcolonialism is that which succeeds the restraints of imperialism—that period during which indigenous cultural retrieval is beginning—the onset of decolonization, of self-determination, the denial of imperial cultural hegemony. It is this cultural retrieval about which I am most interested vis-à-vis the Navajos, who are an apt choice of people on which to focus, for theirs is a particularly courageous, inspiring, and to some extent successful resistance of colonization. In some respects theirs has not even been a retrieval of culture, for some of it was never lost, but was always being practised.

Culture, which, like postcolonialism, requires definition in a discussion such as this, is, as Said defines it, 1) "all those practices, like the arts of description, communication, and representation, that have relative autonomy from . . . economic, social and political realms" (1993, xii), and 2) a "source of identity" (xiii) existing in the form of prescribed intellectual and moral behavior, historical narratives, including traditions, religion, politics, ideology. "The slow and often bitterly disputed recovery of geographical territory which is at the heart of decolonization is preceded—as empire had been—by the charting of cultural territory. After the period of 'primary resistance' . . . there comes the period of secondary, that is, ideological, resistance, when efforts are made to reconstitute a 'shattered community, to save or restore the sense and fact of community against all the pressures of the colonial system'" (1993, 209). For the Navajos this has not been zealous or fanatical; moreover, it has also been more religious and cultural than nationalistic. The Navajos are not, for example, petitioning for secession, and in this they are and historically have always been different from the Taos and other Pueblo peoples.

The relationship between culture and postcolonialism is made clear in *The Long Revolution* by Raymond Williams, who would see the latter as a kind of cultural revolution, for it is cultural identity or uniqueness that is most consequently being retrieved from an imperial hegemony. And to maintain a cultural identity, says Williams, people must be able to "govern themselves, and make their own decisions, without concession of this right to any particular group, nationality or class" (x). Such a revolution must be economical as well, Williams continues, and it must possess "the aspiration to extend the active process of learning, with the skills of literacy and other advanced communication, to all people rather than to limited groups" (xi). For a people whose narratives of identity have been largely oral, Hillerman, one of a small group of artists the subject of whose work is the Navajos, contributes importantly to the dissemination of cultural awareness.

While he has admitted, in *The Blessing Way*, that his work is not scholarly, it does derive not just from his long time residency in the Southwest, but from historical and anthropological sources which he acknowledges in the same novel: sources including Washington Matthews and Clyde Kluckhohn, anthropologists who gathered large amounts of oral material, and whose works were the first to delineate the remarkable complexities of the Navajo culture. More recent sources, also both oral and written, include information gleaned from traditional and nontraditional Navajos (the latter including members of AIM and the Native American Church), the Hopis, the Zuñi and other Pueblos, the BIA, the FBI, archaeologists and related members of academe, and the non-native community. In this, Hillerman becomes author as synthesist, in the Foucauldian sense: not "in the sense of the individual who delivered the speech or wrote the text in question, but . . . as the unifying principle in a particular group of writings or statements, lying at the origins of their significance, at the seat of their coherence" (Foucault 1972, 221). In other words, he creates "links between documents written by others" (Landow 71)—in this sense he is both postcolonial and cultural (contextual)—by utilizing the discoveries, the languages, the perceptions of others, and in so doing is also able to speak to those others.

In these endeavors Hillerman, like many other authors, synthesizes in the Hegelian sense as does a scientist—as did Einstein or Freud, who made the last (albeit perhaps the most significant) of a series of interlocking discoveries about reality in their particular fields. As author, Hillerman need not be Navajo any more than Freud had to be anally retentive or Einstein had to be an atom. Nor does Hillerman have to know everything about the Navajos. As Foucault has advised us, a "discipline is not the sum total of all the truths that may be uttered concerning something; it is not even the total of all that may be accepted" (1972, 223). It also will undoubtedly contain errors, Foucault continues, and it will in all probability not even be pure, but will utilize the discoveries, the language, the perceptions of other disciplines, just as it will also likely speak to those other disciplines.

Raymond Williams has also been telling us this for some time, as has Gérard Genette who discusses the "Idealization of the author," and an even more dangerous form of "Idolatry": the "fetishism of the work—conceived of as a closed, complete, absolute object" (147). And Derrida, too, argues for an "open bordered text," a text that "cannot shut out other texts" (Landow 61), a text which blurs "all those boundaries that form the running border of what used to be called a text, of what we once thought this work could identify; i.e., the supposed end and beginning of a work, the unity of a corpus . . . and so forth" (Derrida 83). And of course even in terms of endings and beginnings we know how the final page of a murder mystery—the "solution"—takes us back to the opening of the narrative or perhaps to some other parts in order to test the solution, in order now to perceive what we did not previously perceive, and so on. With the Leaphorn and Chee narratives, Hillerman pushes us to do even more, to consider phenomena beyond the immediate text: the BIA, Congress, the FBI, the Smithsonian, the world of archaeology, the actual Navajos. We will never again view a Navajo woman selling a blanket in the way we once did. These novels prod us to consider the narratives in terms of integration rather than self-containment, which parallels in a remarkable way the desire of the Navajos themselves: neither to assimilate nor to secede but to integrate to a degree while preserving their own sense of uniqueness, autonomy, and self-determination, all of which they have thus far succeeded in doing through self-containment and isolation. At the same time, Hillerman clearly sees this as no longer feasible nor advisable in exclusive terms: as Leaphorn's mother tells him, the Navajo endure by adapting.

Hillerman often makes clear the benefits of integration over assimilation, in part by describing the plight of those Navajos who have left the reservation and the Navajo way of life: *xojo·*. Drunk, alienated, caught between Navajo and Euro-American cultures, many of those who live just off the Rez live in a kind of purgatory, while those who have attained some degree of assimilation—those living in Los Angeles, for example—are in many respects no longer Navajos, certainly no longer living according to *xojo·*. In *The Blessing Way* Joe Leaphorn describes an Los Angeles Navajo named Horseman as "another poor soul who didn't know quite how to be a Navajo and couldn't learn how to act like a white" (70). In *The Ghostway* Jim Chee makes the point even more dramatically as he contemplates the possibility of a life with Mary Landon. How would they decide where to live, and how would he decide how to live: "Either he stayed with the Navajo Police or he took a job off the reservation. Either he stayed Navajo or he turned white. Either they raised their children in Albuquerque, or Albany, or some other white city as white children or they raised them on the Colorado Plateau as Dinee. Halfway was worse than either way. Chee had seen enough of that among displaced

Navajos in the border towns to know. There was no compromise solution" (7).

David Trotter quotes Franco Moretti, a critic who argues that the detective's tendency is *not* to be "moved by pity for the victims, by moral or material horror at the crime, but by its *cultural quality*: by its *uniqueness* and its *mystery*" (Trotter 68). This is not always the case, of course, and certainly not in Hillerman's works, in which Leaphorn and Chee are deeply disturbed by crimes against the Navajos, and especially by corpses. Chee in particular is never detached, for cultural and especially for religious reasons. He is in fact affected often to the extent of requiring a traditional cleansing to purge himself of the effects of the travesties he has witnessed. The antithesis of the subjective Chee is Leaphorn who, although no less engaged, is extremely cognizant of the ways of the Euro-American world, as he is of his own. He is also a quintessentially empirical detective who has no time for superstition, ignorance, gossip, or reactionism. He is, as a result, often impatient with his own people.

That impatience, however, is insignificant compared to that which Leaphorn and Chee experience in their relations with other agencies who do not possess the knowledge of topography, environment, culture, religion, and so forth, necessary to solve the crimes under investigation. The Navajos not only can succeed at solving crimes such as murder, kidnapping—crimes outside their jurisdiction—they are able to compromise when necessary in contending with the other authorities involved (and indeed often *must* do so in order to get the job done, because non-Navajos, with one or two exceptions, will not defer to their ways). They can be independent, reliable, self-deterministic, even though they are culturally different from their Euro-American counterparts—just as they are different as well from Hopis, Pueblos, Hispanic-Americans, Utes, and Jicarilla Apaches. But none of this is recognized, and most of the investigation of a murder in which Leaphorn and Chee engage is unofficial. Officially, they are expected to follow procedure and respect jurisdiction in a labyrinth of overlapping jurisdictions. In a conflict with a county sheriff, Chee is made to realize yet again that the Navajo Police "lived with jurisdictional problems. Even on the Big Reservation . . . jurisdiction was always a question. The serious felony brought in the FBI. If the suspect was non-Navajo, other questions were raised. Or the crime might lap into the territory of New Mexico State Police, Utah or Arizona Highway Patrol, or involve the Law and Order Division of the

Bureau of Indian Affairs. Or even a Hopi constable, or Southern Ute Tribal Police, or an officer of the Jicarilla Apache Tribe, or any of a dozen county sheriffs of the three states [Arizona, New Mexico, Utah]" (*People of Darkness* 30-31). And on the southwest fringe of the Reservation the problem becomes almost surrealistic, for that area, known as the Checkerboard, is divided into square miles, every other one of which is non-Navajo. Even knowing where the borders are is almost impossible.

CRIME AND CULTURE

The perception Hillerman most obviously recognizes in his novels is the Navajos' desire and quest for self-determination, in religion, in politics, in culture, and in language. One way he constantly conveys his sensitivity to this desire—and to any number of injustices the Navajos have suffered—is to dramatize the fact that the Navajo police can investigate all crimes except serious felonies, which are under the jurisdiction of the FBI. But of course, as I have noted, the FBI agents know nothing of the people, language, history, religion, politics, culture, relations with other peoples, or landscape necessary to solve the murders. Murder in this sense becomes a kind of metaphor for the need to investigate the imperialistic, hegemonic "murder" (and, historically, murder) of the Navajos. In pointing out the greater injustices suffered by the Navajos, Hillerman's crime narratives are not only metaphorical; for the crimes, invariably committed by people seeking revenge or, much more often, material gain, are symptomatic of colonization or, when the criminals are Navajos, of individuals who have strayed from *xojo·*, people not integrating but caught in the terrible paradox of attempted assimilation, since to assimilate, if it were possible, would be to become non-Indian.

In that the Navajo detectives, and their author, are at least as interested in the dilemmas and injustices facing the Navajo people, the quest for answers to social and cultural questions parallels a concomitant quest for the murderer, which in one sense Hillerman recognizes as inextricably related—that is, that a loss of cultural identity (such as is being experienced by other Indians) is in itself a kind of murder. Thus homicide in Hillerman's works becomes a postcolonial metaphor for cultural genocide, as does the destruction of the environment by mining companies, the military, or hydroelectric companies. In *Sacred Clowns* this destruction is about to be extended as a multinational corporation lobbies Washington for permission to turn a part of the Reservation into a toxic waste dump, and in *A Thief of Time*, in which archaeologists are stealing artifacts, yet another form of cultural genocide is occurring.

Given the range and complexity of details presented, it is not surprising that Hillerman does not always get details right—as late as 1986 he was still referring to *xojo·* (or *hozho*, as he now spells it) as *hozro*—but the Navajos themselves generally do not care about the mistakes. What they appreciate is the feeling that their secrets are still safe (Hillerman and Bulow 17). As well, according to a librarian at St. Catherine Indian School, Hillerman's novels "make us feel good about being Navajos" (Hillerman and Bulow 43). In appreciation of what he is doing for them, the Navajo people presented Hillerman with a plaque naming him a "friend of the Navajo because of his respectful attitude toward cultural matters and the dignity with which he invests his Navajo policemen" (Hillerman and Bulow 14). This appreciation derives in part from a lack of discernible colonialist sensibility in Hillerman, although he tends occasionally to romanticize the Navajos, and generally to omit mention of nontraditionalists: those, for example, who live just off the Reservation in poverty and alcoholic dependency. He is also not a liberal concerned with political issues—land or civil rights, freedom of religion—rather, he begins from the understanding of the Navajos as dignified, autonomous, mature, self-determining people who do not need sympathy or even assistance. What they need is an end to their colonized state and a perception as universal as possible of Navajos as individuals equal to all other individuals in America or in the world.

Another Hillerman characteristic is his understanding of multiplicity and a consequent avoidance of what other Euro-American colonists have historically done, which is to see only one Indian culture and only one Indian religion. (Berkhofer points out that in reality pre-Columbian North America constituted a socially and linguistically diverse multiplicity of some two thousand cultures.) In being aware specifically of Southwestern diversity Hillerman is acknowledging considerable differences between Pueblos and non-Pueblos—differences of culture, religion, and language among people who do not share even the same language *group*. There also exists between some of these cultures, for example between the Navajos and the Hopis, or the Taos Pueblos and the Utes, very old but still bitter enmities. This is one reason why some of them have kept their religions secret, so as not to give their enemies the power of knowledge. (The Navajos are a notable exception here, partly because they have been an extremely isolated, nonurban people, and partly because they were once a fearsome tribe, known as "head crushers" by some for their penchant for dropping large boulders on enemies as they passed through narrow canyons.)

But while they may not keep it secret (although in isolation it has hardly been made public either), the Navajo religion is extremely difficult to understand. One essential difficulty the outsider faces is in comprehending the symbolism. As Gladys Reichard has noted: "Where ideas are expressed in symbols, they serve one believer as doorways into the inner courts of understanding, another rather as doors at which thinking stops in favour of literal acceptance" (xv). And even when a reasonable attempt is made to proceed beyond the literal, that attempt is confounded by the fact that symbols are "neither predictably rational nor universal" (Said 1978, 54). Nor are symbols concrete or factual; they are created, and like so much of human life, they are part of what Said calls the "poetic processes" of trying to make "emotional and even rational" sense of the world. So the snake, one person's potential benefactor, is to another merely a slimy reptile, or worse, and one person's reference to a wingèd god is interpreted by another as a reference to a thunderbird because only *his* religion can have wingèd gods.

To know the Navajo religion is to appreciate a complex system of belief which anthropologists such as Gladys Reichard have spent lifetimes attempting to understand. Indeed, as Jim Chee makes clear, it can take a Navajo a lifetime to understand it, in part because it is a "philosophy of life and preservation" (Reichard 147) that makes necessary an exact knowledge of history, including tradition, myths, and most of all, a grasp of a very complex and subtle system of symbols contained within a series of ceremonies and prayers complete enough to provide specific responses to almost any situation in a life. As well, what makes the Navajo religion difficult for the Westerner to grasp is that its fundamental concepts—*xojo·* (harmony) and *sa'a na·yái* (restoration or return to harmony)—are the antithesis of the Christian sense of individuality. That is, when an individual strays from *xojo·*, his or her deviance affects all Navajos in imperceptible but definite ways. The Navajo religion also possesses no concept of an afterlife or of a soul; consequently, the dead are believed to roam this plane of existence as *tcî· ndi·* (or *chindi*, in Hillerman's spelling—spirits or even evil spirits) which, if not avoided, can contaminate a living person, turning him or her into a "witch" or "skinwalker." Normally a Navajo person has no trouble avoiding *tcî· ndi·* but when that Navajo is both a traditionalist and a policeman often investigating murders, as is Jim Chee, we see one of the many cultural clashes, and ironies, experienced by a postcolonial people, and one of which Hillerman is keenly aware.

One interesting feature of the religion of this tribe that inhabits mostly desert land is that unlike the Hopis, the Navajos do not know how to call the rain clouds. Rather, they accept drought as part of *xojo·*—getting in harmony with whatever is going on. Noticing rain clouds overhead, Leaphorn remembers that the Hopis had held a rain dance recently (it is June) [4]: "Perhaps the Kachinas had listened to their Hopi children. Perhaps not. It was not a Navajo concept, this idea of adjusting nature to human needs. The Navajo adjusted himself to remain in harmony with the universe [*xojo·*]. When nature withheld the rain, the Navajo sought the pattern of this phenomenon—as he sought the pattern of all things—to find its beauty and live in harmony with it" (*Listening Woman* 44). The Diné do not accept the idea that God has a personal and special interest in humans—in that sense, theirs is a religion of impersonal gods, I suppose, if an egalitarian interest in all of nature can be described as impersonal.

Another distinct feature of the Navajos is that unlike the encroaching white culture, which tends in practice not to follow its own moral codes, and to dismiss the codes of others as irrelevant, for Navajos there is a strong ethical prescription against cheating, lying, and stealing which is taken very seriously because to a Navajo "ideal and practice are the same." To cheat an individual is to cheat the gods. As Reichard notes: "If one expects to benefit from their services, one emulates them" (130). As Hillerman's characters point out frequently, Navajos tend to commit crimes only if they are drunk, or have departed completely from the Navajo Way. The only other exception, according to Hillerman, occurs when a witch is spotted, either in humanoid form, but clearly exhibiting supernatural powers, or in the form of an animal such as the wolf or hawk. In either case the being is perceived as life-threatening and the inclination is to murder in self-defense. (This is bound to fail, however, for like the European vampire these beings can survive all but the most specific measures—for *tcî· ndi·*, a bullet made of bone.) In Hillerman such a crime is invariably committed or attempted by an older and very frightened person, and is not condoned by the Navajos. The prescribed response to witchcraft is to hold an

Enemy Way during or previous to which, as in a trial or preliminary hearing, several people must provide evidence against an individual. The punishment, furthermore, is left to the *yei* (Holy People or deities).

In the event of a Navajo committing a crime, the Navajos possess a strong sense of justice, but not one based upon revenge or punishment. Rather, for the Diné justice is a matter of retribution and curing—of returning to *xojo·*. Justice, in other words, "is a religious concept," Chee explains to a lawyer, adding that this makes the tribal cop "sort of religious. He honors his people's traditional ways. He has been taught another notion of justice. He was a big boy before he heard about 'make the punishment fit the crime' or 'an eye for an eye, a tooth for a tooth.' Instead of that he was hearing of retribution in another way. If you damage somebody, you sit down with their family and figure out how much damage and make it good. That way you restore *hozho* [*xojo·*]. You've got harmony again" (*Sacred Clowns* 271). "That's why we Navajos have endured," he adds later. "Survived with our culture alive. This philosophy of *hozho* kept us alive" (275).

An example of this means of justice occurs in *Sacred Clowns*. Clement Hoski, who accidentally killed someone and then fled the scene of the accident, has nevertheless met with the family and is now paying them a monthly stipend. When Chee discovers that Hoski was the hit-and-run driver, he advises the other man to get rid of an incriminating bumper sticker which will identify his as the truck involved, so that Hoski will not lose custody of his handicapped grandson Ernie and the family its stipend. In doing this Chee is rejecting the promotion which has been offered any officer who solves this hit-and-run case; he decides in favour of *xojo·* and the Navajo way.

xojo·, which is "the very root and foundation of the Navajo religion" (*Sacred Clowns* 244), and fundamental to daily living among traditional Navajos, is translated approximately as harmony, although it is more commonly referred to as "the Beauty Way" or sometimes as "the Blessing Way." The spirit of *xojo·* is captured in what is perhaps the most fundamental of songs or "chants"—the *yé'· bitcei·* (Night Chant), named after the "grandfather" of the gods, Talking God, who is the leader of the dance. Addressed to an unnamed "male deity" (*xastsebaka*), this ceremony makes a request to the *yei* not to ignore us or to shun us. Show us you believe what we say: that we still walk in harmony with you and Nature. I am healthy, intones the prayer-maker: "Happily I walk. / With beauty before me I walk. / With beauty behind me I walk . . . With beauty all around me I walk" (Matthews 275;

Hillerman *The Blessing Way* 102-103, although Hillerman has Leaphorn using the pronoun "he" rather than "I," for he is remembering the prayer chanted by an old Singer during a Night Chant—now often called The Blessing Way—held for him and his cousin when they were in the Army).

This brings us to another point about Navajo religious ceremonies or chants. There are two main categories: *xojo· dji* and *xata· l. xata· l* describes a chant or series of chants, such as the Enemy Way described in *The Blessing Way*, which specifically attempt to cure or put things right, the latter including the attempt to ward off evil. These chants, performed by "Singers" (*xata· li*), are appeals to deities for a return to strength, health, and harmony. A common benediction ending many songs or prayers in these ceremonies is *sa'a na· yái bike xojo· n*: may restoration (rejuvenation, harmony) be achieved according to (*bike*) the ideal of beauty or harmony. *xojo· dji*, on the other hand, are chants of celebration and instruction for the continuation of a harmonious life. Thus did Leaphorn and his cousin have performed for them a Night Chant (Blessing Way), which is an example of *xojo· dji*.

Hillerman apparently has no problem, although many Euro-Americans do, with the concept of individuality attained through a collective will whereby active participation in tribal society can provide the means by which individuals are able to achieve personal fulfillment and the fullest realization of their own abilities. This sense of belonging is particularly important to the Navajos, who do not live in villages, as do the Hopis and Pueblos, but in family groups separated from each other by the necessity of having large grazing areas for their sheep. This is also how they have been able to survive and prosper, their language and religion intact, in a colonial world. In his lengthy descriptions of landscape and isolation, Hillerman also clearly understands the primacy of land to the Navajos, and at the same time seems to understand that they are not deterministic; they do not, in spite of *xojo·*, see themselves as mere cogs in a mechanistic Cosmos. They may not pray for rain, but they do not believe it folly to resist the inexplicable movements of a mysterious and unknowable Nature. Indeed, the concept of *xojo·* allows them the potential for understanding not granted to prayers of rain. The Navajos in fact believe in prophecies, but they also believe that being in harmony with Nature allows them to affect its direction in some small way, and that, should they maintain a healthy relationship with Nature, they will be rewarded for being responsible and caring inhabitants of a natural world.

The Navajos, then, are a postcolonial people attempting to preserve and practice their ways as delineated in their *Diné Bahanè* (Story of the People). This is made clear in every Hillerman novel, in which invariably at some point the narrator describes part of the religion or tradition being practised. A good example occurs in *The Blessing Way*, in which an extensive part of Leaphorn's investigation of a crime takes place at an Enemy Way, which is described and explained: it is one of many ways of either returning to or maintaining a sense of *xojo·*, in this case by negating the power of a skinwalker or witch: one who has been contaminated by the dead and has, as a result, parted completely with the entire concept of *xojo·*.

CLOSING THE CASE

As I have mentioned before, what the Navajos are attempting to preserve is inextricably related to—and in some respects a consequence of—place, of where they are attempting their preservation. In other words, the *Dinetah* (where the *Diné* live) is to the Navajo what the landscape of the eastern Mediterranean is to Jews, Moslems, and Christians—part of the *Diné Bahanè*. Such a relationship to the land is in many respects alien to Euro-Americans, who even now—in spite of a growing international community of environmentalists propagating another view—perceive landscape as Other without being able to synthesize that Otherness. Luther Standing Bear goes even further: "The white man," he has observed, "does not understand the Indian for the reason that he does not understand America. He is too far removed from its formative processes. The roots of the tree of his life have not yet grasped the rock and soil. The white man is still troubled with primitive fears" (*Blessing Way* 248).

While the primacy of land may suggest otherwise to some, the Navajos also believe in progress—again, contrary to a rather atavistic belief held by many Euro-Americans, who either would have them and all other Indians assimilate or stay the way they once were. But Native Americans never were what earlier colonists perceived them to be. They have always been changing and adapting, particularly in the recent past, because of the need to adapt to colonialist intrusion. They have also used industrial innovations to their advantage, notably in their reclamation of desert described in *Sacred Clowns*, in which Chee proudly looks at the Navajo Agricultural Industries truck gardens: thousands of acres of vegetables where once only sagebrush grew. That they still retain their Navajo ways as much as possible is not a result of atavism on their part, but a strong sense of morality and spirituality. And, too, they have had few choices, for while an Indian cannot assimilate into white society and still remain Indian, it is in fact virtually impossible to assimilate anyway. There are a number of reasons for this; one is that colonialism is centralized. In fact, it is both centralized and divisive, and to the same end—the permanent separation of colonialist and colonized. Indeed, Albert Memmi has argued that colonization is founded upon three ideological components: "one, the gulf between the culture of the colonialist and the colonized; two, the exploitation of these differences for the benefit of the colonialist; [and] three, the use of these supposed differences as standards of absolute fact" (71). The result is an unbridgeable gulf which renders assimilation impossible and antithetical to colonialist interests.

The bureaucratic distance which centralist colonialism maintains is often further entrenched by an ethnic, racialist we/they paradigm. In these terms, we can see that assimilation is not only impossible but paradoxical, for while Native Americans can no longer continue as sovereign peoples, they also cannot expect in any meaningful way to become "American." In point of fact they have been legally forbidden to do so anyway. Before the Indian Citizenship Act of 1924 they were the legal wards of the federal government, but even as citizens of the U.S.A. after 1924, those living on reservations (by far the majority), under the legislative and judicial control of the BIA, are still colonized dependents—in fact still wards—of the U.S. government, subject to federal guardianship, and thus not yet citizens. In 1959 a federal circuit court, dismissing a suit filed by the Native American Church against the Navajo Tribal Council (because Indians cannot file suit without the permission of Congress), declared as the reason for the tribe being excluded from the application of the First and Fourteenth Amendments that "Indian tribes . . . are subordinate and dependent nations possessed of all powers as such only to the extent that they have expressly been required to surrender them by the superior sovereign, the United States" (Deloria and Lytle 205).

As Hillerman repeatedly makes clear, there is no doubt that the Navajos, Hopis, and others are colonized peoples. In fact, since the initial foray into what is now New Mexico, in 1604, by Francisco Vasquez de Coronado, they have had the dubious distinction of being among the first and therefore the longest colonized. They have also been the most often colonized—by the Spanish, the British, and now Americans—and the earliest affected—the first forced to adopt European religious practices, languages, sociopolitical institutions. They have been deprived of their former autonomy, first by the Spanish, and now by Americans who force them to elect "governors" acceptable to the BIA. Along with the Mescalero Apaches, the Navajos were forced by an army officer named Kit Carson on the infamous "Long Walk" of 1864 to Fort Sumner (an event Hillerman's characters often mention). They were displaced from their land for five years in an effort to "subdue" them, and to further this end, the Army killed all the Navajos' sheep and destroyed some 4,000 fruit trees. The Navajos have also suffered the anguish of having much of their ancestral land, rich in oil, gas, uranium, and coal, plundered by mining companies. Others have had vast tracts of their lands flooded as a result of several hydroelectric projects in the area. For political reasons over the decades the Hopis have seen their lands reduced as Congress transferred parts to the Navajo Reservation. And finally, let us not forget that on 16 July 1945, the tribal lands of the Navajos, the Jicarilla and Mescalero Apaches, the Utes, and all the Pueblo peoples were the first ever to be showered with radioactive fallout from the nuclear device that was exploded at nearby White Sands Proving Grounds, New Mexico.

What I have just conveyed would suggest that the dilemma for Indians experiencing such intense colonization involves either preserving an ahistorical state of being we might term "Indianness" or abandoning that in favour of a state of full citizenship we might term "Whiteness." That is indeed a dilemma; it also has nothing to do with what many Indians want and have always wanted: neither a return to pre-Conquest sovereignty nor self-government, which is merely a version of colonialist home rule, but unrestricted sovereignty in contemporary terms, or what now is commonly known as self-determination. In many respects this is a desire for nationhood, which by definition is based upon differences (i.e. uniqueness) of culture, language, tradition. (Evidence of these differences in the U.S.A. lies in the continued existence of many Indian tribes.) Such a definition—actually a new understanding, based upon difference as otherness, not inferiority—is what Frederic Jameson terms an "essentialist" or postmodern model which must replace the obsolete definition based upon political autonomy and ideology and, I would add, the hegemony of reason.

For Indians specifically, nationhood or tribal identity is "primarily a religious conception" fairly similar, according to Deloria and Lytle, to the original notion of Judaism contained within the twelve tribes of Israel (8). And religion, as Hillerman's protagonists make clear throughout his works, is to people like the Navajos "primarily a way of acting," rather than "a way of describing how we should believe—or what we should believe" (Deloria xii). Over the past 300 years these ideas of nationhood and religion have, of course, been changed by white interference, most consequently in terms of land. As such, Deloria and Lytle insist, it becomes important to understand "the primacy of land in the Indian psychological makeup, because once land is alienated, all other forms of social cohesion also begin to erode, land having been the context in which the other forms have been created" (12). And as Luther Standing Bear emphasizes, this relationship, which he expresses metaphorically in terms of being rooted in the rock and soil, is something quite alien to many Euro-Americans, who fail to realize that displacement from a traditional *topos* leads to a crisis of identity, for identity can be "eroded by *dislocation*," or "destroyed by *cultural denigration*, the . . . oppression of the indigenous personality and culture by a supposedly superior race or cultural model" (Ashcroft 9).

As important as land, religion, and tradition are, perhaps even more important is language, for without it religion and tradition lose their meaning and land its profound relation to identity. Language is fundamental both ontologically and epistemologically, a fact not lost on colonialists. Whether cognitively or intuitively, they apparently understand the power of language for, according to Ashcroft, Griffiths, and Tiffin, one of the "main features of imperial oppression is control over language. The imperial education system installs a 'standard' version of the metropolitan language as a norm," which becomes as well the "medium through which a hierarchical structure of power is perpetuated and the medium through which conceptions of 'truth,' 'order,' and 'reality' become established" (7). A notable characteristic of postcolonial Navajos is the pervasiveness of their own language and, as Chee notes at one point, its relation to their reality. Chee prefers to describe himself as *xa· ta· li* because "no English word really expressed it. The anthropologists called them shamans [a point I would dispute], and most [other] people . . . called them singers or medicine men" (*People of Darkness* 15).

As Papin has noted, "the world we [English-speaking people] observe is literally not a substantial world [because] there is no one-to-one correspondence between words and what we experience. As soon as we use nouns—or any other words—we recreate a fixed reality incompatible with the actual events" (1256). At the same time, according to the linguist Bernard Whorf, our view of nature "is embedded in the structure of [our] language." Further, "the division into nouns and verbs, a classification found in English and most other Indo-European languages, creates 'a bipolar division of nature . . . which is thus polarized.' . . . Our languages say [for example] that 'a light flashed,' although the lightening and the flash are one." This separation is not the case with all languages. The Hopi language, for example, with which Whorf was familiar, "is not bound by such grammatical categories and is therefore better equipped to 'manipulate . . . a more verblike concept . . . without the concealed premises of actor and action' [which is a *very* important distinction]. The Hopis use a category very close to our concept of verbs, along with durational inflections, to express events such as 'cloud' and 'storm,'" or even an apparently static phenomenon such as "house," the terms for which are "'inflected for durational and temporal nuances, so that the suffixes of the word for "house event" make it mean long-lasting house, temporary house, future house, house that used to be, what started to be a house'" (Papin 1257). This is a feature common to many Indian languages, including other Uto-Aztecan members, Tanoan, and Navajo/Apachean.

What also makes the peoples of the Southwest remarkable is that from the moment of colonization they resisted, and have continued to resist, a number of efforts to conquer and vanquish them. And they have been successful because they have employed various means of resistance. During the twelve years following the Pueblo Revolt of 1680, before the Spanish returned, the Navajos developed an isolationist policy still in place today. Dividing into small clans, and sometimes smaller extended families, they dispersed with their sheep and corn seed throughout the inhospitable terrain of what is now Arizona and New Mexico where, unlike other tribes in America, they prospered, growing from 60,000 in the mid-nineteenth century to 180,000 today (*A Thief of Time* 140). They did so partly because the Spanish could not conquer a people they could not find. Rejected by American settlers who, by the time they reached the Western Plains, were eager to continue to the California or Oregon coast, the Navajos were able to live for a while in isolation from American interference as well, and thus were able to retain their language, religion, and culture. Not until American geologists arrived, followed by miners and the accoutrements of modern industrialism, were they forced to experience the worst of colonialism, and even then they remained strong, and adapted. Sitting at a Kinaalda ("Adolescent Girl's Ceremony"), Leaphorn recalls once asking his mother "how Changing Woman could have prescribed a Kinaalda cake 'a shovel handle wide' and 'garnished with raisins' when the Dinee had neither shovels nor grapes. 'When you are a man,' she had said, 'you will understand that she was teaching us to stay in harmony with time.' Thus, while the Kiowas were crushed, the Utes reduced to hopeless poverty, and the Hopis withdrawn into the secrecy of their kivas, the eternal Navajo adapted and endured" (*Listening Woman* 146-47).

Part of the adaption of the Navajos and their neighbors has meant becoming bi- and even multilingual, although without also becoming diglossic—bilingual and bicultural. Many of them have been able to resist this because they are tribal people for whom societal and individual arrangements are indistinguishable. (This is of course in stark contrast to the European post-Enlightenment obsession with individuality possessed by most Euro-Americans and entrenched within the American Constitution.)

This is not to say that the Navajos or other Natives in the Southwest have remained impervious in any way to the various European invasions they have experienced. That they have retained anything of their own, including their dignity, is remarkable, but certainly they have not escaped the psychological effects of a pattern of relations which has always characterized the movement of the industrial West into other cultures, a pattern based upon certain assumptions of cultural superiority Gramsci has termed hegemony—a cultural form so predominant that propaganda and coercion are no longer necessary. This is twentieth-century colonialism, the unspoken and, for that reason perhaps, the unavoidable; and it is this form of interaction that constantly and pervasively characterizes the experiences of the people in Hillerman's books. Like the distant, looming thunderheads which always threaten to transform drought into deluge, completely destroying the water-starved crops, the racism, humiliation, indignities, and general cultural malaise which *is* colonialism exists, but Hillerman is too subtle, too aware of the nature of drama, to be either propagandist or proselytizer. And yet what I have in essence been summarizing is evident in his works, in bits and pieces throughout. What stands out are the indignities these people experience daily, including those by a high-ranking officer such as Leaphorn, in his relations with rather remarkably ignorant and solipsistic (and by all accounts, accurately portrayed) FBI agents, bureaucrats, geologists, archaeologists. What is also obvious is the sensitivity, patience, insight, and humor of the Navajos. They have endured, growing from 60,000 a century ago to 180,000 today, and their means of achieving this constitutes a narrative worth relating.

NOTES

1. *xojo·* consists of two distinct, aspirated syllables: haw and zh'. I use the phonetic typography Reichard and others have adopted, based upon Sapir and Hoijer. In this typography, *x* is pronounced as in Spanish; *j* is a voiced aspirant, like *j* in the French *je*; *dj* is a voiced affricative, pronounced as *j* in *judge*; *ts* is a voiceless affricative, pronounced as in *bits*; and a superior dot after a vowel indicates lengthening of the vowel (Reichard xxxi-xxxii).

2. An interesting correlative to this is found in the Navajo religion. Just as the *yei* (deities) are paired—the Twins, Talking God and Black God, and so forth—so, too, do the Navajos believe that if "there is good, and harmony, and beauty on the east side of reality, then there must be evil, chaos, and ugliness to the west" (*Skinwalkers* 75). Thus do the Navajos believe in witches.

3. Hillerman is not unlike C.L.R. James, who has written about black insurrection in the Caribbean, or George Antonius, the author of *Arab Awakening*. Both of these writers have also been concerned with detecting "native or colonial reality that was ignored or betrayed" by its imperial oppressors; both have been dismissed by what Said terms a "metropolitan center" as the works of outsiders. But metropolitan audiences wanting to legitimize only "insiders" are in doing so prejudiced, reductive, narrow-minded. "'In the United States,' according to historian Richard W. Van Alstyne in *The Rising American Empire*, 'it is almost heresy to describe the nation as an empire.' Yet he shows that the early founders of the Republic, including George Washington, characterized the country as an empire . . . and promoted imperial growth" (Said 1993, 295).

4. June is significant. As Hillerman knows, all Hopi religious ceremonies, including rain dances, take place—and can only take place—between December and June (the winter and summer solstices), for only then do the Kachinas, the couriers who relay the various prayers of the Hopis to the deities, reside on earth. As Dockstader and others attest, the August Snake Dance, commonly believed to be a rain dance, has no religion involved, except for very

general spiritualism derived from an appreciation of Nature and the complex interrelationship between people and Nature. Further, the Snake Dance is a biennial Snake Clan ceremony, which would also discount it as a rain dance. As every farmer knows, rain is required every year, and not in August but June, when the seedling corn is in need of moisture.

WORKS CITED

Ashcroft, Bill, Gareth Griffiths, and Helen Tiffin. *The Empire Writes Back: Theory and Practice in Post-Colonial Literatures*. London: Routledge, 1989.

Berkhofer, Robert F. *The White Man's Indian: Images of the American Indian from Columbus to the Present*. New York: Vintage, 1979.

Collier, John. *On the Gleaming Way*. Chicago: Swallow Press, 1962.

Curtis, Natalie, ed. *The Indians' Book: An Offering by the American Indians of Indian Lore, Musical and Narrative, to Form a Record of the Songs and Legends of their Race*. New York: Harper, 1907.

Deloria, Vine Jr. Introduction. *Taos Pueblo* by Nancy Wood. New York: Knopf, 1989. xi-xvii.

——— and Sandra L. Cadwalader, eds. *The Aggressions of Civilization: Federal Indian Policy Since the 1880s*. Philadelphia: Temple UP, 1984.

——— and Clifford M. Lytle. *The Nations Within: The Past and Future of American Indian Sovereignty*. New York: Pantheon, 1984.

Derrida, Jacques. *Deconstruction and Criticism*. Trans. James Hulbert. London: Routledge and Kegan Paul, 1979.

Dockstader, Frederick J. *The Kachina and the White Man*. Albuquerque: U of New Mexico P, 1985.

Foucault, Michel. *The Archaeology of Knowledge & Discourse on Language*. Trans. A.M. Sheridan Smith. New York: Pantheon, 1972.

———. "What is an Author?" *The Foucault Reader*. Ed. Paul Rabinow. Trans. Josué V. Harari. New York: Pantheon, 1984.

Genette, Gérard. *Figures of Literary Discourse*. Trans. Alan Sheridan. New York: Columbia UP, 1982.

Hillerman, Tony. *The Blessing Way*. New York: Harper & Row, 1970.

———. *Coyote Waits*. New York: HarperPaperbacks, 1990.

———. *Dance Hall of the Dead*. New York: HarperPaperbacks, 1973.

———. *The Dark Wind*. New York: HarperPaperbacks, 1982.

———. *The Ghostway*. New York: Avon, 1984.

———. *Listening Woman*. New York: HarperPaperbacks, 1978.

———. *People of Darkness*. New York: HarperPaperbacks, 1980.

———. *Sacred Clowns*. New York: HarperCollins, 1993.

———. *Skinwalkers*. New York: HarperPaperbacks, 1986.

———. *Talking God*. New York: HarperPaperbacks, 1989.

———. *A Thief of Time*. New York: Harper & Row, 1988.

———and Ernie Bulow. *Talking Mysteries*. Albuquerque: U of New Mexico Press, 1991.

Knight, Stephen. *Form and Ideology in Crime Fiction*. London: Macmillan, 1980.

Landow, George P. *Hyper Text: The Convergence of Contemporary Critical Theory and Technology*. Baltimore: The Johns Hopkins UP, 1992.

Matthews, Washington. *Navaho Legends*. 1897; reprint. New York: Kraus Reprint, 1969.

Memmi, Albert. *Portrait of the Colonized*. Trans. Harold Greenfeld. Boston: Beacon Press, 1967.

Papin, Liliane. "This Is Not a Universe: Metaphor, Language, and Representation." *Publications of the Modern Language Association of America* 107.5 (October 1992): 1253-65.

Philip, Kenneth R. *John Collier's Crusade for Indian Reform, 1920-1954*. Tucson: U of Arizona P, 1977.

Reichard, Gladys A. *Navaho Religion: A Study of Symbolism*. Princeton: Princeton UP, 1950.

Said, Edward. *Culture and Imperialism*. New York: Knopf, 1993.

———. *Orientalism*. New York: Vintage, 1978.

Standing Bear, Luther. *Land of the Spotted Eagle*. Lincoln: U of Nebraska Press, 1978.

Stowe, William W. "Critical Investigations: Convention and Ideology in Detective Fiction." *Texas Studies in Literature and Language* 31.4 (Winter 1989): 570-591.

Thompson, Jon. *Fiction, Crime and Empire: Clues to Modernity and Postmodernism*. Urbana: U of Illinois P, 1993.

Todorov, Tzvetan. *The Conquest of America: The Question of the Other*. Trans. Richard Howard. New York: Harper and Row, 1982.

Trotter, David. "Theory and Detective Fiction." *Critical Quarterly* 333.2: 66-77.

Weatherford, J. McIver. *Indian Givers: The Continuing Impact of the Discovered Americas on the World*. New York: Crown, 1988.

White, Richard. *"It's Your Misfortune and None of My Own": A History of the American West*. Norman: U of Oklahoma P, 1991.

Williams, Raymond. *The Long Revolution*. London: The Hogarth Press, 1992.

Zolbrod, Paul G., ed. *Diné Bahanè: The Navajo Creation Story*. Albuquerque: U of New Mexico P, 1984.

CHAPTER FOUR

Lucha Corpi and the Politics of Detective Fiction

Tim Libretti

At one moment in Walter Mosley's detective novel *A Red Death*, Easy Rawlins finds a key piece of evidence, a list of names in an envelope with twenty thousand dollars or so. He tells us, "I left the money but I took the list with me. Sometimes words are worth more than money; especially if your ass is on the line"(181). In addition to its role in the plot, this moment also signifies Rawlins's effective extrication from the instrumentality of the capitalist marketplace, privileging the quest for truth, culture, and knowledge over capital gain. As such, it signifies also Mosley's ability to signify on traditional detective fiction formulas which critics traditionally identify as linked with and underwriting capitalist economic rationality, with the exception of Stephen Soitos, who argues that "African American detective writers signify on elements of the detective genre to their own ends" such as "presenting issues of black nationalism and race pride in new ways"(3-4). Indeed, writers such as Chester Himes in his Gravedigger Jones and Coffin Ed novels, Rolando Hinojosa in *Partners in Crime*, James Welch in *The Indian Lawyer*, Sherman Alexie in *Indian Killer*, Walter Mosley in the Easy Rawlins mysteries, and Lucha Corpi in *Eulogy for a Brown Angel* and *Cactus Blood*—just to name a few authors and works—have all appropriated the popular genre of detective fiction in order to subject to critique dominant cultural and legalistic conceptions of crime and injustice and to forward new conceptions informed by an historical perspective of the racial experience in the U.S.

In solving crimes in these novels, the detectives of color inevitably find themselves looking beyond the isolated individual acts of violence or murder into the deeper sociohistorical causes as a way of uncovering the larger structural and historical patterns of injustice perpetrated against people of color. As Lucha Corpi's character Gloria Damasco says in *Eulogy for a Brown Angel* when four people are killed in a 1970 Chicano uprising in L.A. and their bodies are raised onto slabs for autopsies, "In time, perhaps someone would admit to the *real* cause of what happened that day. But perhaps we already knew the name of that insidious disease that had claimed three, perhaps four, more lives that late August afternoon"(28). The novelistic autopsy Corpi performs, obviously, is one that identifies the disease of racism upholding the exploitive and oppressive racial order of U.S. society and political economy. The system itself and those who endorse, perpetuate, and underwrite it are the real criminals. If, as Franco Moretti argues, traditionally detective fiction has restored social order by finding individuals guilty so that society can declare itself innocent, Corpi's fiction incriminates society itself, but without necessarily uncritically acquitting individuals who commit crimes. Rather, her fiction develops a much more complex relation between the individual and society, recognizing the material and discursive social practices that produce criminals and the discourse of criminality itself.

Yet, as we will see, an overwhelming portion of the corpus of literary criticism of the detective fiction genre repeatedly asserts the conservative nature of the genre and the resistance of the generic formula to innovation and to deployment for a political end that challenges the dominant social order. Thus, the oppositional nature of detective fiction by U.S. writers of color requires some theorization, which this essay will undertake. A larger argument of this essay will also be that these writers have consciously turned to the detective fiction genre as a popular form not to bring the genre into the canon but rather to discuss political issues raised within and by popular political movements. They choose this popular form of the detective novel in order to reach a broader audience, indeed to reach the public who actually participates in these movements. While so much of the impulse behind multicultural criticism has been to legitimate and argue for the literary value of multiethnic literature in relation to the already existing canon and the standards of literary value that underpin that literary canon, the impulse behind the turn to the popular form is precisely to repudiate those literary standards which tend to remove literary practice from the processes of everyday life and from the material realm and struggles of political life—as well as to adopt an anti-assimiliationist stance towards the elitist (and racist) standards of the dominant culture. The question that needs to be explored, however, is how and if this turn to the popular can function radically and in opposition to the racial capitalist order.

In carrying through these arguments and explorations, I will focus schematically on key features of Lucha Corpi's *Cactus Blood* and *Eulogy for a Brown Angel* and make a series of arguments with respect to the ways in which Corpi's Chicana political perspective rethinks issues of criminality and injustice. *Eulogy for a Brown Angel* opens with the murder of a small child, taking place seemingly peripherally to the 1970 Los Angeles Chicano March. In the process of detection, however, the novel really becomes a rethinking and diagnosis of the movement from a contemporary perspective. Gloria Damasco is still working on solving the crime eighteen years later and is beginning to piece together the crime as part of an international corporate plan encompassing areas of the globe from Germany to Brazil, suggesting that the assault on Chicanos/as in the United States is bound up with imperialist aggression towards Third World peoples globally. And, indeed, the murder of the child, while again an event seemingly peripheral to the events of the movement, becomes intimately imbricated in the assault on the movement. As Damasco says, "In the summer of 1970 everything anyone of us did had to be considered according to its political impact on the Chicano community"(64). It is this sentiment that fuels Corpi's rethinking of "criminality" and, in particular, of the way in which she defines the difficult task for the writer of color in using the crime fiction genre. Historically, people of color have been criminalized in the United States, so the writer of color must negotiate carefully between reinforcing this stereotypical criminalization, especially in this case in which the individual murderer of the child—insofar as the cause of murder can be reduced to an individual act—is in fact Chicano, and rethinking criminality altogether. Hence, Damasco supports "the unwritten rule that forbade Chicanos to go public on any issues that could be used to justify discrimination against us . . . In some ways, I realized our movement for racial equality and self-determination was no different from others like it in other parts of the world. But we were a people within nation. Our behavior was constantly under scrutiny, our culture relentlessly under siege"(64). Through her detection, Damasco begins to refocus the investigation of the crime, understanding the crime less as the individual action of the Chicano paid off by European corporate culture and more as a crime that is part of the larger crimes against people of color through the mechanisms of colonialism and internal colonialism. What Damasco finally uncovers, this essay will argue, is the history of racial oppression, and what she demystifies are the ideologies of "race" (criminalization, colonization, discrimination, etc.) which underwrite those mechanisms. Before moving into a discussion of the novel, however, we need to look at the racial mountain that the detective novelist of color needs to ascend in resisting the generic obstacles of the reified formulas of detective fiction.

CHANGING NARRATIVE ENDINGS, EXPOSING HISTORY: THE DIALECTICS OF DETECTION

Critical studies of detective fiction have generally theorized the genre in terms of the formulaic narrative strategies and principles which the works seem continually to reproduce and which inevitably contain and transmit a conservative ideology. This conservatism, the story goes, is the immanent ideology of the detective fiction formulas themselves and is stubbornly resistant to innovation precisely because it is so embedded, or sedimented, in the formal features of the genre. Indeed, as Fredric Jameson has noted in his conceptualization of genre in his discussion of the ideology of form,

> . . .in its emergent, strong form a genre is essentially a socio-symbolic message, or in other terms, that form is immanently and intrinsically an ideology in its own right. When such forms are reappropriated and refashioned in quite different social and cultural contexts, this message persists and must be functionally reckoned into the new form . . . The ideology of form itself, thus sedimented, persists into the latter, more complex structure as a generic message which coexists—either as a contradiction or, on the other hand, as a mediatory or harmonizing mechanism—with elements from later stages. (Jameson 1981, 141)

Such seems to be the case with detective fiction, at least as critical assessments of the genre have attempted to state the case. Franco Moretti, for example, declares detective fiction "the *sui generis* totalitarianism of contemporary capitalism" and "a hymn to culture's coercive abilities," associating the genre wholesale with "an economic imagination interested only in *perpetuating* the existing order, which is also a *legitimate* state of affairs, founded on the authority of the real father and sanctioned by the family tie, which moderates and sprititualizes individual egoism"(155, 140,143). Similarly, Dennis Porter argues, almost tautologically, that the ideology of the detective fiction form is inherently conservative and validates mainstream values because "popular fiction is by definition a form of literature that does not offend the taste and values of its mass audience" such that "a novelist has to go out of his way to avoid confusion and conflict in his reader" and must "always retell the story of a well-ordered world"(5, 219). Even the Marxist critic Ernest Mandel neglects to consider the oppositional possibilities of detective fiction, asserting that "the common ideology of the original and classical detective story in Britain, the United States, and the countries of the European continent remains quintessentially bourgeois." Because, for Mandel, "individual conflicts" are "used as a generalized substitute for conflicts between social groups and layers," "the class nature of the state, property, law and justice remains completely obscured"(215).

This ideological sedimentation, critics suggest, persists and asserts itself even in works of detective fiction that attempt to appropriate the genre for ends that challenge social norms. Indeed, Kathleen Gregory Klein, for example, in her study of the woman detective, argues that a fundamental contradiction persists between the detective fiction genre and feminist gender ideologies, attributing an immanent patriarchal ideology to detective fiction formulas because the work of the detective in the pursuit of crime is to restore order, and historically the dominant social order has been structured patriarchally. She argues that,

> the feminist detective who restores order to a disordered world by investigating murder may be serving justice, but although the justice may be personal, it is also public. Consequently, the feminist detective winds up supporting the exisiting system which oppresses women when she re-establishes the ordered status quo. This contradiction between feminist ideals and detectives' behavior is more apparent when the private eye turns their criminals over to the law; however, no woman detective escapes the prospect of assisting in her own or other women's oppression whether women characters are the criminals, victims, or merely bystanders. Adopting the formula traps their authors. (201)

Each of these critical renderings of the detective fiction formula and its immanent ideology, however, are premised on particular assumptions about the sociohistorical context in which the fiction is produced and to which it is responding—and responsive—and about the composition of the fiction's readership. Porter's approach, for example, is reader-centered, as he argues that "since detective novels consciously set out to please their readers" such an approach "promises to illuminate more fully the genre's hold on the popular imagination"(6). As noted above, the author of detective fiction avoids creating confusion and conflict in his reader, and he/she does so, in Porter's view "by creating a work that embodies in its structure ideological presuppositions that are likely to elicit the reader's recognition and approbation." Thus, the success, or "readability," of a work of detective fiction "is dependent on a relationship of complicity between an author and a reader, involving the acknowledgment of shared community values as well as fixed narrative norms"(6).

But Porter's formulation rests on a rather sociologically naive conception of a socially and culturally homogeneous readership whose generalized consciousness conforms or is thoroughly structured according to the dominant U.S. nation's hegemonic social ideals and values. His theory of detective fiction ignores the fissures and stratifications, the various and variable cultural ethoi, visions, and orientations which characterize and constitute the everyday culture and social life of the U.S. nation and which are deployed in the racist and uneven ordering and organizing of economic life and the relations of production. Specifically, Porter's reader-centered approach rests on an impoverished conceptualization of homogeneous national readerships, ideologies, and cultures. The approach is not only reader-centered but nation-based, as he argues that detective novels are expressions of national ideals and offer "a reaffirmation of national self-worth" and of "national mythic values and of fixed cultural quantities"(216, 220).

Situating the production of detective fiction in the specific conditions and racial order of the U.S. social system and political economy, however, Porter's nation-based and reader-centered approach is problematized by the informing historical narrative of U.S. nation-formation as one of recursive colonization and conquest. Understanding racialized populations in the United States as effectively constituting colonized or internally colonized nations, as an internal Third World, within the U.S. nation-state, we must see that the experience of nationhood as well as the cultural myths and ideals of the internally colonized national populations will differ dramatically, even diametrically, from those of the dominant and colonizing U.S. national culture. Corpi's work registers both this national and cultural differentiation of the Chicano population from and within the U.S. nation-state and dominant culture when her character Gloria Damasco states in *Eulogy for a Brown Angel*, "But we were a people within a nation. Our behavior was constantly under scrutiny, our culture relentlessly under siege." Thus, the "taste and values" of the "mass audience" of the Chicano national readership for whom Corpi might by and large be writing will likely ideologically contradict those tastes and values of the mass audience informed by and affiliated with the hegemonic beliefs, values, and attitudes of the U.S. dominant culture. A society fissured by racial antagonisms and founded and maintained through racial oppression and hierarchy is hardly one characterized by a set of "shared community values." If the detective novel must "always retell the story of a well-ordered world," the narrative conception of a well-ordered world for a Third World readership would not be the reinstitution of society as it is or was, of the racially oppressive status quo. Serving justice for the Third World reader does not mean supporting the existing system but rather engaging in a total transformation of the racist U.S. society and the capitalist and imperialist political economy that motivates racial oppression and exploitation. Indeed, as Sherman Alexie's character Thomas Builds-the-Fire says to the judge who asks if "we can go about the administration of justice" during his trial (ironically, he is on trial for the history of racial hate crimes by Native Americans against European and white American settlers and colonizers), "Is that real justice or the idea of justice?"(100).

The point is that the commonplace theory of detective fiction as an inherently conservative genre fails to recognize that it is based in assumptions about the demographic composition of a readership and the ideological perspective of that readership and that if understood in a different cultural and demographic context, the detective fiction formula could as easily serve a politically radical and social transformative function. Thus, it is not necessarily that these studies, such as Mandel's, eschew the radical possibilities of detective fiction but rather that they tend to focus on a limited number of detective novels constitutive of what one might term, somewhat ironically, canonical detective fiction. Thus, these studies focus on theorizing, on the basis of a limited number of works, the practice, rather than the formal possibilities, of detective fiction.

Indeed, the impulse of detective fiction to explain and in a sense rehearse past events suggests that it could be deployed as the literary form *par excellence* for undertaking an historical materialist interrogation and critique of dominant social forms and values and hence for challenging what Jameson has termed "master narratives," ideological paradigms which contain within their plots a predetermined ending. Cannot writers appropriate the form with its attendant master narrative yet change the ending or else invest that form with a radical content? As Barbara Harlow has noted of Third World writers interacting with western literary forms, "The use by Third World resistance writers of the novel form as it has developed within the western literary tradition both appropriates and challenges the historical and historicizing presuppositions, the narrative conclusions, implicated within the western tradition and its development"(78). Following Harlow's formulation, it would seem plausible that the generic form of the detective novel could be deployed to enact resistance to dominant social forms and ideologies by seeking different historical endings from those contained within the traditional or conventional ideological literary paradigms. Indeed, if we understand that literary genres do not exist solely as ideal forms passed down or inherited through some Eliotic notion of a literary tradition that somehow exists apart from or above material history but are instead conditioned by specific historical situations and developments, then we must see these different historical endings as already implicit in an original deployment of the form, as, in Harlow's words, "contained within the narrative analysis and construction of the conditions and problematic of the historical situation itself"(79). In Alexie's story "The Trial of Thomas Builds-the-Fire," for example, Builds-the-Fire's testimony in his own defense involves recapitulating the history of violence against colonization of Native Americans, such that the conception of justice is one that grows directly out of the historical and cultural perspective which challenges the foundational mythos of "American" nationhood. While Moretti argues that "in detective fiction, as in law, history assumes importance only as *violation* and as such, must be ultimately repressed"(138), in Corpi's detective fiction, as in Alexie's story, history is exposed through the legal process and through the acts of detection and crime-solving.

FALLING INTO HISTORY, RECOVERING POLITICAL INNOCENCE

An extended foray into Corpi's second detective novel *Cactus Blood*, measured against Moretti's critical pronouncements on the operations and social functions of detective fiction, will illustrate my point. For Moretti, the detective formula is informed by a Freudian master narrative propelled by the death instinct, the desire to return to the beginning, to an earlier state of things. As such, he argues, detective novels are inherently antinovelistic in that they lack narrative and thus cannot encode or emplot history or historical development. They assert and restore innocence, reaffirming the status quo by expelling the guilty elements from the fallen world. He writes that,

> detective fiction's characters are inert indeed: they do not grow. In this way, detective fiction is radically anti-novelistic: the aim of narration is no longer the character's development into autonomy, or a change from the initial situation, or the presentation of plot as conflict and evolutionary spiral, image of a developing world that it is difficult to draw to a close. On the contrary: detective fiction's object is to *return to the beginning* . . . 'Innocent' characters must, in fact, demonstrate only that they really are, were, and will be the stereotypes they seem to be: that is, that *they know no history: "It seems, then, that an instinct is an urge inherent in organic life to restore an earlier state of things* which the living entity has been obliged to abandon under the pressure of external disturbing forces . . ." Reinstate a preceding situation, return to the beginning . . . demonstrate, again, that one has always been the same . . . So it is too with the reader who, attracted *precisely* by the obsessively repetitive scheme, is 'unable' to stop until the cycle has closed and he has returned to the starting point. *Bildung*, expelled from within the narrative, is then evaporated by its relationship with the reader. One reads only with the purpose of remaining as one already is: innocent. Detective fiction owes its success to the fact that it teaches nothing. (137-38)

Moretti's theorization of the Freudian formula of, and of the reading process enforced by, detective fiction is one that leaves little room for seeing detective fiction as a viable form for a radical literary practice geared toward challenging and transforming dominant social relations, systems, and values.

Yet in Corpi's detective fiction, while we see that many of Moretti's thematic identifications are quite astute and insightful, we also see that these themes of innocence and historical cycle, while prominent, are developed in such a way as to further the exploration of history and historical process and to motivate a political movement and activism that has grown static. To borrow Harlow's formulation, Corpi borrows the narrative but changes the ending. In *Cactus Blood*, for example, Gloria Damasco is investigating the scene of the death of her friend and long-time Chicano activist Sonny. Poisoned grapes, the fruit which Chicanos historically have boycotted because of the pesticides used which poison and kill the farmworkers who pick them, are found in his refrigerator, and on his video recorder a tape is playing of a Chicano farmworker's strike from 1973 in which Sonny participated. Corpi's narration of Damasco's discovery of the scene provides key insights into the U.S. Third World writer's reworking of the generic formula of detective fiction. She writes,

> It was rather warm inside Sonny's apartment, but my hands felt cold and cramped. Surely my reaction was the effect of the emotions triggered by Sonny's death and Art Bello's film. I had the feeling, nonetheless, that something else was at work in me. A bittersweet desire pulled at my heart and mind. I realized that in the span of Art's film I had grown politically nostalgic. I knew I was wallowing in wistfulness, wishing that things were the way they used to be in the late sixties and early seventies.
>
> Intellectually, I realized it was foolish to long for the most oppressive and repressive times we, as Chicanos, had experienced. But I had the feeling I didn't miss the activism as much as the innocence that had underscored our political zeal and the newness of our commitment. I connected our harrowing experience—the violent repressive actions of the police against us at the 1970 National Chicano Moratorium march in East Los Angeles and during the 1973 United Farmworkers' strike and grape boycott—with the loss of innocence. (21)

If this passage registers Damasco's politically unconscious desire or instinct to return to an "earlier state of things," a time of political innocence, we see here that this return to the innocence of political zeal for which Damasco perhaps waxes nostalgic is hardly one underwritten or motivated by the Freudian version of the death instinct. Rather, the nostalgic yearning to recapture the historical moment when one experienced one's most intense sense of political commitment is portrayed here as a return to the moment of the collective birth of a political id or Eros in the Chicano/a national political subject, and within a Freudian pschyoanalytic framework, it is Eros, the opponent of the death instinct, which is "the force that introduces disturbances into the process of life" and works against the death instinct's leading "organic life back into an inanimate state"(Freud 46,38). Thus, while Corpi's narrative is informed to some extent by the detective novel's traditional deep structure or narrative grammar of a return to the beginning, this return to the beginning, to innocence, is imagined not as the repression of an historical violation but rather as the precondition for entering history and assuming an active role on the historical stage so that one can effect change.

In the above passage, Damasco's self-consciousness already exposes the politically regressive—and psychologically repressive—impulse behind the "wishing that things were the way they used to be in the late sixties and early seventies." She recognizes the dangerous and dehistoricizing potential of nostalgia to figure the past erroneously in edenic terms and recognizes that "it was foolish to long for the most oppressive and repressive times we, as Chicanos, had experienced." Instead, as her thoughts clarify, what she longs for is to recapture in the present the political enthusiasm and commitment of the past in order to revitalize and redirect the Chicano movement. This innocence Corpi figures as a key feature of political vitality which is necessary to face the harrowing experiences and historical violations that mark the present. Corpi's detective fiction thus signifies on the traditional thematics and form of the genre and attempts through this elaborated narrative process of signification—the rhetorical reversal of meaning—both to heal and to re-energize the Chicano political psyche ravaged by the historical violations and repressions of the racial oppression and racist order of U.S. society. While Corpi figures landmark events of the Chicano Movement, such as the 1970 Moratorium march and the 1973 United Farm Workers' strike, as marking the loss of innocence, the typical detective fiction formula of repressing history and social contradictions through the restoration of innocence is reversed as history—and the individual's ability to participate collectively in the making of history through revolutionary social transformation—is actually and ironically recovered through the restoration of innocence. Indeed, Corpi's narrative method of exploring and rethinking the origins and legacy of the Chicano Movement bears features of what Fredric Jameson has termed a nostalgia for the present, an element he sees as a predominant characteristic of a postmodern aesthetic: "this mesmerizing new aesthetic mode itself emerged as an elaborated symptom of the waning of historicity, of our lived possibility of of experiencing history in some active way" and demonstrates "the enormity of a situation in which we seem increasingly incapable of fashioning representations of our own experience"(Jameson 1991, 21). It is precisely in response to this "waning of historicity" and the difficulty of representing and comprehending contemporary experience, it would seem, that Corpi turns to the detective fiction genre and, in a sense, returns to the scene of the crime to detect and recover the political history and impulses of the 1960s and early 1970s.

RECOVERING CHICANA/O POLITICAL CONSCIOUSNESS, SOLVING CRIMES OF HISTORY

Indeed, in *Eulogy for a Brown Angel* Gloria Damasco's quest to solve the murder of a young child at the 1970 Chicano Moratorium march in East Los Angeles continues for eighteen years, suggesting, in a sense, that one cannot have done with history and that it will continue to erupt in and inform the present such that the political models of the past developed to understand experience and resist the conditions of existence defining that experience must not be forgotten. Such a narrative of detection does not only *not* repress history, it calls attention to and continually calls up history. The detection process not only propels and keeps alive an historical conciousness into the present but it also pushes Damasco further back into the past to the very colonization of California itself. Similarly, in *Cactus Blood*, the death of Sonny which motivates the narrative turns out not to be a murder but an accident, if not a suicide, such that the "crime" itself which Damasco seeks to solve throughout the novel turns out to be a red herring. What is important in the narrative, then, is not so much the crime or even its solution as the process of detection itself and the exploration and interpretation of clues because of the psycho-historical therapeutic recovery and analysis to which the characters subject themselves.

In *Cactus Blood*, for example, the central task in solving the putative death of Sonny is finding the character Carlota Navarro, who had been seen leaving his apartment. Yet the search for Carlota, who has nothing to do with Sonny's suicide, figuratively signifies the search and eventual encounter with the Chicana/o historical past as well as with the political exigencies persistently defining the present. As an illegal immigrant and undocumented worker who is raped by the husband of the family for which she works as a domestic and is poisoned when in flight from the family she runs through a pesticide-ridden field, Carlota becomes the embodiment of the Chicana/o history of racial/national oppression and colonization, labor super-exploitation, and sexual violence within the racial patriarchal class structure. What Damasco rediscovers in locating Carlota and learning her history are all of the issues that informed Chicana/o political consciousness and identity and motivated the Chicana/o Civil Rights movements in the 1960s and 1970s. She fucntions as the living voice and repository of historical memory, a point Corpi underlines as Damasco finds Carlota's story on a tape made by her deceased friend Luisa who had been engaged in interviewing Chicanas for a project entitled "The Chicana Experience," which was to document the Chicano Civil Rights Movement from the perspective of Chicanas.

In particular, Carlota registers the tradition of Chicana/o protest and resistance to the conditions of national oppression or internal colonization while also magnifying and questioning the waning of Chicana/o activism and political commitment in the wake of the movement's heyday and in the face of these persisting conditions. While driving with Carlota through Sonoma at one moment in the story, for example, Damasco recounts seeing the houses of General Mariano Vallejo and his brother Salvador Vallejo and engages in an historical reflection which I will quote at length for its usefulness, first, in demonstrating Corpi's incorporation of historical documentary and historical consciousness into the plot of detection and, second, in creating within the plot the setting and context that highlights Carlota's heightened and Damasco's diminishing political sensitivity:

> I had never before been in Sonoma, the heart of the wine country and the site of historical events that changed the fate of Mexicans in California forever. Forgetting the urgent reasons that had brought us to the Valley of the Moon, I let my excitement at being there grow for a moment. Doing research at the Oakland History Room to uncover the lives of the Peraltas, an old Oakland Californio family, I had also discovered the Vallejo family, friends of the Peraltas.

> I saw the mission of San Francisco Solano, which stood kitty-corner to us and the Bear Flag Revolt Monument. The monument had been erected in honor of those who fought against the Mexican Army to take control of California. The building across from the mission and the monument had been the Mexican barracks. I knew they had been occupied by the Bear Flag rebels after the Mexican Army, led by General Vallejo, laid down their arms. A short time after Vallejo's surrender, California became a U.S. territory and every gold-digger's rainbow's end. (173)

Damasco's interior narration here of her perceptions of Sonoma is revealing not just because it uncovers the perhaps often overlooked or repressed history of the colonization of the Californios by "Anglo" settlers but also because of the cultural terms in which this moment of historical documentary is inserted into the narrative. The narrative here swings like a pendulum between the "Anglo" or dominant U.S. cultural and historical perspective and the Chicana/o one. For example, Damasco first describes Sonoma in terms of its importance from an economistic perspective of consumption, in terms of what the land now means within the capitalist economy of commodity production, as "the heart of the wine country," a description that effectively enacts a type of commodity fetishism. This perspective is quickly countered, however, by Damasco's qualification from a Chicana/o perspective that Sonoma is also "the site of historical events that changed the fate of Mexicans in California forever." Similarly, Damasco's vision moves from the Mexican monument of the mission of San Francisco Solano to the monument memorializing the conquest and colonization of California, the Bear Flag Revolt Monument, registering the history of cultural strife and land struggles between indigenous Mexicans and invading "Anglo" settlers in California.

But while the passage itself effectively calls up that historical consciousness and even shrewdly and economically reveals the cultural struggle and the process of the commodification—and commodity fetishism—of the land that resulted in the repression of the Chicana/o historical perspective in the face of the instrumentality of capitalist cultural and economic imperatives, as a narrative representation of Damasco's consciousness it seems significantly to indicate the extent to which she is vacillating between these two cultural perspectives which seem ambivalently and alternately to inform her cultural and historical consciousness. She seems to inhabit a Chicana/o past but an "Anglo" present; that is, she has a clear and committed understanding of U.S. history from the Chicana/o perspective of internal colonization, but this understanding seems to apply only to the events of the past and not to inform her decoding of the present. Her "forgetting the urgent reasons that had brought us to the Valley of Moon" in order to remember the historical research she did (for solving the crime in *Eulogy for a Brown Angel*) exemplifies this dissocation of past and present in Damasco's mind. Even the language she uses here marks this cultural duality, as she speaks of Sonoma, apart from her recovery of California history from a Chicana/o perspective, as the "Valley of the Moon," calling up an almost Jack Londonesque cultural figuration of Sonoma. Damasco fails to realize that solving crimes in the present requires understanding them both as crimes with a history and as crimes of history. Indeed, Corpi implicitly diagnoses her detective's flawed investigative techniques as ahistorical. Damasco must connect past and present, a lost connection which for Damasco, as the ensuing dialogue at this moment in the novel dramatizes, results from a sense her lost political consciousness.

Within the context of the plot, this passage through Sonoma leads to a conversation between Damasco and Carlota in which Damsaco's own depoliticization of the past and, by extension, the diminution of her political commitment in the present become central issues. Carlota refers to Sonoma as "la cuna de traicion" (the cradle of treason), sparking the following interchange between the two:

> "The cradle of treason? Is that what you call Sonoma?" I asked, guessing that Carlota's comment had something to do with the city's historical past.
>
> Pouring coffee into a plastic tumbler, I offered it to her. She took it and drank it in large draughts. "Well," she asked, "wasn't Vallejo our first *vendido* ? I mean—the man sold out to the highest bidder," she emphasized. "And he traded Calfornia for a post in the new state government."
>
> "I hadn't thought about it," I answered. "But I suppose his actions were somewhat opportunistic."
>
> "Do you always have to be so non-committal? When did you abandon your political commitment? Next you'll be calling yourself *Hispanic*," Carlota snapped. (174)

Carlota's final comment here references the fact that the name Chicana/o is much more than a "racial" identity. One identifies oneself as Chicana/o in order to indicate one's political affiliation with and commitment to the Movement. As Rosa Linda Fregoso and Angie Chabram point out, the term "signified both the affirmation of our working-class and indigenous origins, and the rejection of assimilation, acculturation, and the myth of the American melting pot. Implicit in the term Chicano was a strategic relation and a strategy of struggle which thematized the Chicano community and called for social struggle and reform"(205). Thus, for Damasco to call herself *Hispanic* would mean not only betraying the resistance politics of the Chicano Movement but also identifying herself with the dominant U.S. culture and nation, as part of the melting pot, into which, in reality, Chicanas/os and other racial minorities in the U.S. have historically not been allowed to melt. Damasco herself readily admits her loss of political clarity, responding, "'You're absolutely right. I myself have been thinking that I am growing politically apathetic and quite selfish . . . And when this is over, I know I have to do a lot of mental and emotional housekeeping. I just don't think I'm ready to do anything about my political complacency in the middle of this mess"(174-75).

But it is precisely in the middle of this mess that Damasco, because of Carlota, is forced to do that "housekeeping" and reaffirm her commitment to the principles of the Movement. At one point when Carlota and Damasco are escaping a tight spot rushing through a Mexican restaurant, for example, Carlota sees a woman eating grapes, snatches the bunch from her hand, and crushes them with her shoe, while firing questions at the woman: "'Don't you care that farm workers are poisoned and die of cancer every year? That babies are born with birth defects? That people go crazy from the pesticides used on those grapes? Don't you know that you should (. . .) boycott table grapes?'"(177). When Damasco urges Carlota to keep moving, Carlota insists, "'It's important people know (. . .) we're still boycotting grapes and why'"(178). Damasco is forced to agree and finds herself reverting to her activist mode of the 1960s and 1970s, assuring Carlota that they will return to the restaurant and speak to the manager or, if that yields no results, organize a picket line. While on one level these moments might read like incidental interruptions in the detection plot, they actually constitute the return of the historically repressed, the interruption or persistent emergence of the plot of history which becomes not incidental to the plot but rather the central plot itself, demonstrating Ramón Saldívar's analysis that "history cannot be conceived as the mere 'background' or 'context' of [Chicana/o] literature; rather history turns out to be the decisive determinant of the form and content of the literature"(5).

DETECTION AS DEREIFICATION: THE SCENE OF LABOR AS THE SCENE OF CRIME

The detection process, in psychotherapeutically recovering the repressed history of Chicana/o struggle against racial oppression and class exploitation, performs a dereification of consciousness that brings both characters and reader back to the scene of labor that produces our world and is the motor of history. The questions Carlota raises and the history of racial and sexual oppression and labor exploitation she embodies as an undocumented worker, an "illegal alien" in her own colonized land, are ones that the formulaic plot of detective fiction as dicussed by Moretti and others cannot make disappear. Indeed, Corpi recursively brings the plot back to the scene of labor, as when earlier in the novel Damasco's friend Victor, a physician, diagnoses Carlota's illness as caused by poisonous pesticides: "I've read reports in medical journals about the effect of pesticides and herbicides on human beings. Ironically, people still feel it's a problem only for the farm worker . . . I always tell Irma there is a human price to be paid for the unblemished apple of grape. But that's what we consumers demand . . . The proverbial poisoned apple. Amazing, isn't it?"(114). Through the orchestration of character and plot Corpi invokes a perspective of production and critiques the dominant perspective of consumption informing U.S. capitalist culture which is a function of, in Marxist terms, the reification of consciousness and the fetishism of the commodity that effectively mystifies and eliminates labor from the purview of U.S. social vision. Thus, while Moretti argues that "Money is always the motive of crime in detective fiction, yet the genre is wholly silent about *production*: that unequal exchange between labour-power and wages which is the true source of social wealth" and condemns detective fiction as performing "a cultural fetishism"(139, 152), Corpi's detective fiction overturns these conventions by making the solution of the crime the discovery of history itself, of the functioning of the racial patriarchal capitalist system as it has historically and in the present shaped racial and class struggle and criminally impacted individual lives such as Carlota's as well as the collective lives of workers and people of color generally. Indeed, while Mandel identifies the "reification of death . . at the heart of the crime story"(210), referring to the process by which death becomes an isolated, individualized experience divorced from social circumstances or problems, Corpi indicts the systemic structure of racial capitalism and its productive relations which consign people of color to the worst jobs and to inhumane and deadly work conditions.

Corpi thus reworks the typical detective fiction formula by displacing the importance of the individual crime to what she identifies as the larger source of criminality: the social structure itself. No innocence, as in Moretti's narrative, is ever restored. In fact, as the plot progresses it uncovers only more guilt and more evidence of the fallen condition of the social order, as in the scene above when the doctor Victor, speaking of the poisonous apples, invokes the trope of the fall from innocence. Damasco and other Chicanas/os of the post-Movement, post-Lapsarian political environment have forgotten this condition (recalling Adorno's statement to Benjamin that "every reification is a forgetting"[Jay 229]) and need to be reminded of this fallen condition to revivify their political commitment to the ideals of the Movement. Indeed, as Corpi structures the narrative, the crime is not revealed at the beginning of the narrative but rather discovered at the end, inverting the traditional formula of the detective novel. The solution of the actual crime in the novel offers no significant closure because it serves more to motivate the plot than to constitute a central event in the plot.

The murder in the novel, as already mentioned, is not that of Sonny, who presumably committed suicide. The murder in the novel is committed by Carlota's friend Josie Baldomar who, by her confession, accidentally murdered her Anglo husband because, she knew, he had been planning to leave her for another woman. She had been intending to murder him and with these intentions had been at work creating the circumstances that would allow her to frame an old Chicano activist, Ramon Caballos, of whom she is jealous because she views him as a rival for Carlota's affection. During a farmworkers' strike in 1973, Ramon had wanted to explode a pesticide tank and had conspired with Art Bello and Sonny to carry out the mission. Art and Sonny, however, had misgivings, deciding it would be politically counterproductive to the ends of the strike, and attempted to persuade Ramon not to execute his plan. When he did, Art and Sonny, in a moment of ambivalence, testified against him, believing it best for the Movement, although their sense of ambivalence never diminishes and they continue to harbor guilt for having betrayed a comrade. Aware of these events, Josie leaves posioned grapes in the refrigerators of Art and Sonny, steals some significant photographs of the strike hanging on Art's wall, and leaves a rattlesnake in Art's yard to make them believe that Ramon is seeking revenge upon them, her logic being that given such circumstances she will be able to frame Ramon for any murder she commits.

While this is but a partial recapitulation of the complexities of the plot, it should make apparent that the actual murder Josie commits is irrelevant in comparison to the chain of events her attempt to frame Ramon triggers. Damasco, in fact, is never even attempting to solve the murder of Josie's husband but rather the death of Sonny, which she mistakenly believes to have been a murder. But Josie's actions motivate the central elements of the plot, the characters' meditations on their political pasts and their examination of the strength and persistence of their political commitment in the present. Art, for example, must come to grips with his having testified against Ramon. And Sonny, it is speculated, committed suicide after seeing the tape depicting events from sixteen years ago because of a sense of political failure. Indeed, the search for the missing photographs from Art's walls which document past Chicano struggles symbolizes this urgency to recover the pieces of the past and reassess one's present position—and the state of the Movement as well—in light of that history. This aspect of the plot and its relative dissociation from Josie's murder of her husband become clear in the climactic scene near the end which takes place in a Native American ritual site. At this point, Art still suspects that Ramon Caballos is behind Sonny's death and the other events and sees this culmination as a referendum of sorts on the outcomes of the Movement. He says, "I feel as if a cycle that started back in 1973 is coming to a close. I just hope this cycle doesn't end with my own demise . . . For the cycle to end like it began, those of us who were involved in the action of sixteen years ago would have to be here at the same time. Aren't cycles supposed to work that way?"(190).

But the cycle does not end, at least not as Moretti has theorized the cycle of detective fiction as a return to the beginning and to the status quo with nothing changed and nothing learned. Through the ritualized process of detection, the characters work through the difficult political questions of the past, the conflict between Ramon and Art is resolved, and Damasco as well has her political commitment restored. Josie, who exploited the past and the Movement, is brought to book, and the conditions of possibility for a Third World working-class solidarity are renewed. The questions and awareness raised by Carlota remain, not at all dissipated or overshadowed by Josie's being brought to justice, for the novel recasts concepts of justice and criminality in much broader terms. The re-establishment of political solidarity and the re-recognition that, as Damasco asserts early in *Eulogy for a Brown Angel*, "we were a people within a nation," signifies not a closure but a renewed beginning which is not a return to the beginning but a recognition that the conditions of internal colonization persist in the 1990s and that the Third World Movements of the 1960s and early 1970s provide fruitful models of resistance. In the terms in which the novel defines justice, as the end of racial, class, and sexual oppression and exploitation, the quest for justice is just beginning. Apprehending the criminal means overhauling a social and economic system that is itself criminal through and through.

In *Eulogy for a Brown Angel*, Damasco is still trying to the solve the crime of 1971 eighteen years later. Although the individual murderer, a Chicano Vietnam veteran who had turned against the Movement, had been apprehended in 1971, Damasco uncovers in 1989 the conspiracy with which he was linked, a multinational corporation, signifying the continuation of imperialism and global capitalism into what Mandel has termed "late capitalism." In short, she discovers not just that "we were a people within a nation" but that Chicanas/os and other racial minorities still are peoples within the U.S. nation and that an anti-colonial nationalist politics must still constitute the enabling conditions of literary practice and political resistance. Yet, as we have seen, Corpi's novels address the U.S. Third World national audiences and, far from offending their tastes and values, support the Third World political status quo which calls for the revoltionary transformation of the racial and economic order.

WORKS CITED

Alexie, Sherman. *The Lone Ranger and Tonto Fistfight in Heaven*. New York: HarperCollins, 1993.

Chabram, Angie and Rosa Linda Fregoso. "Chicana/o Cultural Representations: Reframing Alternative Critical Discourses."*Cultural Studies* 4:3 (1990): 203-216.

Corpi, Lucha. *Eulogy for a Brown Angel*. Houston: Arte Publico Press, 1992.

———. *Cactus Blood.* Houston: Arte Publico Press, 1995.

Freud, Sigmund. *The Ego and the Id.* New York: W.W. Norton, 1960.

Harlow, Barbara. *Resistance Literature.* New York: Methuen, 1987.

Jameson, Fredric. *The Political Unconscious.* Ithaca: Cornell UP, 1981.

———. *Postmodernism or, the Cultural Logic of Late Capitalism.* Durham: Duke UP, 1991.

Jay, Martin. *Marxism and Totality.* Berkeley: University of California Press, 1984.

Klein, Kathleen Gregory. *The Woman Detective: Gender and Genre.* Urbana: Universtiy of Illinois Press, 1988.

Mandel, Ernest. "A Marxist Interpretation of the Crime Story."*Detective Fiction: A Collection of Critical Essays.* Ed. Robin W. Winks. Vermont: The Countryman Press, 1980. 213-228.

Moretti, Franco. *Signs Taken for Wonders: Essays in the Sociology of Literary Forms.* NewYork: Verso, 1983.

Mosley, Walter. *A Red Death.* New York: Simon and Schuster, 1991.

Porter, Dennis. *The Pursuit of Crime: Art and Ideology in Detective Fiction.* New Haven: Yale UP, 1981.

Saldívar, Ramon. *Chicano Narrative: The Dialectics of Difference.* Madison: University of Wisconsin Press, 1990.

Soitos, Stephen. *The Blues Detective: A Study of African American Detective Fiction.* Amherst: University of Massachusetts Press, 1996.

PART TWO

Gay and Lesbian Crime Fiction

CHAPTER FIVE

Playing the Boys' Game

Phyllis M. Betz

> transgress—1. to go beyond the bounds or limits prescribed by (a law, command, etc.); to break, violate, infringe, contravene, trespass against. b. to break a law or command; to trespass, offend, sin. c. to offend against (a person); to disobey.
>
> 2. to go or pass beyond (any limit or bounds). b. to go beyond limits, to trespass. OED

That the earliest appearances of the word "transgress" are in religious and legal works should not be surprising. These sources succinctly frame the values—moral and social—that define the very nature of transgression, since only when a community's sense of shared belief is defined can trespass be known. To transgress requires the breaking of these most basic ideas of what is and is not proper. By pushing beyond these socially imposed limits, the transgressor becomes the target of the community's anger. The group's accepted ideals of order have been violated and opened to questions, and those guilty of such aberrant behavior are quickly identified by this failure to follow social norms. These individuals become the targets of the community's sanctioned retribution. The response will take various forms, but the common purpose of punishment is the defining of the transgressor as outcast. To be identified as different, to be named other, places the offender and the offense outside the group's protection, and the institutions devised to serve the group become the wall separating the individual from the community.

The expression of the relationship between society and its transgressors appears with greatest clarity in creative literature. Fictional representation allows the frameworks to be defined concretely, often more accurately, through the requisite literary conventions; fiction enables situation and consequences to be emphasized by creating affective narrative situations, as well as believable characters. The fictional environment draws the reader into the particular situation as a participant. By becoming actively engaged in the story, the reader invests in the projected outcome, which most often reflects conservative, traditional ideals of the dominant society. This expectation dominates the reader's experience of popular genres—especially in the mystery novel and its various sub-genres. In crime novels the social order suffers temporary breakdown and is reclaimed at the end through the hero's actions. Crime challenges the social norms that define the particular community values described in such works. Order, conformity, and ordinariness characterize the world restored. The hero, whether public agent or independent, represents allegiance to these standards when the transgressor is successfully ousted; no break with communal systems is tolerated in the fictional worlds of the crime novel. Yet, in the several novels discussed in this paper, this basic premise is overturned as the representatives of the community are also transgressors of its most deeply held values. Who breaks the social standards, how they are broken, and what the consequences such action takes is the subject of this analysis.

It is important to recognize that transgression occurs in a variety of ways, from deliberate to accident as well as from physical to ideological. Those offenses, easily recognized and understood, receive clear-cut responses; the difficulty for the dominant group comes when the transgressor wears the camouflage of the wider community. The greatest perceived transgressive threat to the larger society is the individual who shares in the dominant social codes governing behavior and belief. The person who has absorbed the community's lessons, who accepts these structures, who blends in and is therefore undetectable as offender is potentially the most devastating participant in such a social order. Such a person enjoys the protection allegiance to the larger community brings while at the same time challenges this same community by (ultimately) remaining fundamentally distinct from it. This individual, then, infiltrates the group, thereby representing the potential for dissolution. The successful infiltrator can pass, and by passing, embody the contradictions that are inherent in such a position. One such figure whose public role contradicts her private life and who captures the complexity of the successfully integrated transgressor is the lesbian police office whose public responsibility demands the maintenance of the dominant community standards, but whose private life severs all connections with them.

THE RULES OF THE GAME

Since its inception, the idea of a police force has centered on the relationship between power and authority. Ideally the police system is a formalized conduit for the community's authority to control and regulate its participants. The foundations of the community's authority rest on its definitions of acceptable and deviant behavior. Without the legal and moral determinations of the group, the enforcement power of a police system is nullified. Each depends on the other for security and credibility in that the police organization exchanges maintenance enforcement of societal rules for support and tolerance of its organizational actions. Given this mandate, the police system establishes itself through adaptations of larger social institutions which ensure the smooth transfer of its authority into action. The internal structure of the police, while altered to fits its particular needs, retains strong ties to the dominant social framework. Such mirroring guarantees the continuity of the contractual relationship. The "[p]olice," as Kappeler, Sluder, and Alpert affirm, are

> selected based on demonstrated conformity to dominant social norms and values. They are also socialized into their occupational role and function. Those who become police officers bring to the occupation the perceptual baggage and moral standards common to the working middle class. . . . In essence, police are selected, socialized and placed into a working environment that instills within them an ideology and shared culture that breeds unprecedented conformity to the traditional police norms and values. (92)

Becoming a police officer, then, requires an expected, deep-seated adherence to society's dominant ideals and practices, as well as demands an intense, all-encompassing allegiance to the specific communal values of law enforcement.

These traditional configurations have been, and continue to be, male defined and dominated. Frances Heidensohn's 1992 study of women in law enforcement sets out as a major premise that "male 'ownership' of social control tends to be taken for granted, leaving women perpetual strangers, invaders in the field" (27). Heidensohn's use of the word invaders reinforces the closed world view held by many traditionally male police forces where the hierarchy of the police system is often a direct imitation of military structures. The stereotypic view of policing as an environment restricted only to men because of the continual threat of violence remains. According to this view, women are not capable of exerting—and more importantly, of maintaining—the force necessary to contain it. Typical negative comments point out the tenacity of the stereotypic image of women police officers. As Kappeler, Sluder, and Alpert note,

> " . . . most officers have problems working with female officers and dislike working with them because they believe women don't have the *physical stature* to do the job."
>
> "Female officers generally cannot back up officers." "Female officers sometimes exacerbate the situation because they feel the need to assert themselves or escalate the potential for use of force." (173-74)

Women, however, have always infiltrated police ranks. From the beginning of formalized police systems, the female officer has gained admittance into this closed world by "keep[ing] her mouth shut, accept[ing] the assignments she was given, follow[ing] rules, and maintain[ing] a low profile" (Martin 9). While still disproportionally represented in many forces, and still fighting social biases and barriers, the female police officer is no longer an anomaly. The female officer who expresses allegiance to the law enforcement communal norms gains the approbation of the dominant authority figures. She is allowed to share in the mechanisms of power; she is able to wield authority, knowing her actions and decisions have the necessary internal sanctions. Once accepted, the female officer has been transformed from an interloper. She no longer trespasses into the forbidden; she is a fully integrated member of this community.

The essential point of the female officer's acceptance into the police community is her willingness to play by the rules. She will succeed when she subordinates her individuality to the group, taking on its particular attitudes and beliefs. According to the authors of *Forces of Deviance*, this code mixes publicly stated policy, which includes following proper procedures for arresting and processing criminals, obeying the orders of superiors, and maintaining a professional public demeanor, with a frequently unstated set of private expectations dealing with how officers relate to and work with one another. This second, unspoken, set asks an officer to maintain a code of silence concerning another officer's questionable or illegal activities, to distrust anyone outside a very limited circle, including superiors in the department, to do anything to protect a partner, even as far as lying, and oneself, and to take and give physical and emotional abuse when necessary (110-15).

One common point of reference for the acceptance of women as police officers may be the unspoken but assumed agreement that the police community holds the larger society's views of sexual issues. Women, whether in the department or not, can be the butt of vulgar sexual jokes and threats and harassment; however, their sexual behavior, attractions, and relationships must conform to expected heterosexual patterns. Susan Martin's study of the District of Columbia police force in the late 1970s points out the impact that real or perceived questions about female officers' sexuality has on their professional behavior and self-images as women. Here, even the suggestion of being a lesbian can jeopardize a woman's position in the department. No matter what rank the female office has obtained, the homophobic responses of male officers remains deep.

Acting properly as a police officer enables the lesbian to pass successfully in the wider social world, and, as a police officer, the lesbian automatically appropriates the privileges of the contract that characterizes her profession. She is given the ability to identify those who obey or disobey social regulations; she is allowed to determine the course of response and instigate the requisite action; she enjoys the support of her peers and superiors when the performance and outcome produce a successful arrest of the criminal or prevention of the crime. The emphasis, here, rests on the function of the public role of law enforcement: her transgressive existence receives public sanction. Yet her woman-centered life denies the lesbian the right to participate within dominant fields of social interaction. Outside the closed society of the police station, a lesbian has no access to the various expressions of power available to her as a police officer, nor does she have the authority to take them on. Whatever status the lesbian holds as an officer, she relinquishes it when she moves outside the work environment and into the larger community. In the public sphere the lesbian once again becomes the outcast, the unredeemed transgressor of all social standards. As such she is denied the same protections which, as an officer, she must provide to others.

BREAKING THE RULES I: PASSIVE RESPONSES

In the fictive world of lesbian police novels, the intersection of the major characters' public world and private experience echoes but does not replicate the actual lesbian experience. Sally Munt, in *Murder by the Book?: Feminism and the Crime Novel*, states that "[l]esbian crime fiction provides a site of struggle over definitions of justice, social status, and sexual identity, positing the lesbian at the center of meaningful dissemination" (140). In the lesbian police novel the transgressive position of the main character is successfully integrated into the development and outcome of the crime plot. The character's lesbian identity, in fact, becomes the fulcrum that enables the transformation necessary to bring about the resolution of the overt and subversive conflicts in a particular novel. As Maureen Reddy states:

> Lesbian feminist crime fiction redefines the threat lesbian, and potentially all women, pose to men, which is actually threefold: (1) the threat of indifference; (2) the threat of changing the relations of the sexes by placing women at the center of concern, and (3) the threat of radically altering social power relations through a moral vision that does not assume the value of hierarchical order. . . . (130-31)

The demands of the fiction alter real social structures to meet the genre's requirements. In fiction, the lesbian police officer always succeeds; she is able, through a variety of maneuvers, to be recognized as a transgressor *and* a supporter of the law. The novels examined here present characters in various stages of this process and reveal the impact this integration of private self and public identity has on them by examining the increasing complexity of these characters and their relationships with the multi-layered worlds they inhabit.

Reddy's third assertion underscores the problems of claiming an authoritative role in a police environment. As a woman intruding in a male domain and as a lesbian assuming the prerogatives of the dominant heterosexist culture, the lesbian officer is twice suspect. Yet few of the novels examined for this study confront this dilemma in a straightforward manner. They either drop the issue totally from the story, or the characters replicate the behavior of the officers described by Martin and Wade: keep quiet, do your job, and do it better than the men. The one notable exception is Catherine Lewis' novel *Dry Fire*, which explicitly examines the whole range of power issues facing lesbian officers.

Lewis' story follows the cadet and rookie year of Officer Abigail Fitzpatrick, presenting in realistic detail the conflicts still faced by women in the police force even in the 1990s. Fitzpatrick faces strong antagonism from the instructors in the academy, as well as from her male classmates. In sessions on arrest techniques and self-defense, she is often paired with males. Camp, one of the male recruits, becomes Fitzgerald's particular antagonist, even breaking her rib during a drill. Fitzgerald, however, contributes to the fracture by refusing to cede to Camp's greater physical strength:

> [Camp is speaking] "It hurts. Admit it *this time*. . . . Come on, Fitzpatrick, say it hurts."
>
> "Go to hell." I say. (20, emphasis added)

Fitzpatrick falls easily into the notion that a woman must prove tougher and smarter than male officers. The stance impels her to take risks, some of which bring about the desired arrest and some of which backfire. The novel itself shows Fitzpatrick slowly adapting her own ideas of police practice to the department's, but the novel also reveals how she adopts the dominant value system of the police as she becomes an experienced officer.

Fitzpatrick adheres completely to the black and white divisions of society that police officers traditionally create. The times when she questions a supervisor's direction or takes the initiative in a situation are few and when undertaken, meet with derogatory comments. The harsh reality of police work dominates Fitzpatrick's rookie period: domestic abuse, rape, a suspect who forces an officer to shoot him, accidents, and the other points when society breaks down quickly teach Fitzpatrick the importance of adhering to policy and procedure. Lewis does present Fitzpatrick reflecting on her role as an officer: she replays situations and examines her actions, but does not place herself in a global context. She is not interested in being a model for others; she is interested in being a good cop. As she becomes a more experienced officer, Fitzpatrick continually takes on the mannerisms and attitudes of her fellow officers. After the arrest of a juvenile thief, Fitzpatrick comments: "In the world according to Abigail Fitzpatrick, he should be spending some time in juvenile jail, but there's not exactly a plethora of politicians beating my door down for advice on rampant crime" (240).

Late in the novel, Fitzgerald has completely absorbed the unspoken codes of police society—anyone who is not a cop undermines my efforts—and, at the novel's conclusion, passes these same lessons on to her own rookie.

Surprisingly, Fitzgerald's sexual orientation has little impact on her position on the force. She faces the jokes, and the harassment, of other officers for being a woman, not specifically for being lesbian. However, the homophobic attitudes of her trainers, supervisors, and peers is evident throughout the novel. For example, a trainer at the academy screams, "You limp-wristed pansy! You wimp!" at a recruit to make him fight harder (19). Homosexuality is equated with not being capable of surviving as an officer, and—perhaps not unexpectedly—it is male, not female, homosexuality that is perceived as the threat. Most of the derogatory jibes refer to gay men and gay behavior, not to lesbians. In fact, Fitzpatrick's sexuality seems to be no threat to other officers as demonstrated when one of her supervisors—a woman—even offers to fix her up: "I brought you here for a reason. That cute little server over there is Bonnie, and she'd be perfect for you. She's in my softball league and as sweet as they come" (164). Fitzpatrick's sexuality also seems unimportant in her developing relationship with Morelli, a male officer. Over the course of the novel, the two become close friends, sharing many of the same ideas about police work. Until he asks her to cross the line by lying about an arrest Fitzpatrick helps Morelli pass examinations and covers his sloppy work. His request marks the collapse in their relationship, but it is Morelli's failure to maintain the integrity of being an officer, not Fitzpatrick's sexuality that separates them.

Asserting one's right to belong in the police force is not typical of lesbian police novels. More commonly found is the lesbian officer whose sexual orientation plays either a negligible role in the solution of the crime at the center of the story, or who must integrate her private life more fully into the public sphere. In the first narrative situation, the officer's sexual life is omitted entirely from the text, or is kept on the periphery of events; in the second, the officer's orientation becomes a touchstone for the successful resolution of the investigation. The novels under consideration here offer variations on these key scenarios, describing a complex relationship between having command and having control.

Like Abigail Fitzpatrik, lesbian characters such as Delta Storm and Kate Martinelli are conservative women, committed to the ideals of police enforcement, and direct all their energies to solving the crime. In their novels, the crime—usually murder—takes place in the world at large, where the task is the restoration of civil order. Again, like Fitzpatrick, these officers have little authority in the overall hierarchy. Rarely do they instigate action in an investigation nor do they direct it. They understand their part in the whole system and undertake their duties with confidence. Nor does the struggle to reconcile one's professional role and personal identity so common to lesbian crime novels described by Sally Munt appear in the investigations carried out by these two officers. They define themselves as necessary components of the law enforcement system; indeed, they are rarely pictured outside of this system. Both Martinelli's and Storm's whole identity is confined to being police officers.

Delta Storm, the hero of Linda Kay Silva's series, will deliberately step outside the traditional chain of command, but only when an intimate relationship is threatened. In *Taken by Storm*, for example, Storm's partner, a straight, male officer, has been murdered by a group of rogue cops. Miles Brookman and Delta Storm have been partners for several years, and have developed the intense working/private relation typical of police officers. Brookman's murder becomes an invasion of Storm's private life, and, even more importantly, a revelation of the collapse of the integrity of the police world. Storm will follow her own leads and go outside conventional procedures to discover who the murderers are. Her insubordination, while technically disavowed by her superiors, is quietly abetted by them, because the focus of her efforts is the restoration of the status quo of the department. Storm accomplishes this task by utilizing every access made available to her, using standard department channels and circumventing them as needed. She makes connections with the district attorney and is given greater sanction for her undercover work.

While it leads to success, such reliance on existing authority structures indicates how limited Storm's power to act really is; had she attempted any action without the knowledge and implicit approval of her superiors, Delta Storm would have been forced to leave the department. Such a step is unthinkable to Storm; being anything but a police officer is beyond comprehension: "[O]nce she hit the streets, she fell in love with the job. . . . [she] found it incredibly satisfying to collar a criminal after doing her homework on his patterns, motives, and techniques. She never knew life could be so exciting until she became a cop" (2-3). As the novel comes to its conclusion with Storm successfully identifying and capturing the rogue officers, she receives the highest level of acknowledgement from her fellow officers:

> "Well, we just wanted you to know that the three of us are behind you. You're okay in our book." "Yeah, and if any of the other guys give you any shit, you come to us okay? It's shit like this that gives us all a bad name. We gotta stand by each other." (179)

One cop avenging another, good cops getting rid of bad: Delta Storm follows the rules of the group and gains the expected respect. Storm's sexual identity has little impact on the novel's events—her orientation is apparently known in the department. The only reference to her being lesbian occurs early in the story when Miles Brookman physically assaults another officer who makes a derogatory comment about Storm. That one incident, and its violent resolution, is sufficient to prevent any further discussion of Storm's sexuality. The officer's sexual orientation become incidental to the main plot, or if it intrudes, sexual identity remains centered in the personal sphere.

While questions of romantic involvement between the officer and a suspect/witness include such plot devices as a lover in an ongoing investigation or the stress of the crime on a long-term relationship, like heterosexual police detective fiction, once she is engaged in direct police activity, the lesbian *woman* becomes a lesbian officer. The most clear-cut representative of this strategy is Detective Lucia Ramos in Mary Morell's *Final Session.* Here, Ramos appears on the first page confidently in charge of the investigation; she gives the necessary orders to various scene-of-the-crime technicians, interrogates witnesses, and advances the investigation accordingly. So much does Ramos' professionalism dominate the novel's opening scenes that the cues about her orientation—a quick sexual thought about another woman, allusion to a well-known lesbian science fiction novel—are easily overlooked. Not until page sixty-six is Ramos concretely identified as a lesbian. The revelation has no connection to the investigation, and, most importantly, no impact on her relations with superiors or other officers. Like the successful officers profiled in Wade's article, Ramos has managed to separate the public and private aspects of her life and to maintain the integrity of each without one impinging on the other. Her immediate commander considers her a capable officer and encourages her to follow the unlikely as well as obvious leads. Throughout the novel Ramos enjoys the respect of the various officers in her department: no obvious or subversive homophobic or sexist comments are made. In this fictional world, at least, a lesbian officer is an integral member of a working community. Ramos can move freely from private, romantic life to public role seamlessly. While sources for Ramos' secure position can only be surmised, it is clear that she understands the regulations and follows them. Unlike Delta Storm, Lucia Ramos is a by-the-book officer. Her authority stems from this allegiance to procedures, and every stage of the murder investigation follows the proper chains of command. Ramos is no maverick. She neither breaks down doors not goes into dangerous situations solo, even when her new lover is in danger. As such Lucia Ramos inhabits an ideal world, where respect is a given and where one's sexuality is a non-issue.

BREAKING THE RULES II: ACTIVE RESPONSES

Not all lesbian police novels, however, present such a complete integration of the lesbian into the law enforcement community. More typical is the lesbian officer who must confront the tensions raised by her sexuality, especially when she appears in an authoritative position. Three such characters—Elizabeth Mendoza, Kate Delafield, and Gianna Maglione—embody the contradiction of representing the police hierarchy, whose duty is to maintain the smooth functioning of the dominant heterosexual community, while at the same time creating a satisfying personal life, including the development or sustaining of a loving *and* sexual relationship. For instance, all three women share a key characteristic in that each functions in prominent positions of authority within her particular force: Maglione is a lieutenant of detectives given command of a special Hate Crime Unit, while both Delafield and Mendoza are detectives with enough years of experience to control more of their investigations than Ramos as an officer. All three women have developed a reputation for accomplishment in their particular departments and each enjoys the support of her superiors. However, ability does not always guarantee acceptance as demonstrated by Mendoza and Delafield who both find their investigations hampered by overt and implicit homophobia, in and out of the force. And while all three women are comfortable with their sexuality, each maintains a firm separation between private lives from public roles. During the course of their novels, Maglione and Delafield will be faced with the challenge of bringing their orientation out into the open in the departments and be forced to publicly assert their lesbian identities. Moreover, the reconciliation of the real and perceived tensions from this moment on is an important to the text as is the solution to the crime.

In *Amateur City*, Kate Delafield articulates the dilemma which confronts the lesbian—indeed any woman—who desires to become accepted in a mainstream profession:

> She felt the familiar heavy weariness at being reminded of her singularity. The tired knowledge that always she was silhouetted against her background. . . . She had been the women reluctantly singled out in her division of the Los Angeles Police Department for one advancement after another as LAPD, in stubborn fighting retreat, gradually succumbed to increasing pressures for change. (25)

The most prominent feature of Delafield's, and others, relations with the police structure is the reluctance to be anything more than a good officer, a working member of the larger entity, unlike the many private detectives described by Munt, Reddy, and other critics of lesbian crime fiction who, by being independent, are able to integrate the political and the personal. None of these women desires any particular notoriety in her position; at the same time, by their very nature as women and as lesbians, they assume that silhouetted position Delafield recognizes. These women cannot help but stand apart from the other members of the force, and their ability to take on the appropriate authoritative posture includes some degree of tenuousness. In each case, it is not that their places in the chain of command deny them access to power, but rather their authority to wield that power that is always open to challenge, particularly from those inside the police system. Moreover, the refusal of cooperation—usually presented in subtle ways—has the potential to jeopardize the successful pursuit of the criminal investigation and as such becomes a threat which each woman must overcome as well as solve the crime.

Each detective carries a double burden during the progress of the investigation: first, each is responsible for the successful resolution of the crime. This, of course, is the basic purpose of the contract between the police and the public, but its success requires that the commanding officer has the respect and trust of those under her command, as well as the public's acceptance and participation. The second burden each detective carries is the knowledge of the impact the revelation of her sexuality may have on the investigation. This knowledge demands a continued vigilance on the part of the lesbian detective as each attempts to maintain control of public and private experience. What frequently opens the contractual relationship to challenge is the introduction of a woman who offers the detective the possibility of a romantic involvement. Such an interruption of her professional life reminds the detective, and potentially others, of the transgressive foundation of her existence. What is brought to the surface, as Reddy notes, is the inherent conundrum of the lesbian police officer:

> the female hero does not experience her sexual and emotional attraction to women as an active, open choice she may make, but does perceive her acknowledgement of, and acting upon, that attraction as a matter of choice with strong political implications. (123)

The ability to solve the crime, which all these women have, is the benchmark for becoming an accepted member of the police community. However, as their professional careers reveal, solid police work and a record of successful investigations can neither eradicate the biases against a female in the ranks, nor guarantee acceptance of the lesbian officer's sexual identity. Delafield, Mendoza, and Maglione are self-identified lesbians. Each reveals a past involvement in the early chapters of her story which indicates an awareness and comfort with that identity, and each becomes involved with another woman during the progress of their current investigations. Still, with the exception of Maglione, the romance for these detectives tends to remain subordinate to the main crime plot. What does surface, however, are subtle tensions and outright hostility towards the lesbian officer, and these attitudes expressed by the public (when orientation is known), as well as by the police community, create an atmosphere that has the potential to thwart their success in apprehending the criminal. No longer constrained by closets of their own making, Maglione, Delafield, and Mendoza extend the range of influence. The quality of the connections between these women and their subordinates deepens and is often portrayed outside of the precinct building. The separate aspects of their lives—personal, professional, public—become intertwined in a series of beneficial relationships.

Gianna Maglione's experience represents the idealized version of this situation. She is confident and comfortable with her lesbian identity, and even though her position on the force would suggest otherwise, her sexuality does not prevent a successful working relationship with her special crime unit. This is due in part to her selection of a group of officers who represent racial, gender, and sexual diversity. A large factor is her sense of fairness and respect for fellow officers, her willingness to do the hard, tedious aspects of police work, and her desire for justice, in both the abstract and practical. Moreover, her professional boundaries are respected by her colleagues, particularly Eric Ashby, her second in command. Interestingly, Ashby becomes the impetus forcing Maglione to confront the implications of her identity. Ashby, who knows Maglione is a lesbian, argues early in the book that she publicize the homophobic source for the crimes: all the victims are either gay or lesbian, and as the investigation continues, the motive for the killings is discovered to be the sexual orientation of the victims. He confronts her and challenges her:

> These people thought they were safe, Anna. They thought their lives were their own. They were wrong and now they're dead and that scares the hell out of me and I know it scares you just as much." Maglione's answer indicates ambivalence in terms of identification with the victims and identification as a police officer. She tells Ashby, "I can't catch a killer if I'm spending time worried about keeping my own closet door locked (KS: 25-26).

Throughout the course of the investigation the latter connection dominates Maglione's decisions. When her new lover, a reporter, publishes the story of the investigation, the collision of these divergent allegiances occurs. Here, Maglione's integrity as an officer remains paramount even as the private relationship between these two almost breaks at the story's climax. As Maglione is threatened when she is taken hostage by the murderer, the two sides conflict when "for the first time she wondered whether or not it might truly be better for all homosexuals and lesbians to exit the closet. . . . Keeping secrets is different from keeping privacy" (175). At the novel's conclusion, however, Maglione maintains the basic separation of private and public environments as Ashby accepts the reporter's romantic attachment and Maglione's private relationship is kept out of the news.

Were it not for the crime and its victims, Maglione's sexuality would remain an isolated component of her professional life. But because the victims of the serial murderer are all gay and lesbian and because Maglione shares this identification, her struggle to reconcile the public and personal aspects of her life takes on great significance—how her peers and subordinates respond to this knowledge can make the Hate Crimes Unit a success or failure. Moreover, understanding the importance of the Unit (Maglione has lobbied hard for the Unit's formation and to be appointed its head) focuses her attention on keeping these aspects of her personality separate rather than integrating them. Maglione's attention to the borders, despite the open acceptance of her Captain and others, indicates the deep-seated tensions the lesbian in a command position carries.

In *Amateur City* homosexuality is a subtext, an incidental factor to the solution of the murder, and for Kate Delafield the division of professional and private spheres is instinctive: "I've never pretended to be heterosexual, But I've never made any announcements either, and never will. Why give anyone a weapon? And it *is* a weapon" (180). As noted earlier, Delafield maintains a clearly defined relationship to her co-workers that admits no unprofessional actions. While Delafield's partner indicates sympathy for the death of her long time companion, the sentiment is quietly but completely rebuffed. This distance, however, is bridged as the Delafield series continues. With each new case, Delafield finds these two components of her life forcefully, sometimes dramatically, reconciled. In *Murder at the Nightwood Bar* and, most directly, in *Murder by Tradition*, Kate Delafield's lesbian identity becomes the central factor to the solution of the crime. In previous novels Delafield had refused to become involved with particularly gay-identified issues. She even refused to visit gay bars when off duty. The first novel ends with Delafield specifically connected to the gay community, breaking down her self-imposed isolation. However, Delafield still maintains the separation of her private and public life.

In *Murder by Tradition*, the next to last in the series, Delafield's lesbianism becomes essential to the crime's resolution. As with Maglione, the case involves the death of a gay man, and during the accused murderer's trial, Delafield's sexual orientation become a potential weakness for the prosecution. The defense attorney, who knows of Delafield's sexual identity, attempts to accuse her of bias against his client. During intense questioning, the attorney continually goads her with allegations of conflict of interest and partiality. Here the most dangerous implication for Delafield is not so much having her orientation made public as is the challenge to her professional position and authority. Before the trial begins, Delafield confronts the fear of being publicly outed and acknowledges the pulls on her loyalty. During the trial, when she is asked if she let anything interfere with her investigation, Delafield answers with an assertion of her commitment to the law and fair play. The defense attorney's constant attacks on her integrity are met by objections from the prosecutor, objections which, more importantly, are upheld by the judge. The jury may guess at Delafield's sexual orientation, but the focus is kept on the victim and the accused. When the guilty verdict is returned, Kate Delafield's personal and professional identities are acknowledged and protected.

Elizabeth Mendoza confronts the overt homophobia of her male colleague when she is asked to assist in the investigation of a series of rapes. As with the cases of Delafield and Maglione, the victims of the rapist are all lesbian. Mendoza must first overcome the prejudices of Steve Carson, her temporary partner for this investigation, before she can pursue and capture the perpetrator. Carson feels threatened on two levels: first as an officer whose abilities are questioned when another detective is brought into his case; second, Carson's blatant homophobia is revealed when Mendoza's own orientation is mentioned. His hostility comes through clearly when he and Mendoza meet for the first time: "I don't need any help with the investigation. You two are here simply to make the victims feel more comfortable. . . . So make them feel better however you like. Just don't do it in front of me" (TL:37). His outburst suggests Mendoza's using some kind of sexual overtures to comfort the victims. Mendoza ignores the sexual innuendo, addressing the more important challenge to her authority: "I was a special agent for the FBI for several years . . . I have more investigative experience than you and your new partner combined. I wasn't selected to work these cases because of my sexual preference, but because I'm the best my department has to offer" (37). At this point, Carson grudgingly accepts Mendoza, because he has checked her credentials, and is willing to "overlook" her gender and orientation. Nonetheless, because of police hierarchy, Mendoza's experience requires that Carson acknowledge her authority over him. Moreover, as the case precedes, Mendoza discovers a gap in his procedures that could jeopardize the case. Eventually Carson learns to value Mendoza's experience and to respect her leadership in the investigation.

However, while overcoming his prejudice against Mendoza as his commander is more easily done, accepting her lesbian identity is more difficult even though he can ignore it during the active pursuit of the suspect. The reeducation of Carson's homophobia comes more slowly over the course of the novel. Besides Mendoza, Carson is given a second partner, Officer Ashley Johnson, another open lesbian. Clearly the novel examines the manifestations of prejudice—the extreme hostility of the rapist and Carson's more conventional bias:

> Steve looked over each case and decided that these were definitely hate crimes. The suspect didn't like lesbos. Steve could understand that, he didn't like them either. Shit, women didn't belong doing it with each other. That wasn't normal. It just wasn't natural. (35)

At this moment the two men's views are indistinguishable. However, Carson immediately begins to distance himself from the rapist: "But this guy was sick." He is still unable to recognize that his version of normalcy rests on ignorance. During the investigation Carson will be made to realize the extent of his own homophobia. He will begin to compare his views with others and find his rigid stereotypic judgments being tested. Carson's basic decency comes through as these discoveries drive him to recognize and work to change his perceptions. Interestingly, Mendoza's demand for Carson's professional response (her authoritative demand) acts as a buffer for those often intense emotional situations. Acting like a cop enables Carson to become aware: "You know, Tenny, it was like talking to anybody. . . . I'm not saying I understand any better why women want to be with other women. But a relationship is a relationship, no matter who it's between" (86). This marks the beginning of Carson's turnaround; he can accept sexual difference at least on an intellectual level. The rape of Ashley Johnson brings this recognition into the personal realm. Instead of Carson turning the attack into a vendetta, it is the finely tuned team work of a commander and her partners that brings the rapist to justice.

Whatever her rank, the lesbian police officer's very presence on a force juxtaposes two divergent attitudes. On the one hand, the lesbian embodies all that a society considers aberrant; she flaunts the heterosexual assumptions concerning sexual and emotional attachments. Such behavior demands its practitioner be ostracized from the community because she poses a threat to the traditional definition of community consensus:

> The woman who identifies as lesbian, far from occupying a position of power and prestige, is likely to be stigmatized and socially marginal. She is a member of an oppressed minority group, and her

> way of life is regarded by the general public as dissident and transgressive." (Palmer 70)

As a transgressor, the lesbian is pushed outside the protection society provides; as a transgressor, the lesbian has no power to present societal expectations from defining her existence as deviant. The various institutions of authority that establish a framework of security and stability for a community fail the lesbian in her attempts to function as a member of that community The implied contract that exists between the individual and society is declared void, and the lesbian has no social recourse.

The lesbian who takes on the role of law enforcement officer also assumes the burden of reconciling the contradictory aspects of her existence. The fundamental duty of the police is to assure that the relationships between members of a community and its authoritative institutions are smoothly integrated. A police officer represents the basic and conservative idea of social control; she embodies the power of maintenance and stasis, and she defends the legal structures that define proper behavior. She succeeds only when she "negotiate[s] the existing system and conform[s] to the organizational and occupational norms" (Martin xv). For the lesbian officer, however, this support of the status quo denies her very nature. The lesbian, because she stands outside the law, cannot represent or defend the law.

Yet, as these novels featuring lesbian law enforcement officers show, the ability to integrate these opposing positions is possible without compromise. As Sally Munt points out, "[c]rime fiction is a site for the expression of anxieties about society, and the appeasement of that fear is structurally inscribed in the narrative" (124). Each of the characters considered here has absorbed the ideals of enforcement; each officer is committed to maintaining the laws that hold society together. This allegiance become the point of entry into the power systems of a particular police force. Knowing the rules, knowing how to adapt them to her situation, enables the lesbian officer to survive both in and out of that environment. In fact, many of the characters—like Gianna Maglione and Kate Delafield—discover that they must bring the personal and professional together. Doing this enriches the lesbian's experience in each sphere. The officer gains authoritative stature through her honesty. Challenging the stereotypic expectations of male officers actually stabilizes her position in the police hierarchy. The lesbian officer does not have to outman her fellow officers, but show that she accepts the limits and expectations of her position. The woman acquires visibility and asserts the right to exist in the community, not on the margins. The transgressive definition of the lesbian's private life loosens and frees her from the threat of physical and emotional annihilation. Playing the game, when the rules are clear and the play is fair, establishes new points of reference for the lesbian and society.

WORKS CITED

Forrest, Katherine. *Amateur City*. A Kate Delafield novel. Tallahassee, FL: Naiad Press, 1984.

———. *Murder at the Nightwood Bar.* Tallahassee, FL: Naiad Press, 1987.

———. *Murder by Tradition*. A Kate Delafield novel. Tallahassee, FL: Naiad Press, 1993.

Heidensohn, Frances. *Women in Control?: The Role of Women in Law Enforcement*. Oxford UP, 1992.

Kappeler, Victor, Richard Sluder, and Geoffrey Alpert. *Forces of Deviance: Understanding the Dark Side of Policing*. Prospect Heights, IL: Waveland Press, 1994.

Lewis, Catherine *Dry Fire*. NY: W.W. Norton, 1996.

Martin, Susan Ehrlich. *Breaking and Entering: Policewomen on Patrol*. U of California Press, 1980.

McAllester, Melanie. *The Lessons*. An Elizabeth Mendoza novel. Minneapolis, MN: Spinsters Ink, 1994.

Morell, Mary. *Final Session*. A Lucia Ramos novel. San Francisco, CA: Spinsters Book Co., 1991.

Munt, Sally R. *Murder by the Book?: Feminism and the Crime Novel*. London: Routledge, 1994.

Palmer, Paulina. *Contemporary Lesbian Writing: Dreams, Desires, Difference*. Buckingham: Open Univ. Press, 1993.

Reddy, Maureen. *Sisters in Crime: Feminism and the Crime Novel*. NY: Continum Publishing Co., 1988.

Silva, Linda Kay. *Taken by Storm*. A Delta Storm novel. San Diego, CA: Paradigm Publishing Co., 1991.

Wade, Donna. "Crossing the Thin Blue Line." *The Lesbian News* May 1996: 32+.

CHAPTER SIX

Queering The "I": Black Lesbian Detective Fiction

Stephen F. Soitos

Nikki Baker has written three detective novels featuring Virginia Kelly an amateur detective who is also a lesbian and an African American. The three novels, *In the Game* (1991), *The Lavender House Murder* (1992), and *Long Goodbyes* (1993), take place in Chicago, Provincetown, and the small Midwestern town of Blue River, Indiana, respectively, where Kelly was raised by working-class African American parents. Kelly herself lives in the fast lane of contemporary urban life and works as a investments counselor for the Chicago brokerage firm of Whytebread and Greese, and her first-person narratives deal with the contemporary issues of sexuality, class, and race that confront a well-educated and ambitious black woman. Her unique viewpoint as a black lesbian presents an insider's look at the corporate world while exploring alternative and marginalized lifestyles in the broader context of lesbian subcultures. In this way, the novels become more social critiques than genre crime stories.

HISTORY OF FEMALE DETECTIVES

The history of female detectives has a literary tradition stretching back to 1864 in England with the appearance of *The Female Detective* by Andrew Forrester, which introduced a female police detective named Mrs. Gladden. The same year produced W. Stephen Hayward's *The Experience of a Lady Detective* featuring the female detective, Mrs. Paschal. Although both books have female detectives, they are generally considered to be part of the detective memoir category. The first authentic appearance of a female detective in a detective novel written by a woman occurs in United States with the publication of Seeley Regester's *Dead Letter: An American Romance* (1864), followed in turn by Anna Katherine Green's *Leavenworth Case* (1878), and both precede by a number of years the first appearance of Conan Doyle's detective Sherlock Holmes in 1887. Following Doyle, the female detective continued to appear in print under various guises throughout the late nineteenth and early twentieth centuries.

While the tradition of the female detective is long and varied, critics such as Kathleen Klein in *The Woman Detective: Genre and Gender* (1988) have found much to debate concerning their effectiveness in challenging the male model of the detective. One such area of contention is the way in which detective authors, both male and female, failed to convincingly present a new type of female detective by not creating tension between the female detective gender issues. As Klein states there is no positive correlation between the detective's gender and her professional experience (23). According to Klein, one common pitfall of female authors was typecasting their female detectives directly on male models in the genre, giving their heroines similar attributes and traits: "Modeling the female protagonist on a male prototype establishes the conditions for her failure as either investigator or woman—or both" (162). The difficulty of having a woman work within the system without co-opting her own feminist principles is also problematic in female detective novels as demonstrated by another fatal ploy that sabotaged the effective creation of a unique female detective novel: the infusion of the typical marriage plot in which the female detective falls in love and gets married—often to a male detective—and consequently gives up her career. In the early novels the female detective commonly restores the dominant male social superiority and overall male hegemony at the conclusion of the case. Concerning this early period of female detective writing, Klein states: "Less important as detective novels, these novels function as cautionary tales for readers about the importance of middle class respectability and its rewards" (79).

Other critics, however, including Maureen T. Reddy in *Sisters in Crime: Feminism and the Crime Novel* (1988) and Gloria A. Biamonte in her dissertation, "Detection and the Text: Reading Three American Women of Mystery" (1991), use greater flexibility in examining early detective texts. Both suggest that these novels subvert the genre and critique the dominant male viewpoint in indirect but no less meaningful ways. All critics seem to agree that the publication in the 1970s by a number of female detective novelists, such as Sue Grafton, Marcia Muller, and Sara Paretsky, brought new life to the genre at which point there occurs "a consciously articulated response to social change by women writers who challenge the sexist assumptions of hero formation" (Klein 5). These contemporary female novelists consciously work within the traditions of the detective genre, predominantly the hard-boiled school, "exposing the genre's fundamental conservatism and challenging the reader to rethink his/his assumptions" (Reddy 2). Klein, who focuses mainly on paid professional female detectives, also agrees there are female authors who use amateur detectives to "consciously and carefully tell women's stories through feminocentric plots and structures which challenge the generic restrictions" (229).

After the publication of Pauline Hopkins's *Hagar's Daughter* (1901-1902), which introduces an amateur black female detective, there are no known African American women writing novels with black female detectives until the publication of Dolores Komo's *Clio Browne: Private Investigator* (1988). There is a Chicana detective named Kat, short for Maria Katerina Lorca Guerrera Alcazar, who appears in M.F. Beal's feminist detective novel *Angel Dance*, published in 1977, a groundbreaking novel Klein calls "the earliest of what has become a subgenre of the eighties—the explicitly feminist detective novel usually published by a women's press" (216). Yet it is important to remember that even though there are no known black female detectives between Hopkins's 1901 novel and Komo's 1988 novel, there were a number of black women who were consciously employing the strategies of detective fiction in their more mainstream novels. These writers and novels would include Toni Morrison's *Song of Solomon*, Ann Petry's *The Narrows*, and Gayl Jones's *Eva's Man*.

THE VIRGINIA KELLY SERIES

Nikki Baker's novels are good examples of texts published by a small press for a particular audience which tell womens' stories from a woman's viewpoint. Baker's press, Naiad, based in Tallahassee, Florida, offers feminist and lesbian texts exclusively, while Baker's work, in particular, also underlines the interesting contemporary reality of the detective novel. As the detective novel's sphere of influence and readership widens, more diverse groups find its versatility appropriate to their needs; Baker herself is a female author who introduces a new twist to the growing assortment of amateur female detectives solving crimes in contemporary settings. As I have discussed in my book, *The Blues Detective: A Study of African-American Detective Fiction* (1996), an important aspect of detective fiction is its function as a social document of a time, place and culture. Baker, as an African American female who writes detective novels with a black female detective, has extended the black detective tradition into new areas. By so doing, she joins a growing number of African American detective authors who use the form to explore cultural and social issues. As indicated by other female black detective writers, such as Barbara Neely in *Blanche on the Lam* (1993) and *Blanche Among the Talented Tenth* (1994), the crime text can be used as an interesting vehicle of self-exploration. Moreover, when the detective devices of suspense and intrigue are applied to African American cultural themes, it provokes issues and, at the same time, provides an entertaining and suspenseful plot.

To some extent Nikki Baker's three novels extend the tradition of classical and hard-boiled detective fiction. Creating a black female detective who is a lesbian is a daring move. In the long run, however, the novels make only superficial reference to detective themes and no reference whatever to the African American detective tradition. For example, Baker makes off-hand references to mysteries in her fiction. In *In the Game* Ginny Kelly says that she has "been a hopeless mystery buff since I was a kid. I like mysteries where a regular guy is the hero like Cary Grant in *North by Northwest*, Jimmy Stewart in *Rear Window*, and a million different book and movies they show late at night . . . " (33). This rather vague and exclusively male reference to the detective tradition (cinema version only since no books are shown late at night) is slightly amplified by Ginny's insistence that her life is like a mystery movie. Sam Spade, Marlowe, and detective icons in general are dropped here and there, but none of Ginny's comments mention either the female or the black detective tradition. Consequently, Baker's use of the detective genre is not self-reflective or highly self-conscious. She uses only the simple staples of the genre such as mysterious murder, crime, or assignation to provide a vehicle for her more idiosyncratic interests.

THEMATIC OVERVIEW

Overall, there are three important themes that Baker's work establishes. First, her choice of the detective genre underlines the vitality and continuing diversity of detective fiction. Secondly, the books make revealing disclosures about African American presence in contemporary settings. Finally, the queer philosophy and lifestyle depicted in the novels reinterprets detective conventions by refocusing the locus of investigation on the narrator rather than the plot. Thus, complex social issues concerning personal liberation and social adaptability, as well as the condition of minority relations in contemporary United States, are presented under the guise of mystery novels.

Kelly is an amateur detective whose personal life is in chaotic change. The crimes of the first three novels function as plot devices, backgrounded against the more important issue of Kelly's intense identity quest. The mysteries loosely follow the pro forma constructions of murder and investigation usually adhered to by mystery novelists and established by classical detective writers such as Conan Doyle and Agatha Christie. However, instead of reinterpretating established forms of the genre, Nikki Baker has redefined the "I" in the detective tradition and made it one of marginalized difference in that the detective "I" found in Baker is in continuous struggle with itself and the larger world.

The detective viewpoint, the larger than life "I," is a typical conceit of American hard-boiled detective fiction. However, Baker's novels share little else with the predominately white male hard-boiled tradition which often relies on the detective's professional status and physical violence for plot construction. More importantly, by queering the "I" and radicalizing its persona, Baker has reversed the typical hard-boiled detective approach. Instead of presenting a detective persona consciously adapting the world to its viewpoint and thereby establishing ultimate control, Baker has given us a queer "I" which more often than not questions itself and the viability of its worldview. With the use of the detective persona "I," Baker gives us a black lesbian's viewpoint as she searches for meaning in contemporary American society. In Virginia Kelly's case, the lesbian worldview is of primary importance and provides the framework and the gestalt for the three detective novels.

ANALYSIS OF THE NOVELS

The first novel, *In the Game* (1994), takes place in Chicago and introduces us to Virginia Kelly in her job as an investments counselor.

Virgina Kelly, commonly called Ginny, is a liberated, black female involved in a live-in relationship with a white female named Emily. Virginia struggles to define her place in American society, first as a black women and then as a lesbian. Her problems are presented in the first pages of the novel when she outlines her life in Chicago. She is not happy with her job or her upper-middle-class lifestyle, and while she bemoans a shallow existence based on material accumulation, she can't seem to find a workable alternative. Her relationship with her white lover Emily is rapidly falling apart. Emily is a tax accountant and the two were brought together by Virginia's desperate need for financial structure. Virginia's circle of friends and acquaintances are predominately women with middle-level executive and professional jobs. As an educated black woman from a working-class background, Ginny is successfully pursuing the American dream, yet finds it curiously hollow and comments "I was feeling trapped by my life" (*Game* 4). Her fancy car, gentrified inner-city condominium in a white neighborhood, and her self-avowed pursuit of appearances (learned, she suggests, from her parents) have left her without a center.

Questions of class are inextricably connected with the problems of race in these novels. Virginia's struggle occurs on three fronts: black, female, queer—but not necessarily in that order: "I saw a woman with some brains in a country where women are valued for our bodies. I saw a black face where blackness is valued not at all" (*Game* 135). But race issues for Ginny are predominately personal reflections on the difficult status of blacks in contemporary society. Ginny's analysis contains little historical perspective and no sense of solidarity.

On one hand, she is quite astute when analyzing the pervasive prejudices of Chicago's neighborhood discriminations: "In Chicago, race hate and prejudice cross barriers of class and money. Consequently, middle class neighborhoods as well as slums and housing projects are still segregated for the most part" (*Game* 31). Conversely, the Civil Rights Movement of the 1960s seems like ancient history to her. In *Long Goodbyes*, a novel focusing on Ginny's family and background, her father asks her "Why are you so angry?" (175). Her expository answer reveals an interesting dialectic:

> My parents had told me stories of the 1950s, bus boycotts and protest marches, water hoses and attack dogs, the way other kids grew up on the grim morality of Mother Goose, when all we had was a bourgeois savior who liked his women white and wore silk pajamas just like

> Hugh Hefner. 'How angry were you in the fifties?'I asked him. (*Long* 175)

The black struggles for equality and respect seem like fragments of a shadowy past to her; but the connection she makes between her own lesbian liberation struggles and the black liberation movement of the civil rights era is a valid and important one, for it was out of this earlier movement that gay rights gained momentum. However, Ginny's race consciousness is definitely post-Black Power and solipsistic in nature. While she is concerned and aware of how racism effects her, particularly in the workplace, a broader perspective seems to eludes her.

For example, in the novel *The Lavender House Murder*, which explores lesbian community, outing, and ageism in the hothouse atmosphere of Provincetown, Massachusetts, Ginny is very aware of her exoticism by way of skin color in the predominately white lesbian community. She is also cognizant of the brutal origins of the African American experience as when she reflects on a bas-relief commemorating the Mayflower Compact in Provincetown:

> . . . I can find no memorialized evidence of my own less auspicious landing one hundred years after the mooring of the Mayflower at Provincetown. A legacy of exploitation and adversity, survival and resourcefulness. My absence in history and memorial is not surprising when people want to read stories with happy or unambiguous endings." (*Lavender* 89)

Assuming that the "my" here is representative of a race not an individual family (we are given no other confirming genealogy), Ginny's condemnation of institutionalized racism reveals an interesting perspective. Her sentiment is fittingly bitter, but her overview is not accurate and offers no hint of approaches to negate the ongoing legacy of the past. Historians generally consider the twenty blacks traded in Jamestown harbor by a Dutch captain in 1619 as a primary reference point, although there is much debate on this issue.[1] But more importantly, Ginny's worldview tends to be very narrow. Her blistering asides on matters of race prejudice are without doubt incisive and acerbic but remain victimized, forming circles that inevitably place her in the middle, attacked from all sides with no recourse for action. The claustrophobic, egocentric scope of these novels is both part of their fascination and inherently their greatest weakness: all roads lead to Ginny Kelly's troubled existence. Her vast complaint provides an often confusing and at times self-contradictory succession of fragments that total a self-revealing portrait. In general, while detective novels usually open up into an outside world perceived through the eyes of the detective or his/her trusted assistant, the solitary "I" of detective persona takes on a new perspective in the Kelly series. Here, one finds a perspective far less perspicacious and omnipotent than normal—and a perspective that often implodes back on itself with devastating consequences.

Ginny is frustrated on many levels and acculturization is part of the problem. She reflects on her own upbringing as an:

> African-American princess with the fatal flaw of kinky hair . . . little black girls with their hair on end do not want to hear about black pride when they are taught on movie screens what is beautiful is straight and white and western. (*Lavender* 9)

Indeed there is no question that institutionalized racism has wrecked havoc on the self-esteem of countless minority members. But as a mature black woman in her late twenties who frets fearfully in all three novels over her *old* age, her looks, her image, the reader slowly realizes that Virginia Kelly has accumulated a vast plethora of cultural detriments. Not least among these is her total obsession with self which colors the world she inhabits with negative images of all kinds.

In the Game establishes this point early. The title is a metaphor for business and private life. Her business life is conscribed by racism, antifeminism, and homophobia. She suspects, correctly, that she is a token employee in a predominately white male bastion of commerce and that the glass ceiling is brushing her kinky head. Her critiques in this arena attack isolation enforced from without, but Virginia is also isolated from within. Most, if not all, of her friends are white lesbian females, but the bonds they share are easily shattered. The immanent breakup of Ginny's marriage with girlfriend Em is foreshadowed by the essential mystery of the novel—who killed Kelsey, the lesbian lover of Ginny's friend Beverly. The murder occurs outside a lesbian bar and brings up the issues of gay bashing, closet lifestyles, and career opportunism among gay yuppies. Ginny is drawn deeper into the developing conspiracy of betrayal and jealousy between lesbian lovers and during the process of her investigation makes trenchant comments on social behavior.

Although the murder functions as a plot device, Baker's novel is constructed around the themes of sexual identity and lesbian relationships. This is demonstrated by the fact that after the murder of Kelsey and the implication of Ginny's friend Beverly, Ginny ignores the murder to have a one-sided affair with a white female lawyer, ending her three-year-old relationship with her lover Em. This forty-page digression seems symptomatic of Ginny's take on the world and Baker's approach to the detective novel. Traditional detectives hammer the solution to a crime out of disparate pieces of evidence, generally ignoring in the process personal needs. In Baker's detective fiction the converse is true: Virginia Kelly's needs are of primary importance and the crimes themselves fulfill a secondary function.

Ginny's personal life is paradoxical. She demands respect for her color and her sexual choice. Yet within her own world she is ruthlessly self-serving. When she tires of her affair with Susan, the not so good-looking white lawyer, she disposes of her this way: "I was looking for adventure to prove my life was not a lesbian version of middle-class monogamy. Now I had an adventure and it was enough for a while" (*Game* 89). As a consequence of this flash affair in which she takes advantage of Susan, Ginny loses her marriage with Emily and is in turn stalked by Susan—then seems puzzled by the consequences of her behavior.

Kelly is superb when indicting the ignorant biases of her white, male coworkers who make value judgements about her based on color and sexual preference. Yet she herself manufactures hollow judgements on other people based on superficial characteristics. After sleeping with Susan she relates the common disgusting anecdote about sexual usury:

> There are single baggers where you'll put a paper bag over her head to take her out. There are double baggers. . . . The worst is Coyote ugly, here you will gnaw off your own arm to escape in the morning. . . . From the way Susan held me as she slept I wondered if I hadn't better sneak out while I still could. (*Game* 83)

Gay and lesbian couples have been living the nightmare of zero security and unrecognized relationships for years. This injustice seems strangely opposed to democratic ideals as pointed out in *The Gay and Lesbian Liberation Movement* (1992): "America does not have a federal law protecting the civil rights of lesbians and gay men . . ." (Cruikshank 193). Without official sanction lesbian couples find themselves thwarted at every turn in their desire for conventional acceptance of their existence. In *The Lavender House Murders*, Ginny reflects on what she wants in a relationship:

> What I wanted was a woman as flexible as builder's putty to fill in the empty spaces in my life. I wanted a woman as large as a circus tent to wrap around me and keep me safe, as deep as the potholes in the city streets when the spring thaw comes, to make a home for me in the ugly world. Em could not bend and stretch like a tarp and had not learned to live happily with compromise. (65)

And at times Ginny can sound even more conventional than a traditional heterosexual: "I felt myself succumbing to my middle-class suburban programming: co-habitation, commitment ceremonies, slab houses and screaming babies were looking better and better all the time" (*Goodbyes* 31).

Ginny knows only too well the isolation and the consuming desire for love and companionship that is so difficult to fulfill in any community and particularly difficult in the gay community as it is currently constituted. Moreover, fueling her continued state of frustration is the dilemma of gay "passing" and its converse "coming out" or "outing." The second novel, *Long Goodbyes*, explores Virginia's past, her family relationship, and her first attempts at coming out. Here, it is clear that Virginia Kelly is caught in dangerous trap of appearance versus reality and is living a lie, snared in a web of duplicity and intrigue fabricated around hidden lesbian identity and homophobia. The Blue River high school reunion forefronts crucial problems Ginny has never resolved. For example, her parents suspect her lesbianism but have not been told. One of her old high school friends, a gay man named Emery, has died of AIDS while Ginny has ignored his illness and his last attempts to reconnect with her. Emery is one of the few males in the three novels who is described with sympathy. He took her to her first Gay Pride Parade in San Francisco in 1984 just at the outbreak of the AIDS epidemic. At the time Ginny comments that "AIDS was a disease that happened to people I didn't know" (*Goodbyes* 81). While awareness of AIDS and its devastating effects are not lost on Ginny by the 1990s, she nonetheless manifests a *laissez faire* attitude towards promiscuous and unprotected sex; her understanding of the devastating effects of the disease on the gay community seems beyond her concern. Twenty plus years after the Stonewall Riots of June 1969, the defining moment of gay and lesbian activism, Ginny Kelly has no comprehensive awareness of gay rights battles or the overall gains fostered in the struggle for solidarity and community.[2] In the process of attempting to seduce her old school mate, Rosalee, Ginny Kelly uncovers the hidden underbelly of Blue River's social conventionality. Appearances deceive and the people that Ginny once imagined as having control of their lives and the community are shown to be motivated by less than noble principles. Rosalee's sexual ambiguity becomes the focal point of Ginny's attempts to rediscover the mystery of first love complicated by a blossoming but bewildering urge to come out.

The novel functions as an active palimpsest for the evolving conflicts of a complex lesbian personality. Surrounded by a conventional heterosexual family and community with status quo aspirations and zero tolerance for sexual difference, Ginny confronts the issue of lesbianism alone. She avoids and fights with her parents who cannot accept her choice. She manipulates former schoolmates for her own interests and she generally pretends to be something other than she is. This overall identity crisis is further acerbated by her queerness which she attributes to an essentialism she terms a "genetic wild card" (*Goodbyes* 6).

As Claudia Card discusses in *Lesbian Choices* (1995), this concept of "essentialism," or any reference to the concept of a "lesbian essence," is only one aspect of a debate about sexual identity and preference (17).[3] In *The Gay and Lesbian Liberation Movement* (1992), Margaret Cruikshank offers another:

> Despite these hints of genetic influence, it seems likely that homosexuality has complex social origins. No particular family structure is known to favor its development, however, and homosexuals are as diverse as heterosexuals in their personality types. (26)

In fact, all of Baker's novels deal with the conflict between the personal and public life of lesbian characters who have to hide their sexual orientation for fear of reprisal and discrimination. For Ginny Kelly, the joys and dilemmas of her queer lifestyle are the fulcrum point by which the rest of the world is weighed. However, when it comes to solidarity and commitment to political as well as personal change, Ginny refuses to participate. In *The Lavender House Murders*, the lavender house of the title, first imagined as a sanctuary for lesbian couples in Provincetown, quickly becomes a house divisive in which gay couples fight over past relationships, cling jealously to current ones, and generally take advantage of each other at every opportunity.

Perhaps the most important arena of Ginny's frustration is the battlefield of "outing" as it relates to lesbian community and solidarity. The lavender house of Provincetown is projected to be the idealized home of lesbians, a place where they can be themselves, safe from the attacks of the outside word. But even in this atmosphere there is conflict. Samantha, the older matriarch of the house, has not achieved recognizable stability and while committed long-term friendships among gay women are one of the great triumphs of lesbian lifestyle, this novel focuses instead on the ravages of age, the continued jealousies of possession and sexual intrigue, and the impossibility of trust.

Joan, the white gay activist and political journalist in *Lavender House*, is a good case in point. Joan is strenuously attacked for her political views by Kelly while at the same time she is the focus of Kelly's sexual appetite. Joan, a militant "outist," is killed off early in the novel, and it is possible that the closet-lesbian Senator, hiding with her lover in the back room, might be the culprit. Then again it could be Samantha herself who is jealous over Joan's promiscuous behavior. Or perhaps she is a victim of homophobia, which even in Provincetown rears its ugly head.

Ginny's relationship with Joan has been fraught with conflict. She lusts after Joan as a sexual partner but finds her militant pro-lesbian attitude very threatening. Joan embodies liberation and activism in a devil-may-care confrontational style that forces Kelly to rethink her own situation. For one thing, Kelly has been closeted in her work place:

> I wasn't sure it would improve my employment prospects if my sexual orientation became a topic for lunchroom gossip at Whytebread and Greese . . . somehow I didn't think I needed to advertise my membership in yet another downtrodden minority group. (*Lavender* 40)

The pressures of Ginny's job situation are taking its toll on Ginny's sense of self. Her ambition to succeed in the business world amplifies rather than reduces the difference between Kelly and the white, male dominated world of commerce. Unlike her white, male colleagues she can't be herself and in fact is forced to hide her true identity in an attempt to place herself in the mainstream. Complicating all this is the ambiguous definition of her own needs. She wants commitment but fears committing. She wants sexual encounters but refuses responsibility for acceptance of the personality or wishes of the sexual objects she desires. Ginny tries to seduce Joan and then comments: "But for all my histrionics, it was odd to know that I hadn't even liked Joan much, although, I couldn't deny I wanted to sleep with her" (*Lavender* 47). Joan is every closet queer's nightmare and her arch, in-your-face style aggravates both on a personal and public level. Ginny does not trust her. Nobody trusts her because everyone is hiding something. Consequently she is killed. As Ginny states:

> Her voice was mother-father promising that my Negro rights were well-secured and offering me the chance to fight for newer, whiter, more feminist causes. But I was tired of people saying what was good for them was good for me and I'd heard that pitch before. (*Lavender* 85)

Vivian V. Gordon in her book *Black Women, Feminism and Black Liberation: Which Way?* makes an important point about this issue. As Gordon notes, "White women have historically and consistently welcomed black men into organizational efforts while at the same time excluding black women" (12). Moreover, she cautions, "African American women must reconstruct their supportive linkages, many of which have severed because of their rejection of each other" (24). Virginia Kelly is caught in the same double bind: excluded by blackness and suspicious of solidarity amongst lesbians she is adrift in a world driven by her fickle desires. Her biggest lie, hidden sexual identity, forces her to question everything about herself. Until she finds the courage to declare and join with her sisters in protesting conventional suspicion and hatred, she will remain isolated and bitter.

Claudia Card gives a reasonable account of the optimistic approach to coming out:

> Neither chauvinistic nor sexually exhibitionist, the point of coming out is usually to avoid "passing" and duplicity, to prevent extortion, to make political connections, to get others to see oneself in

> nonintimate contexts as Lesbians see each other in such contexts, or to communicate that one is *not* ashamed and refuses to be shamed. (*Choices* 15)

In effect, Ginny's sexual orientation is her greatest strength and perhaps her greatest weakness. Part of the problem is that she fears recrimination, but she also exhibits personal revulsion and guilt. With her outsider's perspective on societal conventions, she is incredibly insightful about biased behavior, particularly in the subtle and not so subtle ways in which women are victimized. However, by the same token she's capable of complaining about sexual stereotyping at the very moment she's practicing it: "It was a long set and the car girl danced well, I thought, like the way she would fuck. She poured herself across the floor like she was made of warm molasses . . . I had no doubt that we would go to bed" (*Lavender* 64). The sex in these novels is explicit but not pornographic and its humdrum casuality often depicts passionless promiscuous coupling. Kelly frequently has sex with females she dislikes or finds distasteful, often because of their looks or their clothes.

Virginia Kelly is a lesbian female whose sexual preference is not mainstream. But the rest of her world is predominately one of consumerism and value judgements based on appearance. She is ageist, materialistic, and prejudiced against males. How people look, what people wear, what people drive and what and where they eat are all serious considerations for Virginia Kelly's world. Image, clothes, accessories function as indices of value judgements. Her sexual conquests are revealing blends of need and usury, with other females judged mainly by their looks: "Em wanted only the confidence in my stone fidelity, an impossible thing for the weak of faith to give in a world that is full of temptation and so empty of moral support" (*Lavender* 65).

Virginia Kelly takes her place in a long line of dissatisfied sleuths whose personal life is a shambles. The difference is that Virginia's personal life is the real focus of these novels. Kelly is a female in turmoil caught in a vise between personal desires and socialized phobias. The sum of the total is a frightening portrait of a woman on the verge of self-destruction. Part of the problem is that Ginny leads an unconventional lifestyle in sexual choice but manifests conservatism in other aspects. Her mistrust and dislike of many of the people she meets in the novels also reflects some degree of self-hatred. The issue of homophobia is often a two-edged sword and guilt for transgressions against the status quo sometimes masquerades as anger. In her introduction to Bernice Goodman's *The Lesbian: A Celebration of Difference* (1977) Adrienne Rich makes a good point about this: "Homophobia (the fear of same gender erotic feelings, both in oneself and in the world at large) has only begun to be named and identified" (1). These novels underscore the insidious way in which socialized phobias such as racism, homophobia, and sexphobia are endemic in our society, creating in their enveloping wake a terrible legacy which often turns the individual tainted by these poisons into self hating and self-destructive human beings.

In conclusion, Nikki Baker's three detective novels featuring Ginny Kelly are uneven creations that seldom work as effective mystery novels on the genre level. The rejection and questioning of conventional lifestyles is an important reevaluation that hasn't often been pursued in detective fiction. The novels as a unit explore many facets of Kelly's life and we are not left with a happy, unambiguous ending. The books document a process and a exploration. Virginia Kelly's life is in evolution and she is continuously defending her minority status against attacks. As in hard-boiled detective fiction and film noir, the American landscape is presented as a wilderness in which only the toughest and most merciless survive. Virginia Kelly lives in the middle of this wilderness but is trying to find a way out. Her strong points are a relentless searching for meaning and a questioning of a purely existential existence. Hopefully, future novels will demonstrate an evolving consciousness of Virginia Kelly's worldview and appreciation of herself in relation to committed social agendas that by nature and inclination she seems destined to embrace.

NOTES

1. For example, the historian C. Eric Lincoln writes "The first Negroes to arrive in the Western Hemisphere were *not* the "twenty Negars" traded in Jamestown harbor by a Dutch captain in 1619. A Negro, Pedro Alonzo Nino, was the navigator of the Nina, one of the ships Christopher Columbus sailed to the New World in 1492" (10).

2. As a lesbian Virginia Kelly appears devoid of interest in or knowledge of her own tradition. These novels would provide an excellent forum for some historical reification. For example, What is *The Well of Loneliness*?—an early lesbian novel by Radclyffe Hall. What was a Boston Marriage?—a romantic

friendship between women in New England. What was the name and year of the first U.S. Homosexual Group?—*Society for Human Rights*, 1924.

3. Claudia Card's recent book contains an excellent first chapter on the herstory and debate on the themes of lesbian culture. See "What is Lesbian Culture?" pp. 11-35.

WORKS CITED

Baker, Nikki. *In the Game*. Tallahassee, FL: Naiad P, 1991.

———. *The Lavender House Murder*. Tallahassee, FL: Naiad P, 1993.

———. *Long Goodbyes*. Tallahassee, FL: Naiad P, 1993.

Beal, M.F. *Angel Dance,* 1977. Reprint Freedom, CA: Crossing Books, 1991.

Biamonte, Gloria A. "Detection and the Text: Reading Three American Women of Mystery." Dissertation, University of Massachusetts, Amherst, 1991.

Card, Claudia. *Lesbian Choices*. New York: Columbia UP, 1995.

Cruikshank, Margaret. *The Gay and Lesbian Liberation Movement*. New York: Routledge, 1992.

Forrester, Andrew. *The Female Detective*. London: Ward, 1864.

Goodman, Bernice. *The Lesbian: A Celebration of Difference*. Out and Out Books, 1977.

Gordon, Vivian V. *Black Women, Feminism and Black Liberation: Which Way?*. Chicago: Third World Press, 1989.

Green, Anna Katherine. *The Leavenworth Case: A Lawyer's Story*. New York: G.P. Putnam's Sons, 1901.

Hopkins, Pauline. *Hagar's Daughter: A Story of Southern Caste Prejudice*. 1901-02. Reprint. *The Magazine Novels of Pauline Hopkins*. The Schomberg Library of Nineteenth-Century Black Women Writers. New York: Oxford UP, 1988.

Jones, Gayl. *Eva's Man*. Boston: Beacon Press, 1987.

Klein, Kathleen Gregory. *The Women Detective: Gender and Genre*. Urbana: University of Illinois, 1988.

Komo, Dolores. *Clio Brown: Private Investigator*. Freedom, CA: Crossing Press, 1988.

Lincoln, C. Eric. *The Negro Pilgrimage in America*. New York: Bantam Books, 1966.

Morrison, Toni. *Song of Solomon*. New York: Knopf, 1977.

Neely, Barbara. *Blanche on the Lam*. New York: Penguin, 1993.

———. *Blanche Among the Talented Tenth*. New York: Penguin, 1994.

Petry, Ann. The Narrows. 1953. Reprint. Boston: Beacon Press, 1988.

Reddy, Maureen T. *Sisters in Crime: Feminism and the Crime Novel.* New York: Continuum, 1988.

Regester, Seeley (Metta Victoria Fuller Victor). *The Dead Letter: An American Romance.* New York: Beadle, 1867. Reprint. New York: Gregg Press, 1979.

Rich, Adrienne. "Introduction." Goodman, Bernice. *The Lesbian: A Celebration of Difference.* Brooklyn: Out and Out Books, 1977.

Roberts, Dell. *Lesbian Lists: A Look at Lesbian Culture, History, and Personalities.* Boston: Alyson, 1990.

Roberts, J.R., compiler. *Black Lesbians: An Annotated Bibliography.* Tallahassee, FL: Naiad Press, 1981.

Silvera, Makeda, ed. *Piece of My Heart: A Lesbian of Colour Anthology.* Toronto: Sister Vision Press, 1992.

Soitos, Stephen F. *The Blues Detective: A Study of African American Detective Fiction.* Amherst: U of Massachusetts P, 1996.

CHAPTER SEVEN

Gender-Blending, Genre-Bending, and the Rendering of Identity in Barbara Wilson's *Gaudí Afternoon*

Susan Elizabeth Sweeney

Every account of the exploits of C. Auguste Dupin, Sherlock Holmes, Lord Peter Wimsey, Ellery Queen, and other early detective heroes lingers over that climactic moment when the sleuth reveals "who done it"—naming the criminal aloud, disclosing his or her true identity, and sometimes even pointing him or her out with an accusing forefinger. By indicating the guilty party so specifically, and so definitively, the hero has managed once again to preserve the prevailing social order. It is the detective's ability to fix identity, in other words, that produces the conservative ending required by nineteenth-century positivism and Golden Age elitism. In contrast, today's multicultural, feminist, and postmodernist detective stories seek to subvert the social order rather than preserve it. They assert that characters' selves are fluid and multivalent. They argue that identity must be understood in terms of its social construction. Because these stories renounce some of the basic premises of detective fiction, then, they inevitably transform the genre's ideology as well as its expression in literary form. Barbara Wilson's lesbian feminist detective novel, *Gaudí Afternoon* (1991), is a case in point. *Gaudí Afternoon* not only revises the classic mistaken-identity plot in terms of sexuality and gender; it also uses "translation" as a metaphor for crossing the borders of private, social, sexual, and gendered selves.

CASES OF IDENTITY

Before I turn to Wilson's novel, however, I want to gloss the series of adjectives that I have applied to it—"detective," "feminist," and "lesbian"—and explain their relevance to notions of subjectivity. *Detective* stories are usually defined as either tales that feature a detective or tales that focus on the detective process. The typical plot emphasizes a mysterious crime, an investigation conducted by a single individual, and a final solution produced by that investigation. The genre's historical and formal development includes "classic" tales by Edgar Allan Poe, Arthur Conan Doyle, and others, which stress scientific positivism (ca. 1840-1910); primarily British "Golden Age" mysteries, featuring stylized puzzles, stock characters, enclosed settings such as a country house, and amateur sleuths such as Agatha Christie's Hercule Poirot (ca. 1910-1940); the American "hard-boiled" school, characterized by gritty realism, Southern California locales, tough private eyes like Dashiell Hammett's Sam Spade or Raymond Chandler's Philip Marlowe, and a sense of underlying social corruption (ca. 1925-1960); and recent extensions, revisions, or "metaphysical" inversions of all three models (ca. 1960 onwards).[1] The genre's ideology is revealed in the way that it represents such elements as sleuth, criminal, mystery, investigation, and solution. Classic detective fiction, for example, upholds a philosophy of rational individualism. And yet it also presents people as fixed components in an immutable social, political, and economic system; thus Holmes can discern a client's class, occupation, habits, history, and character with a single glance from his hooded eyes.

Feminist detective fiction criticizes both that hierarchical system and its perpetration in popular narrative.[2] As Anne Cranny-Francis points out, feminist writers tend to revise existing literary genres "as part of a conscious political strategy to explore the social construction of women's lives" ("Gender" 69; cf. Godard 46, Humm 237). Authors of feminist detective fiction, in particular, manipulate that genre's narrative formulae in order to expose and alter its ideological assumptions. In other words, feminist detective novelists do more than merely replace a male sleuth with a female one. Cranny-Francis even contrasts hard-boiled "*female* detective novels"—which alter the genre's usual characterization of women by employing female protagonists—with more "radical," "subversive" *feminist* revisions of the amateur-detective plot, which implicitly criticize the genre's "narrative of bourgeois individualism" and its ideologies of gender, race, and class ("Feminist" 176; my emphasis).

Feminist detective fiction, then, revises the very notion of individual identity, especially in terms of autonomy, authority, responsibility, and criminality. As Barbara Godard explains, these detective novels work "to produce a dispersed subject position" rather than a unified subject (50). In particular, they tend to privilege collaboration, relational thinking, and what Carol Gilligan has called a female "ethics of care" over the lonely individualism of classic, Golden Age, and hard-boiled tales. (Wilson's first detective novel, *Murder in the Collective* (1984), is a good example of such concerns: as the title suggests, it addresses tensions between individual and collective enterprise.) Feminist detective novels also define crime itself differently. They often investigate incidents of sexism, homophobia, and violence against women rather than capital offenses. More important, they suggest that these particular instances of wrongdoing are the logical outcome of a society based on women's oppression, and that patriarchy and other hierarchical systems which discriminate against groups of people constitute the real evil behind such crimes. Although feminist detective novels may still name a single person as the guilty party, then, they argue that this individual's actions reflect a broader social practice—and that truly solving the crime would entail changing that practice as well as identifying the individual. Accordingly, these novels extol feminism as both a framework for analyzing such behaviors and an alternative to the system that produces them (cf. Reddy, "Feminist" 175).

Lesbian feminist detective novels subvert the genre's form and ideology even more radically.[3] They replace the masculine world of classic and hard-boiled detective fiction with an explicitly woman-centered one. Lesbian detective novels thus pose additional questions about the nature of identity—especially in regard to desire, gender, social conformity, and "compulsory homosexuality," in Adrienne Rich's famous phrase. What this new subgenre builds upon, Sally Munt suggests, is the traditional notion of the sleuth as both moral crusader and outlaw, as both representative of society and critic of it (120). But lesbian crime fiction makes the investigator's relationship to her society even more ambiguous and problematic. Indeed, it extends the critique of binary gender roles (heterosexual woman versus heterosexual man), already present in other feminist detective novels, by adding a third term: "lesbian." The resulting disruption of gendered dichotomy alters even more drastically the rigid, stylized, Manichaean worldview that is the very basis of detective fiction. As Kathleen Gregory Klein points out, "If the binary of gender—male/female—can be thrown off track by the introduction of a third term . . . then so too can the apparently unchanging pairs of criminal/victim and detective/criminal. . . . If detective, criminal, victim are not either-or identities but fluctuating subjectivities, if crime is both criminal and legal, if detection is both discovery and concealment, what then is detective fiction?" ("*Habeas*" 175).

Lesbian crime fiction also builds upon the inherent eroticism of the mystery's hermeneutic structure; the romantic subplots that Wilkie Collins and Dorothy Sayers added to the genre, and the explicit sexuality of hard-boiled detective stories. Munt notes, in fact, that the novels of M. F. Beal, Katherine V. Forrest, Barbara Wilson, Mary Wings, and others derive not only from the detective genre but also from lesbian pulp romances, which are "preoccupied with issues of sexuality and identity" (121). Traditional detective fiction is preoccupied with those issues, too, but it defines them with regard to ideologies of masculinity and heterosexuality. In lesbian crime fiction, however, both the mystery and its solution are implicitly linked to the sleuth's awareness of her erotic attachment to women. Indeed, virtually every series of novels about a lesbian detective features an account of her "coming out" (Klein, "*Habeas*" 179; Reddy, *Sisters* 123-28).

Such emphasis on the sleuth's discovery or disclosure of her own homosexuality shapes the form and content of lesbian detective fiction. The prevalence of coming out stories shows, in particular, how this subgenre links investigative practices to sexual identity and identity politics. Munt even suggests that the fundamental quest in lesbian detective novels "is an epistemological one: to discover, to know, what is a lesbian?" (143). What it means to be lesbian, after all, is elusive, ambiguous, and private, self-determined as well as socially constructed, and intrinsically linked to all the other x's and why's of one's own identity—more so, for example, than being feminist. And yet, no matter how inherently *individual* one's sexuality may be, acknowledging it means identifying oneself with the way others perceive it. Coming out, then, means coming up against the social representation of one's identity. Speculating on detective fiction's appeal to lesbian writers and readers, Wilson observes that "most of us have been silenced as women [and] as lesbians. The lesbian investigator brings this silence into her work; it protects and opppresses her" ("Outside" 181). By focusing on coming-out narratives, in fact, lesbian detective fiction transforms the familiar search for the person "who done it" into an investigation of how ideologies of gender and sexuality shape individual subjectivity.

At this point in my essay, I feel acutely the responsibility to identify myself as heterosexual. (My reading of Wilson's detective novels may well differ from a lesbian feminist analysis. But Wilson has said that she writes with various readers in mind ("Feminist"); and I believe that *all* feminist critics must recognize and engage with lesbian texts in order to counter sexism, heterosexism, and misogyny in the academy and to ensure that all women's voices can be heard.) As my confession indicates, this subgenre's emphasis on coming-out stories—in which a woman learns to identify as lesbian—can make all readers more aware of their own identities. Lesbian feminist detective novels prompt questions about matters of selfhood, sexuality, and gender that were never addressed by the stock characterizations and rigid classifications of earlier tales.

WILSON, NILSEN, AND REILLY

I now turn to Barbara Wilson's witty, exuberant, delightfully self-reflexive lesbian feminist detective novel, *Gaudí Afternoon* (1990). This is the fourth of Wilson's five detective novels to date: she has published the Pam Nilsen series—*Murder in the Collective* (1984), *Sisters of the Road* (1986), and *The Dog Collar Murders* (1989)—as well as another book about Cassandra Reilly, *Trouble in Transylvania* (1994). She is also an award-winning translator of Norwegian literature; a cofounder of Seal Press; and the author of two other novels, *Ambitious Women* (1981) and *Cows and Horses* (1988), and three story collections, *Thin Ice and Other Stories* (1981), *Walking on the Moon: Six Stories and a Novella* (1983), and *Miss Venezuela and Other Stories* (1989).[4] Wilson has said that she began writing detective fiction because she liked the challenge of working within its formal and ideological constraints: "Wherever there's a genre, someone will try do something different. . . . That's definitely my reason for doing it; it's fun to subvert something that has some rules to it." At the same time, she wanted to subvert the detective formula for feminist ends: "I thought it would be interesting to combine politics with an entertaining genre" ("Feminist"; cf. Wilson, "Outside" 176, Gerard 128).

The nature of lesbian identity is central to Wilson's detective fiction. The Pam Nilsen series recounts not only Pam's inquiry into several murders but also her investigation of her sexuality, her discovery of her lesbianism, and her "navigat[ion of] the coming-out process" (Wilson, "Outside "182). Indeed, precisely because Pam discovers in the first book, *Murder in the Collective*, that she *is* lesbian—in other words, because she realizes something about herself she had not known before—the novel seems to suggest that acknowledging her attraction to other women is tantamount to finding her true self. As Munt points out, then, the Nilsen series appears to trace the revelation of an authentic inner lesbianism, "a fixed, stable, natural essence forming the truth of identity" (125; cf. Gerard 128, Reddy, *Sisters* 123-24).

Wilson may have felt uncomfortable, however, with such an essentialist notion of sexual identity. Even in her first detective novel, as Munt explains, she "problematizes meaning by constantly undermining textual and social conventions; things are never what they seem. 'Identity' is seen as a transitional process of discovery involving contradictory states of desire" (129). In an interview, moreover, Wilson specifies that Pam's coming out in *Murder in the Collective* is not a form of narrative closure, but rather "a kind of opening up in a way that presents whole new problems" and forces Pam to reconsider her position in a patriarchal society ("Feminist"). More important, after three books Wilson abandoned Pam Nilsen, as a detective, for the breezily confident Cassandra Reilly. She explains that she wanted to write "about women who have been out and have been self-identified as lesbians for their whole lives, and Cassandra was good for that. She's just easy and natural about it and doesn't even think twice about anything to do with it" ("Feminist"). Because Cassandra—unlike Pam—already identifies as lesbian, her sexuality is a matter of playful, pleasurable performance rather than earnest self-discovery. Indeed, Wilson calls the Cassandra Reilly novels "comic myster[ies]" (184) or "moral comedies," which are "more frivolous and more sophisticated" than her earlier books ("Outside" 183). And because the new series assumes Cassandra's lesbianism from the beginning, Wilson can investigate more fully the connections between sexuality and other issues: gender identification, "passing," coupling, parenting, aging, ethnicity, nationalist politics, and global feminism. In *Gaudí Afternoon*, in particular, she shows that individual subjectivity belies rigid classification according to sex, sexuality, or gender.

As its title suggests, *Gaudí Afternoon* combines two allusions to twentieth-century modernism: on the one hand, the gender politics, romantic intrigue, and festive atmosphere of Dorothy Sayers' early feminist detective novel, *Gaudy Night* (1936);[5] on the other, the playful, nonlinear, free-flowing form of buildings by Spanish architect Antoni Gaudí. Both allusions are appropriate: *Gaudí Afternoon* is a romantic feminist mystery set in Barcelona, and Gaudí's surreal architecture even plays a role in the plot. But the hybrid nature of the novel's title—its conflation of two different languages, two different artists, and two different art forms—is also fitting. I argue, in fact, that *Gaudí Afternoon* constantly elides such distinctions between genders, genres, and languages in order to underscore the mutability of identity. This strategy is consistent with queer theory and transgender studies, both of which seek, as Ken Plummer puts it, "a world of multiple gendered fluidities—a world at home in a postmodern cacophony of multiplicity, pastiche, and pluralities that marks the death of the meta-narratives of gender" (xvi). The Cassandra Reilly series has been marked, so far, by just such heterogeneity; wordplay, multilingual jokes, intertextuality, narrative framing, and genre parody; "unrestrained physical slapstick and farce, as well as witty repartee" (Wilson, "Outside" 184); and repeated depictions of gender itself as ironic social performance.[6] In order to trace this playful deconstruction of unified subjectivity in *Gaudí Afternoon*, in particular, I want to focus on two aspects of the novel: first, Wilson's use of the detective-story device of mistaken identity, especially in light of sex, sexuality, and gender; second, her reliance on "translation" as a metaphor for subverting binary social constructions of identity.

BLENDED GENDERS

Gaudí Afternoon takes the form of a masquerade in which names, nationalities, languages, genres, genders, and sexualities change before the reader's eyes. Wilson's detective, Cassandra Reilly, is a literary translator, a lesbian, a woman who often passes for a man, and an American with an Irish passport who spends most of her time in Japan, Iceland, and Uruguay (*Gaudí* 3). The mystery that confronts her in *Gaudí Afternoon*, moreover, further emphasizes the mutability of such social categories. The client—a lovely damsel in distress named Frankie—asks Cassandra to track down an ex-husband who apparently violated their custody agreement by absconding to Barcelona with their six-year-old daughter. Cassandra is busy translating a novel, but she adores Barcelona and gladly accepts the opportunity to go there, all expenses paid. Frankie's ex-husband, Ben, apparently fled to the Spanish city with their daughter, Delilah, in lovesick pursuit of a foot therapist named "April Schauer." April, in turn, went to Barcelona because she and her stepbrother, Hamilton, own an apartment there in one of Gaudí's most famous buildings. Cassandra locates Ben, April, and Hamilton soon after she arrives. Little Delilah keeps disappearing, however, as she is abducted first by one parent, then by the other, and then by other interested parties. Finally, Delilah herself refuses to return unless her parents promise to stop fighting.

The emphasis on such "women's issues" as marriage, motherhood, and child custody mark *Gaudí Afternoon* as a feminist detective novel. And yet the novel's plot, as I have just described it, may not seem terribly innovative, resembling as it does a high-concept cross between Hammett's *The Maltese Falcon* (1929) and Disney's film *The Parent Trap* (1961). However, nothing in this novel is as it seems. *Frankie*, Cassandra's winsome client, turns out to be a male-to-female transsexual and female impersonator. *Ben* is not Frankie's husband but Frankie's ex-wife, Bernadette—who is now a lesbian and a bodybuilder. *April*, Ben's new love interest, is also a male-to-female transsexual, a fact that she has kept from Ben because Ben was so upset by Frankie's sex-change. *Hamilton*, April's half-brother, is a gay man who often cross-dresses. It is not surprising, then, that Cassandra—after an unsuccessful attempt to solve Delilah's latest disappearance—dreams that she herself has been captured by a tribe of hermaphrodites (139-41). Indeed, before the mystery is resolved, virtually every character in this novel has been mistaken for or disguised as someone of the opposite gender.

This may be why Klein calls *Gaudí Afternoon* a "so-called detective novel, which is more like a romp through Barcelona on a search for missing persons in plain sight" (*"Habeas"* 183); why Munt complains that it "degenerates into comic gender picaresque" (143); and why even Wilson herself calls it "a farce, a mystery without a murder, a caper" ("Outside" 183). I argue, however, that *Gaudí Afternoon* is an ingenious detective story that cleverly parodies generic clichés in order to deconstruct notions of sexed, sexualized, and gendered identity.

Consider, for example, how Wilson subverts the classic detective-story charge to "cherchez la femme." Cassandra's client, Frankie, is just as lovely, elusive, and deceitful—and, it initially appears, just as red-haired—as Brigid O'Shaughnessy, the femme fatale in Hammett's *The*

Maltese Falcon and a character to whom Cassandra explicitly refers (*Gaudí* 55, 59). But when Cassandra tries, in vain, to track down her own client at the hotel where she is supposedly staying (as Sam Spade also did), she must first describe Frankie to the desk clerk "as a curly redhead and then as a brunette with a pageboy. I even tried describing her as a man. The desk clerk gave me a strange look and grew more adamant." His paraphased response—"No one like that had ever been a guest at this hotel"—suggests not only that he has not seen Frankie in any shape, form, or gender, but also that his establishment does not welcome clients of such indeterminate sex (65). Wilson parodies the stylistic clichés of hard-boiled detective fiction for the same ends. After Delilah disappears yet again, and her mother—boyish, muscular Ben—breaks into tears, first-person narrator Cassandra wisecracks in the time-honored tradition of Hammett and Chandler: "I hated to see a woman go [to] pieces like that, especially one who looked like Arnold Schwarzenegger" (158). Wilson also shows how social constructions of gender provide false clues that lead to mistaken identity. Cassandra herself is "mistaken for a man too many times to count" after she compensates for a bad haircut by cropping her hair (114). When she shares a taxi with Ben, however, the driver addresses *her* as "señora." Cassandra observes wryly: "I was back to womanhood, but only because the world thinks in dyads and Ben was more of a man than me" (103).

In addition to being mistaken for someone of another gender, most of the characters in *Gaudí Afternoon*, including little Delilah, deliberately cross-dress in order to escape detection or circumvent restrictive gender roles. Such disguise is not unknown in detective fiction (Farrer 125, Garber 186); in Doyle's classic "A Scandal in Bohemia" (1891), for example, Irene Adler foils Holmes by dressing as a boy, following him to his lodgings, and boldly accosting him there. In *Gaudí Afternoon*, however, Wilson uses various instances of cross-dressing (unisex clothing, drag, female impersonation, male heterosexual transvestism, and fetishism), as well as the confusion that it produces, to expose the very dichotomy of maleness and femaleness as a social construction. On one such occasion, a transvestite character states outright that "Crossdressing throws our rigid dualistic thinking into chaos" (152). On another, Cassandra's lesbian girlfriend, Carmen, reviles transvestites because "Men should be men" and "Women should be women," whereupon Cassandra immediately retorts: "What about you? . . . Are you a woman if one of the definitions of woman is only being attracted to men?" (68).

Wilson thus "plays with the . . . disguises and false identities so dear to the hearts of crime writers" ("Outside" 183). She uses those familiar devices, moreover, to critique "rigid dualistic thinking" about gender (*Gaudí* 152) and problematize the relation between gender and sexuality (as shown by the exchange between Cassandra and Carmen above). In *Gaudí Afternoon*, in fact, Wilson attempts to tease apart the tangled interconnections of biological sex, psychological sexual identity, erotic sexuality, social gender role, and actual behavior. After Cassandra learns that Frankie is transsexual, for example, she finds that she can detect slight ways in which Frankie "still resembles a man"; but she concludes that Frankie nevertheless is "more feminine than I or many of my woman friends. It wasn't only surgery that had changed her sex, or hormones, it was a conscious choice to embrace femaleness, whatever femaleness is" (82). Frankie's identity as a woman, then, results less from her biological sex—or rather, surgical and hormonal correction of her biological sex—than from her "conscious" identification with other women and her deliberate performance of femininity.

Wilson is equally careful to distinguish between sexual identity and sexuality. Cassandra muses, "I don't think people change their sex for erotic reasons. . . . It must be something deeper, more existential" (73). Indeed, Frankie is apparently attracted to men, whereas April, another male-to-female transsexual, is attracted to women—and Cassandra, in turn, is smitten with her.

In addition to tracing such distinctions among biological sex, sexual identity, and sexuality, Wilson also recounts Cassandra's discovery of the crucial difference between self and gender role. When Delilah disappears once more, Cassandra suspects Frankie of having kidnapped the child; accordingly, she disguises herself as male in order to search for Frankie at a men's gay bar. Although Cassandra doesn't locate Frankie, she does experience a sudden revelation: "it was as if I were at a masquerade ball and everyone, at the very same moment, lifted their masks, and I saw gender for what it was, something that stood between us and our true selves. Something that we could take off and put on at will. Something that was, strangely, like a game" (77). The analogy to a masquerade echoes the novel's overall atmosphere of comedy and carnival as well as its many references to cosmetics, costumes, wigs, masks, props, prostheses, and other forms of disguise.

More important, this passage clearly differentiates between individuals' "true selves" and the gender roles that they perform—whether for pleasure or from necessity.

Wilson, who has said that she expects her novels to offer various readers "a safe way of talking about families and lesbians and feminist ideas" ("Feminist"), also apparently intended *Gaudí Afternoon* to subvert conventional assumptions about the relation of gender and sexuality to parenting. She investigates the connections among biology, psychology, and social roles more closely, for example, when she shows Cassandra puzzling out the relationship between Delilah's parents. Frankie's sex-change and Ben's coming out as lesbian each raise questions about how the roles of husband, father, wife, or mother relate to social constructions of masculinity, femininity, and heterosexuality. In one instance, Frankie tells Cassandra that she considers Ben her ex-husband—despite the fact that Ben has always been female—because "she's so *butch*. She's always been so much more of a man than me" (83). In another instance, Ben's transsexual girlfriend, April, announces that even though "women are supposed to be crazy about babies and children," she personally dislikes them. Her remark subverts gendered ideologies that equate women primarily with reproduction. And yet April herself defines motherhood in terms of femininity and heterosexuality: she complains to Cassandra that she had never imagined Ben might have a child, since Ben looks like "a bodybuilder," "bulldyke," or "boy" rather than a mother (123).

To make matters more complicated, while Ben rejects traditional femininity and compulsory heterosexuality, she does cling to an essentialist definition of motherhood. And even though Frankie is Delilah's biological father, *she* wants to function socially as the child's mother. Ben, who accuses Frankie of "trying to usurp [her] biological role," claims that "the biological mother always feels different than the other parent" (64, 130); transsexual Frankie, who describes herself as "a perfect mother" and says that she abducted Delilah because of "a mother's love," counters that "Motherhood isn't about biology, it's about love" (84, 118, 130). Meanwhile, one of Cassandra's girlfriends wants to raise a family with her, even though Cassandra has no interest in becoming a parent.

Wilson sums up this ongoing, open-ended debate about motherhood's relationship to female biology, female sexuality, heterosexuality, and femininity by revising another classic detective-story device: the interrogation scene. After Delilah disappears yet again, Cassandra questions two elderly Spanish sisters who run the hotel from which a large woman, who claimed to be Delilah's mother, apparently abducted her. Cassandra doubts the sisters' ability to identify a stranger's biological sex accurately, since one of them has already addressed *her* as "señor." Nevertheless, she asks, "'You're sure the lady was a woman?' 'Sí, sí, madres son mujeres, claro,' the second sister said firmly, as if I were an idiot. I guessed she had a point. Mothers were women. At least they used to be" (138).

RENDING GRAMMAR AND BENDING GENRE

This parodic interrogation scene illustrates another aspect of Wilson's feminist critique in *Gaudí Afternoon*. She not only questions essentialist notions of identity that are based on gender, sexuality, and physiology; she also suggests that language cannot adequately express identity apart from its social construction. Wilson has said that she made her detective a translator so that Cassandra could "engage in all the word games and misunderstandings that the juxtaposition of languages can create" ("Outside" 183). In *Gaudí Afternoon*, as we have already seen, Cassandra must deconstruct words like "mother" and "woman" in order to solve the crime. She must also confront Ben's cross-gendered nickname; Frankie's androgynous name, which may allude to the sexually confused young heroine of Carson McCullers' *The Member of the Wedding* (1946); and the recurrent difficulty of grammatically designating Frankie's gender. "I was having trouble following the pronouns," Cassandra says at one point: her transsexual client is designated as "she" by April's brother, Hamilton; as "he" by Frankie's ex-wife; and as either "she" or "he" by Frankie's daughter, depending upon whom she is talking to (62). Cassandra herself can't decide "whether to think of [Frankie] as a 'she' or a 'he' now" (82). In the final analysis, grammar must apparently surrender to individual subjectivity. As Hamilton explains, when Cassandra asks him why "Ben refers to Frankie as he and you call her her," "I call people what they want to be called" (113).

Trouble in Transylvania (1994), the next Cassandra Reilly novel, also investigates grammatical representations of gender. In *Trouble*, Wilson devises another interrogation scene—in which Cassandra questions a tempestuous Romanian waitress named Zsoska—to show that some languages distinguish third-person pronouns by sex, and some don't. Because Zsoska's native languages are Hungarian and

German, Cassandra finds her English sentences to be "frequently impenetrable" due to their "gender-bending method of assigning pronouns" (147). This sexual pun on the *impenetrability* of Zsoska's English stresses how profoundly language is gendered and gendering. In the Cassandra Reilly series, then, Wilson uses the novels' international settings, along with her own extensive experience as a literary translator, to show how language contributes to the social construction of gender.

In *Gaudí Afternoon,* in fact, Wilson employs translation as a model for ways to subvert gendered expectations. In one scene, Cassandra and her Spanish girlfriends—one Castilian, one Catalan—argue about their linguistic differences and about cross-dressing. Her friend Carmen, who disapproves of transvestites and dislikes Cassandra's new masculine haircut, pretends to recite a dialogue from an English lesson: "My name is Carmen. . . . I am woman. Please, what are you? Woman or man?" Cassandra answers, first in English and then in Spanish: "Neither . . . I'm a translator" (74). Wilson thus uses "translator"—like "lesbian"—as a third term that undermines the male/female binary.

Indeed, Cassandra's clever bilingual rejoinder exemplifies the way in which "translation" operates throughout this novel as a metaphor for the subversion and manipulation of rigid gender roles. *Gaudí Afternoon* uses the prefix "trans-" (meaning "across," "beyond," or "through"), for example, to denote various behaviors and practices associated with transgenderism. The novel constantly refers to "translator[s]" (3), "transsexuals" (56), "transvestite[s]" (67), "transplantor[s]" (170), and even a "European Society for Organ Transplantation" (16). These terms overlap in suggestive ways—for example, a sex-change operation might involve "organ transplantation"—at the same time that they allude to related themes such as bilingualism, dual citizenship, and hybrid narrative form. "Translation" also evokes, more broadly, the strategic *trans*gression of any spatial, sexual, gendered, or generic boundary—a practice that Maggie Humm calls "crossing the border," and which she particularly identifies with feminist detective fiction (237). Translation provides a metaphor for gender-blending, then, which pervades the entire text of *Gaudí Afternoon.* But Wilson not only emphasizes this metaphor in wordplay and leitmotif; she extends it even further by describing Cassandra's activity as a working translator within the novel.

Cassandra's actual practice of literary translation evokes various instances of cross-dressing and gender-blending in *Gaudí Afternoon.* It functions, moreover, as a self-reflexive model for her detective process—especially because throughout this novel she is really investigating the mystery of gender. More specifically, Cassandra's work as a translator exemplifies both her own analysis and interpretation of the crime, and the reader's experience of this very book. Indeed, Wilson heightens narrative suspense by alternating episodes of Cassandra's investigation with excerpts from her current project: the translation of a Spanish novel, *La Grande y su hija*, which serves as a mise-en-abyme (that is, an instance of interior duplication) of *Gaudí Afternoon* itself.

La Grande y su hija is a magical realist novel penned by the pseudonymous "Gloria de los Angeles," who is acclaimed as "the new female García Márquez" and as "García Márquez in female form" (4, 31). Its authorship, then, constitutes an instance of *literary* cross-dressing that parallels the many moments of gendered disguise in Wilson's narrative, and also reflects her own efforts to revise the male detective-story tradition in feminist terms. Its text, moreover, resembles that of Wilson's own novel: *La Grande y su hija* is variously described as a genre parody, a feminist "political allegory," a picaresque tale marked by "coincidences and mysterious circumstances," and a narrative that traces a series of disappearances (94, 79). Like *Gaudí Afternoon*, it is a mystery: it features a missing person as well as a strange black bag whose contents will not be revealed, apparently, until the ending. As in Wilson's novel, in fact, these narrative enigmas all relate to gender; that black bag, for example, is hidden from women, guarded by men, and closely linked to male power. Indeed, the main plot of *La Grande y su hija* seems curiously familiar: it traces a daughter's lifelong quest for her mother, just as *Gaudí Afternoon* recounts a series of maternal quests for a missing daughter. More important, it, too, is a fictive meditation on gender, sexuality, and motherhood. In addition, its title, *La Grande y su hija*—which Cassandra translates as *The Big One and Her Daughter*—suggests its filial relationship to the detective novel in which it is embedded. It even contains, in turn, "two stories" that alternate throughout its own narrative (107).

Wilson's metafictional use of two stories, two narrative levels, and two genres associated with different national literatures—Anglo-American detective fiction and Latin American magical realism—constitutes, of course, another kind of translation. Indeed, the prefix "meta-," like the prefix "trans-," means "beyond"; and the practice of metafiction, like translation, entails a transgression of linguistic borders. Wilson's metafiction is thus consistent with the playful intermingling of disparate art forms, genres, and languages—of disparate selves, in other words—that is first manifested in the title *Gaudí Afternoon* and that recurs in various ways throughout the novel. As a miniature, self-reflexive version of Cassandra's own narrative, for example, *La Grande y su hija* resembles the fanciful miniature houses, "shaped exactly to the child's fantasies," that Cassandra's friend Ana designs and builds for children (13).[7] The magical little house that Ana completes at the novel's end—and which she gives to little Delilah, who so needs a home of her own—is consciously based, in turn, on Gaudí's similar use of open-ended "organic form" (142). These interconnections are wonderfully appropriate, moreover, because Gaudí's extravagant, surreal, earthy style is the architectural equivalent of magical realism—as well as an apt parallel for the masquerade of gendered identities in Wilson's own novel.

As its title suggests, then, *Gaudí Afternoon* meditates on and translates between literary and architectural structure. At the same time, however, Wilson also compares an author's or architect's manipulation of organic form to the playful performance of gender. Her novel's epigraph, taken from Rainier Zerbst's *Antoni Gaudí*, makes this connection clear: "For Gaudí, however, nature consisted of forces that work beneath the surface, which was merely an expression of those inner forces" (Zerbst quoted in *Gaudí* 1). Wilson, too, is interested in distinguishing the "inner force" of selfhood from its gendered surface expression.

TRANSPOSED TEXTS AND HYBRID ENDINGS

The conclusion of *Gaudí Afternoon* skillfully increases narrative suspense by transgressing the border between frame tale and embedded text even more flagrantly than before. Cassandra's copies of *La Grande y su hija* keep disappearing, and she keeps being interrupted as she tries to translate its last pages. Such elusive texts recall, of course, another classic detective-story device, one first invented by Poe: the purloined letter. At the same time, the missing books evoke other instances of disguise, deception, and disappearance in the plot of *Gaudí Afternoon* itself, and thus heighten the reader's anxiety that those mysteries be resolved. It appears, moreover, that the ineffable last pages of *La Grande y su hija* are going to reveal, at last, *that* text's central mystery:

the contents of the mysterious black bag which generates male characters' social and sexual power, and which irresistibly suggests, therefore, the very concept—the phallus—that Jacques Lacan articulated in his famous "Seminar on 'The Purloined Letter.'" Even more curious, this black bag, in the novel that Cassandra is translating, resembles the black flight bags, bearing the intriguing logo "European Society for Organ Transplantation," that she notices all over Barcelona. But before Cassandra can finish translating *La Grande y su hija*, it is stolen from her once again, just as she is about to complete this tantalizing sentence: "At long last the mystery of Raoul's black bag was solved! It contained nothing more, nothing less than. . ." (169; Wilson's ellipsis). Cassandra never does discover how that sentence ends. Such lack of closure in the embedded text, moreover, increases the reader's anxiety about the resolution of *Gaudí Afternoon* itself.

By employing these self-reflexive strategies in her novel's ending, Wilson acknowledges how deliberately she has altered both detective fiction's ideology and its expression in literary form. The ending, after all, is the quintessential element of any detective story, the moment whose anticipation shapes the entire preceding narrative, and the aspect of the tale that most decisively affirms the genre's conservative ideology. And yet the dénouement of *Gaudí Afternoon* does not emphasize, as classic or Golden Age stories do, the sleuth's triumphant indication of the guilty party. Cassandra has already managed, of course, to identify the other characters, despite their various aliases and disguises, and to discern their roles in Delilah's disappearances; she has also made important discoveries about herself and her relationships with others.[8] But she cannot figure out on her own what happened to her copies of *La Grande y su hija*. Only on the very last page of *Gaudí Afternoon*, when her friend Ana hands her yet another embedded text (a newspaper clipping about Barcelona pickpockets), does Cassandra learn that she has been the repeated target of a gang of thieves who have not yet been captured—and who use those mysterious black "Organ Transplantation" bags to transport their loot. And even then she learns too late: in the novel's last sentence, Cassandra realizes that *La Grand y su hija* has disappeared once again (172).

The characters' personal relationships may be resolved, then, but the novel's dénouement nevertheless features an embedded mystery about the source of male power that is still unsolved, a series of anonymous criminals who are still at large, a purloined text that is still missing, and a detective who is faced with her own failure to either prevent or detect the book's theft—or, for that matter, to finish reading it. Even more disturbing, the novel's conclusion seems to confuse the black bag of *La Grande y su hija* with the flight bags of the "European Society for Organ Transplantation." By blending together "real" and "fictional" items in this way, *Gaudí Afternoon* ends with an unresolvable transgression of the distinction between its two narrative levels—frame tale and embedded text—which replicates, in formal terms, the novel's subversion of binary gender codes.

Rather than affirm a fixed, unified social order, then, the dénouement of this lesbian feminist detective novel refuses to choose among genders, genres, tongues, texts, sexes, and selves. Even at the end of *Gaudí Afternoon*, the "who" in "who done it" is still lost in translation.[9]

NOTES

1. See my essay on crimes of identity in metaphysical detective fiction.

2. On feminist detective fiction, see Cranny-Francis, "Feminist" and "Gender"; Gerard 122-30; Godard; Humm; Irons; Klein, *Woman* 200-22; Munt; Reddy, "Feminist" and *Sisters*.

3. Lesbian detective fiction's popularity makes it the quintessential lesbian literary genre (Zimmerman 210). Yet some critics seem hesitant to discuss it: A. Wilson's essay on "The Female Dick and the Crisis of Heterosexuality" leaves out lesbianism altogether, and Klein's book on female detectives gives it only two pages (*Woman* 239-41). But see Klein, "*Habeas*"; Munt 120-46; Palmer; Pope; Reddy, *Sisters* 121-46; B. Wilson, "Outside" 176-81.

4. Critics cite Wilson as the foremost writer of lesbian detective fiction, but they tend to summarize her plots rather than analyze them in detail. For an acute reading of the Pam Nilsen series, however, see Klein, "*Habeas*" 175-85; on *Gaudí Afternoon*, see Munt 143-45. See also Cranny-Francis, "Feminist" 171-74, "Gender" 78-83; Gerard 127-28; Munt 129-32; Palmer 18-19; Reddy, "Feminist" 181-82, 184 and *Sisters* 124-46. For Wilson's self-appraisal, see "Outside" 181-86; for bio-bibliographical information, see Troxell.

5. Sayers' title refers, in turn, to an academic gala or festival (*OED*).

6. On gender as performance rather than category or identity, see Butler. For definitions and theories of "gender blending," see Ekins and King.

7. One of Ana's houses, designed for a pregnant woman in the form of a pregnant woman, nicely parallels this interior duplication—particularly because both novel and embedded text are concerned with motherhood. Since both texts

recount searches for mothers and daughters, moreover, it is fitting that the house's "head" is briefly stolen (126).

8. Cassandra's most vital discoveries, such as her revelation at the gay bar, have little to do with crime-solving. As Humm points out, Wilson emphasizes character development and relationships as much as progress toward a solution (246).

9. This essay is dedicated to the memory of my friend, colleague, and mentor Cynthia Jordan (1949-1993), who introduced me to *Gaudí Afternoon*.

WORKS CITED

Butler, Judith. *Gender Trouble*. New York: Routledge, 1990.

Cranny-Francis, Anne. "Feminist Detective Fiction." *Feminist Fiction: Feminist Uses of Generic Fiction*. Cambridge, UK: Blackwell, 1990. 143-76.

———. "Gender and Genre: Feminist Rewritings of Detective Fiction." *Women's Studies International Forum* 11.1 (1988): 69-84.

Ekins, Richard, and Dave King, eds. *Blending Genders: Social Aspects of Cross-Dressing and Sex-Changing*. New York: Routledge, 1996.

Farrar, Peter. "120 Years of Male Cross-Dressing and Sex-Changing in English and American Literature." Ekins and King 123-32.

Garber, Marjorie. *Vested Interests: Cross-Dressing and Cultural Anxiety*. New York: Routledge, 1992.

Gerard, Nicci. "Feminist Genres." *Into the Mainstream*. London: Pandora, 1989. 116-48.

Gilligan, Carol. *In a Different Voice: Psychological Theory and Women's Development*. Cambridge, MA: Harvard UP, 1982.

Godard, Barbara. "Sleuthing: Feminists Re/writing the Detective Novel." *Signature* 1 (1989): 45-70.

Humm, Maggie. "Feminist Detective Fiction." *Twentieth-Century Suspense: The Thriller Comes of Age*. Ed. Clive Bloom. New York: St. Martin's, 1990. 237-54.

Irons, Glenwood, ed. *Feminism in Women's Detective Fiction*. U of Toronto P, 1995.

Klein, Kathleen Gregory. "*Habeas Corpus*: Feminism and Detective Fiction." Irons 171-89.

———. *The Woman Detective: Gender and Genre*. 2nd ed. Urbana: U of Illinois P, 1995.

Lacan, Jacques. "Seminar on 'The Purloined Letter.'" Trans. Jeffrey Mehlman. *Yale French Studies* 48 (1972): 39-72.

Munt, Sally. *Murder by the Book? Feminism and the Crime Novel.* New York: Routledge, 1994.

Palmer, Paulina. "The Lesbian Feminist Thriller and Detective Novel." *What Lesbians Do in Books.* Ed. Elaine Hobby and Chris White. London: Women's Press, 1991. 9-27.

Plummer, Ken. "Foreword: Genders in Question." Ekins and King xiii-xvi.

Pope, Rebecca A. "'Friends Is a Weak Word for It': Female Friendship and the Spectre of Lesbianism in Sara Paretsky." Irons 157-70.

Reddy, Maureen. "The Feminist Counter-Tradition in Crime: Cross, Grafton, Paretsky, Wilson." *The Cunning Craft: Original Essays on Detective Fiction and Contemporary Literary Theory.* Ed. Ronald G. Walker and June M. Frazer. Macomb: Western Illinois UP, 1990. 174-83.

———. *Sisters in Crime: Feminism and the Crime Novel.* New York: Continuum, 1988.

Rich, Adrienne. "Compulsory Heterosexuality and Lesbian Existence." *Signs* 5 (1980): 631-60.

Sweeney, Susan Elizabeth. "Subject-Cases and Book-Cases: Crimes of Identity in Metaphysical Detective Stories." *Detecting Texts: The Metaphysical Detective Story from Poe to Postmodernism.* Ed. Patricia Merivale and Susan Elizabeth Sweeney. Philadelphia: U of Pennsylvania P, forthcoming.

Troxell, Jane. "Barbara Wilson." *Contemporary Lesbian Writers of the United States.* Ed. Vivian Pollack and Denise D. Knight. Westport, CT: Greenwood, 1993. 566-71.

Wilson, Ann. "The Female Dick and the Crisis of Heterosexuality." Irons 148-56.

Wilson, Barbara. "Feminist Mystery Writer Barbara Wilson." Interview with Sheila McIntosh. *Sojourner* 16.10 (1991): 22.

———. *Gaudí Afternoon.* Seattle: Seal, 1991.

———. *Murder in the Collective.* Seattle: Seal, 1984.

———. "The Outside Edge: Lesbian Mysteries." *Para-doxa* 1.2 (1995): 176-86.

———. *Trouble in Transylvania.* Seattle: Seal, 1994.

Zimmerman, Bonnie. *The Safe Sea of Women: Lesbian Fiction, 1969-1989.* Boston: Beacon, 1990.

CHAPTER EIGHT

Subject to Interrogation

Jeffrey Langham

SWALLOWING: CHANDLER'S *THE LONG GOODBYE*

> They're all sizes and shapes when they come in here, but they all go out the same size—small. And the same shape—bent."
>
> —Raymond Chandler, *The Long Goodbye* (1953)

So speaks the figure of the law as embodied by Grenz, the district attorney in Chandler's novel, *The Long Goodbye*. Interrogating Philip Marlowe about his involvement in the escape of a murder suspect, Grenz reminds the private investigator what the system can do to an uncooperative body. While this reminder comes as a threat, and while the police do an excellent job of brutalizing Marlowe, he resists their exertions to make him conform to their will; that is, he refuses to give an official statement—or, in a word, confess. His resistance is not a matter of innocence—in fact, Marlowe is guilty of abetting Terry Lennox by transporting him out of the country—rather, it is a resistance to put into language that which everyone knows. In this sense, Marlowe's involvement evokes what D. A. Miller would call an open secret, in that knowledge is shared but not articulated or avowed. As such, Marlowe's refusal to confess his involvement invests him as an object of a desire that cannot be fulfilled until he offers the police a confession; as a result, Marlowe's refusal would appear to thwart their investigation.

However, the tug of war between the police and Philip Marlowe over a secret everyone knows actually demonstrates the complicity of the "open secret." According to Miller,

> In a world where the explicit exposure of the subject would manifest how thoroughly he has been inscribed within a socially given totality, secrecy would be the spiritual exercise by which the subject is allowed to conceive of himself as a resistance: a friction in the smooth functioning of the social order, a margin to which its far-reaching discourse does not reach. Secrecy would thus be the subjective practice in which the oppositions of private/public, inside/outside, subject/object are established, and the sanctity of their first term kept inviolate. And the phenomenon of the "open secret" does not, as one might think, bring about the collapse of these binarisms and their ideological effects, but rather attests to their fantasmatic recovery. (207)

Marlowe, therefore, by resisting the police, feels that he is not only keeping some fraternal code that binds him to Terry Lennox but that he is maintaining the character of a successful private investigator. As he puts it, "[m]aybe I'm obstinate, or even sentimental, but I'm practical too. Suppose you had to hire a private eye. . . . Would you want one that finked on his friends?" (64). However, at the same time that Marlowe's fantasy of resistance invests him with his professional identity as a detective, it also makes him an unwitting accomplice in the system that threatens to make him small and bent, since his resistance enables the police to manifest itself through the exercise of force. As to the binarisms phantasmatically recovered by the nonconfession that functions here as an open secret, we can add Miller's binary of the police and the criminal, or more to the matter of this essay, the heterosexual and the homosexual. After all, if bodies can come under the pressure of the law in order to confess a truth everyone knows, those very bodies (Marlowe's body in particular) are also sexually (re)inscribed through those pressures ("You think you are a tough guy? We'll see who's tough"). It is not my intention to imply that Grenz, as district attorney, and Marlowe, as suspect, play opposite roles within the hetero/homosexual binary, but to argue that Marlowe's resistance to cooperate with the law actually evokes this binary in a way that is provocative for detective fiction.

As Marlowe discovers first hand, the police force is a system that squeezes bodies into small, bent shapes until it gets what it wants. After it gets what it wants, however, to what extent does the reformation of the witness (small and bent) become the effect of the unproffered confession more than it becomes the effect of coercion? What I want to examine here are the ways that particular systems and modes of resistance to those systems produce particular bodies, both within and as generic texts. Such an examination is more than a matter of looking at how detective fiction represents the law as a system that produces culturally discursive bodies, but rather it is an attempt to situate certain types of detective fiction in a context of systems that extract, produce, regulate, and suppress truths about bodies—in particular, gendered and sexualized bodies. To that extent, this is a study of genre, with the precise understanding of genre as a historically arbitrated category of literature. By "historically arbitrated" I mean to use genre not in the sense of an Aristotelian triad of epic, lyric, and drama, that is, as a term that implies a way of theoretically systematizing literature into universalized categories, or even to talk about the novel itself as a modern genre. Rather, genre will be used as a term to describe a category of cultural products (for instance, popular fiction) that have been determined as such through a history of production (publishing, marketing, advertising, display) and consumption (criticism, review). Therefore, I use genre not only in a phenomenological sense but also with the understanding that, as a culturally inscribed term, genre is ideological.[1] The arbitrary category here is the hard-boiled detective novel, epitomized by Raymond Chandler's *The Long Goodbye* but more recently (re)embodied in Michael Nava's *The Little Death.* By thinking of these texts in terms of genre, our analysis, instead of limiting itself to constitutive differences, rather opens up into an examination of constitutive similarities in order to make sense of the ideological effects of a conventionalized literary form. After all, despite the low estimation of detective fiction in some critical circles, it still enjoys considerable pop-cultural currency; and, as I intend to argue, its popularity may be due to the ideological reinscriptions that the writing and reading of it enact. A more precise question, in this case, would be to ask how the conventions of this particular subgenre address the conventions of heterosexual identification.

The ideology of heterosexual identification within hard-boiled detective fiction has become more pressing as the genre grows beyond the limits of the lonely, straight, male detective. While recently the genre has been opened up by the contributions of such writers as Sara Paretsky and Walter Mosley, who have redefined the detective along lines of gender and race in provocative and exciting ways, my interest in this essay focuses on a growing list of gay detective fiction which has also helped to critique the constitutive role of the straight, white, male detective in the genre.[2] The white woman, the African American, the gay man, and the lesbian, abject characters who once inhabited the periphery of the detective's world, now take the center and appear as discursive subjects. However, within a highly conventionalized genre, gay detective fiction appears to present itself as a problematic co-optation. How then can we account for a subversive potential of recent gay detective fiction? More explicitly, how does a novel such as Michael Nava's *The Little Death* participate in such an economy? What effect does this novel have on the discursive production and circulation of the gay male in at least this particular genre of popular fiction?

I first want to return, however, to the significance of Marlowe's nonconfession, a confession that, because it is never spoken within the conventions of the law, becomes a linguistic gap. What, in fact, does Marlowe have to hide? To what extent does his involvement with Lennox carry a truth about Marlowe himself that he must conceal at all costs? Marlowe's willingness to drive Lennox across the border, and hence away from the law, betrays a relationship that could be read as illicit in more ways than one. Their friendship follows a provocative course of development. The novel begins with their introduction: Marlowe, trying to mind his own business, finds himself compelled to help a drunken Terry Lennox left abandoned by his wife, Sylvia, in front of a restaurant. Marlowe's chivalry appears inflected with gestures of a veiled seduction. He brings Lennox back to his place, fixes him coffee, then drives Lennox back to his apartment, where he turns down Lennox's offer of a drink. On the way home, Marlowe thinks "I'm supposed to be tough but there was something about the guy that got me. I didn't know what it was unless it was the white hair and the scarred face and the clear voice and the politeness. Maybe that was enough" (8). Later, Marlowe, spotting Lennox drunk on a Los Angeles street and close to being arrested for vagrancy by nearby policemen, saves him by picking him up in a taxi and again taking him back to his place. Their friendship established, Marlowe and Lennox meet several times for drinks, Marlowe remaining fascinated by the attention he gets from Lennox, a man of high social standing because of his marriage to a millionaire's daughter. At one point, however, they "break up" at a bar in a scene that reads suspiciously like a lover's quarrel. Lennox incites Marlowe by referring to Sylvia Potter as a tramp and to himself as the "hundred-dollar whorehouse" with "the brass knocker you rap one long and two short and the maid lets you into" (25). Marlowe responds suddenly and walks out of the bar without looking back while Lennox calls out to him. The emotional significance of the scene is later highlighted when Marlowe recounts that ten minutes later he felt remorse. Yet, while Marlowe may have objected to a husband's verbal abuse against a wife not present to defend herself, Lennox's own characterization reveals himself to be powerless, emasculated by his dependence on his wife's money and her apparent sexuality which he cannot, or at least does not, satisfy. It could very well be Lennox's portrayal as the castrated figure, made salient not only by the white hair and the scarred face but by his own words, that prompts Marlowe to say "you talk too damn much. . . and it's too damn much about you" (25) before walking out of the bar. What I want to establish through these above exchanges is the homoerotic dimension of their friendship, one that is present even if articulated only obliquely. Of course, I do not want to suggest that the homoerotic dimension of their friendship is unique to literary representations of male homosociality, since the complex interplay of the homoerotic and the homosocial has already been well established elsewhere and this novel would only provide another example of the phenomenon.[3] Rather I want to clarify the level of their friendship in order to entertain the sexual stake of Marlowe's refusal to confess. In other words, could his refusal also be a disavowal of his friendship in terms of its homoerotic implications?

Despite his refusal to cooperate with the police, what solidifies Marlowe's disavowal is news that Terry Lennox has committed suicide. Satisfied with Lennox's signed confession and his suicide as a literalized admission of guilt, the police no longer need to question Marlowe, who in turn no longer needs to disavow his involvement. This is not to say, however, that Marlowe feels free to make public anything that previously would have implicated him. Rather, Marlowe is allowed to remain silent, to grieve for a friend who both fascinated and angered him. In fact, soon after Marlowe is released from custody, he receives a letter from Lennox written shortly before his suicide, requesting that Marlowe forget about him:

> So forget it and me. But first drink a gimlet for me at Victor's. And the next time you make coffee, pour me a cup and put some bourbon in it and light me a cigarette and put it beside the cup. And after that forget the whole thing. Terry Lennox over and out. And so goodbye. (85)

However, Marlowe finds it difficult to forget Lennox. Although he soon fixes a cup of coffee a few paragraphs later, the second ritual of closure is deferred until Marlowe feels "sentimental" enough. By the time he does have that drink at Victor's, Marlowe's memory of Lennox cannot be easily erased, reinforced rather by the physical threats of other characters, namely Menendez, who want Marlowe to forget. However, Marlowe's romantic idealization of Lennox falls into disillusionment when his investigation uncovers that Lennox is an alias for Paul Marston, thus proving him to be a linguistically shifty character and hence unfathomable as a solitary subject. Lennox, therefore, represents the man that Marlowe cannot bring himself to become. In fact, when it appears evident that Lennox fabricated his suicide and is instead alive and well as Señor Maioranos, yet another character, Marlowe can only acknowledge that "[Lennox] is not here any more. [He's] long gone" (378). As a result, Marlowe's relationship to Lennox becomes one borne out of grief, the rituals of which compel Marlowe to remember and forget his attraction to another man.

As D. A. Miller points out, the "open secret" functions as a mechanism "reminiscent of Freudian disavowal" (207). While it appears as an aside on the narrative workings of the open secret, Miller's observation in fact opens up a theoretical entry, precisely a psychoanalytic one, into how an example of the "open secret" impinges on the construction of Marlowe as a subject.[4] For Freud, disavowal is not merely a neurotic response to a conceptual trauma, such as the death of a loved one, but a constitutive mechanism in the formation of the ego. Judith Butler's writings on discursive formulation of sexual identity also isolate disavowal as an important means by which heterosexuality becomes naturalized, thus showing that disavowal produces subjects precisely as sexualized ones. Thinking of Marlowe's open secret as a Freudian disavowal provides a way of seeing the ideological value of hard-boiled detective fiction in terms of hetero/homosexual identification, and may provide a model for conceiving the subversive potential of particular pulp fiction genres.

In *Gender Trouble*, Judith Butler revisits Freud in order to make a persuasive claim that gender could be understood as an effect of melancholy, recalling that Freud, in "The Ego and the Id," argues that melancholy is the structure through which egos are formed. It is important here to remember that in "Mourning and Melancholia" (1917), Freud distinguishes melancholia from mourning: whereas mourning is a process of libidinal withdrawal from the lost love object and the eventual transferal of the libido to a new one, melancholia differs in that the libido is taken into the ego. Thus melancholia establishes an identification of the ego with the lost object. Although it may appear as mourning, melancholia represents to Freud a "regression from one type of object-choice to original narcissism" (587). However, in *The Ego and the Id* (1923), Freud later comes to recognize that melancholia is not merely an aberrant response to object loss but is in fact a mechanism operational in the Oedipal complex and hence important to ego formation. Just as disavowal of grief through identification involves the incorporation of attributes characteristic of the lost love object, so the ego itself is formed through similar incorporations of love objects around it. In fact, the ambivalence one may feel toward a love object, when internalized, informs the creation of an ego-ideal so that identification with the object leads to self-criticism, the effect of which is a reformation of the ego. If melancholia functions as a mechanism for ego formation, Butler argues, then "this process of internalizing lost loves becomes pertinent to gender formation when we realize that the incest taboo, among other functions, initiates a loss of a love-object for the ego and that this ego recuperates from this loss through the internalization of the tabooed object of desire" (58).

Butler's allusion to the Oedipal complex as a model of gender formation through the repudiations of the mother and the father precisely defines the ego's response to these repudiations as a form of mourning; however, Butler makes clear the differences between these repudiations. According to Butler, "in the case of the prohibited heterosexual union, it is the object which is denied, but not the *modality* of desire, so that the desire is deflected from that object onto other objects of the opposite sex. But in the case of a prohibited homosexual union, it is clear that both the desire and the object require renunciation and so become subject to the internalizing strategies of melancholia" (58-59 emphasis mine). In other words, what Butler's reading of Freud argues is that gender as an effect of melancholia is a literalized disavowal of homosexual love; that is, the ego takes on a gender when it renounces the same-sex parent through a process of identification.

Butler's analysis, therefore, bears on the connection between genre and gender when we consider that, until recently, hard-boiled detective fiction has been traditionally understood as a masculine genre (written by, for, and about men). As such, hard-boiled detective fiction has traditionally offered idealized gender representations. Insofar that those gender representations, namely the detective heroes, most often narrate their stories in the first person, hard-boiled detective fiction also renders the world through a male gaze. In this sense, an analysis of Chandler's *The Long Goodbye* in terms of genre could be facilitated by a model of gender construction in which gender itself is an incorporation. As an ideological artifact of gender representation within popular culture, *The Long Goodbye* appears then to represent a masculine subjectivity constructed through melancholy. Marlowe's grief over the loss of Lennox literally becomes a long goodbye, a novel of a man who cannot admit before the law that he loves—or at least feels for—a man (enough to risk his own life) and therefore literalizes that disavowal through a body that constantly must defend itself against its own objectification. The threat of objectification—that which informs Marlowe's paranoia—insinuates itself as a calculating, cannibalistic gaze. He describes the police as having "watching and waiting eyes, patient and careful eyes, cool disdainful eyes, cops' eyes" (38). Again, he describes himself later as being eaten by one detective's eyes (40). Harlan Potter looks at him "like an entomologist looking at a beetle" (229). Marlowe, therefore, must appear as a "tough guy" by resisting their gaze.

As Judith Butler points out, what helps to solidify the literalization of gender is the fantasy of the real, the natural, that retroactively hides the sedimented history of prohibitions and displaced attachments that circumscribe gender within a heterosexual matrix. The fantasy of the real here depends paradoxically for its articulation on the unspeakability of melancholic incorporation. The literalization of gender appears real because it is not recognized as an effect, but rather the irreducibly natural cause of desires. Moreover, the fantasy of the real has as its effect the compartmentalizing of the body. As Butler's argument goes, "'becoming' a gender is a laborious process of becoming *naturalized*, which requires a differentiation of bodily pleasures and parts on the basis of gendered meanings. . . . Pleasures are in some sense determined by the melancholic structure of gender whereby some organs are deadened to pleasure, and others brought to life" (70). To this extent the "real body" is itself a fantasy, one whose "limits. . . are produced within the naturalized heterosexualization of bodies in which physical facts serve as causes and desires reflect the inexorable effects of that physicality" (71). A consistent, continuous gender is a fantasy constructed from body parts. Insofar as gender informs subjectivity, the subject perceives itself as whole through a double action of libidinizing body parts that give it a gender while disavowing that very zoning in an attempt to establish that it had always been that way, even before the subject's story began.

As it appears in *The Long Goodbye*, the fantasy of the wholly sexed body becomes manifest through Marlowe's vocalizing mouth—the first person narrative voice so common to hard-boiled detective fiction—as he tells a story of how dangerous it is to get involved with anyone. What supposedly makes Marlowe a whole subject, and hence real, is his apparent lack of desire to be attached to anybody, especially another man. After all, Marlowe's desire for attachment to another man (or woman for that matter) would seem to entail his acknowledgment that he is incomplete. Significantly, his first-person narrative constructs the fantasy of a single voice despite the melancholic incorporation of other character's voices, despite the omission of scenes or dialogue that appear not to bear on his story, even despite the formal breaking of the narrative into chapters, especially at critical scenes. Of course, ending a chapter before the climax of a particular scene heightens suspense, but it is precisely such moments of suspense in the novel that produce desire for a continuous voice, and hence the unbroken body of the hard-boiled detective. As Chandler himself notes in his 1950 essay "The Simple Art of Murder," "If the mystery novel is at all realistic (which it very seldom is) it is written in a certain spirit of detachment; otherwise nobody but a psychopath would want to write it or read it" (2). What becomes or appears "real" for Chandler must come via the signs of detachment. The male detective himself must then function as the embodiment of detachment, a peculiar stylization of the real through his resistance to be moved by the corruption around him. Since for Chandler, the detective "must be a complete man and a common man and yet an unusual man" (18), the first-person narration allows Marlowe to speak in a "real" language, the language of the common man, whose authenticity is significantly reliant on an almost poetic use of metaphor. Marlowe, therefore, speaks in the language of detachment.

CHOKING: NAVA'S *THE LITTLE DEATH*

> The sexual aspect of homosexuality was, in many ways, the least of it. The tough part was being truthful without painting yourself into a corner: I am different, but not as different as you think"
>
> —Michael Nava, *The Little Death* (1986)

The continuing development of gay pulp fiction, especially within the subgenres of romance, science fiction, and mystery, appears to trouble any program of gay cultural legitimization. Working against the intuition of reinforcing an albeit problematic gay cultural identity through high culture, the gay pulp novel appears to be sleeping with the bourgeois enemy by its very embrace of low culture. This is especially the case when we consider that the logic of production within high culture is rebellion, autonomy, transgression, originality. The logic of production for the detective novel, however, is often the opposite. As Todorov states in *The Poetics of Prose*, "the whodunit par excellence is not the one which transgresses the rules of the genre, but the one which conform to them. . . [it is] an incarnation of the genre, not a transcendence" (43). Whereas Chandler's participation in a tradition of the detective novel epitomized by the works of Hammett rearticulates a peculiarly masculinized fiction, gay detective fiction may appear to articulate a troubling co-optation. What does the gay detective novel do when it follows the rules, when it attempts to become the incarnation of the genre? In particular, what does Michael Nava's first hard-boiled detective novel, *The Little Death* (1986), do *to* the genre as it participates *in* its formularity?

Michael Nava's first novel nicely illustrates the problematics of gay pulp fiction, precisely because it is not only a hard-boiled detective novel but one that clearly evokes Chandler's *The Long Goodbye*. The parallel between the two novels did not go unnoticed by *Publisher's Weekly* whose blurb appears on the back cover of the book: "This mystery is distinguished by good writing and by skillful adaptation of the genre's traditions. Lawyer Henry Rios's loyalty to wealthy wastrel Hugh Paris strongly recalls the male bonding in Raymond Chandler's classic *The Long Goodbye*." Both novels concern a detective who befriends a man who is down on his luck despite his involvement with a rich family. It is because of their involvement with said rich families that Terry Lennox and Hugh Paris both commit "suicide." Whereas Lennox fakes his own suicide to protect his wife's real killer, Paris is murdered and his death is made to look like a heroin overdose. Both Lennox's figurative death and Paris's literal death attempt to suppress, or perhaps more evocatively, "bury" a family secret. What impels the narratives of each novel, is the suppressed grief of the detective over the loss of another man. *The Little Death* participates in the tradition of the hard-boiled detective novel primarily through its exploration of a previously established thematics of the corrupt family and of grieving masculinity, which are not merely juxtaposed but critically pertain to each other. The novel, however, differs from Chandler's in that Henry Rios is a gay man who has established a sexual relationship with Hugh Paris. The homosexual obliquity of Chandler's novel thus comes to the fore in Nava's. *The Little Death*, therefore, recasts the problematic role grief plays in the construction of identity. If Chandler's novel represents a hypermasculine ideal, one that is constructed through a disavowal of loss, how does Henry Rios as a gay articulation of the masculine detective question the logic of that construction?

Again Butler offers a way of conceiving the subversive potential of genre. If we keep in mind that pulp fiction genres such as detective fiction are formally normative, their production involves, as Todorov puts it, an incarnation of the genre. The highly romantic image of a text as the incarnation of a spiritualized, idealized genre, however, belies that incarnation is in fact an incorporation, and precisely an incorporation of other texts. As such, a text is an incorporation of its genre through signs of a citational reiteration. Similarly, as Butler argues in *Bodies That Matter*, the materiality of a body's "sex" becomes visible through a process of reiterative and citational practices. However normalizing the effects of such practices may be, Butler does see a possible space for subversion: "As a sedimented effect of a reiterative or ritual practice, sex acquires its naturalized effect, and yet, it is also by virtue of this reiteration that gaps and fissures are opened up as the constitutive instabilities in such constructions, as that which escapes or exceeds the norm, as that which cannot be wholly defined or fixed by the repetitive labor of that norm" (10). Reiteration, then, always carries with it the threat of the slipped tongue, the mispronunciation, the miscued line that reveals sex as an unstable construction. Reiteration does not index sex, rather it (re)produces sex at moments when proof of sex becomes required. Reiteration, therefore, calls into question the certainty of sex as a natural given.

Butler reminds us, furthermore, that this ritualized practice is citational. For Butler, the law of sex does not precede its citation but becomes manifest through it. That is, the law exists solely as a citation, a deferral to a fictive past. Authority, therefore, becomes a significant problem. After all, to what authority do we defer, and what authorizes us to cite the law? What makes a gay pulp novel's citation of a highly conventional, and therefore normative, tradition non-normative? In particular, how does *The Little Death* disturb the conventions it evokes when it speaks in the language of the father-texts? Its evocation of

Chandler's text, indeed, would appear actually to reinforce a highly normative model of hypermasculinity. However, as Butler makes clear, such citation is "not enslavement or simple reiteration of the original, but . . . an insubordination that appears to take place within the very terms of the original. . ." (45). It is precisely as an insubordinate act that citation becomes potentially subversive. In the mouth of the other (whether for Butler it is Irigaray citing Plato, or here Nava citing Chandler), the citation dislocates both authority and origin. *The Little Death*, therefore, calls into question *The Long Goodbye's* originary status (and hence its authority) not by disavowing the novel but by evoking it through another voice.

My recourse to Butler's deconstruction of a "naturalized" sex is not merely an attempt to draw a methodological analogy between a particular argument about the law of sex within queer theory and one that could be made about the reiterative, citational nature of genre, but one that is borne out of the recognition that genre itself—and detective fiction, in particular—actually participates in cultural constructions of sexuality. The difficult play of sameness/difference, which Henry Rios in the above epigraph recognizes as the problem of "being truthful" about homosexuality ("I am different, but not as different as you think"), actually describes the relationship of gay detective fiction to the dominant genre of the hard-boiled detective novel. The problem of working within the treacherous line of sameness and difference, which Michael Nava's novel poses as it attempts to make a difference within the tradition of the hard-boiled detective novel, can very well allow for an ideological subversion of rules in the very submission to them.

In fact, the problem of a partial difference has also been articulated within the context of postcolonial theory. Writing on the subversive effects within the rhetoric of cultural imperialism in his essay "Of Mimicry and Men," Homi Bhabha isolates mimesis as a tool employed by colonizers to regulate colonial bodies under the guise of civilizing them. However, the mimesis must be partial for the colonial bodies to remain other, prompting Bhabha to define colonial mimicry as "the desire for a reformed, recognizable Other, as *a subject of a difference, that is almost the same, but not quite*" (126). However, mimicry produces a countereffect, becoming a menace by "its double vision which in disclosing the ambivalence of colonial discourse also disrupts its authority" (129). Returning to Freud's understanding of the partial nature of fantasy as described in "The Unconscious," Bhabha describes mimicry as "a discourse at the crossroads of what is known and permissible and that which though known must be kept concealed; a discourse uttered between the lines and as such both against the rules and within them" (130). As such, the ambivalence of mimicry (same but not quite) figures the colonial as a partial object within colonial discourse, that which Bhabha likens to a fetish, and the result is that mimicry has the residual effect of revealing the "phobic myth of the undifferentiated whole white body" (133).

The relevance of Bhabha's analysis of mimicry to the context of heterosexist discourse can be found in like constructions of homosexuality which are tortuously negotiated in terms of a partial sameness. Same-sex desire is frequently made intelligible through a heterosexual matrix, especially through the still fashionable trope of inversion (a gay man is really a woman trapped in a man's body) which, as Eve Sedgwick reminds us in *Epistemology of the Closet*, "[preserves]. . . an essential heterosexuality within desire itself" (87). Same-sex desire seen through such a matrix, therefore, can only be interpreted as an incomplete mode of heterosexual desire. As recent national debates about same-sex marriage demonstrate, heterosexist responses to attempts to legitimize same-sex desire often label it a mockery (a mimicking) of heterosexuality and as such, an attempt to diminish such institutions as marriage and the family. However, mimicry, regardless of the rhetorical usefulness it may offer heterosexism, carries with it a subversive potential to displace heterosexual authority. Writing from within the context of postcolonial theory, Homi Bhabha notes that when "the look of surveillance returns as the displacing gaze of the disciplined, . . . the observer becomes the observed and 'partial' representation rearticulates the whole notion of *identity* and alienates it from essence" (129). And so it is with gay pulp fiction, whose negotiation with a dominantly heterosexual pulp tradition inevitably unseats naturalized myths of a desire for an originary heterosexual body.

If *The Little Death* calls into question the authority of *The Long Goodbye*, we should remember that what Chandler's novel "authorizes" is a particular masculinity constructed through a process of melancholia. Therefore, what Nava's novel cites in effect is a subject readable through a narrative grief over the loss of homosexual love. However, the similarity between the two pairings (Rios is to Paris as Marlowe is to Lennox) is marked with significant differences. While the homosexual is only a specter evoked in the construction of a straight male identity in Chandler's novel (that is, Marlowe's figurative swallowing of his love for Lennox becomes literalized through his assumption of a body that must be perpetually defended against intrusion), Rios *is* a gay man who loses his lover to murder and struggles to articulate his grief within a world that keeps him from doing so. Whereas Marlowe never sees Lennox's dead body, Rios not only sees the dead body of Hugh Paris but is actually called upon by the authorities to identify it. For Rios, his loss is made viscerally apparent, and despite the unavoidable recognition of his loss, Rios becomes immediately closed off from the means to acknowledge his grief publicly. Returning to his "dark and chilly" apartment, Rios realizes that he has no one to turn to for support, posing the question that could only be rhetorical: "with whom could I share this loss?" (57). Although the question could presume a pain so exquisite that it exceeds articulation (which would be better phrased as "how can I express my loss"), the verb "share" points to the matter of acknowledgment. Who will affirm and sympathize with Henry Rios's pain? Who will ratify his right to grieve? Certainly not the family of the victim, who quickly claims the body and has it cremated, effectively barring Henry Rios from attending the memorial and being publicly acknowledged as the grieving lover.

For the Paris family, the cremation finalizes an utter disavowal. No trace of Hugh Paris should remain in order that they may secure a fantasy of familial stability. Not only does Hugh Paris's status as a gay man form an undesirable skeleton in the family closet, but he threatens to bring out the other family skeletons as well, namely through his knowledge that other heirs have been murdered in order to ensure that the family fortune remains in the hands of his grandfather, the judge. Hugh's murder is an attempt to silence him (dead men tell no tales), and to bury the secrets of family corruption with his body. It is, therefore, not coincidental that a gay male body comes to serve as a repository for family secrets and that his murder and eventual dissolution secures a fantasy of continuity and containment. Hugh's family cannot grieve his loss, for to do so would acknowledge a presence that threatens their own stability. It is in this sense that at least this one heterosexually configured family is constructed through a disavowal of homosexual love.

For Henry Rios, however, the cremation punctuates his loss by its radical dissolution of Hugh Paris. The indices of loss (a body, a gravestone) are no longer localized in any external way; therefore, Rios finds himself internalizing Paris as a dissatisfying lack, "the hole where

[his] heart had been" (168). While Hugh's family literally capitalizes on his death, Henry Rios translates his loss into a debt. Realizing that Hugh was right all along in predicting his own demise, Henry vows that he must "now. . . owe him the truth" (57). Since Hugh Paris himself tells Henry Rios who the murderer will be a few days before his death, the plot of *The Little Death* is not about finding out who killed Hugh Paris. Rather, it is about Henry's attempt to articulate his grief by paying a debt to the dead.[5] For Henry Rios, this entails reviving the dead long enough to disrupt a fantasy of family wholeness purchased by Hugh's subjective dissolution. Despite the family's success in literalizing that dissolution, Henry works to figuratively put Hugh back together, and more importantly make that resubjectivization a publicly articulated event. That is, what will only allow Henry to vent his grief is a subversive investigation into the cultural machinery that disavows the object of his love and his right to grieve it.

The cultural machine in question is the very rich and influential Paris family, a convention of the hard-boiled detective novel recalling the Potter family in *The Long Goodbye*. In *The Little Death*, the Paris family embodies thematic tensions which could be mapped across some obvious binaries: private/public, order/disorder, invisibility/visibility, silence/speech. Silence, invisibility, and privacy are different, although not altogether exclusive, tools for the maintenance of order. They naturalize cultural constructions of order by hiding those constructions. Therefore, such a reproducible system of differentiation as the American family maintains its authority through a fiction of privacy. As a rich family, however, the Parises must maintain some sense of familial stasis despite their public visibility. In order for them to participate in the cultural fiction of family as the site of order and privacy, the Parises must suppress certain family secrets through strategic narrative elisions and obfuscations. In fact, their capital ironically allows them to buy their privacy from the law and the press. As Rios observes, "a hundred years earlier, Grover Linden raised monuments to his wealth, but his heirs bought privacy, the ultimate luxury" (75). Grover Linden, the founding father of the clan, is, according to Henry's fourth grade social studies book, the man who built the railroad. He is also the founder of the law school Henry attended. Not only is he the father of the Linden/Paris clan, but he is also the father of San Francisco, transforming it "from a backwater village to an international city" (46). The social studies book, however, omits the fact that Linden's paternity also resulted in unfair labor practices and other forms of corruption. Hugh's own mother cloaks herself in a series of significant omissions, and at one point in his investigation into the Parises, Henry Rios decides to learn about Hugh's mother by going through some of her books of poetry at the Linden College bookstore. He learns that

> Katherine Paris had published a half-dozen slender volumes over the past twenty years and one thick book of collected poems. Each book was adorned with the same photograph I had seen at Hugh's house and beneath it was the same paragraph of biographical information. . . . Nothing about a crazy husband and a homosexual son; apparently, that information was private. (62-63)

While the poems are described as "just words scattered across the page" (63), Henry Rios likens them to a white canvas passed off as a painting. The biographical paragraph, the photograph, and the unfathomable poems themselves do not produce a "mother" text, or at least a mother who acknowledges that she has a gay son. Nothing about her is revealed: the family remains invisible.

However, what the textbooks and the newspapers hide are the practices of a literalized silencing. As the embodiment of the law, Judge Robert Paris, Hugh's grandfather, maintains his authority by repeatedly calling for the murder of insubordinate family members who themselves become the embodiments of silence. Eventually, however, the force of narrative elisions becomes too great to remain contained within the limits of the Paris family. Other nonfamily subjects meet similar fates in order that they too stay quiet. Disturbingly, Robert Paris as patriarch and judge executes the motto "silence equals death." As such, Robert Paris's murder of Hugh is an attempt to silence what would otherwise be a culturally fatal disclosure: a disrobing of a patriarchal heterosexuality posing in the drag of mother nature. Deliberate plots must appear, therefore, as unavoidable accidents; the machine of patriarchal authority that in fact exceeds Robert Paris himself must remain hidden—for Robert Paris, "dead men tell no tales." The production and the revelation of knowledge stop at the death of the subject, and most importantly the death of a gay subject. Ironically, Robert's attempt to secure the family fortune by killing off the family line enacts what homophobic culture ostensibly fears most in the gay body: that it is the site of sterility, a biological threat to the health of the population, the very antithesis of the family's reproductive functions. The capacity to produce culturally subversive knowledge, especially when the site of that production occurs between two gay male bodies (such as Henry and Hugh) threatens family stability, itself condemned merely to reproduce its own myth of the heterosexual family.

The success of Henry Rios's investigation relies on reproducing the same disruptive narrative the Paris family sought to silence by Hugh's death. Henry Rios, however, must not only recover the truth but must also "resurrect" Hugh Paris as the subjective "I" in a story that nobody wants to hear, including Henry himself. In fact, chapter two begins with Henry Rios waking up to Hugh Paris on his doorstep, wanting to tell him about his family. Hugh reveals that he comes from old San Francisco money, his grandfather hates him, perhaps because he is gay and a drug user, and that he wants Hugh killed because of his inheritance. All Hugh wants is to have Henry "hear [him] out." He wants to tell a story, *the story* rather, and he wants someone to hear it. Henry Rios, however, cannot believe this disclosure. When he must later identify the dead body of Hugh Paris, Henry Rios can no longer ignore the dead man's story and begins a campaign to finish it in an odd collaboration of living and dead. Not only must Henry Rios validate Hugh's story of family corruption but he must also make it publicly readable as the words of a gay man.

What Henry's collaboration with Hugh allows is the subversion of the ultimate silence: dead men *can* tell tales. The project at hand is not to find the murderer but to end the narrative silence of a dead subject through its linguistic resurrection. This resurrection occurs through a textual creation of Hugh's presence. Henry recognizes this himself when he picks up a book of Cavafy, Hugh's favorite poet, and reads the following lines: "I have created you in joy and in sorrows:/ Out of so many circumstances, out of so many things./ You have become all feeling for me" (121). Henry's grief leads him to become the mouth for Hugh's voice. And this subjective incorporation occurs through the reading and writing of texts. Coincidental to the fact that he is the son of a woman of letters, capital L, Hugh becomes a readable subject *through* his own letters:

> It seemed impossible these [letters] could come from Hugh, but the details told. I said to myself that I was now his advocate, not his lover, and an advocate accepts revelations about his client that would send the lover running from the room. . . . It wasn't so bad, Hugh, I

> said, silently. I've seen worse. And the letters contained solid information. (67)

These letters tell a family story the other family members are unwilling to tell. As Henry Rios observes, Katherine Paris, Hugh's mother, though living, proves herself to be a narrative dead end. She becomes as elliptical as her own poems. Hugh, however, though dead, offers "solid information" through the intimacy of personal letters. Recreating the suppressed narrative of the Paris/Smith family, Henry recounts the "final chapter" in Robert Paris's machinations:

> In Hugh's case the judge acted more subtly. He took the boy from his mother, sexually abused him, and then set him adrift in a series of private schools far from his home. The judge made sure that Hugh had all the money he could spend. Rootless, without direction, with too much money and not enough judgment, Hugh became a wastrel, a hype. He very nearly self-destructed. But not quite. He came home, pieced together the story of his grandfather's crimes and suddenly became a serious threat to Robert Paris. So he too was killed.
>
> That was the story. The evidence would not be as seamless or easily put together. It would come in bits and pieces, fragments of distant conversations, scribbled notes, fading memories. (114)

There is nothing remarkable about this revelation. The narrative that Henry and Hugh write together only confirms what we have learned from Hugh the night he visited Henry's house the first time. The difference, however, is that now Henry has a secret which endangers him. *The Little Death*, in keeping with the tradition of the hard-boiled detective novel, removes Henry's immunity. He is, therefore, susceptible to the same fate as Hugh Paris unless he can share his secret.

Although such a revelation is not a secret for the detective or the reader, it still functions as an open secret, because it is made by gay men whose attempts to be heard are effectively thwarted by the Paris's annihilating disavowal. If the family will not hear them, and their own stability relies on their refusal to hear, then to whom must Hugh Paris and later Henry Rios testify? Despite the pleasure of narrative dilation that the open secret affords, *The Little Death* ends the suspense of the open secret by providing a public space for Henry Rios to be heard. Perhaps it is not ironic that his annunciation is only perceivably public if there is a guarantee that an audience residing outside of the novel's cast of characters hears it. After all, Henry Rios must skew the linear alignment of the two binaries public/private and visible/invisible, which has helped to ensure the authority of the Paris family. In order for him to "out" the Paris family, his public audience itself must *appear* invisible so as to become a democratized force that exceeds the Paris's efforts at containment. Their representation in the novel, therefore, relies on a metonymy, a partial presence figured as the people's court. *The Little Death*'s use of the courtroom evokes other hard-boiled detective novels that have used it as well as the press as devices fictionally to defuse the fatal potency of the open secret.

Denied the conventions of grief as a result of the Paris family's disavowal, Henry Rios, therefore, seeks to make the courtroom an arena for his own avowal of loss. Henry Rios recognizes this himself when, after amassing his evidence, he states "at least my part would be over. I would finally be able to exorcise that last image of Hugh lying in the morgue" (115). Eliciting the aid of Hugh's estranged mother as a plaintiff, Henry files a civil suit against the estate of Robert Paris in the wrongful death of Hugh Paris. In the assumption that the very publicity of a civil trial is enough to implicate the Judge, Henry Rios in effect vents his grief through the same system the Judge represents. The law that had served to cloak the subjective silencing of a gay man now allows another gay man to avow his grief, precisely through the form of testimony that legitimizes a subjective "I." Even when the case moves from a civil trial to a criminal one, Henry Rios still is given the opportunity to "exorcise that last image of Hugh lying in the morgue." While the civil court would allow the testimony of the mother and the admission of Hugh's letters into evidence, the eventual grand jury allows Henry himself to testify against the Paris family. Going to court is, in effect, Henry Rios's refusal to incorporate his loss any longer.

What appears to be at the heart of both *The Long Goodbye* and *The Little Death* is a subjectivizing confession. In the case of Philip Marlowe, his refusal to confess that he aided Lennox marks a larger disavowal: his refusal to grieve the loss of another man. As Butler points out, this disavowal is important to the formation of a gendered subject within a heterosexual matrix, so that Marlowe's disavowal of male love invests him with the masculinity that has become iconic within the tradition of the hard-boiled detective novel. In other words, Philip Marlowe's refusal to confess makes him, as Detective Grenz would put it, "a tough guy." Henry Rios, on the other hand, confronts a system that refuses to legitimize his love for another man and the right to grieve his loss. The judge's refusal to confess necessitates the annihilation of a man, namely his grandson, whom he cannot bring himself to love. After all, to acknowledge his grandson as a subject, one with a terrible secret to confess, would be to invite Robert Paris's own virtual annihilation. Henry Rios's desire to confess publicly his love for Hugh therefore makes him a dangerous man precisely because it involves acknowledging Hugh Paris as a subject. Henry's success in creating a space for his grief within the arena of the law, ironically with the help of a taped confession from the murderer, subverts the mechanism of disavowal that calls for his own abjection. As an incarnation of *The Long Goodbye*, Michael Nava's novel rearticulates the hypermasculine private eye in the figure of Henry Rios, who questions the stability of a heterosexual subjectivity through his grief for another man. *The Little Death*, therefore, enacts the subversive *possibility* of working within the very conventions of the hard-boiled detective genre.

NOTES

1. For my use of genre here, I am indebted to Thomas O. Beebee who argues in *The Ideology of Genre: A Comparative Study of Generic Instability* (University Park: Pennsylvania State University Press, 1994) that by seeing genre as ideological, not only do we begin to see a text's genre as its use-value but to understand the inherent instability of genre itself.

2. See also Joseph Hansen's Dave Brandstetter mysteries, especially the first in the series *Fadeout* (1970); George Baxt's Pharoah Love Trilogy; and Steve Johnson's *Final Atonement* (1992). Larry Townsend's *Masters' Counterpoints* (1991) provides a mixing of the erotic, particularly S/M, as a genre with detective fiction. And an excellent example of the potential of lesbian detective fiction is Barbara Wilson's *Dog Collar Murders* (1989). Although each author recasts the gay detective in exciting ways, their efforts do not summarize the extent to which other authors have contributed to gay and lesbian detective fiction. For a more detailed list, see Anthony Slide's bibliography entitled *Gay and Lesbian Characters and Themes in Mystery Novels: A Critical Guide to Over 500 Works in English* (Jefferson: McFarland & Co., 1993).

3. See Eve Kosofsky Sedgwick's *Between Men: English Literature and Male Homosocial Desire* (New York: Columbia UP, 1985), which argues that homosocial desire can be articulated through an erotic triangulation in which

women become the objects of symbolic exchange. In my argument, the charge of their friendship is manifest through the literal and figurative presence of Lennox's wife, Sylvia Potter. In fact, her murder occasions the continuation of their friendship to the extent Marlowe feels compelled to prove Lennox innocent. In another related point, the homoerotic dimension of the hard-boiled detective has not gone unnoticed by Hollywood, which can stand as a useful indication of the cultural recognition of the hard-boiled detective's hypermasculinity as a suspect investiture. One good example is *Murder By Death*, in which Sam (Peter Falk), a parody of Hammett's Sam Spade, becomes a murder suspect after it is revealed that he had been blackmailed with the knowledge that he has been seen frequenting gay bars and that his secretary (Eileen Brennen) acts as a heterosexual decoy.

4. Ironically, the novel itself responds to the use of psychoanalysis. As one detective cynically notes near the end of *The Long Goodbye*, the incorporation of psychiatry within law enforcement may eventually produce a reformed subject:

> We got [psychiatrists] in our hair all the time these days. We've got two of them on staff. This ain't police business any more. It's getting to be a branch of the medical racket. . . . Ten years from now guys like Hernandez and me will be doing Rorschach tests and word associations instead of chin-ups and target practice. . . . Too bad we didn't grab the four hard monkeys that poured it on Big Willie Magoon. We might have been able to unmaladjust them and make them love their mothers. (325)

Not only will a competing system for the regulation of truth come to reform the criminal, the officer fears, but only by emasculating both the criminal and the police.

5. Interestingly, debt as a metaphoric response to the loss of a love object appears elsewhere in detective fiction. In fact, the metaphor of debt becomes literalized in *The Long Goodbye* as the $5,000 dollar bill paid to Marlowe for services rendered which instead reminds him of the debt he owes Lennox whose innocence he seeks to prove. Returning the bill to Lennox who turns out to be alive after all is no doubt Marlowe's own final ritual of mourning over the loss of his romantic fantasy of a "real" man.

WORKS CITED

Beebee, Thomas O. *The Ideology of Genre: A Comparative Study of Generic Instability.* University Park: Pennsylvania State University Press, 1994.

Bhabha, Homi. "Of Mimicry and Man: The Ambivalence of Colonial Discourse." October 28 (Spring 1984): 125-133.

Butler, Judith. *Gender Trouble: Feminism and the Subversion of Identity.* New York: Routledge, 1990.

———. *Bodies That Matter: On the Discursive Limits of "Sex."* New York: Routledge, 1993.

Chandler, Raymond. *The Long Goodbye* (1953). New York: Vintage Books, 1988.

———. *The Simple Art of Murder* (1950). New York: Vintage Books, 1988.

Freud, Sigmund. "Mourning and Melancholia" (1917). The Freud Reader. Ed. Peter Gay. New York: W.W. Norton, 1989.

———. *The Ego and the Id.* 1923. Translated by Joan Riviere. London: Hogarth P and The Institute of Psycho-analysis, 1942

———. "The Ego and the Id." *The Freud Reader.* Peter Gay, Ed. New York: Norton, 1989. 628-658.

Miller, D. A. *The Novel and the Police.* Berkeley: U of California P, 1988.

Nava, Michael. *The Little Death.* Boston: Alyson Publications, Inc., 1986.

Sedgwick, Eve Kosofsky. *Between Men: English Literature and Male Homosocial Desire.* New York: Columbia UP, 1985.

———. *Epistemology of the Closet.* Berkeley: U of California P, 1990.

Todorov, Tzvetan. *The Poetics of Prose.* Ithaca: Cornell UP, 1977.

PART THREE

Community and the Multicultural Detective

CHAPTER NINE

"A Rose by Any Other Name"

A Native American Detective Novel by Louis Owens

Michelle Pagni Stewart

Typically a detective novel begins with a murder, then takes the detective through the process of solving that murder and any others that occur along the way. The reader follows along as the detective uncovers clues, queries suspects, and eventually eliminates all but the guilty party. The novel ends with the detective identifying the killer and the motive, reconstructing the crime and its repercussions, thus neatly tying up all loose ends. Choctaw-Cherokee Louis Owens' *The Sharpest Sight*, however, suggests a reconsideration of the detective fiction genre in much the same way that multicultural authors have argued for a reevaluation of what is "standard" fiction when authored by someone of an ethnic background. While some may argue that Owens' plot, narrative structure, protagonist, and language deviate from "standard" detective fiction,[1] I would argue that *The Sharpest Sight* is indeed a detective novel; that the text does not fit the rubric of the genre as a result of its Native American cultural context and the way that cultural context affects what happens in the novel; and that in order to remain true to literary conventions found in Native American literature—many of which are based on cultural traditions and beliefs such as polyvocalism, circular plots, and an emphasis on the community rather than the individual—Owens creates his own kind of detective fiction simultaneously within and outside of the genre.

As a reader would expect in a detective novel, *The Sharpest Sight* involves a murder and its solution, yet even that convention is problematized. Having seen a vision of his friend Attis McCurtain in a dream, Deputy Mundo Morales claims his Choctaw-Cherokee friend has been murdered. But since a body cannot be found, those in power refuse to believe McCurtain is dead, arguing instead that he has run away. Even when faced with the truth when Attis's body is found, officials label it a suicide rather than a homicide, not wanting to give McCurtain the "privilege" of being a murder victim. Morales is both within and outside of the power structure as he attempts first to prove that his best friend is, in fact, dead, then prove that he was murdered; following that, of course, he must identify the murderer.

This is only part of the complications of Owens' murder plot. In addition to Morales, Attis's brother, Cole, tries to find the body, but because his primary goal is to bury his brother's bones, finding the guilty party is not as important to him. His goal centers on doing right by his brother rather than by the law. He knows Attis would not really benefit by anyone's finding the murderer, even if the guilty party were brought to justice, since "justice" will not bring Attis back to life. Attis's Choctaw father, however, seeks revenge rather than justice, and Mundo must keep careful watch over Hoey McCurtain to keep a possibly innocent man from being killed. Also involved in the search are Luther (Hoey's uncle and thus great uncle of Attis and Cole) and Onatima, who utilize their spiritual knowledge to help Cole in his search so that Attis's spirit can rest in peace. Further complicating the murder plot is the fact that Attis himself is a murderer, having killed Jenna Nemi, his girlfriend, in a confused state. Thus both Dan and Helen Nemi, Jenna's parents, become suspects in Attis's disappearance/murder, while her sister Diana seems eager to distract both Mundo and Cole from their purpose. As Mundo receives assistance from his grandfather's spirit and Cole receives assistance from Uncle Luther and his friend Onatima, their separate searches become simultaneous searches of identity and reconciliation with their friend/brother.

THE NARRATIVE STRUCTURE OF *THE SHARPEST SIGHT*

In this sense *The Sharpest Sight* has a different focus as well as a different method of uncovering the guilty parties, and along the way, the narrative deviates from merely tracing the clues to end with a neat denouement. First of all, while Mundo sees his dead friend's body floating in the river early in the novel, the actual body is not found until later in the novel. This means that Mundo must prove that a murder *has occurred* (often a given in a detective novel). He must prove that Attis has not escaped from the state hospital, running free, as some whites claim (several white newspapers report his being seen in various towns, even after the dead body has been found), but that he lies dead somewhere, as Mundo and Luther have envisioned. Moreover, when the body is eventually discovered, Mundo does not find it in the river as he had envisioned it, but instead Cole finds it in a tree.[2] Thus, Owens's plot does not delineate the pieces of the puzzle which will allow Mundo (and, simultaneously, the reader) to solve the murder. The clues may be present, but they are more subtle than those in typical detective novels, which means that the reader has a more difficult time trying to solve the murder himself or herself. Nor does Morales himself always recognize that he is actually gathering clues, since other duties distract him. Instead, he often finds himself trying to keep Hoey in check, warning Cole of the warrant for his arrest, and trying to avoid Diana's seduction attempts. When Owens finally divulges the guilty party, the announcement is not foregrounded since Morales does not rehash the clues that led to his suspecting the murderer—perhaps because he doesn't, nor is Mundo the one who actually "outs" the killer: consequently, a careless reader might not realize the "mystery" has been solved. In fact, the killer's identification comes ten chapters before the end, making it seem somewhat less significant than the action that follows.

Contrary to the "definitive, complete, and single-minded" ending of the classic detective story (Sweeney 5)[3], many Native American novels have conflicting endings.[4] While we can see something positive—Attis's body is found, and his murderer is identified—we can also see, however, that life will continue to be difficult. The ending of the novel does not indicate whether the murderer will be charged with the crime, even though the act is clearly more premeditated and more clearly an instance of murder than the crime for which Attis had been tried. Owens implicates the racism inherent in the white legal system which seems to accept a white's killing of an Indian but not the reverse. While Mundo has proved Attis was murdered and, therefore, proven his own ability as an investigator, that he stumbles upon the solution rather than actively "solving" the crime allows his colleagues to continue to treat him in a condescending manner. At the same time, we see a positive result in that Hoey, Cole, and Mundo all seem more connected to and proud of their heritage; Mundo even recognizes the previously unspoken fact that he, too, has Indian blood. However, the knowledge that Attis's death will most likely go unprosecuted and that fellow Native American veterans—and Native Americans in general—will continue to be treated differently from other vets, other Americans, leaves the novel's conclusion with the recognition that a typical detective fiction ending with "everything nicely taken care of (at least until the next novel)" would be contrary to the historical reality of Native Americans.

Frederic Svoboda argues that the hard-boiled detective plot is characterized by being action-centered, by attempting to "reconstruct the new promised land" attained by the Western hero, by identifying wrongdoings with society (562), and by focusing on the individual, "chronicling his work" (564). However, these premises run counter to Native American cultural beliefs and literary practices. In fact, neither action nor the individual is valued in Native American culture to the extent it is in the dominant, white, modern culture. Instead, Native Americans value community, which explains why Owens utilizes a number of characters to solve the murder rather than focusing on just one "investigator." Under these conditions, Svoboda's premise that the hard-boiled plot reconstructs the "new promised land" of the Western hero becomes a matter of perspective, for certainly, Native Americans found more promise in the land *before* the Western hero claimed it, attempting to eradicate the Indians while destroying the buffalo herds and land. And while the Native Americans might also *want* to reconstruct the promised land of the past, they lack the power to do so, particularly as an outnumbered group of people working against the white system. Thus, the only aspect of Svoboda's definition that coincides with themes found in Native American fiction is the idea that wrongdoings have resulted from civilization, although Native Americans would posit the blame specifically on *white* society and its attempts at "civilizing" others as it disrespects and eradicates beliefs and practices contrary to its own.

For example, Mundo Morales, who both is and is not a detective, does not attempt to reconstruct the promised land. In fact, he seems daunted by the state of society as well as by the place of Native Americans in it. He seems to realize that finding the murderer will not make any significant changes, since identifying the guilty parties will bring neither equality to the Native Americans nor justice for the death of a Native American. Morales recognizes that those in power do not seem concerned with finding the killer, but instead are more insistent on making sure Attis is actually dead. As he explains to Cole:

> You know, those fat asses in San Luis would like to let this drop. They could just put your brother down as escaped and never have to think about it again. That federal douche bag who's been poking around wants the same thing. They don't want it solved, man, because to them Attis just doesn't matter. . . . now that he ain't around to embarrass nobody they want to just forget the whole thing. (183)

Their embarrassment, however, is not compelling enough to make them change the way veterans like Attis are treated; instead, "they just want to forget the whole thing" (183). The plot and ending of Owens's novel, then, show that while both share features similar to those in detective novels, Owens refuses to assimilate his plot to neatly fit the patterns. Thus, no matter how critics define the plot structure of detective fiction, *The Sharpest Sight* simultaneously fits the definition and goes beyond it, largely because of the aspects which make it a Native American text.

THE INFLUENCE OF NATIVE AMERICAN LITERARY TRADITION

Because storytelling has always been such a significant part of the culture, it is at the heart of many Native American novels. Thus, it seems many Native American novels have multiple narrators or multiple viewpoints, much in the way that stories have multiple tellers, since they generally belong to the tribe rather than to individuals. In fact, in *Other Destinies: Understanding the American Indian Novel*, Owens explains that the communal nature of stories makes the idea of an author alien to Native American culture (9-10). Since storytelling relies on what Owens calls the "syncretic process" of storytelling (9), an oral story is never told exactly the same by different storytellers. Native American texts which attempt to replicate "storytelling" give the reader knowledge of the plot through a variety of eyes, voices, and views. This explains why many Native American texts seem to be less progressive and instead more episodic: each part of the story functions as a mini story which is continued at a later occasion, often with other stories introduced or continued in the meantime. This more disjointed plot line is characteristic of many Native American novels, such as Louise Erdrich's novels, Thomas King's *Green Grass, Running Water*, and Betty Louise Bell's *Faces in the Moon*. Moreover, this disjointed structure emphasizes orality and storytelling and can be seen in other

Native American texts such as Leslie Marmon Silko's *Storyteller* and N. Scott Momaday's *The Way to Rainy Mountain.*

The Sharpest Sight follows in this tradition, even as it moves into the genre of detective fiction. Often, the narrative of detective novels is written in the first person from the point of view of the detective or his/her friend or assistant, what Peter Huhn calls the "individualized narrator" (457). Owens, however, does not rely on a singular or first person point of view but rather unravels the mystery from half a dozen viewpoints,[5] allowing the reader to see events through the eyes of dead characters in several chapters. Through such narration, Owens depicts the polyvocalism which characterizes much Native American fiction, reflecting the roots in storytelling and the community-centeredness of the culture. The latter explains why Owens does not make his protagonist the focus of the novel, contrary to standard detective fiction which generally focuses on the actions and thoughts of the detective as he or she sorts out clues in order to solve the mystery.

Huhn describes the narrative structure of traditional detective fiction as consisting of two separate but intertwined stories: that of the crime (the action) and that of the investigation (which is concerned with knowledge). According to Huhn, until the truth of what happened is known, the crime is absent from the present, which is where the investigation occurs. The story itself begins with stable order in the community, but the crime destabilizes it. As Huhn concludes, "The narrative reconstruction restores the disrupted social order and reaffirms the validity of the system of norms" (452). In contrast, *The Sharpest Sight* is not limited to these "two stories" but instead involves a multiplicity of stories—intertwined yet not neatly tied together or wrapped up in the final pages. Owens's novel does more than merely follow Mundo as he sorts out the truth; it also traces the attempts of Cole, Attis's brother, to find Attis's bones in order to fulfill the Choctaw tradition of a proper burial so that Attis's soul will rest. Having recognized that he is only "kind of" an Indian, since he is unfamiliar with his Choctaw heritage (and in fact learned most of the "Indian stuff" he knows in the Boy Scouts), Cole learns more about his Native American heritage as he undergoes the tests his uncle Luther sets out for him. The novel also deals with Hoey McCurtain's attempts to discover the "truth" behind the history he has learned from the white man's perspective and with Luther's attempts to bring both Hoey and Cole closer to their Native American heritage as Luther and Onatima direct them towards finding that heritage, Attis's body, and the truth of what happened. Another intertwined story ties together Attis, Mundo, and the FBI agent Lee Scott, as it considers the role of Native Americans in Vietnam, the shoddy treatment of vets by the country and the government, and the life-altering effect a stay in Vietnam had on survivors.[6] Moreover, in Mundo Morales, Owens has created a Mexican American with Indian roots who must deal with the racism of those outside his culture as well as within when he must prove to his in-laws that, as a California Chicano, he is worthy of their New Mexico Spaniard daughter.

Thus, *The Sharpest Sight* is concerned with more than the identification of the killer. It deals with a smaller community, but the implications extend beyond the smaller group to encompass other Native Americans, other Mexicans, other veterans, and other less powerful people who remain at the mercy of those who wield the power. Contrary to Huhn's assertion that the narrative "restores the disrupted social order and reaffirms the validity of the system of norms" (452), *The Sharpest Sight* seeks to destabilize the accepted social order and to question the validity of the system of norms, for a Native American novel could hardly do otherwise. As do other Native American authors, Owens wants to make readers aware of the harmful effects that can result when those in power wield it unequally, when those not in power (or not allowed power) are at the mercy of those who refuse to see them as fellow human beings.

His plot also deviates from those of many detective novels in the way he utilizes suspense. According to Sweeney, a heightened sense of suspense, brought on by false clues, false suspects, and parallel investigations, makes the resolution of a detective novel all the more important (5). Yet for Owens, the suspense seems *less* heightened, despite the false clues, false suspects and parallel investigations. This is not to say that readers do not get caught up in the "action" of the novel, but since the action proceeds at a calmer pace and the narrative structure does not narrow down to the identification of the guilty party, the novel does not hinge on the solution of the crimes. Instead, the reader becomes immersed in a multitude of conflicts, connected to the identity of the murderer while also extending beyond it; that these other conflicts are significant explains why the novels proceed beyond the naming of the murderer and why the novels cannot find closure simply because we know "whodunit."

Again, such differences seem to be a factor of different philosophies and mindsets, for while standard detective novels hinge on the detective's deconstructing the mystery, finding a logical and chronological order of causes and effects, and producing a narrative that makes sense of those ordered events (Sweeney 4-5), Native American thought does not proceed in the same "logical" and "chronological" patterns. As Paula Gunn Allen explains, Native Americans view "space as spherical and time as cyclical, whereas the non-Indian tends to view space as linear and time as sequential" (7). This is why, explains Allen, all points are significant for American Indians in contrast to the non-Indian view which posits some points (a climax, for example) as being more significant. Perhaps this different view of time and space also explains why *The Sharpest Sight* is more concerned with the present—and, to some extent, the future as an extension of the present—rather than the past, which Tzvetan Todorov indicates is the focus of detective fiction.[7]

OWENS'S DETECTIVE

Just as Owens's plot makes his novel a hybrid Native American/detective novel, so does his mestizo "detective." A typical hard-boiled detective, according to Manju Jaidka, is an ordinary person without illusions, a womanizer who often gets into trouble, someone with whom the common person can identify (74). Svoboda's definition is more complex: he sees the hard-boiled detective hero as a redeemer trying to get the good to outweigh the bad, an introspective and isolated man who risks violence to himself at every turn and whose sexuality is linked with the savagery of civilization (560-66): think of Raymond Chandler's Phillip Marlowe or Mickey Spillane's Mike Hammer. Again, Mundo Morales simultaneously fits and does not fit this definition. For one thing, he is set apart by his ethnicity, by not fitting into white society, so he is isolated from and thus not identified with the "common man." In addition, he is not a womanizer; he resists Diana's passes, but her sexual interests are not confined to Morales, since she seduces Cole as well. Nor does he have any illusions: his place as someone outside the power system despite his being a part of it has eliminated any hope that things might be different. And furthermore, he is not a redeemer in the usual sense, for if we see him as redeeming Native Americans by proving their innocence and their victimization, this suggests the scales have been tipped in favor of evil—the powerful, corrupt, white society.[8]

Like the hard-boiled detective, Morales is isolated, even within his own community, and he finds trouble by attempting to question the power structure. Svoboda claims the hard-boiled detective is isolated from society because of introspection with regard to "his own values, his place in society, and the values of other people" (561), the same factors that seem to be the impetus behind Morales' own isolation. Even though Morales works as a deputy, people within his department do not treat him with respect or allow him to conduct his own investigation. Neither the head hospital psychiatrist Wagstaff, the sheriff Carlton, nor the federal investigator Scott believes that Morales has seen Attis dead, and they later label Morales a suspect. At one point, Scott and Nemi (a rancher who is not even affiliated with the law) interrogate Morales, treating him as if he were outside of the system rather than someone who is attempting to find the body and the killer. The sheriff actually tells Morales *not* to continue the investigation, which is often said to the private eye who is viewed as opposition to law enforcement. The sheriff reminds Morales that it is not his job to solve crimes: "Your job's to keep punks from stealing chickens and fucking somebody else's sheep. Your job don't have nothing to do with solving jack shit" (198-99). Although he seems to be within the system, Morales is often powerless to find the answers, to right the wrongs. Thus, while *The Sharpest Sight* exhibits many of the conventions of hard-boiled detective novels, ultimately, Morales cannot, as many a hard-boiled detective can, shoot the bad guy and win the battle. Moreover, Morales is not the sole seeker of the murderers; he is aided by others in the community who want to discover the truth, thus emphasizing the communal aspect of Native American culture and literature.

Svoboda compares the hard-boiled detective hero to the Western hero, saying both act as redeemers "who can tip the balance between good and evil" (560). In contrast, rather than tip it toward one side or the other, Native American culture typically seeks to *find* a balance, as does *The Sharpest Sight*. For example, when the murder occurs, the balance of nature and of the world is thrown off, [9] since a dead man's body is missing (Luther's viewpoint) and his death is not avenged (Hoey's viewpoint). The novel begins with descriptions of the flooding river which carries Attis's body downstream as the events of the novel unfold; changes in the river reflect the progression of the investigation and discovery. When Hoey admits that Attis had essentially died in the war, that "they killed him and gutted him over there. What came back was just part of him" (142), he sadly mourns the loss of his son as well as the loss of the traditions that might have helped bring his son back. Shortly after, Owens gives a description of the quickly receding river, suggestive of the ebbing of the traditional Native American way of life. Luther's observation that "things aren't very simple. . . . I think this *shilup* is only a small part of something much bigger now, and it's all tangled up" (244) is indicative of Owens's recognition of the imbalance in the Native American way of life—in part because of the loss of tradition and in part because of the inability of Native Americans to fit into the white world where the whites will never see Indians as equal human beings.

Dreams in *The Sharpest Sight* foretell the plight of the Indians. In traditional Native American belief, dreams are messages from the spiritual world, the medium through which people on earth can receive the truths of the other world (Lincoln 100-08), a belief which is reflected in Native American literature. In Owen's novel, dreams function like detectives' hunches in that Mundo Morales's dream and Luther's vision set in motion the search for Attis's dead body. Hoey McCurtain also sees his son dead in a vision and thus seeks the help of Morales, who himself receives help from his visions of his dead grandfather. In this, again, the novel is emphasizing the communal nature of Native American belief, the way the characters work together to solve the murder. As important, the novel emphasizes other significant Native American beliefs—the extent to which the past is tied to the present as well as the respect given to the elders; even in death (as is the case with the old man), their visions help the next generations to find the truth.

THE LANGUAGE OF THE DETECTIVE

Many critics focus on the language of hard-boiled detective fiction heroes, as well as of the authors in regard to their heroes. In many cases, the narrator is the detective or a sidekick, according to Scott R. Christianson, who claims that the detective talks constantly, talks tough, and talks smart, asserting his power through his language, for behind his tough words is the potential for violence (151-54). Yet while Christianson's views of the way language functions in detective fiction may seem at first to problematize Owens's novel as belonging to the genre, since it does not fit Christianson's description, the discrepancies in the novels instead suggest the Native American influence on the detective novel.

While detectives are infamous for talking, Native Americans believe power is gained not through language but rather through silence, in part because historically they have too frequently been deceived by whites who say one thing ("we're only trying to help you"), but whose actions belie their words ("but if we can help ourselves at your expense, all the better"). That the Native American character Mundo Morales is not a narrator who traces the unfolding of the mystery reflects his hesitancy to trust others he works with by divulging what he knows; but more importantly, they do not seem to value his word, so he remains stoic when dealing with the sheriff or the federal agent. According to Native American custom, once spoken, a word cannot be taken back, which indicates potential for good *or* harm. Native Americans believe in the "great and inherent power of the word" (Standiford 183), that words make things happen (Lincoln 92). This helps to explain why Native Americans often hesitate to speak too quickly. Yet Morales is not as reticent as the "detective" Stace Red Hawk in Linda Hogan's *Mean Spirit*, in part because he is not as connected to his Native American heritage as Cole and Hoey, and even they are admittedly distanced from their roots. Morales's disconnectedness is shown when he keeps referring to Attis by name, something which both Cole and Hoey warn him against, since speaking the name of the dead will not allow him to rest in peace.

As Christianson asserts, hard-boiled detectives are known *as* talkers; moreover, they are tough talkers who have the ability to back up their words with violent action if necessary. Contrary to Western stereotypes, in many Native American novels, talking tough—especially to someone who is within the power structure—almost guarantees Native Americans will be the *victim* of violence rather than the person committing it. In fact, one doesn't even have to talk tough to incite violence: Mundo is accosted at the pool hall when he seems to be too close to the truth. Unlike hard-boiled detectives, Native American characters do not talk tough in part because the culture places too great a value on language for words to be bantered about. Moreover, the characters acknowledge the futility of speaking out: it will not change what has happened and will only give the killer a target for the next death.

Christianson claims that inherent in detective novels is the use of language as a means of wielding power. Yet while "'Language as power' means . . . the use of language to assert control over one's self and over situation, and to make some sense of the chaotic and fragmented quality of experience" (Christianson 159), this is not true of Owens's detective novel. Just as Morales recognizes what little control he has, other characters in the novel recognize their own lack of control. At the conclusion, even though the crime has been solved, the characters have not been able to make sense of their experience, nor can they exert any control over their selves or their situations. Mundo Morales does not garner the respect he deserves as an officer of the law, even though he had been correct in claiming Attis had died and even though he discovers the murderer. Moreover, it is clear that the attitudes the whites take throughout the novel will not be changed by the events. When agent Scott tells Cole some jokes about Navajo eating dogs, Cole tries to rectify his misperception: "Navajos don't eat dogs . . . [o]nly a few Indians, like some of the Sioux, ever ate dogs," to which Scott promptly replies, "Okay, here's another one, then. What's a Sioux picnic? . . . A puppy and a six-pack" (169), proving he has completely missed the point Cole was making. Furthermore, because the whites are afraid of Attis and want him controlled, which indicates that finding Attis's body seems to be more important to those in power than discovering who killed him, the situation of Native Americans—Native American vets in particular—will not be any different in the future.

In addition to wielding power through language, the hard-boiled detective also has a penchant for wisecracks and glibness—in part an attempt, Christianson asserts, to stand up to or against something or someone, "an assertion of personal autonomy" (158). Yet, while much Native American literature is characterized by humor, particularly by those who laugh at themselves to make light of their situation or to detract from their powerlessness in the dominant system, humor used by Owens is stark. In fact, in a genre that is known for wit and humor, this novel seems almost to avoid it, perhaps because Owen does not want readers to dismiss the seriousness at the heart of the situation. For example, the novel depicts the way Vietnam wreaked havoc on already fragile minds, and as importantly the racism of those who cannot treat Indians as equal human beings. The feds constantly treat Attis and Cole differently because of their background, even though neither is close to his Indian heritage; in the same way, they refuse to treat a Mexican/Native American deputy with the respect due him as an officer of the law.

This is not to say, however, that Owens's novel is devoid of humor, which would not be consistent with Native American storytelling. Owens utilizes humorous details such as "The Tiptoe Inn" and Luther's phrase "moral turnipitude," and we find humor in the interchanges between Luther and Onatima, in the helplessness of the government men as they search for Cole, and in the way the Native American characters retell *Moby Dick*, *Huckleberry Finn*, and *Hamlet*.[10]

AT THE HEART OF OWENS'S NOVEL

Ironically, then, in a genre which characteristically relies on humor and wit, Owens downplays the Native American literary convention of humor most likely because of the content of his novel. While he deals with murder—as detective novels do—he deals with a metaphorical killing as well: of a people, a heritage, and citizens. Thus, more is at stake than merely finding the guilty party so justice can be served. While detective novels frequently involve a game which encourages wit and word play, Owens emphasizes that the events at the heart of the novel are *not* a game. To consider them as such will prove detrimental to the Native American culture as a whole—and thus, by extension, to the American culture. This is no laughing matter, his underlying seriousness warns.

According to Dorothy Sayers, detective fiction writers try to get readers to believe lies so as to delay discovery of "the truth" (Jaidka 82). The whites in *The Sharpest Sight* seek to keep the truth from the Native Americans, which thus posits the Native American characters in Sayers' reader position, since the whites want to delay the Native Americans' discovery of the truth, of the guilty parties. While detectives often find themselves in a similar position, since characters in detective novels frequently lie to hide their guilt, the situation is even more hazardous for the Native Americans in Owens's novel. Since those people who are *supposed* to be seeking the truth lie to them, the Native Americans are put at a greater disadvantage. The federal agents in *The Sharpest Sight* also seem less concerned with helping Mundo and Cole find the truth than with burying the proof of the harm they have wrought on otherwise peaceful citizens. For, in fact, the agents are seeking Cole for draft evasion, hindering him from his search and from helping Morales; in addition, they too readily defend one of the prime suspects, Dan Nemi, suspecting Morales himself rather than the rancher whose alibi may or may not vindicate him.

Stefano Tani defines the anti-detective novel as one that has a nonsolution or a parodic solution, with a tendency toward disorder and irrationality (37-46). Because the detective does not solve the crime, he argues, the detective "avoids the trap of repetition/serialization" (46). Just as the label "detective fiction" fits yet does not fit *The Sharpest Sight*, so does Tani's notion of the anti-detective novel fit yet not fit his Native American novel. For while Owens's novel does not come to a solution for the problems of the Native Americans in the novel, it does identify the murderer; while the novel gives a solution to the crime, it also "avoid[s] . . . the trap of repetition/ serialization" because of the nature of the story. For even if Mundo were to solve other murders in future novels, the confluence of conflicts and events found in *The Sharpest Sight* could not be replicated; thus, a second novel could not be patterned after the first.[11] However, just as Tani argues that the anti-detective novel is not a "continuation of the genre but . . . a transgression of it" which will lead to a renewal of the genre as well as "the constitution of another genre" (41), so is *The Sharpest Sight* a transgression of the detective genre which should encourage readers to rethink their notions of what is "standard" in detective fiction. Simultaneously, readers should recognize that the Native American influences at work within the plot, as well as the structure, enable the novel to transgress the boundaries of the detective genre. In discussing Tony Hillerman's use of Indian culture, Jane Bakerman says we must be careful that the discussions of Indian culture do not overshadow the detective novel aspect (10).[12] However, this seems to ignore the very thing that makes *The Sharpest Sight* unique and interesting, its Native American culture and literary traditions, the very thing that makes it a Native American detective novel.[13]

NOTES

1. Originally, this argument was made in respect to both Owens's *The Sharpest Sight* and Linda Hogan's *Mean Spirit*; just as Owens's novel is both simultaneously like a detective novel but also transcends the classic definitions for the genre, so does Hogan's *Mean Spirit*. However, because the collection has another essay dealing with Hogan's novel, it was decided I concentrate on Owens's novel. That the argument can be made about more than one novel, however, strengthens my premise about Native American detective novels.

2. At this point, Owens subtly indicates the extent to which the government men fail to understand contemporary Native Americans. When the agent Lee Scott discovers Cole with his brother's bones, he at first labels what Cole is about to do a *primitive* ritual (my emphasis). Later, as he is expressing what he thinks to be a shared perspective on death, he explains he was sent to "make sure that your brother never surfaced again. . . . [the government was] afraid he was loose and was going to dance the ghost dance some more and remind people" (254). After having fought for his country in Vietnam, Attis is still considered an outsider, the unknown "other" that must be eradicated because his mindset is different from that of the mainstream.

3. Granted, the hard-boiled detective novel has a more ambiguous ending than a classical detective novel might have. Ultimately, however, even if the society around him still remains corrupt, the hard-boiled detective is able to put back in order the pieces of the case on which he was working.

4. Louis Owens, in *Other Destinies: Understanding the American Indian Novel*, discusses the somewhat hopeful yet ambivalent endings of John Joseph Mathews' *Sundown* (60) and D'Arcy McNickle's novels (89), claiming that N. Scott Momaday's *The Ancient Child* and James Welch's *Fools Crow* are two of the few novels whose endings display "full recoveries" (127). That is not to say, however, that all Native American novels have conflicting endings. Betty Louise Bell's *Faces in the Moon*, for example, ends on a more positive, self-affirming note, with Lucie proud of her heritage and ready to fight to right past wrongs.

5. Similarly, in *Mean Spirit*, Hogan's shifting point of view includes over a dozen characters.

6. In dealing with war veterans, Owens follows a literary tradition which he himself discusses in *Other Destinies: Understanding the American Indian Novel.* Although veterans of World War II, N. Scott Momaday's Abel from *House Made of Dawn*, Leslie Marmon Silko's Tayo from *Ceremony*, and Louise Erdrich's Russell from *The Beet Queen* are, like Attis, displaced veterans who cannot find a place for themselves in either culture, the Indian or the white. See Owens's first chapter, particularly page 31.

7. See Tzvetan Todorov, "The Typology of Detective Fiction." *The Poetics of Prose.*

8. These descriptions also apply to Cole McCurtain, especially in Owens's subsequent novel *Bone Game*, in which Cole becomes the "detective" in another mystery. This novel also displays aspects similar to *The Sharpest Sight* and, as such, would also support my argument.

9. This can be seen in Hogan's novel as well: it begins with a description of the dry spell forecast by Michael Horse, which foreshadows the numerous

deaths about to be committed or, perhaps more accurately, about to be recognized as actual murders, since many Indians up to this point had been looking the other way when their friends mysteriously turned up dead. The imbalances in nature correspond with the deaths: the flood of crickets in Nola's room occurs soon after the deaths of John Stink and John Thomas, for example, and Belle's limping is later discovered to occur whenever something sacred is killed. Hogan connects nature and the earth to the Native American people, describing the underground explosion as "the rage of mother earth" (189) and connecting the "rains crying" with the killing the sacred eagle (271). The disturbed bees and the dead buffalo are as foretelling of the troubled situation of the Indians as is the fact that Michael Horse is losing his second sight, which makes his predictions no longer reliable.

10. Thomas King's *Green Grass, Running Water* also retells some of the "great white classics" as he inverts the stories that often portray the "other" as savage. For example, he depicts the Native American sidekick of the Lone Ranger, Hawkeye, Robinson Crusoe and Ishmael as being the real force behind the duo, rather than the white man who took—and got—all of the credit. Owens's play with these stories is reminiscent of King's.

11. In fact, in *The Bone Game* (1994), Owens writes another detective novel, but this one centers on Cole, with Mundo Morales mentioned only in passing. And while the guilty party is identified, Cole is not the one who uncovers the truth. So, in fact, Owens is not serializing his detective stories, even if they do have characters in common.

12. Tony Hillerman is a bit controversial within the Native American culture because he is not actually Native American, although he does have knowledge of the culture. In fact, in Sherman Alexie's *Indian Killer*, the Indian characters denigrate Jack Wilson, a character who seems to me to have been written with Tony Hillerman in mind.

13. I would like to thank Kathy Patterson, Linda Gill, and Renee Pigeon for reading drafts of this paper. I greatly appreciate their insight and assistance.

WORKS CITED

Alexie, Sherman. *Indian Killer*. New York: Atlantic Monthly P, 1996.

Allen, Paula Gunn. "The Sacred Hoop: A Contemporary Perspective." *Studies in American Indian Literature*. Ed. Paula Gunn Allen. New York: MLA, 1983. 3-22.

Bakerman, Jane S. "Joe Leaphorn and the Navaho Way: Tony Hillerman's Indian Detective Fiction." *Clues: A Journal of Detection* 2.1 (1981): 9-16.

Bell, Betty Louise. *Faces in the Moon*. Norman: U of Oklahoma P, 1994.

Christianson, Scott R. "Tough Talk and Wisecracks: Language as Power in American Detective Fiction." *Journal of Popular Culture* 23.2 (1989): 151-62.

Hogan, Linda. *Mean Spirit*. New York: Ivy Books-Ballantine, 1990.

Huhn, Peter. "The Detective as Reader: Narrativity and Reading Concepts in Detective Fiction." *Modern Fiction Studies* 33 (1987): 451-66.

Jaidka, Manju. "Let's Play FOOJY: The Politics of Detective Fiction." *Clues: A Journal of Detection* 14.1 (1993): 69-86.

King, Thomas. *Green Grass, Running Water*. Boston: Houghton Mifflin, 1993.

Lincoln, Kenneth. "Native American Literatures: 'old like hills, like stars.'" *Three American Literatures.* Ed. Houston A. Baker, Jr. New York: MLA, 1982. 80-167.

Momaday, N. Scott. *The Way to Rainy Mountain.* Albuquerque: U of New Mexico P, 1969.

Owens, Louis. *Bone Game*. Norman: U of Oklahoma P, 1994.

———. *Other Destinies: Understanding the American Indian Novel*. Norman: U of Oklahoma P, 1992.

———. *The Sharpest Sight*. Norman: U of Oklahoma P, 1992.

Silko, Leslie Marmon. *Storyteller.* New York: Seaver Books, 1981.

Standiford, Lester A. "Worlds Made of Dawn: Characteristic Image and Incident in Native American Imaginative Literature." *Three American Literatures.* Ed. Houston A. Baker, Jr. New York: MLA, 1982. 168-96.

Svoboda, Frederic. "The Snub-Nosed Mystique: Observations on the American Detective Hero." *Modern Fiction Studies* 29 (1983): 557-68.

Sweeney, S.E. "Locked Rooms: Detective Fiction, Narrative Theory, and Self-Reflexivity." *The Cunning Craft: Original Essays on Detective Fiction: Contemporary Literary Theory*. Eds. Ronald G. Walker and June M. Frazer. Malcom, IL: Western Illinois U-Yeast Printing, 1990. 1-14.

Tani, Stefano. *The Doomed Detective: The Contribution of the Detective Novel to Postmodern American and Italian Fiction*. Carbondale: Southern Illinois UP, 1984.

Todorov, Tzvetan. "The Typology of Detective Fiction." *The Poetics of Prose.* Trans. Richard Howard. Ithaca, NY: Cornell UP, 1977.

the lower east side, and the fellow explains to Levinsky what a "topsy-turvy country" the New World is for Jews: "He went on to show [Levinsky] how the New World turned things upside down, transforming an immigrant shoemaker into a man of substance, while a former man of leisure was forced to work in a factory here. In like manner, his wife had changed for the worse, for, lo and behold! instead of supporting him while he read Talmud, as she used to do at home, she persisted in sending him out to peddle" (97). As it turns out, Levinsky himself needs little urging to give up Talmud for the more lucrative garment industry. In contrast to many of the male characters derived from Jewish folklore who populated European Yiddish literature at that time, Cahan's American Jewish male takes charge of his economic fate rather than letting himself be the plaything of it.[2]

Yet once Levinsky absorbs the rules and behavior of American individualism and entrepreneurial capitalism a congenial mate inevitably proves difficult to find. Dora Margolis, whose seduction by Levinsky comprises the longest section of the novel, is traditional and mothering and equally committed to assimilating American cultural values, but she is already married. Adultery and the breakup of Dora's marriage, though exciting to Levinsky as a kind of corporate "takeover," is ethically repugnant to her. Levinsky can neither return to the orthodoxy embodied by Fanny Kaplan, to whom he is briefly engaged out of nostalgia for Antomir, the Russian town that both he and the Kaplans are from, nor can he cross the political divide that separates him from the socialist Miss Tevkin, Levinsky's last romantic obsession in the novel who spurns him not only for his politics, but also because he is simply too old for her. The last chapter, "Episodes of a Lonely Life," underscores Levinsky's ambivalence about his new found freedom in America—the price of that freedom is eternal bachelorhood. Only when he entertains the thought of marrying a Gentile widow do readers glimpse a deep seated reason for his enforced isolation: "I saw clearly that it would be a mistake. It was not the faith of my fathers that was in the way. It was the medieval prejudice against our people which makes so many marriages between Jew and Gentile a failure. It frightened me" (527). Levinsky, an assimilated, wealthy, irreligious male, is frightened by the private prejudices which threaten to undermine his public successes, and because he desires to be a really good success he never marries. Nevertheless, the bachelor Levinsky is a fruitful literary character, the father of Bellow's, Malamud's and Roth's alienated protagonists (so often single, widowed, or divorced) who model Levinsky's design for an American Jewish manhood—outsiders in the midst of plenty, misogynists in the eyes of some.

In Faye Kellerman's detective fiction, the character of Peter Decker is Levinsky's literary grandson, but in Kellerman's hands he is also a mass cultural representation of the assimilated American-Jewish male who now longs for meaningful spiritual and romantic attachments. The noir-tough, Jewish cowboy image of the orphaned and adopted Peter Decker is meant to invoke how alienated from the traditional Jewish world American-Jewish males have become. Like Peter Decker, they might as well have been raised by gentiles. Of course, the attraction which the Orthodox Rina Lazarus feels for the apparently non-Jewish Decker is revealing as well. To her, Decker is the idealized pairing of gentile male virility with Jewish *sechel* (wisdom), an intellectual and spiritual gift that Rina helps him to recognize. In that sense the relationship between Decker and Lazarus is a kind of cultural "intermarriage," a coded reference—and solution—to the current bane of contemporary American-Jewish life. As her last name implies, Lazarus signifies the contemporary perception that Jewish tradition is being resurrected and embodied by American Jewish women, but her character also perpetuates gender divisions that are part of and a response to assimilation (indicated by Kellerman's consistent use of "Rina" for her female character but "Decker" for her male character, a usage I will maintain in this essay in order to foreground those gender divisions). Thus, just how Decker and Rina will accommodate each other and make a home together living in an edgy Los Angeles is one of the mysteries in Kellerman's series. Moreover, once we read her detective stories as reflective of these social and gender conflicts among the American Jewish middle class, it is clear that the the real crime endemic to American Jews is biological merger, the final phase of cultural assimilation. Therefore, despite the fact that Decker is the detective and solves all the crimes in Kellerman's stories, Rina Lazarus is the spiritual hero of the series—and thus its real hero—because it is she who saves Decker from biological merger by explaining and adamantly defending the mystifying fences that Orthodox Judaism erects around Jewish women and between Jews and gentiles.

PRIVATE EYES AND PUBLIC IDENTITY

The social function of Kellerman's detective fiction is evidenced in its relationship to the subgenres of American Jewish popular fiction and modernist detective fiction. Arnold Band, citing Neal Gabler's *Empire of Their Own: How the Jews Invented Hollywood,* has pointed out that American Jewish popular fiction (mass market fiction, musical comedies, Hollywood films, television and radio programs, and so forth) is a continuation of the identity shaping project begun by the early film moguls who articulated the dreams and desires of a burgeoning American Jewish middle class (217). Like the Zukors, the Foxes, the Mayers, and the Warners, writers of American-Jewish popular fiction fabricate an America and a picture of Jews that reflects contemporary middle class life and concerns, and so help create the basis for an American Jewish identity palatable for mass consumption by both Jews and non-Jews. Appropriately, *The Ritual Bath* (1986), the first book in Kellerman's series, opens with advice on how to make a potato kugel, a clever introduction that uses a kind of ethnic shorthand in order to signify the identity of this contemporary popular fiction: "'The key to a *good* potato kugel is good potatoes,' Sarah Libba shouted over the noise of the blow dryer. 'The key to a *great* potato kugel is the amount of oil" (1). This reference to a middle-class "kitchen Judaism" enables Kellerman—aware that the lineaments of Orthodoxy are foreign not only to non-Jews but also to most American Jews—to begin her fiction about a complex American-Jewish subculture by referring readers to a familiar American Jewish domestic context.[3] Using the potato kugel as a touchstone of middle-class American Jewish cultural identity, Kellerman is able to imbue her fiction, from the start, with the same homey "authenticity." More intriguingly, in light of Decker and Lazarus' impending first meeting in this novel, Sarah Libba's qualitative distinction between kugels can also be read as a metonym for the story's theme of a qualitative distinction in American Jewish identity between Jewishness (a good kugel) and "authentic" Judaism (a great kugel), the difference between the two being a matter of cultural/culinary proficiency. Though perhaps fanciful, my reading is meant to illuminate one of the ways Kellerman's popular fiction reshapes images associated with a mass-marketed American-Jewish identity. Other aspects of that identity are also reflected and similarly revised, as we will see.

As a detective fiction, the Peter Decker and Rina Lazarus mysteries represent an interesting improvisation on what Woody Haute calls "pulp culture," an evocative term for the social and capitalist critiques embedded in modernist detective fiction (9). The pulp culture detective, according to Haute, is a private detective in public places, and Haute interprets the individualist ethos of the private detective who is unwillingly drawn into the mysteries of the public world as a "hard boiled" proletariat response to modernization—to the bureaucratization of society, the spread of capitalism, the breakdown of older social norms, rapid urbanization, and the centralization of political power. Think of the famous passage in Raymond Chandler's *The Long Goodbye* in which Philip Marlowe gazes out his open window and meditates on the nimbus of light hanging over nighttime Los Angeles:

> Twenty four hours a day somebody is running, somebody else is trying to catch him. Out there in the night of a thousand crimes, people were dying, being maimed, cut by flying glass, crushed against steering wheels, or under heavy tires. People were being beaten, robbed, strangled, raped, and murdered. People were hungry, sick; bored, desperate with loneliness, or remorse or fear, angry, cruel, feverish, shaken by sobs. A city no worse than others, a city rich and vigorous and full of pride, a city lost and beaten and full of emptiness.
>
> It all depends on where you sit and what your own private score is. I didn't have one. I didn't care. (224)

Neither the powerful nor the powerless are spared in this passage. Yet pulp culture private detectives, whose authors felt the chilling effect of American anti-communism, Cold War censorship, and the moral ambiguity of the atomic era, do not advertise their assessments of the public world as a part of the service or information they provide for their employers. A passage such as the one above is always an interior monologue, a private judgement and dismissal. Haute argues that the detectives in pulp culture fiction were subjective critics of capitalism and state power, as well as of human foibles: "Consequently, pulp culture writing retained the basic themes of proletariat writing: the corrosive power of money, class antagonism, capitalism's ability to erode the community, turning its citizens into a disparate band of self centered and alienated individuals . . . ." (10). These detectives were men, of course, who privatized the investigative process and its solutions, whose only advertisements were for themselves as the worldly-wise isolates of pulp and noir fame.

When Peter Decker is introduced to readers in chapter two of *The Ritual Bath,* the tone of Kellerman's prose echoes the rhythms and wording of the pulp detective fictions, and Decker himself expresses the sentiments of a "hard boiled" detective:

> Decker dragged on his cigarette, looked out the window, and surveyed his turf. Los Angeles conjured up all sorts of images, he thought: the tinsel and glitter of the movie industry, the lapping waves and beach bunnies of Malibu, decadent dope parties and extravagant shopping sprees in Beverly Hills. What it didn't conjure up was the terrain through which they were riding.
>
> The area encompassing Foothill Division was the city's neglected child. It lacked the glamour of West L.A., the ethnicity of the east side, the funk of Venice beach, the suburban complacency of the Valley.
>
> What it did have was lots of crime. (11)

But Decker is a cop, a public detective, and in truth Kellerman's detective fiction is more accurately defined as a police procedural. Still, Decker exhibits some of the classic signifiers of the pulp culture detective in *The Ritual Bath*—he doesn't want to get involved in this new case (40), he feels alienated (65), he's willing to bend the law when it gets in his way (106), and he has no respect for the callously wealthy and powerful(159). What Kellerman's play on the pulp detective stereotype underscores is the American Jewish male's assimilation into the heart of modern America's state structure. Paradoxically, Decker is a version of the pulp detective who is a part of the machinery of power—a somewhat jaded but loyal insider. As the agent and enforcer of that power he really represents the successful embourgeoisement of the American Jewish male in the public world.[4] Indeed, what makes the pulp culture detective such a wonderful medium for Kellerman's revision of a long-standing *topos* of manhood in American Jewish fiction is that both are premised on the ambivalence of professionally successful social loners. Kellerman's fiction, therefore, profits from the dramatic tension generated between the "private" detective and the "public" detective, and between the private Jew and the public Jew, which Decker's character holds in check. That tension is both attractive and problematical; it is a part of the frisson he brings to his relationship with Rina, but it is also a source of Decker's need for the solace of Judaism.

PETER DECKER

Kellerman develops Decker's character in *The Ritual Bath* through actions and revelations that touch on these tension building oppositions, playing on the audiences' assumption that he is a Gentile interested in Rina and Judaism. Privately, Decker is disturbed by the rape at "Jewtown," the name by which outsiders and the police refer to Yeshivat Ohavei Torah (literally, the seminary of the lovers of Torah, an undergraduate and postgraduate level institution). It is a community of law-abiding citizens, and he "wished he had a city full of 'em" (8). Like Marlowe, however, he knows that L.A. is a city of a thousand crimes, and that the yeshiva cannot remain immune to L.A.'s baleful influence. Decker notes in an interior monologue that, as with other neighborhoods in Foothill division, the yeshiva is populated by "[p]eople scratching by, people not getting by at all . . . .These people weren't the wealthy Jews portrayed by the media. It was possible that the yeshiva held a secret cache of diamonds, but you'd never know it by looking at its inhabitants. They dressed cheaply, buying most of their clothes at Target or Zody's, and drove broken down cars like the rest of the locals" (12). The private Decker knows and respects these locals. Urban figure though he is, he owns a horse ranch just a few miles from this neighborhood, in a suburban area that is the border between city and country.

Publicly, Decker plays the tough cop, interested only in upholding the state's laws, suspicious of everyone, even the yeshiva's residents (14). The Orthodox treat this tall, red-headed Gentile warily, and his looks impress Rina as those of a seasoned hunter: "He was a big man, she thought, with strong features and, despite the fair skin and ginger hair, dark penetrating eyes. He looked intimidating yet competent, a man who'd know how to hunt an animal like a rapist. Although she knew size had nothing to do with apprehending a criminal, she was still glad he was big" (17). Unlike the other Orthodox women, however, Rina has looked into Decker's eyes (ultra-Orthodox men and women do not shake hands or look directly into the eyes of the opposite sex, unless they are husband and wife); Rina here signifies her difference from the rest of the community, both by her action and her ability to intuit Decker's "dark," private interior through the windows of his soul.

Rina's initial attraction is reciprocated by Decker, who bends the rules governing the performance of his public duties in order to maintain private contact with her. Since Sarah Libba will not submit a statement to the Gentile authorities (on grounds of religious modesty), Decker's case is stalled. Rina volunteers to bring Sarah Libba to the stationhouse, but she arrives alone, and, technically, there is no reason for Decker to join Rina for a picnic in the park. Lamely, he offers the excuse that talking with Rina there is preferable to talking with her in a hot interrogation room. While Decker continues to present himself as the concerned public servant, he also impresses Rina with his knowledge of Jewish kitchen culture, the first overt betrayal of his private cultural proficiency. Biting into, yes, a potato kugel, Decker shares a significant moment with Rina:

> "You know what it tastes like?" Decker said. "It tastes like a latke. A big, thick latke."
>
> That took her by surprise.
>
> "That's exactly what it is."
>
> "Not too bad for a goy, huh?"
>
> She laughed.
>
> "You've picked up an expression or two, Detective."
>
> "Or three or four. My ex-wife was Jewish. But not like you," he qualified. "She and her parents were very Americanized. But her paternal grandparents stayed . . . ethnic. It was her grandmother who used to make me latkes." (53-54)

Decker's comments reveal a private understanding of Jewishness as a kind of ethnicity whose identity is vouched for by certain foods, but whose "authenticity" has been "Americanized," and therefore made different from Rina's much more exacting, and exact, Judaism. That is indeed an impressive observation for a *goy,* and that observation, as well as Decker's admission that he was once married to a Jewish woman (before his devotion to his job led her to divorce him) and that he was a lawyer before he was a cop, signal to Rina that beneath Decker's public persona is a "private" detective capable of reading the subtle clues that describe "authentic" Jewish cultural and religious difference. After this scene, readers know that Decker's romantic desire to see Rina again is bound up with his curiosity about the Orthodox Judaism of the Yeshiva, a curiosity for information that goes beyond what is necessary for his case.

In that sense, Kellerman reshapes the figure of a pulp culture detective—and, by extension, the figure of the unattached American Jewish male which that detective is an analogy for—by giving Decker an education. Decker, the worldly-wise, individualist detective, becomes Decker the student of a Judaism that Rina will reveal (to him and to readers) as multiple and diverse, a revelation that diffuses Decker's single goal-object in the story, solving the case. This transformation of roles is foreshadowed by Rabbi Schulman's remark early in the novel: "You're a wise boy, Detective. You don't mind me calling you boy, do you? I call all my *bochrim*—my pupils—boys. At my age everyone around me looks like a boy" (27). Later, Decker's willingness to learn—to reconsider his preconceptions and his own psychological motives (insofar as readers are made privy to them)—is the key to his transformative relationship with Rina. When Decker meets Rina's parents, he learns the difference between the black-hatted and dark-suited Jews at the yeshiva and modern Orthodox Jews such as Mr. and Mrs. Elias. The Eliases, Hungarian Jews who live in Beverly Hills, are affluent and European, their clothing and manners influenced more by their class than by their religion. Rina also teaches Decker the differences between Misnagdim (the Lithuanian-Jewish culture of the yeshiva) and Chasidim, explaining that among Misnagdim, Yeshivat Ohavei Torah is itself different, being liberal and less restrictive than other Misnagid yeshivas. In turn, this prompts Decker to exclaim, "Rina I wish you wouldn't lump me and billions of other people into one gigantic category. I'm more than just a gentile." Of course, at this point readers assume that Decker is referring to his private, pulp sensibilities, and contrasting them with his outward appearance as a representative of the law. Only later do readers understand that Decker is alluding to his biological identity. Still, it is clear that Decker's willingness to become a student is an attempt to begin interrogating his discrimination between his private life and his public life.

Additionally, "hiding" Decker's private identity enables Kellerman to oppose the image of Decker the Gentile with images of Orthodox Jewish males, thus reflecting and reshaping stereotypes of the Jewish body as well. Decker's size and hair coloring are signs that Kellerman manipulates in order to fool readers into reading him as a Gentile, and how she clothes his body adds to the deception. When Decker shows up at Rina's house in order to take her sons to a Dodger game, Kellerman purposely images Decker in casual attire as a way of suggesting that Decker is more than just a detective but not at all the picture of a Jewish male:

> Rina was taken aback by Peter's appearance. Her image of him until now had been that of a "professional detective" in a shirt, slacks, and tie. This afternoon he wore a white T-shirt, sloppy cut-off shorts and sneakers, and a baseball cap perched atop his thick patch of orange-red hair. He looked so all-American, so working class. So goyish. . . . Immediately, Rina wondered if she hadn't erred in her judgement. (126)

Decker's immodesty, sloppiness, and "working class" body validate the middle-class Jewish stereotype of the American *goy* and suggest the degree to which Decker is culturally assimilated. Conversely, the Jewishness of Rabbi Schulman, the head of the yeshiva, is imaged through his evidently Jewish body:

> The rabbi was a tall man, not as tall as Decker, but at least six one. Decker put him in his early seventies. Much of his face was covered with a long salt-and-pepper beard, and what wasn't hidden by hair was a road-map of creases. His eyes were dark brown, clear and alert, the brows white and furry. For a man his age he was straight-backed, slender, and a fastidious dresser. His black pants were razor pressed, his white shirt starched stiff, and the black Prince Albert coat carefully tailored. Crowning his head was a black felt homburg. (25)

To Decker, whose range of associations are limited by Kellerman to the Gentile world, Rabbi Schulman's appearance is "regal, like an archbishop." To many readers, however, his appearance is still that of the typically bearded and wrinkled Jew, whose fastidiousness may recall the turn-of-the-century cartoons that pictured such bearded and furry-browed men attired in the clothes of the upper class in order to satirize their ambitions of becoming socially acceptable. Kellerman's point, appropriate to the detective fiction, is that these images are indeed manipulable, and thus deceiving. In a nice twist, Decker is told by one of his fellow detectives that "Jews, in general, look like Jews," and that despite Rina's "button" nose and Decker's "Jewish" nose, "I can tell that [Rina] is Jewish and you're not" (219). In another kind of twist, it turns out that Rabbi Schulman really is a sophisticate, a collector of Jewish ritual art and an expert in American jurisprudence. Other characters elaborate on Kellerman's point. Shlomo Stein, a student at the yeshiva who is a suspect, is imaged as a typical student wearing a white shirt and black velvet yarmulke, but his "Van Dyke" beard gives him away. He is, in fact, a former cocaine dealer who has returned to his orthodox roots. When afterwards another suspect at the yeshiva tells Decker, "Detective, Jews don't murder, Jews don't rape. Your people murder and rape, not mine" (187), readers are prepared to accept Decker's moral for Kellerman's point: "If God was so sure that righteous Jewish men and women wouldn't murder, why did He bother with the sixth commandment?" (187). Appearances deceive, but the Jewish God, like all good detectives, is not taken in by them.

Once readers begin to appreciate that Jewishness is not necessarily signified by public appearances, orthodoxy's emphasis on one's private intellectual and spiritual development provides Kellerman a lens that brings Decker's Jewish potential into focus. Granted, Decker has an enlightened, egalitarian relationship with his female partner, Marge Dunn; he takes excellent care of his horses and his dog; he makes his own rough-hewn furniture; and, as Rina asks, exasperated by her own attraction to him, "why did he have to be *so* good with the children?" (137). But this evidence is not as significant in revealing Decker's true potential to readers as are events that demand ratiocination and serious moral judgement. As an adolescent, Decker impulsively defends a Jewish boy against a group of bullies. When he explains his altruism to his Baptist adoptive parents they respond with platitudes about protecting oneself and turning the other cheek. "Who are we to judge the infidels," says Decker's mother. But Decker has already judged the ambivalence of his parents' responses and his schoolmates' avoidance of him after the fight. Thinking it through, Decker "had learned for a brief period what it was like to be a pariah" (65). In another example in chapter fifteen, after Rabbi Schulman has warned Rina to stop seeing Decker, the detective twice surprises Rabbi Schulman with his ability to apply "Jewish" reasoning to morally troubling situations. Here is Decker trying to convince Rina not to divulge his list of suspects at the yeshiva to Rabbi Schulman:

> "Rina, you once told me that saving a life takes precedence over everything in Judaism," said Decker. "By talking, you'd be endangering your life."
>
> The old man's lips turned upward in the hint of a smile. "It's a strange world when a gentile enlists halacha for the purpose of persuasion. I give you credit, detective." (151)

Later, trying to convince Rabbi Schulman that he must take in the mentally disturbed yeshiva student found wandering near the murder scene, Decker quotes scripture:

> "Rabbi, this is the twentieth century. If the cup was found on Benjamin, Benjamin is going to be tried for theft. And try as he may, Judah can't do a damn thing about it."
>
> The old man looked perturbed.
>
> "Rina has been teaching you Torah?"
>
> "I learned that in Bible school. That's the Christian equivalent to your place."
>
> "*Lehavdil.*" The rabbi cranked open the window. (154)

In scenes such as these, Decker reveals his *sechel,* his proto-Jewish "brains," but this word implies more than just intelligence or a reified Jewish essence. It refers to an intellectual/spiritual component within humans that refines and purifies their physical dimension, but which is available only through Torah, only by connection to the wisdom of Jewish teaching and tradition.[5] Kellerman does not mean to suggest that despite outward appearances all Jews have an essential, unassimilatable nature, an old antisemitic stereotype of the Jewish body (Gilman 194-209). Kellerman makes a point of having Rina articulate one of the themes of the series when she tells Decker, "It takes a lot more to be a Torah Jew than just an accident of birth" (200). Only when a human being is attracted to the study of Torah (even if, in Kellerman's formulation of this Jewish concept, that attraction is galvanized by a beautiful Jewish woman) can that human come into possession of a unique spiritual gift. Decker's backround and Baptist bible schooling indicate that even Gentiles have access to this gift. When Decker finally reveals to Rabbi Schulman his biological identity, the rabbi asserts that "[s]omething pulled you to us" (231), implying not only fate but also that some force was at work bringing the physical to the spiritual—though Decker believes that force is his lust for Rina. Nevertheless, by the time Decker tackles the rapist/murderer at the end of *The Ritual Bath* (who turns out not to be Jewish), Rabbi Schulman and many readers are certain that Decker's physicality has been refined by his spiritual education, setting him on the road to religious piety and a better integrated American Jewish identity. Emphasizing this idea of connection (physical and spiritual, private and public, the individual's embrace of community, Decker's literal embrace of Rina), Kellerman has Rabbi Schulman invite a reluctant Decker to join the celebratory dance that the men of the yeshiva have broken into in celebration of the capture of the rapist/murderer. Rather than face a news-hungry media alone, Decker elects to be a dancer in the dance: "Okay, Rabbi. Show me what to do" (277).

Most importantly, Kellerman's reshaping of the figure of the unattached American Jewish male gives that figure, as Adrienne Rich would describe it, a "womanly series of choices" (27) that lead him back into a Jewish community.[6] It would have been simple for Kellerman to refashion Decker's gentile male virility into the figure of a "Rambowitz," as Paul Breines calls the tough Jew pulp fiction heroes of the seventies and eighties (58).[7] Indeed, given his imposing physique and the fact that he is an exemplary fighter and (inadvertent) agent of revenge in *The Ritual Bath,* Decker shares a number of traits with Breines's tough Jew. In Kellerman's hands, however, Decker never abuses his power in order to achieve some kind of premeditated or political revenge. Decker chooses to use his power, as a man and as an agent of the law, in order to transform his life and to protect his family. In fact, his desire to serve and protect his family is so obsessive throughout the series that Cindy Decker, his daughter from his first marriage, eventually rebels against his overprotectiveness in *Grievous Sin* and *Justice.* In that light, Decker's power recalls Adrienne Rich's redefinition of power as "not power of domination, but just access to sources," that is, the power to reclaim and to live out a spiritual and ethical tradition such as Judaism, and to protect those who wish to do the same (quoted in DesPres 205). Choosing solidarity, education, and faith, Decker's character exemplifies a feminist sensibility of nurturing the world of human beings rather than exploiting dominion over it. The oppositions that Decker's character is able to come to terms with because of these choices—worldly-wise pulp detective *and* 'boy' pupil, successful professional *and* religiously committed suitor—are part of Kellerman's fabrication of an American Jewish identity that reflects middle-class readers' desire for a tough "family values" hero who is wise to the mysteries of America (an America that is itself a fabrication of pulp culture detective fiction) but which reshapes that identity by defining toughness as the willingness to embrace an exacting Jewish faith.

RINA LAZARUS

In contrast, the character of Rina Lazarus is more conventional and less developed than Decker even as late as *Sanctuary* (1994), the seventh installment of Kellerman's series. In *The Ritual Bath,* Rina is introduced, tellingly, as the Bible teacher for the children at the yeshiva. When Decker first sees her his pulp-flavored observation captures her "traditional" looks: "There was something classic about her face—the oval shape, creamy skin, full, soft mouth, startling blue eyes. Doll her up and she'd blend nicely into high society" (19). With her black hair, Rina's beauty suggests stereotypes of the Jewesses' body, but Kellerman, to her credit, undermines that stereotype by periodically focusing reader's attentions on her unexpected and "startling" qualities. Rina is willing to talk to Decker alone at the scene of the crime, an initiative that is considered immodest by the other women at the yeshiva (21), and ultimately she rebukes them for their narrow-minded and judgmental attitudes (273). Though she is in an almost continual state of fear throughout the novel, Rina is still capable of physical force (100) and still takes chances that place her in danger because she does not want to be dependent and helpless (261).

Hence, it is all the more disconcerting that Rina spends the majority of her stage time in the rest of the series cooking, crying, tending to her children and teaching Judaism to Decker, but we must remember that Kellerman fashions Rina as a standard bearer of middle-class "norms." Raised modern Orthodox, Rina's first marriage and her move into the yeshiva after her husband's death has deepened her commitment to Orthodoxy, but these changes did not made her a fanatic. When she recounts her religious odyssey to Decker, Rina's description of her upbringing iterates both modern Orthodoxy's virtues in maintaining Jewish identity and its position as the cultural middle-ground of Jewish religious practice:

> "We were modern Orthodox. Which is to say I grew up with a strong Jewish identity. My mother was far less strict with the rules than my father. That led to a lot of fights. So in keeping with Freudian psychology, my oldest brother—the *doctor*—married a girl much less religious than he, and I married a boy much more religious than I. We all marry our parents, don't we?" . . . "On the other hand," she continued," my middle brother—I'm the youngest—was a lost soul. My parents didn't know what to do with him, so he was shipped off

> to Israel. The Chasidim got to him, and now he's at a Satmar yeshiva, the most religious of the three of us." (117-18)

With her knowledge of Freudian psychology and her frank admission of the personal reasons and rebellions that make one more or less religious, Kellerman has created in Rina a character who helps to place modern Orthodoxy, considered by the majority of assimilated middle-class Jews a part of the religious right, into a middle position long associated with Conservative Judaism. Given that reading, Rina's brothers seem to represent the movement towards secular or religious extremes. Rina's "norming" of modern Orthodoxy thus clarifies how extreme Decker's own assimilation is, and, more fundamentally, how attractive extremes are to Decker's personality. Rina says as much when she evaluates Decker's potential in *The Ritual Bath:*

> "You know, Decker, you would have made a great yeshiva *bocher."*
>
> He broke up.
>
> "No, I'm serious. You have all the external trappings. You're intelligent, curious, hardworking. You ask the right questions. You're even a lawyer. A yeshiva is like a Jewish law school with ethics and morals thrown in. Anyone who's ever studied both will tell you that Jewish law is much harder and more challenging than American law."
>
> "I missed my calling, huh?"
>
> "You laugh, but I can tell, Peter. If you'd been born Jewish and raised in an Orthodox environment, you would have been a fanatic." (121)

Rina thus represents a middle-class American Jewish culture of religious moderation comparing and contrasting itself with Decker's Southern Baptist, American law-schooled, pulp culture "extremist," thereby revealing the cultural differences between her and Decker.

Throughout the series, Kellerman assiduously develops Rina's "middle" position and her casting of modern Orthodoxy as the normative American Jewish religious identity. Though she used to keep her hair clipped short and hidden under a wig when she was married to her first husband, Rina allows her hair to grow out, and only covers it with a kerchief when she marries Decker. Rina continues to wear dresses that conform to a rigorous interpretation of feminine modesty, dresses that cover her from neck to ankle, but allows her children to go camping and to Dodger games with Decker, as long as they bring along their own kosher food. Most provocatively, in *Milk and Honey* (1990) Rina sleeps with Decker before they are married. The mitigating circumstances, however, are threefold: Decker is already trying out daily ritual observance; Rina has consented to marry Decker; and both are suffering from severe sexual deprivation. Kellerman here accedes to a pop cultural convention regarding romantic relationships: love—the fact that Decker is clearly Rina's *bashert* (divinely destined partner)—rationalizes their impulsive act.

More significantly, in *Sanctuary* Rina's middle-ground modern Orthodoxy is portrayed as coeval with moderate American political values in scenes where Kellerman contrasts it with the religious Zionism of the Israeli settler movement. Her spiritual appreciation of, and personal attachment to, the sacredness of the *Ma'arat HaMachpelah,* the Cave of the Pairs (Adam and Eve, Abraham and Sarah, Isaac and Rebecca, Jacob and Leah), is made clear when she visits Hebron and prays in the shrine: "Something ethereal came over her, a sense of personal history. As if she were looking through her parents' scrapbook. . . . These people weren't fairy-tale characters or mythological creatures, they were real people. And like all real people, they had lived, they had died" (310). But as a representative of the middle, Rina is also pragmatic:

> Though Rina knew that Hebron was still a *Jewish Holy City,* would always be a *Jewish Holy City,* it was time to be realistic. Hebron was no longer *Jewish* and hadn't been for fifty years. It was a typical overcrowded Arab village that bred rage and hatred against Jews. It had become such a hotbed of politics, Rina wasn't sure who was securing its borders—the IDF, the Israeli Police, the Palestinian Police or UN troops. (283)

Kellerman has Rina articulate a very American response to the Israeli-Palestinian conflict, a response that echoes the American middle-class ideals of moderation and tolerance which middlebrow readers of Kellerman's series expect to be validated. Later, Kellerman has an Israeli soldier echo Rina's moderate position, as if to paint the average Israeli as a blue and white version of middle-class red, white, and blue sentiments: "Many pray here—Arab and Jew. I don't think you're a crazy fanatic. . . . Here there has been too much bloodshed caused by small minds. I talk to the settlers, try to tell them that bloodshed and revenge is *their* way, *their* customs, *their* laws. It is not *our* way" (311). Clearly, Rina's embodiment of a normative American Jewish religious identity is based upon a middle-class disavowal of extremism of any kind, cultural or political.

Rina is also an embodiment of spiritual renewal, but in the role of spiritual hero her character reveals its limitations even as it mirrors the contemporary perception that American Jewish women have become agents for Jewish renewal in America. Kellerman addresses this perception in *The Ritual Bath* by first clarifying Rina's attitude toward sex and sexuality. In the beginning of the novel, Decker treats Rina as if she must be sexually naive or prudish, assuming that Orthodox Jews are as puritan about sex as are religious Protestants. Rina first explains to Decker that she abstains from premarital sex and observes the customs of bodily modesty not on moral grounds "but because we believe that the body is private and not some cheesy piece of artwork that's put on public display" (93). Then, in a key passage in *The Ritual Bath,* Rina explains the significance of the mikvah (ritual bath) to Decker:

> "You know what a mikvah really symbolizes, Peter?" She became animated. "Spiritual cleansing. A renewal of the soul. For twelve days, starting from the first day of a woman's menses, she and her husband are forbidden to have sex. When the twelve days are up, if she hasn't bled for the last seven days, she immerses herself in the mikvah, and then they can resume marital relations, renew their physical bond. That means for at least twelve days every month a husband and wife are off-limits to each other. I bet that seems nuts to you, doesn't it?"
>
> He smiled. "In a word, yes."
>
> "And yet it seems so *normal* to me." (93)

Rina's explanation of the mikvah suggests that it is the woman's unique responsibility to maintain spiritual housekeeping in order to renew the soul, and that such renewal is dependant on observing and respecting limits. Rina's explanation—since it completely avoids mentioning when and how men make use of the mikvah—implies that such renewal is domestic woman's work, and it perfectly articulates "the bourgeois gender division that placed religion and the inculcation of religious sensibilities within the female domain" (Hyman 36).[8] One can't help but be disappointed by Kellerman's missed opportunity (here and elsewhere) to allow Rina a fluid, feminist reading of American Jewish womanhood appropriate to that image of the mikvah. Still, Rina's animation and personal engagement in a religious observance whose proscriptions she respects offers readers the possibility of a more generous reading. Rina's vital relation—through her body and her sexuality—with her faith, and her use of that vitality in an attempt to teach Decker something important about Judaism and about spiritual healing, evokes, briefly and incompletely, Miryam Glazer's notion of "spiritual romanticism" (439), a feminist spirituality which she observes in the works of a number of contemporary American Jewish women writers.[9]

Unfortunately, Kellerman is not interested in Rina's overturning middle-class American Jewish gender divisions or reclaiming the mystical power of Jewish female spirituality in a way that truly transforms her character. And if a review of a later book in her series, *Prayers for the Dead* (1996), is any indication, neither are most of her readers. Writing for the *Los Angeles Times,* Margo Kaufman notes:

> As always, Kellerman is most fascinating when she's explaining the nuances of Judaism. (I've learned more from her books than I did in 12 years of Sunday school.) For example, "Wiping the dish, Rina thought about the Jewish concept of *shalom bais,* the keeping of marital peace. So important a tenet, a person was allowed to do everything in his or her power to keep home and hearth tranquil, even if it meant slight variations on the truth." Whether this concept justifies Rina jeopardizing her husband's investigation is arguable, but the book is first-rate. (8)

Rina, whose name in Hebrew means "joy," is a character whose primary role is to bring joy and peace to Decker and to teach him the "norms" of Judaism (as Kellerman shapes them for her middlebrow audience) so that *he* may be transformed into a public representative of Judaism. Thus, Rina is referred to by other characters as either Decker's girlfriend or wife, but Decker's colleagues dub him "Rabbi," a nickname he retains throughout the series. Kellerman underscores the gender division between the two characters by writing "Rina" when designating her female character but using the patronymic "Decker" when designating her male character. Additionally, Kellerman uses the symbol of the mikvah in *The Ritual Bath* only in order to identify Rina as a woman and her place as a woman in the Jewish community. When Rina meets Decker, Kellerman no longer needs that overt symbol of femininity because Rina has a man; Rina is never seen in a mikvah again in the rest of the series. In short, Rina, as Kellerman has constructed her, is the sort of female popular fiction character whose function is to empower her man, and in that sense Rina needs Decker as much as Decker needs her.

TYING THE KNOT

Rina's relationship with Decker, then, leads inevitably to a kind of "intermarriage," and not only in the sense Kellerman toys with in *The Ritual Bath.* True, Rina and Decker appear to be a coded reference to the overwhelming intermarriage rate among American Jews. Rina and Decker's attraction to each other registers the potential for romantic attractions between Jew and Gentile even among the most Jewishly identified American Jews. Yet the surprise of Decker's biological identity is not simply a "cheap trick" as some students of mine have insisted. If the cultural chasm between assimilated Jew and observant Jew is as wide as that between these two fictional characters, then by analogy any marriage between two such disparate Jews is a kind of cultural "intermarriage." Therefore, the solution to such an "intermarriage," as Kellerman formulates it in *The Ritual Bath,* is the "conversion" of the "non-Jewish" partner. Decker's willingness to embrace Jewish practice—to choose solidarity, education, and faith—is that conversion experience. Kellerman, by making Decker's choices and his struggle to understand Judaism and become an observant Jew the central character transformation of her mystery series, thus provides mass cultural evidence which supports Julius Lester's recent, trenchant observation about contemporary American Jewish life. "The convert's experience is becoming a paradigm for being Jewish," says Lester, an African American convert, "regardless of natal origin" (64).

Kellerman's mystery series is thus the continuing story of Decker's conversion from unattached individualist to Jewishly identified family man through the loving tutelage of his fiancee, and then wife, Rina. It is a narrative that consequently "intermarries" the individualist pulp culture detective to a middle-class, "family-values" American Jewish religious identity. Furthermore, the crime Decker investigates in each mystery is really a pretext for Kellerman to appropriate pulp culture's capitalist critique of America and transform it into a moral critique of secular American society. By doing so she exposes its vapidity as well as the real crime that Rina the spiritual hero prevents in this series—biological merger with such a society and the loss of a distinctive identity that provides a moral compass with which to plot one's path through life.

For example, in *Sacred and Profane* (1987), the second book in the series, Decker must learn to balance the separations that Judaism makes between love and lust as well as between Judaism and the secular, public world. These separations are made tangible to Decker when he celebrates the Sabbath and appreciates the haven it is from the horrors of his case, a double murder of two young girls caught up in a pornography ring. It is the Havdalah blessing marking the end of the Sabbath that provides the title of the book: "Blessed art Thou, Oh Lord, who has made a distinction between sacred and profane" (122). But that spiritual haven does not insulate Decker from his revulsion for the pornographers who steal young girls' lives and the powerful people who keep them in business, or from his confusion about how to resolve his lust for Rina with his love for her. Decker has abstained from sex with Rina because both have not yet resolved their fears and doubts about marrying, but Decker, used to the sexual mores of his assimilated lifestyle, does not yet know how to deal with his carnal desires in a Jewishly appropriate way. So how will Decker balance love and lust as well as his new Jewish life and his public life? According to Rabbi Schulman, Decker must find the answer in faith—not faith in Rina but faith in God. Trying to find relief for his soul through Rina is what is confusing Decker. In that sense, the sexual perversion of the case Decker investigates is a critique of the way sexual desire is perverted in contemporary American society into a substitute for true personal comfort, and the way a woman's body is perverted by pornography into a goal-object. Though Decker considers giving up the religious life he has embarked on (and suggests to Rina that they settle for a "mixed" marriage), Rina helps him understand that balancing his private and public lives, his love and his lusts, means renouncing the professional detective's instinct for "a neat little solution" (239), for a goal-object. Being a really good Jew is not the same as being a really good detective. When Rina and Decker decide to temporarily separate at the end of the novel, Kellerman brings home to readers the message that separation, in Judaism and in this relationship, is not an end but simply part of an ongoing balancing act that describes the long, spiritual process of creating enduring attachments.

By the time Decker and Rina tie the knot off stage and reemerge in New York on honeymoon in *Day of Atonement* (1991), Decker has learned that spiritual success requires a different standard of measurement than professional success, and that only through faith in God will he be able to balance his pursuit of both. Accepting the separation between himself and his biological mother, Frieda Levine, as well as learning the true meaning of repentance, preoccupies Decker even as he comes to the rescue of his biological family in *Day of Atonement.* He learns that he cannot force Frieda to come to terms with her abandonment of him, and that the only "solution" to what is long past solving is to grant her forgiveness when she asks for it on the eve of Yom Kippur (354). Concurrently, Kellerman continues to portray secular America as corrupted and corrupting. Hersh Schaltz, the megalomaniac serial killer and kidnapper in *Day of Atonement,* is the product of a dysfunctional Orthodox family who finds the secular world murderously liberating, and who does not "steal" Noam Levine, Decker's half nephew, so much as "trap" him, luring him away from his warm Jewish home in Boro Park by playing on the boy's curiosity about the secular world. In *Milk and Honey* even Gentiles are affected by this corruption. As Pappy Darcy says about his all-American family farm: "Once it was the Promised Land for me, God's land of milk and honey. Not no more, misters. Not no more" (365). Creating a family in the face of these private and public revelations is difficult at best, as *Milk and Honey* and *False Prophet* (1992), with their respective tales of family skeletons and pagan, New Age seductresses, attest.

Therefore, when Rina finally gives birth to Hannah in *Grievous Sin* (1993), the accomplishment seems heroic, spiritually and physically; after all her defences and explanations of the ritual and spiritual separations that Orthodox Judaism requires, she has, through the birth of their child, guaranteed the continuity of family and identity that redeems the meaning of Decker's life. Rina's heroism does not come easily. Her daughter's birth is a difficult one, and after the delivery she loses her uterus. Giving way momentarily to religious doubt, she calls on Rabbi Schulman to tell her what to do, echoing Decker's action at the end of *The Ritual Bath.* Rabbi Schulman lectures her on what prayer can and cannot accomplish, and on the important understanding that control over human destiny is out of our hands:

> In reality, how much control do we have over our lives? Life is a loan from *Hashem* [The Name]. We are put here by His design; so shall

> we leave by His design. . . . There are times when *Hashem* is willing to deviate from His original plans, times when He has forgiven the most grievous of sins. Our prayers are not empty words, Rina Miriam. Though the world may seem very dark now, *Hashem* has an open ear for you. You may ask. You may not get, but you may *ask.* (73)

The point of prayer is that it articulates human hope, weighting the words of prayer with the fullness of human desire, but without guarantee of their fulfillment. Rina, the spiritual hero, is the real hero in Kellerman's series because she brings home to Decker, through the birth of their daughter, evidence of hope's fulfillment even as she accepts that she has no control over her life, as the danger attending her delivery proves. Decker has embraced Judaism, but his detective's instincts still lead him to believe that he can achieve some sort of control over his and his family's Jewish future. As he chases down the nurse/kidnapper of a baby born in the same hospital and at the same time as his own, readers see that the desire for control is what has corrupted the nurse. Tandy Roberts is a control freak who is addicted to body-building as a way of achieving control over herself, but she fails to gain control over her mental illness or the sense of betrayal that fuels her actions. Decker himself must learn to give up his belief that he can control and protect his daughter Cindy, who places herself in danger despite his order that she keep out of his case (265).

Hence, Decker may be a success as a detective, solving all of the crimes in the series, but he remains dependant on Rina's heroic example to maintain his hope and trust in the ultimate efficacy of his private conversion, despite his lack of control over past and future. Kellerman underscores this point in *Grievous Sin* by juxtaposing Decker's desire to be a "successful" Jew in order to atone for his biological parents' mistakes with the corrupted desires of Tandy Roberts who thinks of herself as a "martyr" of the cultural revolution of the 1960s. Like the other "addicts" of that grievous decade—addicted to sex, drugs, Jesus, and now body-building—Roberts justifies her rebellion against middle-class norms as an attempt to rectify and atone for her parents' perceived sins, but that only exacerbates rather than solves her personal problems. In contrast, Rina's example and Decker's experience reveal the wisdom of a Judaism that asks individuals to atone only for their own sins, because, as Decker muses at the end of the novel, "some things are just out of your control" (390). Once

Decker appreciates that he is responsible only for his own struggle to avoid biological merger, the grievous sin of American Jews, he discovers that time and God are what heal all his other wounds. Real American Jewish men, in Kellerman's reworking of American Jewish manhood (and in marked contrast to David Levinsky), are consciously aware that though secular culture promises us the possibility of control over our lives, it fails to deliver on that promise. Such men recognize that Judaism makes no promises; it asks only that we trust in God, in ourselves, and—as Decker is surprised to learn when his adoptive, Baptist parents decide to visit him and his new baby despite their initial disapproval of his marriage and conversion—in our families. Thereafter, the books in Kellerman's series read as if, in the words of the Jewish sage Hillel, everything else is commentary.

As an example of American Jewish popular fiction, the Peter Decker and Rina Lazarus mysteries reflect the current reappraisal by American Jews of the project of cultural assimilation, embraced so wholeheartedly by the immigrant generation. Kellerman's middle-class audience, Jewish and non-Jewish, shares the contemporary disillusionment with American individualism and its secular, consumerist culture. Kellerman herself, along with multicultural writers of both literary and popular fiction, shares in the contemporary project of recuperating and reshaping images and traditions from the past as models for a meaningful hybrid-American ethnic identity. Kellerman's audience, however, is not about to embark on a wholesale transformation of their lifestyle, and in that respect Decker and Rina embody a recommitment to the ethical values of those traditions as long as they are compatible with middle-class expectations. Kellerman's series thus reflects the mix of curiosity and unease that many in her audience have about hybridity and an increasingly multicultural America. Like Decker, they find it hard to accept that so much about their lives and the life of their country is beyond their control. To justify their faith in the future may require more than a popular fiction, but for now Kellerman intrigues her audience with an American Jewish detective's interrogations of manhood and society in America, and comforts them with Decker's validation of marriage as the solution to the unsettling mysteries of family and hybridity.

NOTES

1. Rabbi Yitzchak Etshalom, in his online commentary on Maimonides' "Laws of Prayer," explains: "The Torah commands a general Mitzvah without defining those actions which we must do to fulfill it. The Rabbis create a structure through which we can fulfill this command of the Torah. By mandating that we visit the sick, for example, the Rabbis have given us a vehicle for fulfilling the Torah's command of 'Love your fellow as yourself'" (Part II). Similarly, by mandating marriage the Rabbis have given Jews a vehicle for fulfilling the command "be fruitful and multiply."

2. See, for example, S. Anski's play *The Dybbuk.* Khonnon, a poverty stricken Kabbalist and disappointed bridegroom, "wins" his bride by dying at the end of the first act after fate has seemingly stolen his intended from him (38). In the second act, he responds to his circumstances by transforming himself into a dybbuk, a ghost, as if to suggest that the only "action" available to a Jewish male is in the spiritual and not the material realm (39-68).

3. Jenna Weissman Joselit notes in *The Wonders of America: Reinventing Jewish Culture, 1880-1950* that in American Jewish recipes "what counted was not the authenticity of the recipe but its symbolic power and presentational value as a touchstone of authentic Jewish culture" (217).

4. "Embourgeoisement" is Jonathan Webber's term for the social adaptation of middle-class values and behavior. Webber lists a number of features of contemporary Jewish life that are included under this rubric, including "the abandonment of a traditional Jewish work ethic that had not connected personal achievement or status with occupation," "the movement out of the inner-city ghetto to the more affluent suburbs," and the consequent redefinition of religion as "Jewish ethnicity" or "Jewishness" (255). Embourgeoisement is itself one aspect of modernization.

5. Rabbi Shaya Karlinsky, in his online translation of and commentary on Rabbi Judah Loew's sixteenth-century exegesis of the *Sayings of the Fathers,* words the Maharal's discussion of *sechel* thusly: "A human being who lacks Torah has two characteristics. First, he is empty and void of wisdom. He lacks the element of 'sechel' (the intellectual/spiritual component) that should be found in the human being. Secondly, his human physicality is less perfect due to this lack of wisdom. (While he could have a more purely phyiscal strength, which would appear to indicate a superior physical dimension, this aspect of his physicality is really animal physicality, since it is built purely on physical strength. If we focus on what is unique in the human being, even his material dimension is more perfect when it is imbued with 'sechel.'). . . . When man's physical dimension is connected to the 'sechel' (imbuing the material human

being with a spiritual/intellectual reality), then that physical body is refined and purified. It is clear that the body of an animal is of a more material nature than the body of a human being, for the animal has no 'sechel' (spiritual/intellectual dimension). The more connected man's body becomes with this 'sechel,' the more refined that physicality becomes. And the more refined and elevated the physicality becomes, the more piety it will manifest, with this person doing acts of kindness to all" (Chapter Two, Mishna 6, Part I).

6. "Womanly series of choices" is from Adrienne Rich's poem "Sources," and refers to choices that reflect feminist revisions of patriarchal traditions.

7. Breines' quick definition of tough Jews is "Jews who fight, who are violent in the public political sphere" (ix). In contrast to the stereotype of gentle or weak Jews, images of tough Jews in popular fiction reflect a newfound Jewish nationalism engendered by Israel's military victory in the 1967 Six Day War: "What occured in the Middle East in early June 1967 transformed the way American Jews thought not only about Israel but about the Holocaust, politics, their parents, grandparents, children, Jews, non-Jews, and, not least, themselves and their bodies" (58). For an analysis of weak Jews in American popular culture see Berger 93-107.

8. In chapter one of *Gender and Assimilation in Modern Jewish History,* "Paradoxes of Assimilation," Paula Hyman explains how the project of assimilation helped shift responsibility for educating Jewish children from fathers to mothers, and notes that the outcome, "permitted Jewish men to pursue success in the worlds of commerce and civic affairs and to assume leadership positions within the Jewish community while relegating the transmission of Jewish knowledge and identity to the domestic sphere and to women, who, incidentally, had fewer educational and material resources to accomplish the task" (48).

9. "Spiritual romanticism" is Miryam Glazer's term for Jewish women's imaginative spiritual exploration and re-vision of a rationalist, egalitarian American Judaism. The writers Glazer refer to—Anne Roiphe, Nessa Rapoport, Tova Reich, and Rhoda Lerman—write narratives that "are evolving a new spiritual romanticism, rooted at once in the experience of Jewish womanhood and in a mystically imaginative Judaism . . ." (443). Glazer's essay is useful in suggesting what Kellerman could have done with the character of Rina, not in identifying Rina's putative feminism.

WORKS CITED

Anski, S.. *The Dybbuk.* Trans. Joseph C. Landis. *Three Great Jewish Plays.* Ed. Joseph C. Landis. New York: Applause Books, 1987.

Band, Arnold. "Popular Fiction and the Shaping of Jewish Identity." *Jewish Identity in America.* Ed. David M. Gordis and Yoav Ben-Horin. Los Angeles: Wilstein Institute, 1991.

Berger, Maurice. "The Mouse That Never Roars: Jewish Masculinity on American Television." *Too Jewish?: Challenging Traditional Identities.* Ed. Norman L. Kleeblatt. New York: The Jewish Museum/New Brunswick, New Jersey: Rutgers U P, 1996.

Breines, Paul. *Tough Jews.* New York: Basic Books, 1990.

Cahan, Abraham. *The Rise of David Levinsky.* New York: Penguin Books, 1993.

Chandler, Raymond. *The Long Goodbye.* New York: Ballantine Books, 1978.

DesPres, Terrence. *Praises and Dispraises: Poetry and Politics in the 20th Century.* New York: Penguin Books, 1989.

Etshalom, Rabbi Yitzchak. "Shiur P'tichah." *Rambam's Hilkhot T'fillah.* Online. Rambam Archives. Project Genesis: http//www.torah.org, 1996.

Gilman, Sander. *The Jew's Body.* New York & London: Routledge, 1991.

Glazer, Miryam. "'Crazy, of Course': Spiritual Romanticism and the Redeeming of Female Spirituality in Contemporary Jewish-American Women's Fiction." *People of the Book: Thirty Scholars Reflect on Their Jewish Identity.* Ed. Jeffrey Rubin-Dorsky and Shelley Fisher Fishkin. Madison, Wisconsin: The U of Wisconsin P, 1996.

Haute, Woody. *Pulp Culture: Hardboiled Fiction and the Cold War.* London: Serpent's Tail, 1995.

Hyman, Paula E.. *Gender and Assimilation in Modern Jewish History.* Seattle & London: U of Washington P, 1995.

Joselit, Jenna Weissman. *The Wonders of America: Reinventing Jewish Culture, 1880-1950.* New York: Hill and Wang, 1996.

Karlinsky, Rabbi Shaya. *Maharal Derech Chaim.* Online. Maharal Archives. Project Genesis: http//www.torah.org, 1996.

Kaufman, Margo. "Happiness Is a Warm Subplot." *Los Angeles Times,* 22 Sept. 1996: Book Review, 8.

Kellerman, Faye. *Day of Atonement.* New York: William Morrow and Company, 1991.

———. *False Prophet.* New York: Fawcett Gold Medal, 1992.

———. *Grievous Sin.* New York: Fawcett Gold Medal, 1993.

———. *Milk and Honey.* New York: Fawcett Gold Medal, 1990.

———. *Prayers For the Dead.* New York: William Morrow and Company, 1996.

———. *Sacred and Profane.* New York: Fawcett Crest, 1987.

———. *Sanctuary.* New York: Avon Books, 1994.

———. *The Ritual Bath.* New York: Fawcett Crest, 1986.

Lester, Julius. "What Do American Jews Believe?" *Commentary,* 102.2 (August 1996): 63-65.

Rich, Adrienne. *Your Native Land Your Life.* New York & London: W.W, Norton & Company, 1986.

Webber, Jonathan. "Modern Jewish Identities: The Ethnographic Complexities." *Journal of Jewish Studies* 33.2 (1992): 246-267.

CHAPTER ELEVEN

Do We Need Another Hero?

Caroline Reitz

In 1992 I taught an undergraduate seminar on female detective fiction. Wanting to underscore that we had come a long way, baby, I began with the masculinist heroics of Hammett and Chandler. My mostly female—indeed mostly feminist—class howled indignantly at the macho individualism of these hard-boiled detectives and clamored to move on to the surely more enlightened works on the syllabus, such as those of Sue Grafton, Sara Paretsky, and Patricia Cornwell, writers who had female sleuths. By the end of the semester, the students were regularly applauding the individualist heroics of these "different" detectives—and I was rethinking my sense that we had gone anywhere at all. We had simply exchanged one individualistic hero for another and called it feminism. Scholarship on both heroes and detective fiction suggests that my class and I were experiencing a common translation problem; that of a dominant tradition, the figure of the hero, into a nondominant practice, the detective with a difference.[1] Hero and man are traditionally equated, as Victor Brombert writes in *The Hero in Literature*, "the very concept of man is bound up with that of the hero" (11). At the same time, Kathleen Klein laments in *The Woman Detective*: the hero is "a man, and, I would argue, only a man—who makes his own rules and then lives by them, no matter how difficult that may be" (234-35). Both are correct in that traditionally the hero has been an individual white male who, by virtue of being exceptional, both represents society and is set above it.[2] As Klein and other critics maintain, the genre of detective fiction is equally "bound up" with the traditional hero and the individualist ideology he embodies: as Dennis Porter explains, "the myth of the hero is built into the structure of the detective formula itself" (154-55).

As the weeks—and heroes—went by, and as the final papers on "Kay Scarpetta: Feminist Hero" poured in, I wondered "Do we need another hero?" What difference does *difference* make? And then I found Barbara Neely, whose African American domestic worker cum sleuth, Blanche White, showed me that we don't need another hero, we need an *Other* hero, a figure whose identity challenges not only the whiteness and/or maleness of the figure, but also the traditional notion of the hero as an exceptional individual representing a community he can stand above. Neely personifies this challenge in Blanche, who meets head on the difficulties heroism presents for nondominant communities and movements—such as the exclusive history of the concept and the logic of individualism that this history implies—and who raises many of the questions the Other hero must address if she is to avoid being just another hero. A brief introduction to the two Blanche mysteries, *Blanche on the Lam* (1992) and *Blanche Among the Talented Tenth* (1994), illustrates how Neely revises some of the hero's—and the hero-centered genre's—traditional assumptions.

We first meet Blanche as she is bolting out of the courthouse door after being unfairly sentenced to thirty days in prison for a couple of bounced checks. Blanche has returned to Farleigh, North Carolina, her childhood home, to make ends meet in a supposedly safer environment for her dead sister's two kids. When these loose financial ends send her fleeing from the courthouse, she takes cover in a week-long job in service to a rich white family at their vacation home outside of town. This family has as much to hide as they do to spend. The book's cover warns that "keeping other people's houses clean can be murder," suggesting Blanche's own problems with the law pale beside the transgressions of her new employers. Not only that, Blanche has been on the lam before. She returns to Farleigh in the first place to escape the perverts of New York City, one of whom tried to lure her niece, Taifa, and nephew, Malik, into a van with a Run-DMC tape. Moreover, she is in New York only after running away to California for a year, fleeing the obligations of motherhood her sister's death placed on her. Blanche, under these circumstances, is at the center of colliding social forces, indeed. The already rugged terrain of race, class, and gender in the first novel becomes more insidious in the second novel, as Blanche follows her wards to Amber Cove, an exclusive, all-black resort. While solving the mysteries of the resort, Blanche must negotiate conflict not only between black and white, rich and poor, male and female, but within those communities as well.

However, the Other hero does more than simply visit the now familiar sites of conflict of race, class and gender. Difference in Neely's work is more than a superficial makeover of tradition. This paper argues that the Other hero, both as a theoretical figure and in the character of Blanche White, ruptures the binaristic logic of surface variation/deep adherence to heroic convention that has limited contemporary attempts to remodel the figure and the genre.[3] Such a figure is needed to reinvent a tradition that, rather than tolerating or at best incorporating "difference," understands difference as fundamental to the hero's collective individuality, an identity that cannot be defined apart from the community. In other words, the Other hero illustrates that difference, rather than being an obstacle to heroism or simply the material for a predictable variation, is the stuff heroism is made of. Neely shows that difference enables not only heroism but the practice of detection itself in her discussion of Blanche's "Night Girl" persona in *Blanche on the Lam*. Here, the "eggplant black" Blanche White, teased since childhood for her extra-dark color and doubly white name, is encouraged by an insightful aunt to consider her liabilities as assets. "It's only them that's got night," her aunt tells her, "can become invisible" (59). Signifying on the painful legacy of invisibility documented by Ralph Ellison, Blanche capitalizes on her invisibility to see beneath the surface of a society divided by and within race, class, gender—divisions symbolized by the crimes she solves. Just as "Night Girl" makes use of "the part of her so many people despised" (59), Blanche as Other hero must use rather than transcend the pitfalls and possibilities of the social conditions of her existence.[4] With Blanche, Neely alters the traditions of both the hero and the genre, while offering an alternative to the current compromises of contemporary nondominant detective fiction.

As the word "compromises" suggests, the revision of the individualistic hero and the hero-centered genre of detective fiction is not only a tall order, but a familiar one. Even multicultural detective fiction, which deliberately challenges these traditional heroic requirements (white, heterosexual male), is identified and marketed as a genre of exceptional individuals: an Easy Rawlins or a Pam Nilsen mystery, the latest Kinsey Millhone, V. I. Warshawski, or Tamara Hayle—indeed, Blanche White. While writers of detective fiction have challenged the traditional concept of the hero by placing, for example, exceptional women or people of color at the center of their texts, the variations on the hero presented by contemporary mystery writers have not substantially changed the figure's individualist assumptions, suggesting that the logic of individualism may be a more durable characteristic of tradition than the challenges presented by differences of gender and race. Maureen Reddy concedes that the genre's essential conservatism threatens feminist values in that "crime novels tend to celebrate traditionally masculine values and to reinforce conservative social attitudes" (5), while Klein argues that the genre's boundaries can be as limited as the hero's. "Adopting the formula traps their authors," Klein writes, "either feminism or the formula is at risk" (200-01).[5] But where Klein sees an either/or scenario, some writers see the possibility of resistance. Lee Edwards, for example, describes the hero as "a figure who, at least *in potentia*, might oppose that most embracing of all cultural institutions, patriarchy itself" (14). Nevertheless, even hopeful assessments of the possibility for reshaping traditional roles have a compromised quality. Discussing "fourth-generation" detective writers working in the shadow of Chandler and Macdonald, David Geherin argues that for these writers to be successful, they must combine "respectful adherence to the conventions of the genre with their own individual talents" (2-3).

It makes sense, then, that Reddy questions "Have the rules changed or do they remain the same, with different players at the game?" only to answer, "Both" (11). A different player—a female detective, for example—both disrupts convention by threatening the "masculine values" of the traditional crime novel, and at the same time abides by the even more sacred rule ("respectful adherence") for the traditional hero: individualism. To borrow a phrase from Eve Kosofsky Sedgwick, contemporary attempts to create a hero with a difference are "kinda subversive, kinda hegemonic."[6] Sedgwick's phrase captures both the aspirations and the frustrations of the nondominant writer's balancing act, the difficulties of keeping "other" from becoming "another." Navigating between the Scylla of subversion and the Charybdis of hegemony can be a strategic position for the nondominant writer and critic.[7] However, the modifying "kinda" suggests a certain predictability about this strategy. Sedgwick's phrase implies that even the dynamics of revision can become static. A nondominant reinvention of the detective, such as Neely's Other hero, thus requires not only a reexamination of the tradition of the hero and the requirements of the genre, but a look at the compromises within feminist and African American theories of subjectivity, as well.

HEROISM AND NONDOMINANT THEORY

The possibilities for and limitations of challenging traditional figures and genres are much examined in African American, feminist, and postcolonial critical theory.[8] Henry Louis Gates Jr.'s concept of "repetition with a difference" (3) in African American literature and literary theory acknowledges the necessity for incorporation into tradition. "Canonical Western texts," he explains, "are to be digested rather than regurgitated, but digested along with canonical black formal and vernacular texts" (6). While this merger with "received (European) 'literary' forms" results in "new (and distinctively black) genres of literature" (12), Gates's emphasis on canon formation illustrates an enduring investment in traditional forms. Similarly, Deirdre David's discussion of women and the British Empire, using Homi Bhabha's conception of "mimicry," underscores the transformative possibilities of repetition in that "the subaltern figure interrogates the master text in such a manner that the colonizing power must endlessly re-form itself against the native de-forming mimic countertext" (34). While these authors do see tradition (here, the hegemonic Western canon) being altered by its contact with "countertexts," the conceptual implications of "repetition" and "mimicry" illustrate the incorporative gusto of tradition and the perhaps inevitable canon-abilizing of "different" texts/figures. Kinda subversive, kinda hegemonic.

Given these compromised options—the entrapping formulas and figures, resistance *in potentia*, mimicry, repetition with a difference—arguing that Other heroism manages to avoid the stasis implied in the "kinda" is a large claim. Claiming Other heroism for Blanche White is an equally large claim. In order to see how Neely manages to succeed where others have, if not failed, at least become predictably subversive, we must first look closely at the assumptions of "heroism" and their theoretical implications for the non-dominant community.[9] The hero has always been a paradoxical figure, at once "typical," in that he stands for a community and "exceptional," in that he stands above it. Traditionally, "he" is an individual paradoxically distinguished from "his" community by virtue of being designated its "representative." At the same time, such a figure becomes even more complex for nondominant groups, where access to power—the space that marks the difference between the typical and the exceptional—is much more difficult. While any hero must acrobatically bridge the contradictions of exemplarity—being both superior and common, particular and general—for the nondominant hero, the "common" and the "general" have a historical specificity, in that neither he, nor she, nor their community have access to "universal" representation. In addition, collective organization is obviously crucial to the social change he/she seeks. Moreover, in light of tokenism, the individual success story, far from being a victory for each member of a nondominant community, can represent the very failure of real institutional or social change.[10] And yet one of the goals of the women's movement, an example of collective organization of a nondominant group, has been to celebrate exceptional women. Cheri Register, for example, in determining what functions literature must perform in order to be "useful to the movement," writes that "provid[ing] role models" is a major concern (quoted in Gallop 106), while in their study of the female hero in literature, Carol Pearson and Katherine Pope explain that recovering female heroes is crucial feminist work. According to Pearson and Pope, "the new scholarly interest in recovering myths about strong female heroes is beginning to restore female heroes to their rightful place in the culture" (227). Certainly feminist movements are at least part of the reason for the overwhelming success of female detective fiction, with mystery bookstores devoting entire sections to "strong women."

Even so, the problem that the figure of the hero presents for feminism is apparent in the very term itself. Literary critics deciding whether to use the term "hero" or "heroine" for female protagonists have always had to weigh the pros of eschewing a nonstandard term, heroine (the suffix "ine" seeming derivative and dependent), with the cons of adhering to a masculine-gender term. This terminological discomfort suggests a philosophical one as well in that a feminine version of a masculine concept does not disturb its deeper individualist ideology: "The battle for female individualism," Gayatri Chakravorty Spivak writes, "plays itself out within the larger theater of the establishment of meritocratic individualism" (265). Moreover, Spivak laments, the language of "feminist individualism" has come to be recognized as the "language of high feminism within English literature" (273). Heroism, as it has been traditionally conceived, necessarily elevates the individual above the community. "This goes against our basic philosophy," Sookie Stambler explains, "we cannot relate to women in our ranks towering over us with prestige and fame. We are not struggling for the benefit of the one woman or for one group of women. We are dealing with issues that concern all women" (quoted in hooks 6). Lillian Robinson concurs, adding "It is not role models we need so much as a mass movement, not celebration of individual struggle so much as recognition that we are all heroes" (quoted in Gallop 138). In her critique of feminism's heroicization of Anais Nin, Estelle Jelinek makes the point bracingly clear: "hero-worshipping should be anathema to all serious radicals and feminists" (323). But, Jane Gallop argues, this is all academic: "Whether in some ideal, superior version of feminism, 'serious' feminists would completely shun 'hero-worshipping,' in the real 'popular' form that feminism is usually found, we tend to celebrate exceptional individual women" (138). But in order to understand Neely's creation of an Other hero, a hero that is not "exceptional," we need to reconsider the question—not whether we should have heroes, but what it means that their struggle, in Spivak's words, "plays itself out within the larger theater of the establishment of meritocratic individualism" (265). It's no easy question and the answer involves the history of the traditional hero.

THE TRADITIONAL HERO

The hero as a Great Man was often thought of but never so permanently expressed as in Thomas Carlyle's representation of the figure in his *On Heroes, Hero-Worship, and the Heroic in History* (1841). Carlyle opens his lectures with the famous statement that "Universal History, the history of what man has accomplished in this world, is at bottom the History of the Great Men who have worked there" (1) and he places exceptional men at the forefront of society, where the Great Man directs rather than is directed by social forces. While Carlyle conceives of the hero as more a creator than as an expression of history, even he eventually turns to the idea of the hero as both a Great and a common man. G. F. W. Hegel's slightly earlier conception of the hero in *The Philosophy of Fine Art* recognizes the hero's necessary immersion in society, acknowledging that while "under the present condition of the civilized world a man may act independently for himself in many directions, the fact remains that in whatever direction he may turn he is still only a member of a fixed order of society" (199). Yet as Georg Lukacs points out in his study of the hero in the work of Walter Scott, the Hegelian heroes (like the Carlylean) are "total individuals who magnificently concentrate within themselves what is otherwise dispersed in the national character, and in this they remain great, free and noble human characters" (206). Such heroes then, while concentrating national characteristics within themselves, can, nonetheless, act as free individuals.

The logical extension of this freedom from society is alienation, always posited as a requisite stage of the hero's journey, and Joseph Campbell's famous formulation in *The Hero with a Thousand Faces* suggests that the hero's development begins with departure from his community. The modern conception of the hero, particularly evident in the detective genre, more often shows an alienated hero or an antihero torn between acting for the society of which he is a part and needing to reject it altogether. Raymond Chandler sums up the paradoxical position of the modern detective hero: "The detective is the hero, he is everything. He must be a complete man and a common man and yet an unusual man" (398). The contradictions of this position—representation and alienation, common and unusual—are central to the pain of the modern hero's exile. Nevertheless, these formulations still privilege the individualism of the hero enough to suggest that society is something he *can* leave, that, going back to Reddy's definition of the necessarily male hero, rules are something he can make up for himself.[11]

Lukacs's conception of "the mediocre hero" in Scott provides an important alternative to this individualist conception of the hero as able to be either fundamentally or at least temporarily distinct from society. Lukacs sees the social forces of modern life as dominant, "everywhere colliding" and inescapable (206). Traditional heroes, in his analysis, are "passionate partisans" of warring sides in social conflict, whereas mediocre heroes "have an entirely opposite function. It is their task to bring the extremes whose struggle fills the novel, whose clash expresses artistically a great crisis in society, into contact with one another" (206). This sense of the hero as the "contact zone" of colliding social forces, unable to pick up and depart for a journey into noncommunal selfhood, is crucial to my definition of the Other hero, which draws on Mary Louise Pratt's definition of "contact zone" as "social spaces where disparate cultures meet, clash, and grapple with each other, often in highly asymmetrical relations of domination and subordination" (364). While Pratt is speaking literally in terms of geography ("contact zone" is often synonymous with "colonial frontier"), her use of the term recognizes that individual writers and texts are equally the spaces where these cultures meet.

What Lukacs's conception of the hero and Pratt's definition of the contact zone recognize is the impossibility of the individual operating outside of social forces. While this might seem like reinventing the

Althusserian wheel, with the individual always already interpolated by ideological state apparatuses, what the Althusserian formulation doesn't recognize—and what an examination of Neely's construction of Other heroism must—is how the social relations between the individual and the collective change when considering a "non-dominant" individual. In this case, the inextricable connection between individual and society and the particular burdens of representing that society carry particular significance. While this link can be for better, in that one represents the aspirations of a community struggling for social power and recognition, it can also be for worse, in that part of what inevitably bonds the hero to his/her community are the limitations placed on it by dominant society. As a member of a non-dominant community, one never has the option of autonomy from the social constructions of dominant culture.[12] Believing in the myth of the heroic individual who discovers himself in alienation from the community can dangerously lead to reproducing the exclusivity of the very tradition one is trying to change, to an incorporation into the individualist ideology the traditional hero represents.

BLANCHE WHITE IN THE CONTACT ZONE

In Other heroism, both the alienation-and-return model and the predictable balancing act implied by Sedgwick's "kinda" are replaced by the continual collision of differences so volatile that the logic of individualism can never emerge. Barbara Neely's Other hero, Blanche White, inhabits and embodies this contact zone. Neely's novels illustrate a world dominated by the "contact zone" of race, class, and gender, but what is crucial for Neely's novel, and for the Other hero in general, is how those chaotic social forces are characterized. Rather than the Patriarchy or the white, middle-class world posing the sole threat which must be fought, guerrilla-like, from the outside, the social forces of Neely's novels render such binaristic, us-against-them characterization impossible. It is true that Blanche, as a black female domestic worker, is the contact zone for many stereotypical conflicts of race, class, and gender. The hair on the back of her neck bristles signaling danger when Everett, her "too rich, too white, too male" employer in the first novel, enters the room (*Lam* 37). Blanche has learned to sense the presence of her employers and she has a reason to expect danger. In her attempt to get "some of her sold self back," Blanche takes "liberties with her employers' space" (63), sitting in their front rooms, looking out their windows, listening to their stereos. Once, while taking a bath in a customer's tub, she is discovered by the employer's brother and made to pay, Blanche reports, in a "painful and private way" (63). Her position amidst many colliding social forces keeps her from reporting it to the police: "Even if they'd believed her and cared about the rape of a black woman by a white man, once it came out that she'd been attacked while naked in her employer's bathtub, she'd never have been employed in anybody's house in town again" (63). She senses danger even from supposedly harmless white men, such as Mumsfield, the mentally handicapped cousin of Everett's wife, Grace. Blanche worries that Mumsfield, for whom she feels an instinctive tenderness, will give her a dreaded case of "Darkies Disease," an affliction whereby "you convinced yourself that you were actually loved by people who paid you the lowest possible wages" (48). The "real danger in looking at customers through love-tinted glasses," Blanche explains, is that "you had to pretend that obvious facts—facts that were like fences around your relationship—were not true. Mumsfield was a grown white man in whose home she was presently hiding from the police" (48-49).

While racism, class prejudice, and sexism are facts of Blanche's contact zone, Neely does not build the fences of these facts in the predictable places. Conflict doesn't happen just between black and white, rich and poor, man and woman, but within those individual communities as well. In the beginning of the second novel, *Blanche Among the Talented Tenth*, Blanche contemplates the recent marriage of Leo, her ex-boyfriend, who found someone else when he finally realized Blanche would never marry him. Blanche explains her position: "all the married women she knew worked hard in somebody else's house, field or plant and came home to take care of a full-grown man and a houseful of kids who seemed to think her labor was their due" (11). Perhaps predictable expectations from her small-town, high school sweetheart, but Blanche finds herself equally stereotyped by a prominent African American feminist, Mattie Harris. For most of the novel, Mattie Harris is Blanche's Mata Hari, helping her get to the bottom of the mysterious events at Amber Cove, an all-black resort in Maine. But when Blanche's version of events clashes with Mattie's, the famous feminist insists that she "will not be spoken to in this manner by some poor, uneducated, ignor . . ." (221). Blanche interrupts to point out to her—and to the reader—that "there's more than one way to be poor, more than one kind of education and a whole lot of ways to be ignorant" (221).

There's also more than one way to be black, as Blanche discovers at Amber Cove, where she has gone in the first place to discover if her wards, Taifa and Malik, are becoming "color-struck." Blanche believes that Taifa is wrongfully making individual distinctions, here based on skin color, about a community—the same mistake, Blanche will argue, made by W. E. B. Du Bois, whose essay "The Talented Tenth" gives Neely's second novel its name. While Du Bois significantly altered the color of the hero in 1903 when he wrote that "the Negro race is going to be saved by its exceptional men," his emphasis on individual talent replicated the elitist logic that made racism so successful in shaping social structures in the first place. What Du Bois's formulation, as well as the feminist individualism that Spivak laments counts as feminism these days, does not recognize—and what the Other hero must—is that the concept of the individual as it has been traditionally conceived, potentially free from society, can never be the same concept for non-dominant communities for precisely the reason that community is never anything the individual can entirely leave, especially when, like Blanche, one is the color of night. In the second novel, Neely points out the racism (and colorism) inherent in Du Bois's "talented tenth." Here, Blanche investigates the problem of elitism inhering in representation when she vacations at an exclusive all-black resort frequented by patrons who would have once been referred to as the "talented tenth." Blanche laughs: "It's been a long time since I heard that old Du Bois's thing about the light-brights being the natural leaders of their darker brethren" (65). Because Neely continually underscores Blanche's imbrication in the implicitly talentless ninetieth, she provides a fundamental reformulation of the concept of the individual that surface variations of the traditional figure have not been able to achieve. Neely is able to differentiate, as feminist legal theorist Zillah Eisenstein argues nondominant communities must, between "a theory of individuality that recognizes the importance of the individual within the social collectivity and the ideology of individualism that assumes a competitive view of the individual" (quoted in hooks 8). The key word here is "within" which implies that the individual, for all its history to the contrary, can never be outside of multiple colliding social forces.

Neely begins *Talented Tenth* alluding to money Blanche received from "those white folks in North Carolina for not putting their nasty business in the street" (7), for keeping most of her discoveries about the rich white family to herself and her friends. Thanks to this money, her niece and nephew are now happily enrolled in a prestigious school in Boston, where they all have relocated. Blanche worries that they are developing the prejudices towards dark-skinned blacks that she has had to endure from people of all colors her whole life. Remembering being called "Ink Spot and Tar Baby" (*Lam* 59), she presses Taifa on her newfound desire to stay out of the sun so she won't get darker. "Well, you know, Mama Blanche," Taifa confesses, "if you have dark skin, people laugh at you and say you smell bad and nobody wants to be your friend" (*Tenth* 85). Blanche's personal experience with being on the wrong side of many kinds of prejudice has given her a larger view of social dynamics that allows her to identify sexism on the part of women or racism on the part of African Americans as just a surface variation on a traditional theme.

Amber Cove is certainly full of intraracial prejudice. Mattie explains to her that there are two types of guests at the resort, the "Insiders," who have had family cottages there for generations, and the "Outsiders," who stay at the Inn. "This Insider/Outsider business ya'll got going here," Blanche comments, "Don't it remind you of something?" (47). It reminds Blanche of "the same kind of bull hockey reasoning white people used to keep us out of everything they wanted for themselves! Next you gonna tell me the Outsiders like it this way" (48). Blanche recognizes that Amber Cove's all-black exclusivity does not significantly change the rules but merely the players of the game. "She wondered," Neely writes,

> how soon after the first baby was born of the rape of a black woman by a white man did some slaver decide that light-skinned slaves were smarter and better by virtue of white blood? And how long after that had some black people decided to take advantage of that myth? (67)

With all the light-skinned guests acting color-struck, the "eggplant black" Blanche designates herself "race representative." But she undermines the individualism implicit in "representative" by emphasizing that her racial identity is made up of many things other than color. She contemplates what it would be like to be able to pass for white, but "she couldn't make the leap to wanting to step out of the talk, walk, music, food and feeling of being black that the white world often imitated but never really understood. She realized how small a part her complexion played in what it meant to her to be black" (20).

Here, Neely makes the important point that the issue is not whether light-skinned blacks are superior, a la the logic of Amber Cove, or inferior, not as "representative" of the race as Blanche, but that a fixation on any kind of color prejudice, because it individualizes, obscures rather than clarifies identity.

For Blanche, identity is constructed by the collision of many defining categories. Blanche is in the middle of many colliding forces: between her feminism and the type represented by Mattie, between her view of color and those of the Amber Covites, between her understanding of the freedom of domestic work and the prejudices of those around her, from her dangerous or dismissive employers to the elitist guests at the resort to her own mother, who had hoped Blanche would be a nurse. The result is that Blanche's sense of self is the result of continually shifting relationships between and within her color and her sex, her class position, and her sexuality. Like Eisenstein's definition of an individuality "that recognizes the importance of the individual within the social collectivity," Blanche's individuality recognizes the importance of the social collectivity, and all its shifting relations, within the individual. Blanche underscores the necessity of this connectedness between individual and community in her description of Christine and David, the parents of Taifa and Malik's friends and their hosts at the resort. Though Christine and David are wealthy professionals, they could have been, Blanche explains, any type

> of competent hard-working colored folk who believed in the race and felt some responsibility to move it, and therefore themselves, forward. She wondered what their mamas and daddies had taught them about being a well-off black person in a world of poor blacks that made it possible for them to remain connected in a way she doubted any of the other Insiders were (75).

Neely's novels are realistic about the limitations these colliding social forces place on Blanche. But rather than portray these forces as obstacles to be surmounted, as restraints from which to seek independence, Neely places them at the foundation of her narrative voice, the mysteries and their solutions, Blanche's detective ability, and, indeed, her heroism itself.

Feminist analyses of writing by women have argued for the significance of the first-person narrative. Feminist discourse, Spivak suggested, speaks in the idiom of individualism. Writing in the first person may be a way for the female author to rebel against a third person narrative format which, according to Sandra Gilbert and Susan Gubar, "allows—even encourages—just the self-effacing withdrawal that society fosters in women" (548). Women's stories, feminists agree, must be told in women's voices. "It is obvious," Klein explains, "that the male first-person narrator cannot truthfully tell a woman's story, but neither can an implicitly phallocentric third person narrative voice which cleaves to the generic formula" (228). The third-person narrative voice, however, is hardly contemporary detective fiction's formula. If speaking in the first-person is an act of female authority, it would appear to be an easy victory for the writer wanting to make a feminist intervention in the detective genre; practically all contemporary detective novels are told in the first person. Again, Neely presents a challenge both to tradition and to feminist revisions of tradition. Neely's far-from-phallocratic third-person narrative voice challenges a feminism that articulates itself in the individualistic voice of first-person narration. Blanche's reality, Neely suggests, is collective and cannot be spoken in a single voice. But Neely's use of the third-person does not have the universal implications of traditional novelistic narration. The communities that speak through Neely's third-person narrative are historically specific, such as African Americans brought to this country as slaves or women struggling against oppression.

Like the collective voice of Blanche's experience, her community is always imbricated in the secrets that both generate and solve the mysteries. Unlike works by some white women detective writers, such as Patricia Cornwell, Neely's fiction does not show crimes originating with individual psychos nor are they solved by individualist heroes. Blanche plays an important—but not the only important—role in investigating a crime. This is particularly true of the second novel, where the setting of the all-black resort creates a world in which criminal, sleuths, victim, suspects and innocent bystanders are from within a diverse African American community.[13] But even in the first novel, where it would be easier to read Blanche as a black sleuth solving the crimes of the white world, Blanche's ability to piece together the puzzle requires that she recognize that these are not separate worlds, that they are woven together through the blood and sweat of history. Blanche is part of a network of past and present domestic help whose grasp of social dynamics, and hence investigative powers, permeate the boundaries of black and white, rich and poor. As

Blanche points out, "a family couldn't have domestic help and secrets" (95). For example, Miz Minnie, an old friend of Blanche's family, is both a sounding board and a source of information: "Because she knew the black community," Blanche explains, "Miz Minnie also had plenty of information about the white one" (115). In order to solve the mysteries, Blanche must utilize her community's knowledge of the long history of race relations and the strange interdependence it engenders. In this case, a key figure in the mystery turns out to be a light-skinned African American woman passing for white. Blanche must also discover the secret of the old African American gardener's loyalty to the rich white family, a story of obligation—they inadvertently saved him from the Klan decades earlier—that requires his life. The mysteries of Amber Cove spring from the internal racisms of the place; deadly crimes originate in the cover-up of past shame over skin color and parentage.

As the mysteries themselves result from interdependence of different worlds, the solutions require a collective effort even beyond the old girls' network. In *Talented Tenth*, Blanche approaches the larger mysteries of her own life and the specific ones of Amber Cove with the help of her ancestors. Blanche has always been connected with her various communities, but "the older she got, the stronger her need to be connected to something that was larger than the world as she knew it" (60), a recognition that causes her to turn "her tendency to talk to her dead grandmothers into ancestor worship" (61). Just as Blanche provides a reinterpretation of the hero that requires difference and collective individuality, her ancestor worship is a version of traditional hero worship, while radically challenging the individualist concept of the Great Man. Blanche connects her desire for communion with a larger community with her racial identity, feeling that "It was as much a part of her African heritage as the heavy dose of melanin in her body" (60). Blanche's ancestors constitute her "race memory," a connection with a community in the past that anchors her in her present communities. Blanche looks to the past for both memory and promise. As an Other hero, she experiences the collisions between past, present, and future as both liberating and binding. While the ancestors brace her for solving the mysteries of her collective individuality, they link her to "a pain so old, so deep, its memory was carried not in her mind, but in her bones. It was not always useful to be in touch with race memory. The thought of her losses sometimes sucked the joy from her life for days at a time" (*Lam* 111-12).

Blanche's detective powers, rather than being some mystical second sight or congenital curiosity, are rooted in the social conditions of her existence; her heroism, unlike the traditional figure, is not born of a departure and a return but of a recognition of her indissolubility from a community of both pain and promise. In Blanche's "Night Girl" persona, Neely reconciles not only the traditional contradictions of heroism, but also the tensions between individual and community that have limited other nondominant writers' reformulations of the genre and the figure. Blanche fulfills the aspirations of her underrepresented communities—and solves the crime—because she uses, rather than transcends, her social condition. Like the name she refuses to change, a name that perversely reminds her that she is doubly black in a white world, and like the service job that she maintains despite other options, Blanche's heroism is not because she rises above the collisions of her social position, but because she stays put.

Though not always geographically. The end of *Blanche on the Lam* has Blanche, still the wandering Night Girl, on the move again. She heads to Boston to face the challenges of "what it meant to be a black woman trying to control her own life" (214-15), a life, the reader now knows, to be composed of many lives, past and present. She knows that her brushes with individual and systemic violence have changed her, but she also knows that she is "still capable of negotiating enemy territory" (215). As the second novel illustrates, this enemy territory is all the more challenging for being neither predictable nor static. But because Neely's reformulation of the traditional hero—her portrait of Other heroism—places the contact zone of social forces within the individual rather than below the triumphant individualist, neither is Blanche.

NOTES

1. "Nondominant" is the not entirely satisfactory term I use to suggest any community, or member of that community, that is not culturally dominant, i.e., not white, male, middle-class, heterosexual. "Minority" or "nonmajority" can imply numeric rather than cultural subordination, which we know is not necessarily the way power functions; for example, black South Africans were a numeric majority even when excluded from cultural power. I use "difference" occasionally to suggest all kinds of differences from the dominant culture. Similarly, "Other," as in the Other hero—the subject of this paper—is meant to be an inclusive term that might at times mean female or African American or

both. While this inclusiveness might seem to ignore the specificity of difference, thereby reproducing a classic blindspot of feminism, that is the "absence of race-determinations in a certain sort of feminism" (Spivak n.280), my point in this paper is that the collision of multiple differences, the contesting relations between and within specific communities constitute an "Other" heroism that includes potentially all kinds of difference in response to the traditional construction of the hero.

2. The hero, as Brombert points out, has been in existence since the beginning of stories about humanity. The history of this concept of the hero, crystallized by Thomas Carlyle and extended through modern day examinations by Joseph Campbell and the authors collected in Brombert, is discussed below, pp. 8-11.

3. While a consideration of other contemporary detective fiction, such as the works of Patricia Cornwell, Sue Grafton and Sara Paretsky, is beyond the scope of this paper, I would argue that these writers are examples of nondominant writers whose attempts to remodel the genre are limited by a deeper adherence to the convention of heroic individualism. This is not to say that they are limited in the same way or to the same extent. Certainly the emphasis on individuals as both the source and solution to crime is far greater in Cornwell than the other two writers. Nevertheless, an individualism persists in the work of even these explicitly feminist writers which limits the difference, here of gender, to a surface variation.

4. As the "Night Girl" persona materially liberates Blanche from being limited by her color, the nickname metaphorically liberates her. Just as the gay community has reclaimed and reformulated the derogative name "queer" into a symbol of gay pride, Blanche wears proudly her doubly white name and embraces the appellation "Night Girl," where the first three letters of both words can be anagrammatically read as "nig-gir."

5. While Klein never wavers from her understanding of the detective genre as essentially conservative, her "Afterword to the Second Edition" recognizes several writers of detective fiction who have managed to transcend some of the obstacles to make feminist interventions.

6. Sedgwick used this phrase in a 1992 paper she delivered at Brown University on Henry James and gay identity. The paper appears as a chapter in her most recent book, *Tendencies*; the phrase does not. It is perhaps fitting that this phrase is without specific attribution as Sedgwick's point was that this has become a universal and therefore predictable way of reading resistance.

7. Nondominant critical theory presents many figures for this "subversive/hegemonic" balance. Rosi Braidotti's figure of the acrobat literally suggests the trope of the revisionary balancing act. See her *Patterns of*

Dissonance (New York: Routledge, 1991). Henry Louis Gates Jr.'s "trickster" and Gloria Anzaldúa's "mestiza" are more familiar figures of this "borderland" between difference and tradition.

8. For work on the role of race in the formation of subjectivity, see the recent collection of essays *Female Subjects in Black and White: Race, Psychoanalysis, Feminism* (U of California P, 1997), Elizabeth Abel, Barbara Christian, and Helene Moglen, eds. Regrettably, this essay was written before a consideration of this collection was possible.

9. The oxymoronic undertone of being "predictably subversive" is exactly what I want to be suggesting here about "kinda subversive/kinda hegemonic" readings of difference. While there is nothing necessarily bad about the interplay between these two terms, predictability can work against the "subversive" aims of challenging tradition, such as in the case of the individualistic hero.

10. I'm referring to the phenomenon of "tokenism," whereby having an individual woman (a person of color, etc.) occupy a position of power can be a sign of a *lack* of (a decoy for) real institutional recognition. The link between the increasing recognition of individual sports heroes (Jackie Joyner-Kersee, Gail Dever, Shannon Miller, and Kerri Strug, to name a few) and the rise of support for women's athletics is illuminating in that it illustrates that individual success can lead to greater public attention while still not representing institutional progress. Women's sports, despite its heroes and growing popularity, are still greatly underrecognized and underfunded relative to men's sports.

11. Even critics who see the hero's individuation from society as contradictory still assert that such an individualist option does exist. Frederick Garber, writing of the Romantic hero's relation to society, suggests that "the hero may insist that he makes up his own rules (*and there is always some sense in which he does*), but the very nature of society and of the structure of his own personality find points of antagonism which prove to be elements in a mutual attraction as well as a necessary repulsion" (my italics, 226).

12. Feminist historian Denise Riley explains that "feminism never has the option of putting forward its own uncontaminated, self-generated understandings of 'women'" (68).

13. The African American community similarly structures all aspects of the crimes in Valerie Wilson Wesley's Tamara Hayle series. An African American female "cop-turned-struggling p.i.," who quit the Newark police because her teenage son was roughed up when mistaken for a criminal, Tamara Hayle is a contact zone for the contesting forces of gender and race. Unlike Blanche, however, Tamara Hayle, at least in the first two books of the series, seems to

follow a more individualist model, a la the hard-boiled female detective, in investigating and resolving crime.

WORKS CITED

Braidotti, Rosi. *Patterns of Dissonance.* New York: Routledge, 1991.

Brombert, Victor, ed. *The Hero in Literature*. Greenwich, CT: Fawcett, 1969.

Campbell, Joseph. *The Hero with a Thousand Faces.* New York: Meridian, 1956.

Carlyle, Thomas. *On Heroes, Hero-Worship and the Heroic in History*. Ed. Carl Niemeyer. Lincoln: U of Nebraska P, 1966.

Chandler, Raymond. "The Simple Art of Murder." *Detective Fiction: Crime and Compromise*. Eds. Dicken Allen and David Chacko. New York: Harcourt Brace Jovanovich, 1974.

David, Deirdre. *Rule Britannia: Women Empire, and Victorian Writing*. Ithaca: Cornell U P, 1995.

Edwards, Lee R. *Psyche as Hero: Female Heroism and Fictional Form.* Middletown, CT: Wesleyan U P, 1984.

Gallop, Jane. *Around 1981: Academic Feminist Literary Theory.* New York: Routledge, 1992.

Garber, Frederick. "Self, Society, Value, and the Romantic Hero" in Brombert 213-27.

Gates, Henry Louis, Jr. *Black Literature and Literary Theory.* New York: Methuen, 1984.

Geherin, David. *Sons of Sam Spade: The Private Eye Novel in the 70s.* New York: Frederick Ungar, 1982.

Gilbert, Sandra M., and Susan Gubar. *The Madwoman in the Attic: The Woman Writer and the Nineteenth-Century Literary Imagination.* New Haven: Yale U P, 1979.

Hegel, G. F. W. *The Philosophy of Fine Art* in Brombert 186-201.

hooks, bell. *Feminist Theory: From Margin to Center.* Boston: South End, 1984.

Jelinek, Estelle C. "Anais Nin: A Critical Evaluation." *Feminist Criticism: Essays on Theory, Poetry, and Prose*. Eds. Cheryl L. Brown and Karen Olson. Metuchen, NJ: Scarecrow, 1978.

Klein, Kathleen. *The Woman Detective: Gender and Genre*. Urbana: U of Illinois P, 1995.

Lukacs, Georg. "Sir Walter Scott" in Brombert 202-12.

Neely, Barbara. *Blanche on the Lam*. New York: Penguin, 1992.

———. *Blanche Among the Talented Tenth.* New York: Penguin, 1994.

Pearson, Carol, and Katherine Pope. *The Female Hero in American and British Literature*. New York: R.R. Bowker, 1981.

Porter, Dennis. *The Pursuit of Crime: Art and Ideology in Detective Fiction*. New Haven: Yale U P, 1981.

Pratt, Mary Louise. *Imperial Eyes: Travel Writing and Transculturation*. New York: Routledge, 1992.

Reddy, Maureen T. *Sisters in Crime: Feminism and the Crime Novel*. New York: Continuum, 1988.

Riley, Denise. *"Am I That Name?": Feminism and the Category of 'Women' in History*. Minneapolis: U of Minnesota P, 1988.

Roller, Judi M. *The Politics of the Feminist Novel*. New York: Greenwood, 1986.

Spivak, Gayatri Chakravorty. "Three Women's Texts and a Critique of Imperialism." *Critical Inquiry* 12 (Autumn 1985): 243-261.

CHAPTER TWELVE

An Un-Easy Relationship

Walter Mosley's Signifyin(g) Detective and the Black Community

John Cullen Gruesser

Only a handful of people would recognize the names of Venus Johnson and Sadipe Okukenu, two of the earliest black detectives to appear in African American fiction. More but by no means a large number of readers are familiar with the detective teams of John Archer and Perry Dart and Coffin Ed and Grave Digger Jones. Today, however, the popularity of Ezekiel (Easy) Rawlins,Walter Mosley's private eye who has so far appeared in five mysteries, reportedly extends all the way to the White House (Muller 300-01). Focusing mainly on *Devil in a Blue Dress* (1990), the originary novel in Mosley's series in which Easy decides to become a detective, this essay draws upon Henry Louis Gates, Jr.'s theory of Signifyin(g) to indicate how and to suggest why the author emulates and diverges from earlier detective fiction. Although *Devil* adheres quite closely to the hard-boiled formula, it innovatively casts Easy as a signifying detective, adept at juggling linguistic and social codes to deceive and outwit both white and black characters. Mosley goes further, however, signifying on the conventions of the genre in order to meditate on black freedom and the relationship between the individual and the community in African American society.

For the black writer of any era, detective fiction presents at least two challenges. First, as an enormously popular form with a number of major and minor conventions, the crime novel would seem a restrictive vehicle for an African American author aspiring to do more than simply entertain readers by satisfying their expectations. Second, because the genre requires the detective to solve the crime or crimes and thereby restore the established order, the mystery is notoriously conservative. As a result, the question for black crime novelists becomes how to preserve the integrity of their detectives. No matter how brilliant or brave they are, black sleuths in the pay of white clients or the white power structure risk coming off as lackeys. In short, African American mystery writers must strike a difficult balance between genre conformity and genre subversion.

Two of the earliest black detectives in African American fiction appear in Pauline Hopkins' *Hagar's Daughter* (1901-02) and John E. Bruce's *The Black Sleuth* (1907-09), novels serialized in black periodicals (the *Colored American Magazine* and *McGirt's Magazine* respectively). Hopkins only turns to the mystery genre in the last third of her narrative, when a young, black maid, Venus Johnson, cracks a case that Chief Henson, the head of the federal government's detective agency, has been unable to solve. In Bruce's novel, the Yoruba detective Sadipe Okukenu, employed by an international detective agency, manages to sniff out a criminal conspiracy before it even occurs. Rudolph Fisher is credited with writing the first African American detective novel published in book form. His *The Conjure-Man Dies* (1932), introducing the black detective team of Perry Dart, a police detective, and John Archer, a physician, takes place in Harlem. In the 1950s and 1960s, Chester Himes likewise used Harlem as the setting for eight novels featuring the black police detectives Coffin Ed Johnson and Grave Digger Jones.

By setting his books in the corrupt, violent, and ethnically-diverse milieu of postwar Los Angeles, Mosley places Easy on the familiar turf of the hard-boiled detective. Like his white counterparts created by writers such as Raymond Chandler, Easy is tough, street smart, fiercely independent, and yet vulnerable to the attractions and deceptions of women. Yet Easy, like Perry Dart and John Archer and Coffin Ed and Gravedigger Jones, operates in a distinctly black environment. He lives (at least initially) in Watts, has access to black nightspots and organizations the police and white operatives cannot infiltrate, belongs to an extensive network of black Houstonians transplanted in Los Angeles, and comes to describe his role as a sleuth as a matter of doing "[p]rivate investigations" for "[p]eople I know and people they know" (*Devil* 214) rather that a strict fee-for-sevices-rendered form of employment. In the five Easy books published thus far—*Devil* (1990), *A Red Death* (1991), *White Butterfly* (1992), *Black Betty* (1994), and *A*

Little Yellow Dog (1996)—Mosley has taken Easy from 1948 to 1963, stopping in 1951, 1956, and 1961 along the way. In each installment, Easy tells his own story in his idiosyncratic voice from a vantage point at a considerable temporal distance—internal evidence suggests the 1980s—from the events he describes. This enables Easy to reflect on how things (and he himself) have changed in the intervening years and thereby either overtly or subtly comment on the progress or lack thereof that has been made by African Americans in the last forty years. Apart from his use of a signifying African American detective who operates in a black environment, Mosley remains remarkably faithful to hard-boiled crime writing; however, he innovatively uses the detective genre to illustrate the conflict between personal and racial freedom by detailing how Easy's decision to become a private investigator complicates his relationship with his friends and the black community generally.

SIGNIFYIN(G) AND DETECTION

Before examining *Devil in a Blue Dress* in detail, I would like to discuss Henry Louis Gates, Jr.'s theory of Signifyin(g) to establish its utility in indicating what is distinctive about Easy as a detective and Mosley as a mystery writer. Gates' *Figures in Black: Words, Signs and the "Racial" Self* (1987) and *The Signifying Monkey: A Theory of Afro-American Literary Criticism* (1988) have had a profound impact on the study of African American literature. Rejecting both a purely discursive and a strictly political and/or essential definition of African American writing in favor of one that combines both of these elements, he proposes a non-Western rhetorical strategy as the defining gesture of the field. Gates discards the repudiative theories of African American literature proposed by Houston Baker and Robert Stepto in the 1970s as well as Addison Gayle and Ron Karenga's Black Aesthetic in favor of "Signifyin(g)," a revisionary, double-voiced response to the "discourse of the black"—Gates' term for texts by whites and people of African descent that portray black characters. In an effort to map out a tradition that is distinctively black but avoids the essentialism of Negritude, the Black Arts movement, and Afrocentrism, Gates argues that black American writing does not simply repudiate assertions of black inferiority by either imitating white literature or refuting its assumptions, nor does it reflect a distinctive black essence; instead, it is a counterdiscursive strategy associated with the African American trickster figure of the Signifying Monkey, which ultimately derives from the Yoruba trickster and messenger of the gods, Esu-Elegbara.

Conceiving *Figures in Black* and *The Signifying Monkey* as companion volumes, in the former Gates relates African American literature to mainstream white literary theory, reviews the history of black literary criticism, and proposes a theory of Signifyin(g) rooted in the black vernacular tradition, while in the latter he elaborates, illustrates, and situates this theory in a specifically black (primarily African American but also African and diasporic) context. In *Figures* Gates laments and endeavors to remedy African Americans' aversion to theory, an aversion that is nevertheless readily understandable given the manner in which theory has for centuries victimized people of African descent. Rather than responding with a theory of their own, according to Gates, black American writers and critics up until at least the Harlem Renaissance strived to counter accusations of black inferiority by demonstrating their literacy and refuting the charges leveled against them. This involved writing texts that adhered to mainstream white formal and stylistic conventions, publishing biographies of blacks responsible for great achievements, and producing propagandistic literary works that had few if any aesthetic aspirations. The emphasis on content and disregard of form and technique continued in the 1930s, 1940s, and 1950s when the influence of Marxist ideas resulted in what Gates punningly calls the "race and superstructure" school of black literary criticism, reaching its "zenith of influence and mystification" with the Black Arts movement in the 1960s (*Figures* 31).

Gates focuses on two works of African American literary criticism from the 1970s that in different ways fall short of providing a rigorous and comprehensive theory of black American literature in *Figures*. The first is Houston Baker's *Long Black Song* (1972), outlining his repudiative theory of black American literature. Gates discerns two problems with Baker's emphasis on repudiation. First, like so much of African American literature and criticism, it focuses on the content of a literary work rather than its structure, technique, and rhetoric. Second, by making black American writing dependent on the white theorizing about culture to which it responds, rather than proposing an autonomous (black) source for African American literature, Baker is himself doomed to go to battle against—and have his argument shaped by—those same assertions of black inferiority. Gates takes issue even more strongly with Addison Gayle's *The Way of the New World* (1975), which elaborates the Black Aesthetic. Once again content dominates over form in this strictly ideological criticism, which regards language and literature as expressions of a black essence. According to Gates, the major problem with Gayle's theory is its refusal to recognize that literature is a linguistic system and not an expression of external reality and that blackness is a trope.

Regarding strictly discursive or rigidly essentialized descriptions of the field as dead ends, Gates proposes a more theoretically rigorous alternative that combines aspects of each approach. After calling for attention to key concerns of traditional mainstream white literary criticism and poststructuralist theory that have largely been ignored in African American criticism, he introduces his theory of Signifyin(g) which is intended to address these deficiencies. Unlike Baker's repudiation theory in which African American literature opposes but is nonetheless dependent upon white literature, Gates's Signifyin(g) "is indigenously black and derives from the Signifying Monkey Tales," which themselves derive from the African trickster Esu-Elegbara (48). Moreover, instead of being obsessively thematic, like Baker's, Gayle's, and black American critical theories generally, "Signifyin(g) is a uniquely black rhetorical concept, entirely textual or linguistic, by which a second statement or figure repeats, or tropes, or reverses the first. Its use as a figure for intertextuality allows us to understand literary revision without resource to thematic, biographical, or Oedipal slayings at the crossroads; rather, critical signification is tropic and rhetorical. Indeed, the very concept of Signifyin(g) can only exist in the realm of the intertextual relation" (49).

Acknowledging that "all texts Signify upon other texts" and suggesting that this intertextual, revisionary concept may be useful in studying other literatures, Gates nevertheless regards his notion of Signifyin(g), which graphically represents the linguistic difference between white and black pronunciations of the word "signifying," as distinctively black because of his belief that "black writers, both explicitly and implicitly, turn to the vernacular in various formal ways to inform their creation of written fictions. To do so, it seems to me, is to ground one's literary practice outside the Western tradition. Whereas black writers most certainly revise texts in the Western tradition, they often seek to do so "authentically," with a black difference, a compelling sense of difference based on the black vernacular" (*Signifying* xxiv, xxii). Indeed, repetition with a (black) difference is another definition Gates offers for Signifyin(g).

If blackness is merely a trope, however, this problematizes Gates' attempt to delineate a specifically black tradition of Signifyin(g). If there is no racial essence, as Gates argues, then the "identifiable black Signifyin(g) difference" that makes African American literature distinctive had to be created by the material conditions in which a particular group of people (arbitrarily) designated as black found themselves. In other words, the black tradition Gates writes about had specific historical and political causes. Despite his protestations to the contrary, beneath the esoteric terminology of the Yale deconstructionists, a major purpose of Gates' project in *Figures in Black* and *The Signifying Monkey*, in fact, is to outline a *history* of black American literature from the eighteenth century to the present. At least in its relationship to white writing, Gates's theory of Signifyin(g) involves a historically-based and politically-motivated response to the dominant discourse that calls the terms of that discourse, as well as its own, into question.[1] Despite this inconsistency, a major strength of Gates' theory of Signifyin(g), with its focus on the rhetorical strategies black American authors use to revise the discourse of the black, is its ability to account for not only literary movements and genres that develop in response to earlier ones but also revisions within specific genres.

HARD-BOILED, WITH A BLACK DIFFERENCE

Comparing Easy to a prime example of the hard-boiled detective, such as Chandler's Philip Marlowe, reveals how closely Mosley adheres to the conventions of the tradition;[2] however, Mosley repeats the dominant white American detective story with a black difference, illustrating Gates' theory of Signifyin(g). Although tough-guy private eyes frequently disguise their actual intentions to achieve their goals, Easy deceives people and wears masks to an even greater extent than Marlowe and his cohorts. The hard-boiled hero operates in a world where appearance and reality seldom mesh. The detective by definition is a seeker of truth, but he himself is not always truthful in achieving this end. A hard-boiled sleuth such as Marlowe will normally identify himself and his profession; however, the seediness of his office and his lower-middle-class standard of living can cause people to underestimate him, and he occasionally finds it expedient and prudent to disguise his true intentions when gathering information or pursuing a criminal. Nevertheless, the hard-boiled lifestyle and moral code perfectly suits a man like Marlowe. For Easy, in contrast, deception is the rule rather than the exception and the role of a detective is much more of a consciously chosen pose than an expression of his true nature. I do not mean to minimize the role deception plays in Chandler's novels or Marlowe's participation in it. As Liahna Babener correctly observes of Marlowe, "[n]ominally on the side of truth, the detective becomes in effect an agent of deceit. He gives consent to the lies because in the end they are both pervasive and invincible" (143).[3] My point is that, as Babener also remarks, Marlowe is only "something of a pretender," not a consistent signifier like Easy. Not only in his relations with whites, like Bruce's Sadipe, but especially in his dealings with blacks, Easy is a trickster who employs signifying methods common in African American folk tradition.

In Mosley's 1948 Los Angeles, a black man does not acquire a detective's license and hang a shingle advertising his services as a private investigator. With no models on which to pattern himself, Easy must invent a detective persona that will work in his milieu. When DeWitt Albright, a veritable Moby Dick of murderous whiteness, surfaces in Joppy's bar asking Easy to do some investigative work for him, Easy knows he is in deep, uncharted waters; nevertheless, the one hundred dollars Albright offers is too tempting for the recently unemployed Easy to refuse. Unlike Marlowe, to survive and succeed Easy must invent a method for dealing with not only Albright, and the corrupt, white power brokers who employ killers like him, but also the violent, oppressed black community in which he lives. The method Easy chooses is based on the well-established African American strategy of signifying.

As Easy explains at the end of *Devil*'s second chapter, he can speak in two languages: "I always tried to speak proper English in my life, the kind of English they taught in school, but I found over the years that I could only truly express myself in the natural, 'uneducated' dialect of my upbringing" (10). This ability links him to the great trickster, the Signifying Monkey, a figure that "seems to dwell at th[e] space between two linguistic domains"—the European American and the African American (Gates, *Figures* 245). In the many versions of the story of the Signifying Monkey, the mischievous Monkey persuades his friend the Lion that their friend the Elephant has insulted him. When the Lion seeks satisfaction from the innocent Elephant, he is soundly thrashed. The Lion returns to punish the Monkey but cannot reach him in the trees. Thus, through words alone the Monkey succeeds in diminishing the status of the King of Beasts. Some of the specific varieties of signifying delineated by Gates and the critics on whom he draws include ribbing, complaining, and lying; implying without specifically stating; ridiculing a person or situation; exposing and overturning pretense; and pitting neighbors against one another simply by telling tales (*Figures* 238-40). Each of these types of signifying can be found in some form in Easy's interactions with either whites or blacks in *Devil.*

Mosley may in fact be slyly alluding to the Signifying Monkey tales in the remarkable seventeenth chapter when Easy in desperate straits penetrates the facade of white power and respectability in search of answers and a means of changing the rules of a game that is rigged against him. Convinced that once he has what he wants Albright will kill him, Easy violates both the social and linguistic codes that segregate whites and blacks when he goes to a company significantly named Lion Investments in search of Maxim Baxter, whose card Albright has given him. Things come into clearer focus for Easy when a bronze plaque informs him that Todd Carter, Daphne Monet's former boyfriend and the person who has hired Albright to search for her, is the president of the firm. The rules of propriety dictate that a poor black man like Easy has no business entering the offices of Lion, much less demanding to see its senior officers. These rules also dictate that menials should never discuss the personal lives of the kingpins. Easy, however, has no intention of observing propriety, and by exposing the hypocrisy of such niceties when people have been killed and more lives are on the line, he cuts through the layers of subordinates insulating the president and gains direct access to Carter.

Dressed in his best suit and courteously addressing the secretary in standard English, Easy is nevertheless rebuffed. When he produces the card, he is told Baxter is too busy to see him and he must state his business then and there, to which he replies, "Mr. Albright hired me to find Mr. Carter's girlfriend after she ditched him" (111). This calculated breach of decorum and slip into slang produces the desired effect, enabling Easy to speak with Baxter, but now he will be satisfied with nothing less than an interview with Carter. Like the secretary, Baxter tells Easy his request is impossible and chides him for for openly discussing Carter's business. However, Easy refuses to acknowledge the validity of such social codes and shifts completely into Black English: "I said I don't wanna hear it, Mr. Baxter. It's just too much goin' on fo' me t'be worried 'bout what you think ain't right" (112). Yet it is not until Easy bluffs that Carter's reputation is in jeopardy that Baxter relents and leads Easy up to his boss' posh office: "'All I'm 'a tell ya is that he might be runnin' Lion from a jail cell if he don't speak to me and real quick too.' I didn't exactly know what I meant but it shook up Baxter enough for him to pick up his phone [to call Carter]" (113). Easy's ensuing conversation with the president of Lion is crucial because he learns that Albright's real objective is the $30,000 Daphne stole from Carter and forges an alliance with a powerful businessman who late in the novel will legitimize the story he tells to the police. In his masterpiece of signifying at Lion, Easy manipulates linguistic and social codes and invents a story to gain access to and momentarily achieve equality with one of the most powerful men in Los Angeles, thereby greatly increasing his chances of surviving and sorting out the mystery.

However, Easy's signifying does not occur exclusively or even primarily in his dealings with white people. What makes him a successful detective in Watts is his ability to exploit his Southern roots and manners to gain information from people, often without their realizing his true objective. We see what quickly becomes Easy's modus operandi as a detective in the fourth, fifth, and sixth chapters of *Devil* when he goes to John's illegal club looking for Daphne or information about her and later winds up making love to Coretta James, the girlfriend of his passed-out friend, Dupree Bouchard. Through casually talking with Hattie, who controls access to the club, Easy learns of the grisly death of Howard Green. Moments later, after calculatingly buying an old foe, the bouncer Junior Fornay, a beer, Easy finds out who Green was working for. Unable to get anything about Daphne out of Junior, Easy nonchalantly asks Dupree, Coretta, and his friend Odell Jones "if they had seen a white girl Delia or Dahlia or something" (37).[4] A few hours afterward, in Coretta's arms, he learns that the two women are friends and Todd Carter is Daphne's former boyfriend.

In an extended passage in Chapter 18, Easy explicitly acknowledges his role playing in a description of his unsuccessful search through the shadiest places in Watts for the man he assumes is Daphne's current lover:

> During the next day I went to the bars that Frank Green sold hijack to and to the alley crap games that he frequented. I never brought up Frank's name though. Frank was skitterish, like all gangsters, and if he felt that people were talking about him he got nervous; if Frank

> was nervous he might have killed me before I had time to make my pitch.
>
> It was those two days more than any other time that made me a detective.
>
> I felt a secret glee when I went into a bar and ordered a beer with money someone else had paid me. I'd ask the bartender his name and talk about anything, but, really, behind my friendly talk, I was working to find something. Nobody knew what I was up to and that made me sort of invisible; people thought they saw me but what they really saw was an illusion of me, something that wasn't real. (128)

Easy's ability to signify is his greatest asset as a detective. In a world where appearance rarely reflects reality, Easy creates masks for himself more consistently and consciously than his hard-boiled predecessors like Marlowe in order to deceive others and find the truth. Unlike Bruce's Sadipe Okukenu, whose Ellisonian invisibility is imposed by and limited to the white world in which he operates, Easy deliberately makes himself invisible in the black world as well as the white. Similar to Hopkins's Venus Johnson, who dresses as a boy to uncover the place where her father, one of the villains of *Hagar's Daughter*, is hiding her kidnapped grandmother, Easy disguises himself to fool people. However, where Venus' disguise is physical, Easy's is linguistic and rhetorical.[5]

However, rather than merely imitating hard-boiled fiction, Mosley signifies on it, problematizing and particularizing the form by emphasizing how Easy's decision to pursue the independent life of a detective makes his relationship with his fellow blacks more difficult. Although the active, autonomous life of a private investigator provides Easy with a degree of freedom he has never experienced before, the role-playing it entails greatly complicates his relationship with friends, acquaintances, and the black community generally. As Raymond Chandler indicates in his admonition that "[a] really good detective never gets married. He would lose his detachment, and this detachment is part of his charm" ("Twelve Notes" 59), sleuths, particularly the hard-boiled variety like Marlowe, are by definition loners.[6] The question for Easy becomes can he and must he live disengaged from the black community in segregated, postwar America in order to be a detective? Although *Devil* refuses to provide a conclusive answer, it presents two major foils to Easy that help to clarify his position—one who apparently will never change and one whose compulsion to deceive others ensnares her. Easy's ambivalent relationship with his deadly old friend Raymond Alexander (a.k.a. Mouse) and his encounters with *Devil*'s femme fatale underscore the tensions caused and the dangers posed by his new profession. In contrast to the static Mouse, who represents the past Easy tries to but can never quite escape, Easy has gone through many changes, having served in World War II, moved to Los Angeles, bought a house, and become a detective. Like Easy, Daphne Monet, the devil in a blue dress, disguises herself; however, instead of being liberated by the role she plays as a white woman for white and black men, she is imprisoned by it. Although Easy survives and even prospers by the end of *Devil*, subsequent novels will return to the thorny question of whether Easy Rawlins the detective can maintain his friendships and remain engaged with the black community.

As the long passage describing Easy's search for Frank Green quoted above reveals, Easy takes great delight in his detective work despite its enormous risks. It appeals to him because of the independence, intellectual challenge, and financial gain it offers him. Even though his friend Joppy does not own the building that houses his small bar and it stinks because it is surrounded by a slaughterhouse, Easy admires his ability to call his own shots: "Joppy had six tables and seven high stools at his bar. A busy night never saw all his chairs full but I was jealous of his success. He had his own business: he owned something" (8). Similarly, Easy is fiercely proud of his house, the only thing of importance he has ever owned, and his need to meet his mortgage payment convinces him to take the investigative work Albright offers, despite his misgivings. Even though Easy has no illusions about Albright, almost immediately pegging him as a coldblooded killer like Mouse, he can't help but admire Albright's independence and defiance of conventions. He also realizes that now that he has invested in a house—and the version of the American dream it represents—the friendships that characterized his youth are no longer sufficient for his needs:

> When I was a poor man, and landless, all I worried about was a place for the night and food to eat; you really didn't need much for that. A friend would always stand me a meal, and there were plenty of women who would have let me sleep with them. But when I got the

> mortgage I found that I needed more than just friendship. Mr. Albright wasn't my friend but he had what I needed. (21)

The tension here at this key moment when Easy decides to become a detective is between, on the one hand, Easy's definition of himself and what he requires to be be reasonably happy and have pride in himself—a degree of independence, some property of his own, and a modicum of status—and, on the other, Easy's relationship to his former life, his friends, and his community.

As it turns out, Easy can get his position back at Champion Aircraft and thus keep his house without working for Albright. However, when Easy compares his old boss, Benito Giacomo, and the type of life he offers with Albright and the prospect of becoming a detective, he finds he cannot beg for his old job:

> I tried to think about what Benny wanted. I tried to think of how I could save face and still kiss his ass. But all I could really think about was that other office and that other white man. DeWitt Albright had his bottle and his gun right out there in plain view. When he asked me what I had to say I told him; I might have been a little nervous, but I told him anyway. Benny didn't care about what I had to say. He needed all his children to kneel down and let him be the boss. He wasn't a businessman, he was a plantation boss; a slaver. (66)

After refusing to submit to Giacomo and thereby failing to be rehired, Easy experiences a feeling of elation: "My chest was heaving and I felt as if I wanted to laugh out loud. My bills were paid and it felt good to have stood up for myself. I had a notion of freedom when I walked out to my car" (67). Although he associates the new life he has chosen with independence (in contrast to the slavery his old boss offers), this independence is qualified—"a *notion* of freedom"—hinting at the tensions his career as a detective will entail.

The tenuousness of Easy's freedom becomes eminently clear in two widely separated scenes in *Devil*. Shortly after leaving Champion and exalting in his newfound freedom, Easy is arrested by the police, taken to the 77th Street station, and beaten while being questioned about Coretta's death. A nearly identical deflation occurs at the end of the novel. Having just sold his story to police bigwigs (with the help of Todd Carter), Easy leaves City Hall reveling in what he believes is his independence: "I took the stairs. I thought I might even walk home. I had two years' salary buried in the backyard and I was free. No one was after me; not a worry in my life. Some hard things had happened but life was hard back then and you just had to take the bad along with the worse if you wanted to survive" (212). However, before he reaches the bottom of the steps, Miller, one of the two policemen who interrogated him earlier in the novel, confronts Easy and threatens to harass him constantly unless he provides information about the remaining unsolved murder. Recognizing the seriousness of Miller's threat, Easy fingers the real killer, Junior Fornay. Although Junior is not his friend and he appears to have little choice but to hand Junior over if he wants to keep the life he has created for himself in Los Angeles, turning a fellow black in to the police represents a watershed moment for Easy, as his ambivalent and ambiguous statement reveals: "It might be that the last moment of my adult life, spent free, was in that walk down the City Hall stairwell. I still remember the stained-glass windows and the soft light" (213). At least two types of freedom, personal and racial, have come into conflict, and Easy has no option but to choose between them. Looked at from another perspective, Easy here learns his limits. Remarkably, given the odds against him, he has come out ahead, having solved the mystery, turned a profit, and protected Mouse and Daphne. But his success comes at a price. He can't save everyone; the police need a fall guy (and who better than the real murderer and one of Easy's old enemies?) Although it is a very good compromise in many ways for Easy, it is still a compromise and thus limits Easy's sense of himself and the ideal of true freedom he has set for himself.

The whole issue of friendship becomes and remains tricky for Easy in his career as a detective. Orphaned at age eight, Easy has no family he is connected to (although he will marry, unsucessfully, and have a child in *White Butterfly*, and beginning with *Black Betty* will construct a family of orphans like himself that eventually comprises Jesus, the abused two-year old Mexican boy from *Devil*; Feather, the mixed-race daughter of a murdered stripper from *White Butterfly*; and Pharaoh, the irascible canine from *A Little Yellow Dog*). Thus, more than for most people, friends are important to Easy, but whether he can have and hold onto them while working as a detective becomes a major issue. Other than Joppy, who betrays him, Dupree, who stops being his friend because he suspects Easy of being involved in Coretta's death, and Odell, Easy's only friends are Primo, a Mexican he met while working as a gardener, and Mouse, his pal from the streets of Houston. Significantly, Primo (like Chaim Wenzler, the communist labor organizer, and Saul Lynx, the private eye who takes a bullet for Easy, whom Easy befriends in *A Red Death* and *Black Betty* respectively) is not part of the African American community and thus Easy can be himself with him. Although Easy minimizes the differences between himself and Primo,[7] Easy's detective work does not complicate their relationship in the same way it does with someone like Dupree because Primo isn't black and does not live in Watts.

ALL YOU GOT IS YOUR FRIENDS

Epitomizing the tension between personal independence and engagement with the black community brought about by Easy's decision to become a detective, Easy's relationship with Mouse stands as far and away the most important and complex friendship in *Devil* and one of the most innovative features of Mosley's mystery series. Looked at as allegorical figures, Easy can be read as representing those black Americans who hope to improve themselves and participate more fully in post-World War II America while remaining wary about their status and the promises the future seems to offer; Mouse, on the other hand, can be seen as black America's segregated and often violent and amoral past. Easy, in fact, leaves Houston, first for the war and then five years later for Los Angeles to escape Mouse and his own personal past, which Mouse in many ways stands for. Whenever he is reminded of Mouse, Easy shudders. And yet, when he finds himself over his head with Albright, the police, and Frank Green, it is Easy who makes the call to Houston trying to locate Mouse. In another set of parallel scenes Mosley includes in *Devil*, Mouse arrives just in time to save Easy from being killed, first by Frank Green and later by Joppy and Albright.

Never having learned to read or write (in contrast to Easy, who is a reader, gets his G.E.D., and in later novels takes community college courses), Mouse has remained the same person during the twenty years Easy has known him.[8] After rescuing Easy from Frank Green, one of the first statements Mouse makes is "Easy, you changed," referring to Easy's self-assurance and bold, new lifestyle. Even though he has just been handed back his life and has not yet properly expressed his gratitude for this, Easy so fears Mouse and what he represents that he regrets summoning him: ". . . Raymond, I did call ya, but that was when I was low. I mean I'm glad you saved me, man, but your kinda help ain't nothin' I could use" (152-53). Easy has been trying to create a new life for himself and has embarked on a career that he believes offers him real independence. Mouse's fortuitous arrival and the assistance he renders Easy not only reminds Easy of his past life but illustrates the limits of Easy's independence. Mouse tells Easy that he cannot go it alone, that he must rely on his friends, and that he has bought into a false white dream of freedom and self-improvement:

> Nigger cain't pull his way out the swamp wit'out no help, Easy. You wanna hole on t'this house and git some money and have you some white girls callin' on the phone? Alright. That's alright. But, Easy, you gotta have somebody at your back, man. That's just a lie them white men give 'bout makin' it on they own. They always got they backs covered. (153)

Although it comes from a tainted source, an inflexible man who is an amoral killer, Easy cannot and does not take the argument Mouse advances here lightly.[9] At the climax of *Devil*, in a scene that parallels the rescue of Easy from Frank Green, Mouse appears again at precisely the right time to assist Easy when he is outgunned. In short order, Mouse disarms and ties up Joppy, mortally wounds the fleeing Albright, and kills Joppy execution-style to convince Daphne to hand over the $30,000. Once more, Easy's response to Mouse is a conflicted one. Although happy that he and Daphne have survived, Easy is horrified, though not surprised, by Mouse's coldblooded murder and rapacity.

If the immutable, amoral Mouse, a living reminder of Easy's past, represents one dangerous path for Easy, then the ever-changing Daphne Monet, whom Easy encounters in the present (story time) of the novel, embodies another. According to Chandler, "The only effective kind of love interest is that which creates a personal hazard for the detective" ("Casual Notes" 70). In Daphne, Mosley creates not only a love interest that puts Easy's life in jeopardy but, signifying upon a key motif of both classic and hard-boiled detective fiction, an uncanny double for Easy. Like Easy, Daphne is adept at deception, possessing the ability to change her accent, looks, and personality at will. When they first meet, Easy has difficulty reading Daphne's features. She has "[w]avy hair so light that you might have called it blond from a distance, and eyes that were either green or blue depending on how she held her head" (89). Daphne initially affects a French accent and asserts she is "just a girl" in need of Easy's help; however, after they discover the murdered body of her friend Richard McGee, the accent vanishes and Daphne transforms into an aggressive sexual predator: "She leaned back and smiled at me for a moment and then she kissed me again. This time it was fierce. She lunged so deep into my throat that once our teeth collided and my canine chipped" (95).

Although Daphne's ability to change herself gives her great power over men, including Easy, she lacks the ability to control her role playing. As becomes clear in Easy's second and most extended encounter with Daphne, she needs others to accept the fantasy version of herself that she creates. If a man comes to know the real person behind the mask, she must leave him. According to Easy, "Daphne was like the chameleon lizard. She changed for her man. If he was a mild white man who was afraid to complain to the waiter she'd pull his head to her bosom and pat him. If he was a poor black man who had soaked up pain and rage for a lifetime she washed his wounds with a rough rag and licked the blood till it staunched" (183). Not only is Daphne's power to deceive limited to men, but she has essentially only one role to play—that of a white woman—for either a white or a black man.[10] Daphne wants to keep Easy in the fantasy world she has created for them in the secluded house Primo owns. After hours of lovemaking, she asks him whether he feels the private world of pleasure and pain she has constructed:

> "Do you feel it?"
>
> "Yeah, I feel it."
>
> She released me. "I don't mean that. I mean this house. I mean us here, like we aren't who they want us to be."
>
> "Who?"
>
> "They don't have names. They're just the ones who won't let us be ourselves. They never want us to feel this good or close like this. That's why I wanted to get away with you."
>
> "*I* came to you."
>
> She put her hand out again. "But I called you, Easy; I'm the one who brought you to me." (182)

Daphne's obsession with not only escaping the unnamed people who would keep her and Easy from being themselves but also taking credit for the fantasy they are acting out reveals how little actual control she wields over her role playing. Not yet knowing Daphne's past or understanding how much her sense of herself is controlled by others, Easy tells her that they can ignore other people and stay together so long as they love each other. Daphne, however, knows this is impossible.

In the climactic confrontation scene of the novel, Mouse once again forces a character to face up to his or her past. Turning his attention to the money after tying up Joppy and shooting Albright, Mouse addresses Daphne as "Ruby" and tells her that her half-brother, Frank Green, is dead. Even though the news that the white Daphne Monet is really a mulatto triggers an earth-shaking epiphany for Easy, he still fails to understand the ramifications of this information and his possession of it. Like Carter before him, the knowledge of Daphne's true identity disqualifies Easy as her lover:

> "What's wrong?"
>
> "You know what's wrong. You know who I am; what I am."
>
> "You ain't no different than me. We both just people, Daphne. That's all we are."
>
> "I'm not Daphne. My given name is Ruby Hanks and I was born in Lake Charles, Louisiana. I'm different than you because I'm two people. I'm her *and* I'm me." (203)

Despite Daphne's assertion of the difference between them, they are really quite similar. Both were born in Louisiana, both migrated to Los Angeles, and both play roles to deceive others. What distinguishes them is Easy's ability to manipulate the masks he wears rather than being manipulated by them, as has happened to Daphne. Nevertheless, her fate remains one into which Easy in his role as a signifying detective could fall at any moment.

At the close of *Devil's* crucial twenty-ninth chapter, Mouse perceptively pinpoints Daphne's tragedy: "She wanna be white. All them years people be tellin' her how she light-skinned and beautiful but all the time she knows she can't have what white people have. So she pretend and then she lose it all. She can love a white man but all he can love is the white girl he think she is" (205). Resistant to any kind of change and with his own agenda of winning Easy back to his amoral approach to life, Mouse accuses Easy of being "just like Ruby" and betraying his race: "That's just like you, Easy. You learn stuff and you be thinkin' like white men be thinkin'. You be thinkin' that what's right fo' them is right fo' you. She look like she white and you think like you white. But brother you don't know that you both poor niggers. And a nigger ain't never gonna be happy 'less he accept what he is" (205). Mouse is only half right, however. Daphne, in trying to deceive other people with her mask of whiteness, has indeed deceived herself, allowing a mask imposed by others to imprison her and render her unable to form meaningful relationships with other people. In his attempt to define himself, Easy, on the other hand, has been able to pursue the precarious, uncharted path of the signifying detective, successfully managing the personae he has created for himself to outmanuever both blacks and whites. Yet the choice that Easy makes to lead the independent life of a private investigator comes at a cost. Although his signifying liberates him on a personal level, it complicates his relationship with his friends and the black community as a whole, leaving him sensitive to Mouse's largely self-serving accusation of race betrayal.

In the novel's final chapter, Easy remains troubled about the imperfect justice that has been meted out and the role he has played in effecting it. Sitting with his longtime friend Odell, he expresses his concern that because of him one killer, his old friend Mouse, will once again escape retribution while another will be punished:

> "Odell?"
>
> "Yeah, Easy."
>
> "If you know a man is wrong, I mean, if you know he did somethin' bad but you don't turn him in to the law because he's your friend, do you think it's right?"
>
> "All you got is your friends, Easy."
>
> "But then what if you know somebody else who did something wrong but not so bad as the first man, but you turn this other guy in?"
>
> "I guess you figure that that other guy got ahold of some bad luck." (215)

Although the sustained laughter of the two men that follows suggests that Odell succeeds in mollifying Easy's troubled conscience, Mosley will make sure that such moral dilemmas continue to haunt Easy. Having lost Joppy and Dupree in solving the mystery in *Devil*, in the next novel, *A Red Death*, Easy sees his friendship with Odell vanish because of his detective work. This leaves him with the one friend he feels the most ambivalent about, Mouse, a living reminder of Easy's past who through his words and actions denies the validity of Easy's efforts to better himself and lead the independent life of a signifying detective.

NOTES

1. For a critique of *The Signifying Monkey* that identifies Gates' "*nostalgia* for tradition" (137) as the aporia in his argument, see Adell.

2. For a helpful discussion of hard-boiled detective fiction and its conventions, see Cawelti.

3. This is especially true of *The Big Sleep* (1939), which could easily be entitled *The Big Lie*, because of Marlowe's decision not to reveal Rusty Regan's murder in order to protect his fragile employer General Sternwood.

4. Mosley may be alluding to James Ellroy's *The Black Dahlia* (1987), a police procedural based on real-life events that like *Devil* is set in Los Angeles in the late 1940s and emphasizes the era's racial and ethnic tensions.

5. It has long been my pet theory that the first name of Mosley's hero derives from the twelve-year-old title character of of Rudolph Fisher's stories "Ezekiel" (1932) and "Ezekiel Learns" (1933), a wide-eyed but clever young boy newly arrived in Harlem from the South and born within a year of Easy Rawlins, who in the latter story witnesses a petty crime and stealthily intervenes to insure that justice is done. However, given the major role played by signifying in Mosley's mysteries, the similarity between the names Easy and Esu, the Yoruba god of interpretation whose African American manifestation, according to Gates, is the Signifying Monkey, is intriguing.

6. As I discuss below, although Mosley will violate this rule in *White Butterfly*, the failure of Easy's marriage to Regina ultimately serves to vindicate Chandler.

7. Easy observes that the events in *Devil* occurred in 1948 "before Mexicans and black people started hating each other. Back then, before ancestry had been discovered, a Mexican and a Negro considered themselves the same. That is to say, just a couple of unlucky stiffs left holding the short end of the stick" (177).

8. By the fifth installment in the Easy Rawlins series, *A Little Yellow Dog*, Mouse has begun to change. He has learned to read, takes a steady job, stops carrying a gun, and starts talking about finding religion. It may, in fact, be precisely these changes that are responsible for Mouse's apparent death in this book, which is set in 1963 and is pervaded by disillusionment about the future and the prospect of change, a disillusionment typified by the Kennedy assassination.

9. Evidence that Mouse's argument has a profound effect on Easy surfaces late in the novel when, after being knocked out by Joppy and Albright, Easy has a dream about a great naval battle in which Mouse pulls him away from line

and yells, "We gotta get outta here, man. Ain't no reason t'die in no white man's war" (194).

10. To use poststructuralist terminology, Daphne/Ruby, the signifier, chains herself to a single signified, white Daphne Monet.

WORKS CITED

Adell, Sandra. *Double-Consciousness/Double Bind: Theoretical Issues in Twentieth-Century Black Literature*. Urbana: U of Illinois P, 1994.

Babener, Liahna K. "Raymond Chandler's City of Lies." Fine. 127-49.

Baker, Houston, Jr. *Long Black Song*. Charlottesville: U of Virginia P, 1972.

Bruce, John E. *The Black Sleuth*. 1907-09. John E. Bruce Collection. Reel 3. Schomburg Center for Research in Black Culture, New York.

Cawelti, John G. *Adventure, Mystery, and Romance: Formula Stories as Art and Popular Culture*. Chicago: U of Chicago P, 1976

Chandler, Raymond. *The Big Sleep*. 1939. *The Raymond Chandler Omnibus*. New York: Modern Library, 1975. 1-139.

———. "Casual Notes on the Mystery Novel." *Raymond Chandler Speaking*. Eds. Dorothy Gardiner and Katherine Sorley Walker. Boston: Houghton, 1977. 63-70.

———. "Twelve Notes on the Mystery Story." 1977. *Hardboiled Mystery Writers: Raymond Chandler, Dashiell Hammett, Ross MacDonald*. Eds. Matthew J. Bruccoli and Richard Layman. Dictionary of Literary Biography Documentary Series. Vol. 6. Detroit: Gale, 1989. 56-61.

Ellroy, James. *The Black Dahlia*. New York: Mysterious, 1987.

Fine, David, ed. *Los Angeles in Fiction: A Collection of Essays*. Rev. ed. Albuquerque: U of New Mexico P, 1995.

Fisher, Rudolph. *The Conjure-Man Dies*. 1932. New York: Arno, 1971.

———. "Ezekiel." 1932. *The City of Refuge: The Collected Stories of Rudolph Fisher*.

———. "Ezekiel Learns." 1933. *The City of Refuge: The Collected Stories of Rudolph Fisher*. Ed. John McCluskey, Jr. Columbia: U of Missouri P, 1987. 44-47.

Gates, Henry Louis, Jr. *Figures in Black: Words, Signs, and the "Racial" Self*. 1987. New York: Oxford UP, 1989.

———. *The Signifying Monkey: A Theory of Afro-American Literary Criticism*. New York: Oxford UP, 1988.

Gayle, Addison. *The Way of the New World*. Garden City: Doubleday, 1975. Ed. John McCluskey, Jr. Columbia: U of Missouri P, 1987. 40-43.

Hopkins, Pauline. *Hagar's Daughter: A Story of Southern Caste Prejudice.* 1901-02. *The Magazine Novels of Pauline Hopkins.* New York: Oxford UP, 1988. 1-284.

Mosley, Walter. *Black Betty.* New York: Norton, 1994.

———. *Devil in a Blue Dress.* 1990. New York: Pocket, 1991.

———. *A Little Yellow Dog.* New York: Norton, 1996.

———. *A Red Death.* 1991. New York: Pocket, 1992.

———. *White Butterfly.* New York: Norton, 1992.

Muller, Gilbert H. "Double Agent: The Los Angeles Crime Cycle of Walter Mosley." Fine. 287-301.

CHAPTER THIRTEEN

Bubblegum Metaphysics

Feminist Paradigms and Racial Interventions in Mainstream Hardboiled Women's Detective Fiction

Priscilla L. Walton

In Orania Papazoglou's *Wicked, Loving Murder*, novelist and amateur sleuth, Patience C. McKenna draws attention to the plight of the romance writer[1]:

> They *know* people are trying to make them look stupid. They *know* critics are lurking in broom closets, waiting for a chance to blame the decline of Western civilization and the erosion of world capitalism on the latest Silhouette Desire. They *know* there are traitors in their midst, spies, Quality Lit thugs who swoop into the world of love and lust to make a few thousand dollars under a pseudonym and then swoop out again, to surface in the pages of the *Village Voice* with articles accusing category romance of destroying the future of the women's movement. (32)

While McKenna is speaking specifically about the romance genre, her comments about the climate in which formula writers create also apply, largely, to other genres like detective fiction, thrillers, and westerns.[2] This disdainful perception of popular culture was brought home to me when I (naively) sang the praises of my favorite female sleuths to a number of colleagues and their partners, and then were taken aback when, after dutifully skimming the novels, they eyed me suspiciously and pronounced: "But, this is trash." It would seem, at least drawing from this example, that McKenna's construction of the "Quality Lit thugs" is not far off the mark.

To "do" popular culture, be it as consumer or creator, leaves one open to cultural derision. Readers of formula texts are often ridiculed for their literary preferences, since their reading materials are regarded as simplistic forms of entertainment (as opposed to mind-enriching instructives). Genre fiction is posited as lacking the seriousness of "High" art, and is construed frequently as an addictive "habit," a vice that needs to be hidden. Janice Radway discusses this phenomenon in her significant 1984 study, *Reading the Romance*, and Sparkle Hayter weaves it into her novel, *What's a Girl Gotta Do?*, when her protagonist, Robin Hudson, eschews the flaws of her ex-husband:

> I know lots of his secrets: that his given name is Heinrich Albert Stedlbauer IV, changed to Burke Avery for television; that at home he belches without excusing himself and secretly reads Judith Krantz. I know his guilty pleasures. . . . (31)

The guilt that accompanies their generic pleasures haunts readers and creators of popular culture, who continue to encounter questions about the merit of the works ("But this is trash!"), in part because such texts are not "individualized" after the fashion of "High Culture" literature. Given their market-driven basis, formula works are viewed, almost by definition, as conservative and limited modes of expression. Accordingly, genre writings are texts into which readers may dip (while on vacation, say, at the beach), but in which serious readers should not immerse themselves.

Concomitantly, hardboiled women's detective fiction, which is published by mainstream publishing houses, often troubles feminist and antiracist critics. Although some scholars laud the feminist and multicultural proclivities of women's popular crime novels, others contend that these proclivities get lost in translation—the texts' political ends overwritten and negated by their conventional means. And, indeed, the controversies surrounding the female hard-boiled arise from its relation to (and necessary complicity with) a "macho" tough guy mode, an (inter)relation that has led to queries about its efficacy in affirming political agency. Drawing upon those critical positions which contest traditional perceptions of formula works, in order to argue for the possibilities afforded by the mass media, I would suggest that the feminist multicultural appropriation of the hardboiled mode pushes at textual and cultural boundaries, and serves as a practical application of political tenets expressed in a popular form. Hence, in my view, the novels embody a triptychal movement, for they incorporate a theoretical interrelationship of alternative politics, fictive practice, and the reading public.

"EVEN BUBBLEGUM HAS A METAPHYSICS" (T.W. ADORNO)

As a form, popular culture has a conflicted history. In many ways, it has functioned as High Culture's "Other," or the derided and defamed Low(er class) counterpart that affirms the artistic superiority of the privileged aesthetic medium. Yet, popular culture is also the creative form that has continued to appeal to mass audiences, and thus the form that has been most fiscally successful. Perhaps precisely because of its financial viability, it remains a medium that raises eyebrows when designated as a serious object of pursuit. French sociologist Pierre Bourdieu suggests, in *The Field of Cultural Production*, that there is an inverse correlation between the artistic and the economic terrains. That is, in his terms, "the artist can triumph on the symbolic terrain only to the extent that he [or she] loses on the economic one, and vice versa"; hence, the artistic world is "the economic world reversed" (169). In other words, and in a traditional High Culture sense, those texts that are considered "Art" are generally not financially successful, and those that are, are not deemed to constitute "Art."

Historically, however, the rise of mass-market publications, beginning with the introduction of the dime novel in the nineteenth century, the emergence of pulp magazines in the early twentieth, the evolution of genre fiction, and the later "bestseller," substantively has formed the bulk of readings directed at the mass public. This phenomenon, nonetheless, was perceived as dangerous by the Marxist-oriented theorists of the Frankfurt School, founded as the Institute for Social Research in the 1920s, since they regarded the mass-produced forms as an outgrowth of High Capitalism—forms that, in effect, served as opiates of the masses. As Theodor W. Adorno argues, in *The Culture Industry*:

> Today the commercial production of cultural goods has become streamlined, and the impact of popular culture upon the individual has concomitantly increased. This process has not been confined to

> quantity, but has resulted in new qualities. While recent popular culture has absorbed all the elements and particularly all the 'don'ts' of its predecessor, it differs decisively inasmuch as it has developed into a system. Thus, popular culture is no longer confined to certain forms such as novels or dance music, but has seized all media of artistic expression. . . . Above all, this rigid institutionalization transforms modern mass culture into a medium of undreamed of psychological control. The repetitiveness, the selfsameness, and the ubiquity of modern mass culture tend to make for automatized reactions and to weaken the forces of individual resistance. (137-38)

Adorno's is not a simple analysis, nor is it an elitist dismissal of popular culture's potential. But theorists like him perceived the "individualized" construction of High Culture as the means by which the populace would be educated—and, hence, elevated. The Frankfurt School, in effect, could not see beyond the market-driven nature of mass culture to its potential as a subversive artistic form, precisely because it was inconceivable to them that mass culture could be either artistic or subversive. Adorno was concerned with the political potential of "the populace" which he saw as demeaned and derided by the capital-driven "cultural industries." And, while many critics have taken issue with Adorno's position (see Modleski's *Studies in Entertainment*), suffice it to say here that one of the problems with his argument is the idea that mass culture is a form imposed from above to which the public can only respond by consuming passively. In general, formula texts have been regarded as banal because they are consumeristic and mass-produced. But, as Patience McKenna notes, at one point in *Wicked, Loving Murder*, there is also an elision in traditional conceptions of High Culture, for "it's all a business . . . even ['High'] literary publishing" (Papazoglou 10).

The current situation, wherein the bulk of the public who read (a percentage that is rapidly diminishing) read formula fiction of one sort or another, cannot be ignored. Yet the myth persists that if one is reading the popular, then one is not "really" reading. Genre fictions are often posited as conventional, rather than individualistic works, and condemned because they are required to follow a formula; consumers of mass media, therefore, are constructed as passive, even "addicted" souls, who are at the mercy of the vagaries of the cultural industries. But overlooked in this view are the ways in which the dynamics of the formula in question are complicated and contradictory; that is, while formula texts must be recognizable to their audience as a "type" or genre of fiction, they must also add to that genre. The hard-boiled form, itself, demonstrates this paradigm, for in subverting the "rules" of the British cosy, it gave rise to a "new" subgenre. Shifting the locale and the ideological movement of the British formula, the originary hard-boiled transferred the class stratification of the cosy from an upper-class to a lower-class milieu, and to an urban, as opposed to a "country house" environment. The hard-boiled form followed its own "generic rules" which are summarized by Arthur Asa Berger:

> The tough guy detective has to solve the crime to avoid being suspected or convicted by the dumb cops. In the same way, the individual must prove himself or herself by being a success in the world; otherwise there is doubt that cannot be allayed. [Such heroes are] paradigmatic . . . and reflect basic American personality traits and philosophical beliefs. . . . [The hard-boiled hero] shows the virtue of a principled individualism for . . . the rules motivating his behaviour . . . [demonstrate] what political scientists call *a theory of obligation*. He may be cynical and skeptical and stoical, but he also has a sense of duty and loyalty. (116-17)

These hard-boiled innovations in mystery fiction spoke to a particular time—the late 1920s and the early 1930s (and in *film noir*, to the 1930s and 1940s)—wherein the affirmation of the "common [White] man" was particularly meaningful in a world of increasing corporatization, a world that also witnessed a flux in gender roles. In their time, therefore, they worked to affirm the social function of many of the readers to whom they were targeted, helped to ease their transitions into a transformed social situation, and to confront the problems that ensued from it. Consequently, in his analysis of formula fiction, John G. Cawelti points to four major functions that genre works fulfill:

> 1. Formula stories affirm existing interests and attitudes by presenting an imaginary world that is aligned with these interests and attitudes. . . .
>
> 2. Formulas resolve tensions and ambiguities resulting from the conflicting interests of different groups within the culture or from ambiguous attitudes toward particular values.

3. Formulas enable the audience to explore in fantasy the boundary between the permitted and the forbidden and to experience in a carefully controlled way the possibility of stepping across this boundary.
4. Finally, literary formulas assist in the process of assimilating changes in values to traditional imaginative constructs. . . . [L]iterary formulas ease the transition between old and new ways of expressing things and thus contribute to cultural continuity. (35-36)

As Cawelti contends, formula fiction serves different and conflicting needs: it both affirms norms and values at the same time that it enables readers to assimilate changes. It is, therefore, both conservative and innovative—and at the same time. While the overall movement of the particular genre may work to affirm the ideological norms of its consumers, subtle changes within it also reflect changes in the social climate and provide a means of working through those changes in a "controlled fashion." Significantly, then, Cawelti demonstrates the ways in which formulaic conventions speak to a cultural demand; and, importantly, as he goes on to add: "allowing for a certain degree of inertia in the process, the production of formulas is largely dependent on audience response" (34).

The idea that the audience participates in the construction of a genre itself contradicts the idea that the readers of popular works are simply passive consumers. At the same time, and as aforesaid, the genre also affirms its readers and their belief systems. Thomas Schatz quotes Henry Nash Smith on the Western, to demonstrate how writers of the Western celebrated certain cultural values and myths:

> Smith's fundamental thesis is that these authors participated, with their publishers and audience, in the creative celebration of the values and ideals associated with westward expansion, thereby engendering and sustaining the Western myth. He contends that the public writer is not pandering to his market by lowering himself to the level of the mass audience, but rather that he or she is cooperating with it in formulating and reinforcing collective values and ideals. (11)

Extending Smith's thesis, Schatz moves to a discussion of the ways in which consumers often participate in the construction of these texts, and even set market trends:

> In underscoring the relationship of pulp Western novels to a mass audience and hence to American folklore, however, Smith's study adds an important dimension to our discussion. He suggests that these novels were written not only for the mass audience, but *by* them as well. Produced by depersonalized representatives of the collective, anonymous public and functioning to celebrate basic beliefs and values, their formulas might be regarded not only as popular or even elite art but also as *cultural ritual*—as a form of collective expression seemingly obsolete in an age of mass technology and a genuinely "silent majority." . . . The basis for this viewpoint is the level of *active but indirect audience participation* in the formulation of any popular commercial form. (11-12)

With a commercial genre, reader input (through demand and consumption) is consequential because the bottom line of trade publishing is sales. As a result, the ideological service that the originary hard-boiled novels performed had to shift with the times, since the subgenre's initial movement to affirm the "common [White] man" and "his" code of ethics ceased to speak to a wide readership. But other aspects of the genre did.

I SHOP, THEREFORE I AM

By 1982, the date in which the hard-boiled female investigator emerged as a cultural phenomenon[3], women had entered the consumer market on a different level. No longer simply procurers of "household" artifacts but women with disposable incomes, their status as consumer, in part, generated the shift from tough guy to tough gal hero. Indeed, in "Murder Most Foul and Fair" (1990), Katrine Ames and Ray Sawhill note that the advent of the active female detective arose in part because female readers were clamoring for strong women characters:

> As the women's movement grew, so did the demand for female protagonists. Carol Brener, former proprietor of the Manhattan bookstore Murder Ink, remembers customers so desperate "they didn't even care if the killer was a woman, as long it was a strong character." (*Newsweek* 67)

Moreover, in an article in the *Voice Literary Supplement*, B. Ruby Rich comments on the appeal and the sales potential of the subgenre:

"Women's and gay bookstores, from Old Wive's Tales in San Francisco to the new Judiah's Room in Greenwich Village, report that woman-detective novels are walking out the door as fast as they arrive on the shelves" (24). Rich's observation is confirmed by a 1990 article, "Crime Marches On," in *Publishers Weekly*, that indicates:

> [T]he woman as tough professional investigator has been the single most striking development in the detective novel the past decade. "Books with a woman as central sleuth are very popular with us right now," says St. Martin's Ruth Cavin. "For us at Walker," says Janet Hutchings, "our biggest sellers last year were those with strong female characters."
>
> "Women writers in general are selling better than ever before," says Susan Sandler of the Mystery Guild. . . . "Having a woman detective puts special demands on the writer to be more imaginative." (Anthony 28)

Reader impact on this trend, therefore, would suggest that consumers, while the target market of industry, also play an active role due to their purchasing power. As subjects, these readers can effect a shift in the form of generic conventions, a shift that affirms the subject position they have assumed: "Just the fact that these books exist feels like an achievement. . . . The woman-detective genre can take on anything currently being peddled at airport bookshops or supermarket checkout counters, accommodating any style or level of quality" (Rich 26).

Without a doubt, consumerism is a problematic space from which to construct subjectivity, but, with women buying books (as consumers) and demanding strong female characters (as subjects), their buying power influences the publishing industry's offerings. And such publication shifts can move to empower women and to ease *their* problems in entering what had been heretofore a "man's world." As Rich comments:

> The woman who's been happily seduced by years of soap operas, *telenovelas*, and romance novels now gets a different thrill—the old formulas turned inside out, with gutsy heroines instead of trembling maidens, yet with the same page-turning appeal intact. Each volume offers itself to the willing reader like a safe-deposit box of feminist possibilities, a place where real problems can be play-acted and strategies tested. (24)

Rich's suggestion that each volume may offer feminist possibilities is insightful, but the ways in which the series format of the novels generate both feminist and antiracist possibilities is also integral, since it allows subversion to take place in the mass marketplace.

PAPERBACK WRITER

What is particularly crucial to the subgenre of the feminist hard-boiled, and arguably to other forms of formula fiction like science fiction, westerns, and so on, is that they *do* depart from the individualistic movement of High Culture. Umberto Eco notes that, traditionally, the "products of the mass media were equated with the products of industry insofar as they were produced *in series*, the "serial" production was considered as alien to the artistic invention" (162). Yet, precisely because it *was* alien to "artistic invention," serial formula fiction enabled readers to adapt a different reading strategy. As John Fiske observes:

> The reader of the aesthetic text attempts to read it on *its* terms, to subjugate him- or herself to its aesthetic discipline. The reader reveres the text. The popular reader, on the other hand, holds no such reverence for the text but views it as a resource to be used at will. (106)

Moreover, the series formulation of genre fiction also engenders innovations in the form because it encourages the readerly involvement of which Fiske speaks. Not surprisingly, then, Fiske goes on to contend that "genres are the result of a three-way contract between audience, producer, and text" (108).

As noted earlier, formula fiction, according to critics like Cawelti, both affirms the values of its consumers at the same time that it eases their transition into a changing world. In relation to feminist detective fiction, that series structure helps to open the texts (and their political message) to readers who might otherwise not read "social problem" works. Rich, for example, is speaking primarily to small press novels, which cater to a specialized audience. That audience has been expanded by the wealth of female dicks appearing in the mainstream press. Certainly, because the mainstream market seeks to attract a larger audience than small press offerings, it is generally more "middle of the road" in its construction, and the politics within it are sometimes more muted than those which can be found in a text produced by a publisher like Naiad. But, although small women's press novels may push at boundaries more radically than their mainstream counterparts, the mainstream texts (given the greater distribution possibilities of the big publishing houses, the novels' ready availability, and their visibility in nonspecialized bookstores) reach a much broader audience. It is important to remember, here, that mainstream fiction seeks to affirm the values of its wide readership; however, it is also important to recognize that, at the same time, such fiction can push at the construction of those values. Indeed, the very series structure of the female hard-boiled P.I. novels plays an integral role in shifting readerly expectations: the series formation of these novels means that one individual novel need not, itself, perform all of the subversions possible within the subgenre, but that it might as part of an ongoing series—a series that functions in tandem with the other female P.I. series in print—for it is joined in its project by the wealth of other authors writing in the mode.

If Cawelti is right in his argument that formula fiction eases transitions into a changing world, then series novels make that transition easier. Hence, rather than a problematic element of the texts that detracts from their "individuality" (an argument Papazoglou's "Quality Lit Thugs" might put forth), the series structure can be viewed as crucial to the political potential of women's detective novels. In turn, the very series formulation of these works lends itself to a broad collective of readers and writers, as their series structure enables the novels to transmit their political messages gradually and in a "controlled fashion," enabling them to work to empower the female subject on a variety of levels and in a number of different ways.

The series structure of the novels allows their authors more room to explore their characters and to confront diverse issues and concerns. As Laurie King, author of the Kate Martinelli series notes, "Because I write about people and how they move and change, 300 pages isn't enough to complete a good, strong character. A series is a sort of mega-fiction: 3,000 pages, divided into 10 episodes!" Dana Stabenow, who pens a succession of novels featuring Inuit investigator, Kate Shugak, also comments on the character possibilities engendered by series writing:

> I love writing series fiction. I love being able to peel back another layer of a character with every book, to allow them to tell me things

> about themselves I never knew, to watch them grow. The challenge is to keep the characters fresh. The reward is when a fan says, "I miss Kate. When do I get to visit with her again?"

In turn, Valerie Wilson Wesley, author of the Tamara Hayle novels, the first female African American private eye series in the mainstream, stresses her preference for series novels, and explains her position: "I like series writing. I think that it allows you to develop a character in ways that you may not be able to in a different kind of book. . . . In each book I reveal more about Tamara's character and her past . . . because I think we're all so much a part of our past in our present . . . and I think a series allows you the freedom to do that, not only with your main character but also with other characters (2). As these writers suggest, then, the series formulation of detective novels enables authors to explore various aspects of their protagonists and minor characters, granting them more room for writerly development.

SERIAL SUBVERSIONS

It is, in large part, the series structure of the feminist hard-boiled which allows its proponents to use the venue it affords to tackle social issues in an entertaining fashion. The ongoing series structure means that one book need not evoke every possibility afforded by the subgenre, but that a variety of cultural problems can be interwoven into the series. Writers like Wendy Hornsby, for example, can fold left-wing politics into one book, confront child prostitution in a second, and tackle police corruption in a third. Clearly, social issues are important aspects of the novels for their authors. As Kathy Hogan Trocheck notes of her Callahan Garrity novels: "Issues of race, class and gender always seem to be important in my books. Race especially, since my books are set in Atlanta, the capital of the New South. . . . I can't seem to not write about the issues affecting the society I live in." Authors also see the benefit of writing in a popular format, since it allows them to reach an audience that might not otherwise read their books. Elizabeth Pincus, author of the Nell Fury books, observes: "I like the idea of writing in a popular genre, something that would be very accessible to readers while being political/contemporary at the same time. Dare I say subversive . . ." (her ellipsis). Sandra Scoppettone comments that her Lauren Laurano series "seems to have crossed over in the mystery field. . . . I want to entertain and I also want to show that lesbians are just people . . . that there's nothing so frightening here, and basically just to show the characters as regular people, leading a life. I guess that's the major thing" (11-12). Hard-boiled detective fiction, in so doing, generates a "common space" wherein concerns and social issues can be addressed and then assimilated by readers who would not necessarily read about them in other venues. Valerie Wilson Wesley finds (in a fashion similar to Scoppettone) that her novels act as crossover texts, alerting readers to problems of which they may be unaware:

> I think my readers are primarily, at this point, African American women. It also crosses over, because many white women enjoy my books too and some white men. . . . White readers read black mysteries, black mystery readers read white writers. So it's not the same kind of barriers that I think often separate us when we choose our literature. . . So it's not the same kind of lines, of fences that we build. And I think that's a good thing. To be able to cross into other people's worlds and walk in their shoes for a while. (5-6)

Consequently, while the particular social concern the author examines might be wrapped up in a single novel, and, to some extent, that novel confirms a liberal conception of issues that can be resolved individually, the texts also frequently point to the inability of the main character to resolve the social ills, and thereby draw attention to the systemic nature of the problems. Indeed, Linda Grant, author of the Catherine Sayler series, prefers her novels "to leave the ends open so there's something to think about, because all these things do have a million open ends. That's the interesting part." Sometimes, however, the concerns the author confronts are less successfully received than others. When Sara Paretsky addressed miscegenation in her series in 1990 (through V.I.'s romantic involvement with African-American police officer, Conrad Rawlings), reader response to this romance was so great that she noted in an interview on the TV program, *Imprint*, "I wished I'd never done it." Yet, by the same token, she did raise an issue that forced readers to think about the implications of interracial relations. Valerie Wilson Wesley, whose first novel appeared in 1994, encountered a different reaction from her readers, and by placing racism at the heart of her texts, she believes that she opens its problematics to a wide variety of readers:

> When I write about Tamara I'm writing from my own experiences, for example, with the police. I mean I scarcely know a black person who has not had some kind of horrible experience with the police and that includes me and my family . . . I think a lot of times many White Americans are not aware of just how this happens and how often it happens. But I think a lot of readers say, "Does that really happen in the black community?" And I think that people learn about what people experience and they learn about the trials of racism *etcetera, etcetera*, or sexism. And I also learn about what we have in common, they learn the differences and the similarities. And I think that's a good thing, that mysteries teach you that. They teach you that consciousness, and you learn it because the book is in the first person and you can't help but identify. So I think that that's another good thing that they do. And then I think I like to be a part of that. I like opening the world. (6)

A significant aspect of the wealth of series P.I.s available is that one author need not confront all problems meaningful to her on her own; she can be joined in her effort by a number of other authors. As a result, the series formulation takes the pressure off a writer in her own series, at the same time that it enables her to refer to other novelists, and thus to engage concerns from within a community of writers and readers.

In this fashion, mainstream women's crime writing opens feminist and multicultural concerns to a broad spectrum of readers. As Cawelti argues, formula fiction in general embodies a "controlled space" that allows for the exploration of alternative perceptions and constructions, and through which social concerns and cultural fears can be probed by a wide readership. Accordingly, the ways in which questions of sexuality and race have filtered into the mainstream market testifies to how general readers are engaging with these issues, and to the market's attempt to incorporate their cultural ramifications.

REVISING THE SCRIPT

Despite the complications discussed above, white heterosexual authors are often condemned for liberal tokenism. Sally Munt dismisses the mainstream feminist hard-boiled for what she perceives as its affirmative action approach to sexuality and race:

> Many of the crime texts written by White feminist authors have offered a 'positive images' strategy which inverts the traditional binary of the form wherein White equals good and Black equals bad. . . . Treatments progress from a tokenistic smattering of one-dimensional goodies, usually minor, helpful characters, offering little more than a nod to literary equal opportunities, to, in Paretsky, for example, a plurality of ethnic identities which operates to romanticize a multi-cultural melting pot, excising real conflicts and differences between groups. (90)

But Munt's position here incorporates an essentializing gesture, since it implies that only writers of color are concerned with race, that race impacts only on "the Other," and thus that all antiracist work must be left to the "Other" to perform.

Munt does laud small press publications, and she makes a valid point that alternative presses have made and continue to make efforts to publish female detectives of color. But, contrary to the critic's assertion, these detectives are as visible in the mainstream as they are in alternative press publications. M.F. Beal's *Angel Dance* (published by Daughters in 1977), featured Kat Guerrara, one of the first female detectives of color. However, also in 1977, Marcia Muller began to publish her Sharon McCone series, introducing a protagonist who is part Shoshone, a cultural location that is often overlooked in critical discussions of race in mainstream novels.

In the small presses, Beal was followed by Delores Komo's Clio Browne (*Clio Browne: Private Investigator*, Crossing Press, 1988), Nikki Baker's Virginia Kelly (Naiad 1991), and Penny Mickelbury's Gianna Maglione and Mimi Patterson (Naiad, 1994). Yet, concomitantly, in the mainstream are writers like Valerie Wilson Wesley, Eleanor Taylor Bland, Chassie West, Dana Stabenow, and Gloria White. The emergence of female authors and detectives of color in both markets, then, suggests that the mainstream is as willing as the small presses to include their writings. And, while both may well be at fault for their limited minority authorship, it is interesting that Valerie Wilson Wesley finds writing in the mainstream productive because it enables her to reach a large audience:

> Because part of a mystery is escaping anyway, I think that there's a sense of travelling in someone else's shoes. These novels take you into a different world for a while. I like the openness of mystery

> readers. I'm an African-American woman—or, I should say, I'm a Black woman—because the books have been published in England and Germany, and I understand that they're really catching on in Great Britain. . . . I think that a lot of White women who read them say, "Well you know I get into the character and she's just like me." So I think that these books enable readers to get into different worlds. (5-6)

The different world Wilson Wesley opens to her readers is the world of prevalent racism. Her protagonist, Tamara Hayle, is a former cop who quit the force because the systemic racism she had to confront within it proved too much for her to bear. As a P.I., she can investigate problems, particularly those that relate to the African American community, which the police force have written off. In *When Death Comes Stealing*, Tamara inquires into the death of a young African American male:

> Some lazy cop, tired at the end of the day or late for lunch, had proclaimed that Terrence Curtis had lived and died a junkie, and there was no more to be said about it. But I knew different now. If he'd died of crack, he hadn't been an addict, and I was hot for a minute, angry again at the bullshit so many cops put down when it comes to black folks—the official incompetence, the easy way out. (36)

The reluctance of institutional law enforcement to interrogate the problems of people of color is a matter of concern for many female detectives. In Gloria White's novels, her half-Latina protagonist, Ronnie Ventana, often confronts racism, and, in *Charged With Guilt*, she goes to San Francisco's Hispanic underworld for help, an underworld that exists because the Hispanic community has experienced frequent rejection at the hands of the police, and, consequently, is reluctant to turn to them for help. In order to investigate the crime in question, Ronnie must request assistance from an old friend of her father's, and her ability to shift between cultures opens doors to her that would be closed to a white investigator:

> Santiago Rosales had decided to set up his bar on Ellis Street. Not that it was really a bar. It was an exchange. People went to El Ratón Podrido for information, to make connections, to score goods and

> weapons. They went there for things they couldn't get anyplace else. And Santiago never turned anybody away. . . .
>
> I reached the bar and, when the bartender ambled over, I said, "I need to see Santiago."
>
> He raised his eyebrows and lowered his eyelids. He didn't need to say a word. It was obvious he needed to hear more before he'd consider letting me through.
>
> "Ronnie Ventana," I said.
>
> His surly face broke into an unexpected grin. "Ah, *sí*. 'Cisco's daughter. *Cómo no! Pase, pase. Por aquí.*" (283-85)

The difficulties of acting within the police force are crucial aspects of Chassie West and Eleanor Taylor Bland's novels. In West's *Sunrise*, police detective Leigh Ann Warren is so tired of the pressures placed on her by the Washington police force that she returns to her hometown in North Carolina for respite. While there, she helps to ensure that a proposed mall does not recklessly upset the old African American cemetery. In turn, Eleanor Taylor Bland not only dramatizes the problems an African American female police officer experiences on the force, but also foregrounds the difficulties her protagonist, Marti MacAlister, encounters from the "public" in the commission of her job. Bland documents, in *Dead Time*, the responses that greet MacAlister's appearance at a crime scene:

> "Well, *she* certainly isn't a police officer. I thought they were only letting in people on official business."
>
> A tiny dark-skinned woman with at least five slips hanging below a short, fuzzy blue robe answered.
>
> "Hah. Got cop written all over her. Now ain't that a sight, Betty? Black and a woman and not wearin' no uniform." (21)

While the the above writers often place the effects of racism at the heart of their texts, it does not necessarily follow that "white" publications simply perpetuate racial stereotypes. Indeed, writers like Rochelle Majer Krich and April Smith often problematize ethnic and racial identity. Smith's *North of Montana* and Krich's *Angel of Death* work to complicate stereotypical perceptions and put pressure on "normative" perceptions of race and ethnicity. The respective protagonists of *North of Montana* and *Angel of Death* experience identity crises: throughout the course of the novels, Ana Grey, the FBI agent hero of Smith's text, confronts her Hispanic heritage, and Jessie Drake, the P.I. of Majer Krich's, learns of her Jewish background. Moving from a privileged "inside" White Anglo-Saxon Protestant position to an "outside" status, the protagonists must come to terms with ancestries they have not recognized as their own, at the same time that they must reconstruct their pasts and its impact upon their presents. Examining intersections of race, ethnicity, and subjectivity, Smith's and Majer Krich's novels provide for performative critiques of stable identities—and they do so within the venue of mass market fiction.

Since Munt has cited Sara Paretsky as a perpetrator of "liberalist pluralism," whose novels "romanticize" the melting pot, it seems fair to turn to Paretsky, at this juncture, for an analysis of her efforts to counter stereotypical inscriptions of race and sexuality. Because V.I. Warshawski is white, a whiteness readers have been conditioned to expect in their detectives, Paretsky's focus on race may go unnoticed. But V.I.'s is not a whitewashed world, and she is not a member of the WASP elite. The child of a Polish father and an Italian immigrant mother, V.I.'s first-generation, "new"-world status signals her ex-centric position. She frequently draws attention to her background and the disposition it has created: "I guess my ideals died the hardest. It's often that way with the children of immigrants. We need to buy the dream so bad we sometimes can't wake up. (*Killing Orders* 86-7).

V.I.'s background makes her more aware of cultural marginalization, and her awareness is apparent in her responses to the people she encounters over the course of her investigations. In *Bitter Medicine*, V.I.'s perception of the marginalization of Philippa Barnes, of the Department of Environment and Human Resources, foregrounds the systemic racism in government bureaucracies. Dr. Barnes explains: 'The bureaucracy in a place like this just about kills you. If I had charge of the whole program, instead of just a piece of it—' She folded her lips, cutting off the sentence." V.I. goes on to comment: "We all three knew that having a sex-change operation—and perhaps dyeing her skin—was the only way that would happen" (165-6).

The narratives of the feminist hard-boiled provide their readers with fantasy fiction that has repercussions beyond their immediate textual performances. Hence, to dismiss the texts too easily is to ignore some of the cultural needs they fulfill, for the emergence of readily available strong female heroes engenders more than simple readerly pleasure. When reading through the anthology, *Theorizing Black Feminisms*, I was struck by the words of Andrea Rushing, in her essay,"Surviving Rape." Rushing writes that, after her sexual assault, she took great pleasure in reading books about new-style U.S. women detectives, Sue Grafton's California-based Kinsey Millhone and Sara Paretsky's V.I. Warshawski.

> Week after week I gulp, as if drowningly desperate for air, their plain-spoken stories about acid-tongued, fast-thinking, single and self-employed women who not only dare to live alone, but scoff, sneer, seethe when men try to put them in their "weaker sex" place. Parched and starved, I read and reread Sue Grafton's alphabet adventures, but Sara Paretsky's books became my favourites because her Chicago-based private investigator is even more bodacious and sassy than my pre-rape self. And, in stark contrast to television and movie renditions of women as powerless victims of men, she both withstands and metes out physical violence in every single book. Murder mysteries restore order to worlds thrown out of balance. . . . (137)

Rushing's experience highlights the integral role that fantasy plays in affirming one's sense of self, and the possibilities it offers for a re-construction of that self. And the fantasies embodied in the re-visioned novels also validate their authors' aspirations. For Sara Paretsky, the Warshawski series fulfilled her fantasies of creativity:

> I had had a fantasy about writing a book for a long time. In fact, I wrote my first story when I was six, but I grew up in a family where girls became secretaries and wives, and boys became professionals. I wasn't expected to have talents. (Shapiro 67)

While this is not to contend that the fiction makes women's lots more bearable or manageable, it is to underscore the power of fantasy inscriptions, wherein an independent street-smart tough gal private eye can flourish, and inspire both reader and author alike.

Despite protests to the contrary, then, textual and extra-textual evidence indicates that women's hard-boiled novels are distinctly *unconventional* in content and in formulaic movement. And a crucial aspect of the wealth of series P.I.s available is that one author need not confront all problems of import to her on her own; she can be joined in her effort by a number of other authors. Consequently, the series formulation takes the pressure off a writer in her own series, at the same time that it enables her to refer to other novelists, and thus to engage concerns from within a community of writers and readers.

RE-CASTING THE DICK

The community of writers and readers functions as a support network and as a lobby group. Because female writers of genre fiction were often ignored in major review publications that could alert readers to their existence, Sara Paretsky began the activist group, Sisters in Crime, in 1986. As Ames and Sawhill summarize:

> By 1986, probably a third of American mysteries were by women, but women were getting less than a fifth of the reviews. Sara Paretsky, concerned about issues including the number of books that reveled in "the graphic abuse of women," founded Sisters in Crime. The watchdog and networking organization has more than 600 members. (Its self-help brochure: "Shameless Promotion for Brazen Hussies.") Women are more frequently reviewed now. And Kate Mattes [of Kate's Mystery Books in Cambridge, Mass.] says, "Publishers are saying, 'Gee, we ought to promote these women.' They hadn't before. If I had a book signing, generally the author got herself here and paid for it." (67)

Sisters in Crime succeeded in generating more extensive promotion from publishers and put pressure on publications for wider review coverage. These reviews are particularly important, since, as Linda Grant notes, often public libraries require at least two reviews before considering the acquisition of a text. Without the reviews, the librarians could not order the books, and, as a result, many mystery readers who depended on libraries for their texts could not gain access to them.

On another front, the writers have been aided in their demand for greater visibility by concerned bibliographers. In 1994, librarians Jean Swanson and Dean James produced a compilation of female authors, *By a Woman's Hand*, that consists of author entries and brief summaries of their writings, along with notes at the bottom of each entry, offering readers' advice (i.e. "If this writer interests you, you might also want to look at the following writers"); in so doing, they alert readers to other authors writing in a similar venue. Also in print now are bibliographies like Willetta L. Heising's *Detecting Women: A Readers' Guide and Checklist for Mystery Fiction Written by Women.* Heising's compilation lists female authors by subgenre, profession, and so forth, and features (at an additional price) an accompanying pocket-size volume that readers can take to their bookstore or library to follow up on the suggestions provided in the larger book.

Interestingly, the feminist hard-boiled, in itself, performs as a locus for the commingling of writer and reader through the characterization of the active female investigator. Linda Grant, for example, uses her novels to acknowledge her gratitude to other writers (of whose texts she acts as a reader). Dedicating *A Woman's Place* to Susan Dunlap, the author of the Jill Smith and Kiernan O'Shaughnessy series, Grant's acknowledgement performs a dual purpose: it expresses her personal indebtedness to a sister author; and it also points to the growing community of female writers engaged in feminist detection. At the same time, the novels themselves often draw attention to other female sleuths, effecting a self-reflexivity in the genre, which also points readers to alternative female dicks with whom they can compare the one they are reading. Authorial acknowledgements of the growing writerly community pervade many of the narratives, which self-reflexively draw attention to the presence of other female investigators. Although the tough gal P.I.s often compare themselves and their differences to their male predecessors, they also point outward to the role models provided by female writers. Embedding various readerly codes which draw attention to how writers of the subgenre are also its readers, texts like Elizabeth Pincus's *The Two-Bit Tango*, contain passages like the following, wherein protagonist, Nell Fury, announces: "I'd stayed up late reading the night before, wanting to find out if Kinsey Millhone would go to bed with this fellow Dietz. Then I woke early out of anxiousness—whether for Kinsey or myself, I wasn't sure" (87). Lesley Grant-Adamson, one of the few hard-boiled women novelists in England, bestows on her character, Laura Flynn, a friend named "Anna Lee," thereby intertextually commemorating Liza Cody's character of the same name, and her position as the first hard-boiled feminist detective in the British mainstream.

Metatextual references are also scattered throughout Sandra Scoppettone's novels. The ability to recall other female P.I.s helps Scoppettone's detective, Lauren Laurano, for it furnishes her with role models who authorise her in her investigations. In *Everything You Have is Mine*, Laurano is heartened by the self-inquiry: "Would Kiernan O'Shaughnessy leave without talking to this woman, even if there was nothing to gain?" (244). She also keeps herself on-track with the reminder: "Meg Lacey would never get sidetracked this way" (277); and self-deprecatingly examines a disguise by querying: "I wonder if Kat Colorado would ever dress like this" (284).

References like Grant's, Pincus's, Grant-Adamson's, and Scoppettone's serve as reminders of the importance of the texts' communal enterprise, an enterprise that opens spaces for other female writers, as well as for female readers. And the political impetus that propels the novels inspires female writer/reader societies like Sisters in Crime to work together to bring the concerns of female readers and writers to the attention of the publishing market and the public. The ongoing efforts of female detective authors and their readers, then, designate the feminist hard-boiled as a collective site in which readers, writers, and characters meet. Indeed, the emergence of the active female investigator has repercussions beyond the intervention of a woman into mainstream narratives, for her authorial presence offers alternative realities to the readers who consume them, and whose purchasing power provides for the emergence of a new class of working women writers, who are able to support themselves through consumers' consumption of their novelistic endeavors. This ongoing process is both exemplified in the interactive nature of the texts, and in the interactive community to which they give rise, a community that en/genders an extended circle of partners—and sisters—in crime.

NOTES

1. This article has been culled from a forthcoming book, *Detective Agency: Women Re-Writing the Hard-boiled Tradition*, co-authored by myself and Dr. Manina Jones of the University of Western Ontario. I am deeply indebted to her for allowing me to use material from the collaborative book, and for her help in formulating my ideas here. Without her, this article would not have been written.

2. I would suggest, however, that the derision directed at romances differs somewhat from responses to other genres as a result of gender perceptions. Thrillers, westerns, and detective fiction, traditionally, have not been perceived as "women's" genres in the same way as romance fiction (see Modleski, Mumford, Radway,), and thus, suffer rather less at the hands of literary critics; but, neither are they deemed "respectable."

3. While Marcia Muller broke ground with her private investigator, Sharon McCone, in 1977, 1982 proved to be the year in which women detectives began to form a counter-tradition. It was in 1982 that Sue Grafton penned her debut

novel, *"A" is for Alibi*, the first novel in the alphabet series, which presents Kinsey Millhone to the public, and that Sara Paretsky produced her premier novel, *Indemnity Only*, which introduces V.I. Warshawski.

WORKS CITED

Adorno, Theodor W. *The Culture Industry*. Ed. J.M. Bernstein. London: Routledge, 1991.

Ames, Katrine, and Ray Sawhill. "Murder Most Foul and Fair." *Newsweek*. May 14, 1990: 66-69.

Anthony, Carolyn. "Crime Marches On." *Publishers Weekly*. April 13, 1990. 237.15 (1990): 24-29.

Berger, Arthur Asa. *Popular Culture Genres*. London: Sage Publications, 1992.

Bland, Eleanor Taylor. *Dead Time*. New York: Signet, 1993.

Bourdieu, Pierre. *The Field of Cultural Production*. Ed. Randal Johnson. New York: Columbia UP, 1993.

Cawelti, John G. *Adventure, Mystery and Romance: Formula Stories as Art and Popular Culture*. Chicago: U of Chicago P, 1976.

Eco, Umberto. "Innovation and Repetition: Between Modern and Post-Modern Aesthetics." *Daedalus* (Fall) 1985.

Fiske, John. "Popular Discrimination." *Modernity and Mass Culture*. Eds. James Naremore and Patrick Brantlinger. Indiana: Indiana UP, 1991: 103-16.

Grafton, Sue. *"A" is for Alibi*. 1982. New York: Bantam Books, 1987.

Grant, Linda. Telephone Interview conducted by Manina Jones. December 18, 1995.

———. *A Woman's Place*. New York: Charles Scribner's Sons, 1994.

Grant-Adamson, Lesley. *Flynn*. London: Faber and Faber, 1991.

Hayter, Sparkle. *What's a Girl Gotta Do?* New York: Penguin, 1994.

Heising, Willetta L. *Detecting Women: A Readers' Guide and Checklist for Mystery Fiction Written by Women*. Chelsea, MI: Purple Moon, 1995.

King, Laurie R. Letter Interview with Manina Jones. October 22, 1995.

Krich, Rochelle Majer. *Angel of Death*. New York: Mysterious Press, 1994.

Modleski, Tania. *Loving With a Vengeance: Mass-Produced Fantasies for Women*. New York: Routledge, 1982.

———, ed. *Studies in Entertainment: Critical Approaches to Mass Culture*. Bloomington: Wisconsin UP, 1986.

Muller, Marcia. *Edwin of the Iron Shoes*. New York: Mysterious, 1977.

Mumford, Laura Stempel. *Love and Ideology in the Afternoon: Soap Opera, Women and Television Genre*. Bloomington: Indiana UP, 1995.

Munt, Sally R. *Murder by the Book?: Feminism and the Crime Novel*. London: Routledge, 1994.

Papazoglou, Orania. *Wicked, Loving Murder*. New York: Penguin, 1985.

Paretsky, Sara. *Bitter Medicine*. New York: Ballantine, 1987.

———. *Indemnity Only*. New York: Ballantine, 1982.

———. "Interview." See Richler, Daniel.

———. *Killing Orders*. New York: Ballantine, 1985.

Pincus, Elizabeth. Letter Interview with Manina Jones. November 27, 1995.

———. *The Two-Bit Tango*. San Francisco: Spinsters, 1992.

Radway, Janice A. *Reading the Romance: Women, Patriarchy, and Popular Literature*. 1984. Chapel Hill: U of North Carolina P, 1991.

Rich, B. Ruby. "The Lady Dicks: Genre Benders Take the Case." *Voice Literary Supplement*. June, 1990: 24-27.

Richler, Daniel. "Interview." *Imprint*. Toronto: TVOntario, 1992.

Rushing, Andrea. "Surviving Rape." *Theorizing Black Feminisms*. Eds. Stanlie M. James and Abena P.A. Busia. London: Routledge, 1993.

Schatz, Thomas. *Hollywood Genres*. New York: McGraw-Hill, 1981.

Scoppettone, Sandra. *Everything You Have is Mine*. New York: Ballantine, 1991.

———. Telephone Interview conducted by Manina Jones. October 11, 1995.

Shapiro, Laura. "Sara Paretsky." *Ms*. (January 1988): 66ff.

Smith, April. *North of Montana*. New York: Alfred A. Knopf, 1994.

Stabenow, Dana. Letter Interview with Manina Jones. November 25, 1995.

Swanson, Jean, and Dean James. *By a Woman's Hand*. New York: Berkley, 1994.

Trocheck, Kathy Hogan. Letter Interview with Manina Jones. November 26, 1995.

Walton, Priscilla L., and Manina Jones. *Detective Agency: Women Re-Writing the Hard- boiled Tradition*. Berkeley: U of California P, 1997.

Wesley, Valerie Wilson. Telephone Interview conducted by Manina Jones. November 15, 1995.

———. *When Death Comes Stealing*. New York: G.P. Putnam's Sons, 1994.

West, Chassie. *Sunrise*. New York: HarperCollins, 1994.

White, Gloria. *Charged With Guilt*. New York: Dell, 1995.

PART FOUR

Multicultural Detective Fiction and the Literary Canon

CHAPTER FOURTEEN

Chester Himes and the Institutionalization of Multicultural Detective Fiction

David Schmid

Over the last twenty years, the rise in popularity and influence of a body of texts we might denominate as "multicultural detective fiction" has seemed unstoppable and absolute. More detective fiction by people of color is being published than ever before, and it is selling more than ever before. In another sense, however, multicultural detective fiction remains as excluded and marginal as it has ever been. In spite of (or perhaps *because* of) its success, the academy remains seemingly impervious to the charms of multicultural detective fiction and as determined as ever to preserve itself in the lifeless amber of antiquated notions of 'high' versus 'low' culture. As a result, multicultural detective fiction, along with other genres of popular fiction, has yet to make the slightest dent in the academic literary canon.

This neglect of popular fiction by the Western Canon (note the use of capital letters) comes as no surprise. What is perhaps more surprising is that popular fiction in general, and multicultural detective fiction in particular, is similarly neglected in canons that might be expected to be more open to such writing, that is, in the so-called 'minority' literary canons. This essay focuses on the neglect of the writer Chester Himes in African American literature anthologies and the African American canon as a way of considering the problems raised by the institutionalization of multicultural detective fiction. At issue, I shall argue, is not only on what terms detective fiction can be canonized and anthologized, but whether we, as critics and readers of detective fiction, should even seek such institutional status at all.

Revisiting the issue of canon formation and its relation to popular fiction may seem superannuated in the 1990s. In one sense, the "canon wars" are a relic of the 1980s, a product of the time when we optimistically believed that it was possible to make fundamental changes to what texts were taught in the academy. One would think that we have now moved beyond a concern with the canon, and yet the recent publication of the *Norton Anthology of African American Literature* (Gates and McKay) suggests otherwise, prompting my argument that questions of canonicity—and specifically of minority canon formation—are of crucial importance when considering multicultural detective fiction.

Chester Himes began writing in the 1930s while serving seven-and-a-half years of a twenty-year sentence for armed robbery in the Ohio State penitentiary. He published short stories exclusively for the first third of his career and then, in 1945, with the publication of his first novel, *If He Hollers Let Him Go*, published five novels, generally described as 'social protest' naturalism in the tradition of Richard Wright, over the next ten years. Himes emigrated to France in 1953, and spent the rest of his life in Europe, until his death in 1984. What at first glance appears to be a radical shift in his writing, the publication of his first detective novel, *For Love of Imabelle* in 1957, was to be the first of nine novels that Himes would call his "Harlem domestic series." The series, published over the next twelve years, began at the suggestion of Marcel Duhamel, the editor of the *Série Noire* crime fiction series for the French publishing house, Gallimard: according to Himes, Duhamel asked him to contribute to *Série Noire* in 1957 and "in desperate need of money, I began to write detective stories" (Fuller 11). Nearly all of these novels were published first in France, and then in the United States, and all were considerably more popular in Europe than in the United States.

While I cannot think of any other writer with a comparable oeuvre who is still as neglected and underappreciated as Chester Himes, before detailing that neglect, and offering my interpretation for its reasons, I want to establish Himes's place in the field of detective fiction, and why he deserves so much more critical attention.[1]

CHESTER HIMES'S CONTRIBUTION TO THE CRIME FICTION

While Himes downplayed this aspect of his work, his detective fiction is innovative in several ways. Claiming in an interview with John Williams that "I haven't created anything new whatsoever; I just made the faces black, that's all" (314), Himes's 'Harlem domestic series' in fact contains a number of radical reworkings of the hard-boiled crime fiction genre. The most fundamental and obvious of these is that Himes's detective heroes, Grave Digger Jones and Coffin Ed Johnson, *are* black, when the traditional model for the hard-boiled detective hero has been a white male.

It is not only the blackness of Himes's detectives that makes them innovative, however, it is also the fact that there are two of them. By having two main characters, who in many respects are practically indistinguishable from each other, Himes contradicts another central tenet of traditional hard-boiled crime fiction, the detective as a lonely, romantic, sentimental *individual* :

> . . . in the main tradition of the hard-boiled detective story, the figure of the vulnerable but tough, wise-cracking but sentimental, private eye is the consciousness that holds the characteristically first-person narrative together. Coffin Ed Johnson and Grave Digger Jones are not this sort of hero, as both their doubling and their names indicate . . . The two characters are not "individuals," nor does their relationship fit any of the conventional pairings of sleuth and sidekick (Denning 11).

Himes believes that the individualism seen in Raymond Chandler's Philip Marlowe, for example, is simply not an option on the streets of Harlem. The only way that Grave Digger and Coffin Ed can overcome the ambiguities of their position as both African Americans and cops is to work as a team, in a symbiotic relationship that extends beyond their work to every aspect of their lives (Schmid 259).

But perhaps the most innovative aspect of Himes's detective fiction is not its character or setting but its ideology. By introducing the concept of absurdity to detective fiction, Himes constructs a totally original point of view on the problems of crime and punishment. Himes's emphasis on absurdity comes out of his perception of the essential absurdity of racism. At the beginning of the second volume of his autobiography, significantly titled *My Life of Absurdity*, Himes argues that, "Racism introduces absurdity into the human condition. Not only does racism express the absurdity of the racists, but it generates absurdity in the victims. And the absurdity of the victims intensifies the absurdity of the racists, ad infinitum" (1). What Himes means by 'absurdity' in this context is that racism is completely irrational. There is no intrinsic property of the color of one's skin that should inspire hate; therefore, racism is absurd.

A sense of the general absurdity of life permeates every aspect of Himes's detective fiction, from his plots to the action in the novels. A typical Himes plot, rather than being a showcase for the detective's ratiocinative powers in solving a complex case, is instead an exercise in mayhem. Although the novels usually begin with Grave Digger and Coffin Ed trying to solve a single crime, things quickly mushroom out of control. By the end of the novel, after a lot of Harlem's inhabitants have met their maker in often very grotesque and funny ways, the best that Himes's detectives can hope for is to have restored order, rather than to have 'solved' anything.

The dark comedy and the chaos that exist throughout Himes's detective novels show his belief in the essential absurdity of racism, its power to produce ridiculous and extravagant follies. But Himes also knew racism was deadly serious, for it constituted so much of reality for black people: "[r]ealism and absurdity are so similar in the lives of American blacks, one cannot tell the difference" (quoted in Margolies, *Which Way?* 68). Muller has summarized how Himes translates his knowledge of absurdity into his detective fiction:

> Himes took the critique of culture inherent in the tough-guy or hard-boiled detective fiction of Chandler, Hammett, and other writers of the 1930s and 1940s and transformed the genre into an absurdist parody of the search for order and values in a capitalist and racist world. . . . More than his predecessors, Himes uses his two detectives not so much to solve crimes and preserve order as to test the impossibility of sustaining meaning in a sociocultural world that is inherently irrational and absurd. (85)

But to fully appreciate how Himes reveals the absurd nature of racism, and to understand the depth of his literary achievement, one needs to assess the entirety of Himes's literary output, not just his detective fiction. This is especially important because one reason Himes's crime novels have been unjustly neglected is that they are too easily dismissed as potboilers, the ephemeral literature Himes turned to when he gave up the attempt to write 'serious' naturalistic fiction. It is inaccurate, however, to divide Himes's career up into his 'serious' writing, and his 'popular' writing. As Michael Denning points out, Himes "had a long-standing interest in the detective story form, having subscribed to *Black Mask* magazine while in prison in the 1930s when he was first beginning to publish stories" (10). Moreover, several of Himes's early stories, while not 'detective fiction' in the strict sense of the term, had a background of crime and criminals (Bailey 62). Even Himes's so-called 'serious' early novels were sometimes packaged as hard-boiled narratives. For example, a publisher's ad in *The Crisis* described *If He Hollers Let Him Go* as having "unparalleled courage and a James M. Cain punch" (362). I think this is more than publisher's hype, and that Himes's Los Angeles novels can be appropriately described (as they have been by Mike Davis, in *City of Quartz* (43)) as a variety of L.A. *noir*.

This continuity between Himes's 'serious' fiction and his detective fiction comes across even more strongly in *My Life of Absurdity*, when Himes recounts Duhamel's offer to him to write detective stories. Duhamel, who had translated Himes's first novel, *If He Hollers Let Him Go*, into French, advised Himes to write a detective story in the same style as that novel, "Short, terse sentences. All action. Perfect style for a detective story" (102). Himes's response to this suggestion was to think to himself: "I had started out to write a detective story when I wrote that novel, but I couldn't name the white man who was guilty because all white men were guilty" (102). Writing the "Harlem domestic series" therefore finally gave Himes a way to apportion guilt, if not innocence. When Himes began writing his first detective novel, there was thus a significant degree of continuity between this 'new' venture and his earlier work. This is true not only in the sense that his early and later share a similar criminal background, but also in the sense that Himes continued to explore many of his favorite themes from his early work in the detective novels.

THEMATIC CONTINUITY IN HIMES'S WORK

Chief among the themes shared by both the early and later work is violence. A. Robert Lee has noted that "violence identifies all of Himes's fiction, violence both quietly corrosive and loudly expansive.

The nine "Harlem domestic stories," take up and magnify the violence of the earlier books" (13). Himes's attitude toward the political necessity and utility of violence for black people remained remarkably consistent throughout his life, and in fact, intensified as he got older: "I have always believed—and this was from the time of *If He Hollers* . . . was published—that the Black man in America should mount a serious revolution and this revolution should employ a massive, extreme violence" (Fuller 18). This belief in violence comes out of Himes's view that violence is absolutely constitutive of American culture: ". . . there is no way one can evaluate the American scene and avoid violence, because any country that was born in violence and has lived in violence always knows about violence. Anything can be initiated, enforced, contained or destroyed on the American scene through violence" (Williams 329). Clearly, the detective fiction genre offered Himes a particularly appropriate avenue for exploring the cultural significance of violence in America. Indeed, Himes once said that he started writing detective stories because "I wanted to introduce the idea of violence. After all, Americans live by violence, and violence achieves—regardless of what anyone says, regardless of the distaste of the white community—its own ends" (Williams 337).[2]

All of Himes's fiction explores, in one way or another, his characters' responses to violence in general and to the violence of racism in particular. And yet, having said this, it must be emphasized that the theme of violence is explored differently in Himes's early novels than in his detective novels. For one thing, there is far more actual violence in Himes's crime fiction. In his early novels, such as *If He Hollers Let Him Go* and *Lonely Crusade*, the violence is mostly in the heads of Himes's protagonists. As Ralph Reckley has pointed out, the protagonists of Himes's early novels are always fantasizing retaliatory violence against those who oppress them, but the fantasy is never translated into reality. In the detective fiction, the fantasy is abundantly, overwhelmingly realized and in the process, "Himes legitimizes black violence" in his detective novels (Reckley 99).

But it is not only that the Harlem novels contain *more* violence than the early work, they also contain a different approach to violence, a difference conveniently summarized by Edward Margolies: "Rather than write the kind of novels in which his black protagonists suffer the pain, indignities and humilities of racism, he has turned for the most part to broad burlesque even farce to suggest the absurdity, the human waste, the dehumanization for whites as well as blacks" (*Experiences*

426). In other words, rather than write 'protest' novels about the shattering impact of racism, Himes chooses, in his Harlem novels, to use humor to reveal and attack the absurdity of that racism.

In emphasizing the role of humor, however, we must also be careful to do justice to the development of the Harlem domestic series over the course of nine novels. While it is true that early entries in the series, such as *The Crazy Kill* (1959) and *The Big Gold Dream* (1960), are exercises in absurdist mayhem, full of scenes of very graphic and often very funny surreal violence, by the times Himes published *Cotton Comes to Harlem* (1965) and *Blind Man With a Pistol* (1969), that violence begins to take on a social protest resonance similar to Himes's earlier work, although still with a humorous flair (see Lundquist 116). While it would not be true to say that Himes returns to writing social protest fiction, then, it is certainly true that, by the end of his career, Himes was able to fully explore the potential of the detective story form to articulate a radical political message while at the same time still writing an 'entertaining' and funny story.

Over the course of a career spanning nearly fifty years, Himes wrote and published a formidable array of fictional and nonfictional works. Taken together, they offer an unparalleled exploration of the urban scene and of the causes and consequences of violence in African American literature. A novelist, short-story writer, essayist, and autobiographer, Himes is one of the major figures in African American letters and yet, as I have mentioned, he is virtually ignored by those who anthologize and canonize black literature. What could be the reasons for this neglect? Before answering that question, I will first establish the extent of that neglect by describing what, if any, of Himes's work has been anthologized over the years.

THE NEGLECT OF CHESTER HIMES

The results of a random sampling in the State University of New York at Buffalo libraries reveal that the following anthologies contain nothing by Himes: Abraham Chapman's *Black Voices* (1968), James A. Emanuel and Theodore L. Gross's *Dark Symphony* (1968), Leroi Jones and Larry Neal's *Black Fire* (1969), Darwin T. Turner's *Black American Literature* (1970), Arthur P. Davis and Michael W. Peplow's *The New Negro Renaissance* (1975), Richard A. Long and Eugenia W. Collier's *Afro-American Writing* (1991), and Deirdre Mullane's *Crossing the Danger Water* (1993). Other anthologies only contain a few pages of Himes, either a short story or an excerpt from a novel. Here are a few examples: Sterling A. Brown, Arthur P. Davis and Ulysses Lee's *The Negro Caravan* (1969) contains one short story, "The Night's For Cryin'"; Edward Margolies's *A Native Sons Reader* (1970) contains one short story, "Morning After"; Ruth Miller's *Black American Literature* (1971) contains a seven-page excerpt from Himes's novel *Pinktoes*; Arthur P. Davis and Saunders Redding's *Cavalcade* (1971) contains one short story, "Rape!"; Richard Barksdale and Kenneth Kinnamon's *Black Writers of America* (1972) contains one short story, "Salute to the Passing"; Herbert Hill's *Soon, One Morning* (1972) contains a twenty-page excerpt from Himes's novel *Lonely Crusade*; and Herb Boyd and Robert L. Allen's *Brotherman* (1995) contains a four-page excerpt from *Lonely Crusade.* It is revealing to note that nowhere, not even in those anthologies where Himes is scantily acknowledged, is any of his detective fiction anthologized. This pattern of neglect is maintained in the new *Norton Anthology*, which contains only one short story by Himes, "Salute to the Passing."

This neglect of Himes by the anthologizers of African American literature is matched by the hostility that Himes's work inspired in both black and white critics for the vast majority of his career. One factor in Himes deciding to move to Europe in 1953 was the negative reaction to his work in the United States. Himes always had a conflictual relationship with reviewers and it wasn't until the early 1970s, with the publication of his autobiography, that he began to be treated with the respect he felt he deserved. The criticism of Himes's second novel, *Lonely Crusade*, which told the story of a black union organizer, Lee Gordon, in the shipyards of Los Angeles during World War II, was particularly harsh. Himes found himself being assaulted by communists, fascists, white racists, blacks, and practically every reviewer within those extremes (Lundquist 13). For example, in the November 1947 issue of *Ebony* magazine, in an editorial entitled "Time To Count Our Blessings," Lee Gordon was described as: " . . . a good example of many Negroes who suffer from what psychiatrists would call a color complex. Gordon and his creator Himes are infected with a psychosis that distorts their thinking and influences their every action in life" (44). *Lonely Crusade* was excoriated not only in the mainstream black press, but also in the Communist press. Lloyd Brown, in a review published in *New Masses*, said that Himes's novel should "be buried deep beneath a rising mountain of protest, boycott and condemnation" and that the "self-hate and shameless abasement of Chester Himes, who panders to every depraved element of white chauvinism, is based upon his complete acceptance of white ruling-class ideology" (Brown 20, 19). Removing himself from the United States somewhat tempered the criticisms Himes was subjected to, but criticism tended to be replaced by neglect or dismissal over the years, as his detective stories were denigrated as 'potboilers' not worthy of serious critical consideration.

The first significant factor to consider in Himes's neglect in the African American canon is Himes's position as a misanthrope. What James Lundquist politely refers to "his vicious conception of the black ghetto and his ungenerous view of human nature" (24) does not come close to suggesting the depth of Himes's hatred for white people and his pessimism about whether the situation of black Americans will ever improve. Himes's novels are full of black-on-black violence that takes place between intimates, family members, business associates, and total strangers. These incidents tell the reader that yes, blacks are victimized by racism, but that they are also more than capable of victimizing others. Some critics, such as Stephen Soitos, have tried to apologize for Himes's misanthropy by claiming that, by attacking black values, Himes hoped to improve those values (162). Whether or not this is true, Himes himself certainly was never shy about defending his often negative portrayals of black people. In Himes's words:

> It is no longer enough to say the Negro is the victim of a stupid myth. We must know the truth and what it does to us. If this plumbing for the truth reveals within the Negro personality, homicidal mania, lust for white women, a pathetic sense of inferiority, paradoxical anti-Semitism, arrogance, uncle tomism, hate and fear and self-hate, this then is the effect of oppression on the human personality (*Dilemma* 57).

In other words, Himes's honesty always has a purpose—to reveal the extent of damage to the black psyche caused by racism. Himes was never interested in writing books that were apologies for black people and that should require no apology, unless one makes the problematic assumption that black artists, or any other artists for that matter, are under an obligation to produce only "positive" representations of their "people."[3]

The detective fiction indicates that Himes was not only a misanthrope, but also a misogynist and a homophobe. Stephen Milliken has accurately noted that the "function of . . . women in the novels is, quite simply, to be desired and to be frightened. They offer literary thrills that have obvious and direct affiliations with the realms of sex and sadism" (250). In this sense, Himes is securely plugged in to the hard-boiled tradition. Similarly, Soitos notes that "Himes reserves his most vitriolic attacks for black gay men. . . . Most homosexuals in the Harlem stories end up mutilated and dead" (158). While in no way detracting from the truth of Soitos's observation, it should also be noted that practically *everybody*, not just gay men, finishes a Himes detective novel either mutilated or dead! Nevertheless, objections to the content and ideology of Himes's fiction could partly explain its neglect.

As I have already indicated, Himes would undoubtedly have defended himself from these charges of misanthropy, misogyny, and homophobia by claiming that he was just telling the truth as he saw it. In 1946, responding to criticism of *If He Hollers Let Him Go*, Himes declared that "it is my small, self-appointed task to write the truth as I see it. As long as this nation is what it is and its human products are what they are, then that is what I will write about, beautiful or not" (*If He* 13). Several critics have concurred with this idea that hostility to Himes's work can be explained by his unflinching honesty. For example, Houston Baker, Jr., in a review of the first volume of Himes's autobiography, *The Quality of Hurt*, argues that Himes's honesty is not likely to make him popular: "Chester Himes is not likely to receive accolades for *The Quality of Hurt*. . . . Nor is Himes an apt candidate for kudos from the Black critical establishment when he casts the slings and arrows of scorn, bitterness, and rage at some of the Black greats of the past and the Black masses, past and present" (90).

Himes himself was certainly aware of what his honesty had cost him in terms of his public and critical reputation, but he refused to back down. Instead, he chose to go on the attack. In a talk entitled "The Dilemma of the Negro Novelist in the United States," Himes offered a characteristically forthright explanation of the hostility to his work by describing the situation of an imaginary novelist clearly intended to be himself:

> If this novelist, because he has prepared an honest and revealing work on Negro life anticipates the support and encouragement of middle-class Negro people, he is doomed to disappointment. He must be prepared for the hatred and antagonism of many of his own people, for attacks from his leaders, the clergy and the press; he must be

> ready to have his name reviled at every level, intellectual or otherwise. This is not hard to understand. The American Negro seeks to hide his beaten, battered soul, his dwarfed personality, his scars of oppression. He does not want it known that he has been so badly injured for fear he will be taken out of the game. The American Negro's highest ambition is to be included in the stream of American life, to be permitted to "play the game" as any other American, and he is opposed to anything he thinks will aid in his exclusion (54-5).

It is possible that Himes's unstinting criticisms of Black people may be another reason why his work is not more highly regarded. In my opinion, however, Himes's status can be explained not just by *what* he wrote, but *how* what he wrote has been positioned in relation to other African American texts, and this is where the logistics of anthologization become significant. Himes tends to suffer, as do other writers like Ann Petry, from a more or less forced association with Richard Wright. This association tends to obscure whatever is original in Himes, and makes him instead a more or less interesting offshoot of the great man. As A. Robert Lee has trenchantly noted: "Despite his persisting and highly particular talents, Chester Himes continued to be footnoted a Wrightian exponent of Black American literary protest given to reworking an inherited vein of angry naturalism. This blunt evasion of forty years of craft and resource speaks worlds of criticism's stubborn unseeing before Black imaginative achievement and of its insistence of notions of hierarchy and diagnosis largely inappropriate, dull and racist" (13). Deborah E. McDowell and Hortense Spillers, in their headnote to the section "Realism, Naturalism, Modernism 1940-1960" in the *Norton Anthology*, recognize this problem when they say that "standard literary histories, which tend to focus exclusively on the traditional genres of narrative poetry, and drama in their "high-cultural" varieties, obscure the range of popular cultural forms in which African American writers achieved considerable successes. Chester Himes and Frank Yerby, for instance, were among the few writers of the period whose ambitions ran to popular fiction" (1319). But although McDowell and Spillers correctly identify the problem, they do nothing to address it; indeed, they perpetuate it by anthologizing none of Himes's popular fiction and nothing by Yerby at all!

All of the reasons I have listed thus far play a part in explaining the neglect of Himes, but I believe the primary reason for the neglect of Himes by the African American critical establishment is that Himes is perceived as a 'popular' writer. To be more precise, those who anthologize and canonize African American literature have not proven themselves adept at including any forms of popular culture that cannot be connected to 'folk' or 'vernacular' forms of expression. Although it is never stated explicitly, it seems that any form of fiction that can be seen as 'mass' rather than 'folk' culture is denigrated and overlooked for that reason.

MASS CULTURE AND THE AFRICAN AMERICAN CANON

The hostility of the 'canonizers' to mass culture would certainly explain why multicultural detective fiction has not received a warmer welcome, but it must be said that the exclusion of Himes's detective fiction from the canon on these grounds is ironic for several reasons. First, although African American literature anthologies generally give a prominent place to the vernacular, defined by Robert G. O'Meally in the *Norton Anthology* as: "the church songs, blues, ballads, sermons, stories, and, in our own era, rap songs that are part of the oral, not primarily the literate (or written-down) tradition of black expression" (1), there is no recognition that hard-boiled detective fiction of the type Himes writes is an American vernacular form, in the sense that it belongs to and was developed in America, and is therefore indigenous to America (Soitos 26). Moreover, African American writers have taken this vernacular form and added various black vernacular forms to it, so that it should be relatively easy to insert a writer like Himes into black literary traditions.[4] Milliken has noted that Himes "introduced major elements of black folk art into the subgenre [of the detective story]. His remarkable combinations of humor, pathos, sex, horror, and just plain home truths are very similar to those of the bitter and beautiful blues lyrics and to the traditional black humor that is essentially laughter at black degradation, laughter curiously close to tears or to howling rage" (251).

The second reason that Himes's exclusion from the canon is ironic is that, although Himes's hard-boiled detective fiction is not included in the *Norton Anthology*, one of the general editors of that anthology, Henry Louis Gates, Jr., has made use of hard-boiled conventions in some of his critical essays on canonization. For example, the opening essay of Gates's 1992 collection, *Loose Canons*, is called "Canon Confidential: A Sam Slade Caper." In the form of a first-person, hard-boiled narrative, Gates wittily and satirically explains the existence of the traditional canon as the product of a kind of protection racket: "Seemed there was some kind of a setup that determined which authors get on this A list of great literature. Payout was all perks, so far as I could make out. If you're on this list, they teach your work in school and write critical essays on you" (*Canon* 3-4). This piece naturally leads me to ask the following question: if hard-boiled conventions are good enough to use in writing *about* canonization, why aren't hard-boiled writers considered good enough *for* canonization? One answer to this question, of course, is that it is not a question of 'good' or 'bad' but merely a question of how much can be included in any anthology. It goes without saying, however, that the process of choosing what does or does not go into an anthology is highly overdetermined, and that absences from an anthology are anything but arbitrary or accidental.

John Guillory has noted that "judgments with canonical force are institutionally located," (*Cultural* 29) and Gates is certainly keenly aware of the power of the Norton anthology. In another essay in *Loose Canons*, entitled "The Master's Pieces," Gates speaks of the purpose of the Norton anthology as being to "define a canon" (31) and argues that "a well-marked anthology functions in the academy to *create* a tradition, as well as to define and preserve it" (32). In the Preface to the Norton anthology itself, Gates and Nellie McKay claim that the anthology is comprehensive: " . . . our anthology contains the texts that, in the judgment of the editors, define the canon of African American literature at the present time" (xxxvii). Bearing in mind the apparent comprehensiveness and authority of the Norton anthology, we would do well to pay attention to what Gates describes as his principle of selection for this anthology. Although Gates acknowledges the value of the approach to anthologization that tries to "include as many authors and selections as possible, in order to preserve and "resurrect" the tradition" ("Master's" 32), he goes on to describe how he and his co-editors have a different approach: "Our task will be to bring together the "essential" texts of the canon, the "crucially central" authors, those whom we feel to be indispensable to an understanding of the shape, and shaping, of the tradition" (32). This of course, brings me back to my original question: what is it about Himes that makes him *in*essential, marginal, rather than central, surplus, we might say, to requirements? When Gates argues that "We've got to make discriminations within the corpus of black literature, and to keep that which is worth keeping" (quoted in Guillory, *Cultural* 352), what is it about Himes that makes him 'unworthy'?

We can arrive at answers to these questions by referring to Pierre Bourdieu's concept of the field of cultural production, which he defines as "the site of struggles in which what is at stake is the power to impose the dominant definition of the writer and therefore to delimit the population of those entitled to take part in the struggle to define the writer" (42). In order to understand how this field or site of struggle is structured, I can do no better than to refer to Stephanie Girard's very useful summary:

> The field of cultural production is delimited by two subfields that function as opposing poles: the field of restricted production, associated with elite culture, represents the space in which cultural producers produce for one another; and the field of large-scale production, associated with mass culture, represents the space in which cultural producers produce for the public at large. In the field of restricted production, commercial success is suspect and critical recognition and consecration by other members of the subfield paramount; in the field of large-scale cultural production, commercial success, and lots of it, is essential and critical recognition unimportant and frequently negative. Since each subfield defines one pole of the field, there is a large space between the poles where the definition of what constitutes "legitimate" art is openly contested (162).

My argument is that the field of African American literature in general, and the African American canon in particular, constitute a field of restricted production in Bourdieu's sense of the term. In other words, with the exception of hugely successful authors like Toni Morrison, what guarantees canonization in this field is not popular success but "critical recognition and consecration by other members of the subfield." Himes's detective novels, which are clearly located within the field of large-scale production, for that reason do not attract such recognition and consecration, and are therefore very unlikely to be canonized. Himes is a particularly interesting writer to apply Bourdieu's model to, however, because he has produced work in both subfields. His early, naturalistic, 'social-protest' novels such as *If He Hollers Let Him Go*, and *Lonely Crusade* could be categorized as 'restricted production' texts, while his detective novels such as *The Heat's On* and *Cotton Comes to Harlem*, are 'large-scale production' texts. Bearing this division in mind, it should come as no surprise that when Himes is anthologized at all, it is his 'serious,' more 'restricted' work that is preserved for posterity. To put it another way, and to refer back to Girard's summary, we might say that Himes's work falls in that 'in-between' space between the two poles of restricted and large-scale production. This is how Himes falls between the cracks of the canonizing and anthologizing project.

But why should the African American canon be so hostile to popular fiction? Why should cultural products designed for mass consumption be viewed so negatively? My argument here is admittedly speculative, but I want to suggest that minority literatures go through a similar process of acquiring legitimacy as a field of study. Anthologies play a crucial part in making a field 'legitimate,' because of the way they help form what Guillory has described as an 'imaginary canon.' In this sense, the *Norton Anthology of African American Literature* can be seen as the crowning moment of legitimation for this field. The problems arise when we consider what standards are used in defining this legitimacy. As Cornel West has noted, African American canon formation, "despite its limited positive effects, such as rendering visible Afro-American texts of high quality . . . principally reproduces and reinforces prevailing forms of cultural authority in our professionalized supervision of literary products" (198).[5] Similarly, John Guillory has argued that the project of 'opening the canon' quickly becomes "an unreflective annexation of non-canonical works to a hegemonic tradition—a phenomenon of cooptation" ("Canonical" 483). For these reasons, despite the fact that I have been protesting Himes's exclusion from the African American canon in this essay, his addition to the canon will not resolve any of the problems I am raising.

Adding Himes, or any other multicultural detective fiction writer, to the canon will do nothing to change the assumptions behind 'canonicity' itself. In other words, the constitution of an 'alternative' canon in no way guarantees that alternative standards are used in putting this canon together. Rather, the same ideas of what constitutes 'good' and 'bad' literature are present in both the African American and traditional canons because they share a common understanding of the relationship between the 'popular' and the 'canonical.' For both 'minority' canons and the 'traditional' canon, identifying and then excluding the 'popular' is the *sine qua non* of canonicity itself. As John Guillory has noted in *Cultural Capital:*

> The distinction between serious and popular writing is a condition of canonicity; it belongs to the history of literacy, of the systematic

> regulation of reading and writing, as the adaptation of that system's regulatory procedures to social conditions in which the practice of writing is no longer confined to a scribal class . . . Thus the generic category of the popular continues to bear the stigma of nonwriting, of mere orality, within writing itself, since popular works are consumed, from the point of view of High Culture, as the textual simulacra of ephemeral speech (23-4).

The 'popular,' then, defines the limit of canonicity, the boundary at which the project of 'opening up the canon' must stop. If it goes beyond that point, it is believed, the 'canon' runs the risk of losing those qualities that give it any coherent degree of 'canonicity' at all. Ultimately, therefore, rather than protesting the exclusion of popular fiction from the canon, I am more inclined to problematize and perhaps discard the very concept of canonicity itself.

Having said this, Himes's exclusion from the African American canon is still worth discussing because of the light it sheds on the institutional status of multicultural detective fiction as a whole. By understanding how Himes's exclusion from the African American canon may be the price African American literature has to pay in order to legitimize itself, we arrive at a better understanding of why multicultural detective fiction's popular success may never be matched by a similar degree of academic prestige. Hopefully, we will also come to appreciate how irrelevant this prestige really is.

NOTES

1. One might note at this point how depressing it is that a 'defense' of Himes is still necessary. As Gilbert Muller has noted: "That an author who wrote seventeen novels, dozens of collected and uncollected stories and essays, and a significant two-volume autobiography should be largely unknown offers a chilling prognosis for the state of our literary culture today" (ix).

2. It is worth mentioning Himes's description of himself when writing his detective novels: "I was very happy writing these detective stories, especially the first one, when I began it. I wrote these stories with more pleasure than I wrote any of the other stories. And then when I got to the end and started my detective shooting at some white people, I was the happiest" (Williams 315).

3. In *My Life of Absurdity*, Himes says of his first detective novel that "Maybe it was an unconscious protest against soul brothers always being considered victims of racism, a protest against racism itself excusing all their sins and major faults. Black victims of crime and criminals might be foolish and harebrained, but the soul brother criminals were as vicious, cruel and dangerous as any other criminals—I knew because I had been one" (111). In Himes's work, honesty is a sword that cuts both ways; if it tells the truth about racism, it also tells the truth about acts generated but not excused by racism.

4. As Soitos notes: "References to music/dance, language, and food are laced into the detective text, forming what I call a *blackground.* This blackground is specific to black detective texts and is composed of all the aspects of African American culture that help to define its uniqueness. For example, Chester Himes embroiders his descriptions of Harlem with black vernaculars such as blues and jazz, language use, food, and dance. Himes's description of the cityscape and portraits of characters from the streets typically command more attention than the crimes that motivated the plot. Vernaculars in this sense create their own subtext and extend the notion of the black detective tradition as they are repeated from novel to novel" (37-8).

5. Despite the fact that West's trenchant critique of African American canon formation can easily and accurately be applied to the new *Norton Anthology of African American Literature*, that anthology features just one review on its back cover. That review describes the anthology as "A classic of splendid proportions." The words, heavily ironic in this context, are those of Cornel West.

WORKS CITED

Bailey, Frankie Y. *Out Of The Woodpile: Black Characters in Crime and Detective Fiction.* New York: Greenwood Press, 1991.

Baker, Houston, Jr.,Rev. of *The Quality of Hurt*, by Chester Himes. *Black World* July 1972: 89-91.

Barksdale, Richard, and Kenneth Kinnamon, eds. *Black Writers of America: A Comprehensive Anthology.* New York: Macmillan, 1972.

Bourdieu, Pierre. "The Field of Cultural Production, or: The Economic World Reversed." *The Field of Cultural Production: Essays on Art and Literature.* Ed. Randal Johnson. New York: Columbia UP, 1993. 29-73.

Boyd, Herb, and Robert L. Allen, eds. *Brotherman: The Odyssey of Black Men in America.* New York: Ballantine, 1995.

Brown, Lloyd L. "White Flag." Review of *Lonely Crusade*, by Chester Himes. *New Masses* 9 (Sept. 1947): 18-20.

Brown, Sterling A., Arthur P. Davis, and Ulysses Lee, eds. *The Negro Caravan: Writings By American Negroes*. New York: Arno Press, 1969.

Chapman, Abraham, ed. *Black Voices: An Anthology of Afro-American Literature*. New York: NAL, 1968.

The Crisis. Publisher's advertisement for *If He Hollers Let Him Go*, 52.12 (December 1945): 362.

Davis, Arthur P., and Saunders Redding, eds. *Cavalcade: Negro American Writing from 1760 to the Present*. Boston: Houghton Mifflin, 1971.

Davis, Arthur P., and Michael W. Peplow, eds. *The New Negro Renaissance: An Anthology*. New York: Holt, Rinehart and Winston, 1975.

Davis, Mike. *City of Quartz*. New York: Vintage, 1992.

Denning, Michael. "Topographies of Violence: Chester Himes's Harlem Domestic Novels." *Critical Texts* 5.1 (1988): 10-18.

Emanuel, James A., and Theodore L. Gross, eds. *Dark Symphony: Negro Literature in America*. New York: Free Press, 1968.

Fuller, Hoyt W. "Traveler on the Long, Rough, Lonely Old Road: An Interview with Chester Himes." *Black World* 21.5 (March 1972): 4-22, 87-98.

Gates, Henry Louis, Jr. "Canon Confidential: A Sam Slade Caper." Gates 3-15.

———. *Loose Canons: Notes On The Culture Wars*. New York: Oxford UP, 1992.

———. "The Master's Pieces: On Canon Formation and the African-American Tradition." Gates 17-42.

———. and Nellie Y. McKay, eds. *The Norton Anthology of African American Literature*. New York: W.W. Norton, 1996.

———., and———. "Preface: Talking Books." Gates and McKay xxvii-xli.

Girard, Stephanie. "'Standing at the Corner of Walk and Don't Walk': Vintage Contemporaries, *Bright Lights, Big City*, and the Problems of Betweenness." *American Literature* 68.1 (March 1996): 161-85.

Guillory, John. "Canonical and Non-Canonical: A Critique of the Current Debate." *English Literary History* 54 (1987): 483-527.

———. *Cultural Capital: The Problem of Literary Canon Formation*. Chicago: U of Chicago P, 1993.

Hill, Herbert, ed. *Soon, One Morning: New Writing By American Negroes, 1940-1962*. New York: Knopf, 1972.

Himes, Chester. *The Big Gold Dream*. New York: Avon, 1960.

———. *Blind Man with a Pistol*. New York: Morrow, 1969.

———. *Cotton Comes To Harlem*. New York: Putnam, 1965.

———. *The Crazy Kill*. New York: Avon, 1959.

———. "Dilemma of the Negro Novelist in the United States." *Beyond the Angry Black*. Ed. John A. Williams. New York: Cooper Square Publishers, 1969. 51-8.

———. *For Love of Imabelle*. Greenwich, CT: Fawcett, 1957.

———. *The Heat's On*. New York: Putnam's, 1966.

———. *If He Hollers Let Him Go*. Garden City, New York: Doubleday, Doran. 1945.

———. "If He Hollers Let Him Go." *Saturday Review* 29.7 (February 1946): 13.

———. *Lonely Crusade*. New York: Knopf, 1947.

———. *My Life Of Absurdity*. New York: Doubleday, 1976.

———. *The Quality of Hurt*. New York: Doubleday, 1972.

Jones, Leroi, and Larry Neal, eds. *Black Fire: An Anthology of Afro-American Writing*. New York: William Morrow, 1969.

Lee, A. Robert. "Violence Real and Imagined: The World of Chester Himes's Novels." *Negro American Literature Forum* 10.1 (Spring 1976): 13-22.

Long, Richard A., and Eugenia W. Collier, eds. *Afro-American Writing: An Anthology of Prose And Poetry*. 2 vols. New York: New York UP, 1991.

Lundquist, James. *Chester Himes*. New York: Frederick Ungar, 1976.

Margolies, Edward, ed. *A Native Sons Reader*. Philadelphia: Lippincott, 1970.

———. "Experiences of the Black Expatriate Writer: Chester Himes." *CLA Journal* 15.4 (June 1972): 421-27.

———. *Which Way Did He Go?: The Private Eye in Dashiell Hammett, Raymond Chandler, Chester Himes, and Ross Macdonald*. New York: Holmes & Meier, 1982.

McDowell, Deborah E., and Hortense Spillers. "Headnote: Realism, Naturalism, Modernism 1940-1960." Gates and McKay 1319-28.

Miller, Ruth, ed. *Black American Literature, 1760-Present*. New York: Macmillan, 1971.

Milliken, Stephen F. *Chester Himes: A Critical Appraisal*. Columbia: U of Missouri P, 1976.

Mullane, Deirdre, ed. *Crossing the Danger Water: Three Hundred Years of African American Writing*. New York: Doubleday, 1993.

Muller, Gilbert H. *Chester Himes*. Boston: Twayne, 1989.

O'Meally, Robert G. "Headnote: The Vernacular Tradition." Gates and McKay 1-5.

Reckley, Ralph. "Chester Himes." *Dictionary of Literary Biography*. Volume 76, 89-102.

Schmid, David. "Imagining Safe Urban Space: The Contribution of Detective Fiction to Radical Geography." *Antipode* 27.3 (1995): 242-269.

Soitos, Stephen F. *The Blues Detective: A Study of African American Detective Fiction*. Amherst: U of Massachusetts P, 1996.

"Time To Count Our Blessings." *Ebony* November 1947: 44.

Turner, Darwin T., ed. *Black American Literature*. Columbus, OH: Charles E. Merrill, 1970.

West, Cornel. "Minority Discourse and the Pitfalls of Canon Formation." *Yale Journal of Criticism* 1.1 (Fall 1987): 193-201.

Williams, John. "Chester Himes: My Man Himes." *Flashbacks: A Twenty-Year Diary of Article Writing*. Garden City, New York: Doubleday, 1973. 292-352.

CHAPTER FIFTEEN

“Maybe I killed my own blood”

Doppelgängers and the Death of Double Consciousness in Walter Mosley’s *A Little Yellow Dog*

William R. Nash

> “Yet, henceforward art thou also dead—dead to the world and to its hopes. In me didst thou exist—and, in my death, see by this image, how utterly thou has murdered thyself.” Edgar Allan Poe, “William Wilson: A Tale”

> “One ever feels his twoness. . . .” W. E. B. Du Bois, *The Souls of Black Folk*

Of all the features of Walter Mosley’s fictional world, the single most interesting is the relationship between his two main characters, Ezekiel “Easy” Rawlins and Raymond “Mouse” Alexander. The recent publication of *Gone Fishing*, the “prequel” to the mystery stories, is proof positive of that fact. Actually the first of Mosley’s novels, *Gone Fishing* chronicles Easy and Mouse’s journey towards the murderous encounter with Mouse’s stepfather, daddyReese Corn, that Easy constantly refers to in the meditations on his malevolent friend that appear in the mystery novels. Mosley’s initial attempts to publish this manuscript in 1988 were unsuccessful; however, with all of Mosley’s mystery novels selling well and Mouse apparently dead at the end of the most recent, *A Little Yellow Dog*, *Gone Fishing* is quickly gaining an audience among readers eager to explore this relationship more fully and likely disconcerted by the shocking turn of events in *A Little Yellow Dog*.

Mouse's apparent death is much more than a striking plot twist, however. Mosley deliberately parallels Mouse's death and the changes that it begins working on Easy with the death of Sweet William Doakes, Mouse's double in taste, actions, and appearance and probably, unbeknownst to Mouse, his biological father. In a sequence that resonates strongly with Edgar Allan Poe's "William Wilson," Mouse's self-defense killing of his doppelgänger sets in motion his "death of self," a process of transformation that makes him into a thoughtful, domesticated, and dependable carbon copy of the younger Easy Rawlins. As Mouse changes, Easy simultaneously moves closer to identification with the values of the younger Mouse, taking up the role of violent rebel that he has so long resisted. That evolution halts abruptly after Mouse's fatal encounter with the gangster Sallie Monroe. In a way, the death of each double sets a process of evolution in motion, as the surviving member of the pair radically changes his values. Furthermore, those changes set other changes in motion, as we see when Easy begins his movement back towards the streets as Mouse self-domesticates. Ultimately, however, the apparent death of Mouse paves the way for a resolution as Easy finds a way out of his street mentality and embraces a new world.

This change provides a resolution to a dilemma that is much larger than just the scope of *A Little Yellow Dog*, as we see the unwilling detective turn between his new domestic life and the world of the streets throughout not only this novel but much of the Easy/Mouse saga. At the end of *A Little Yellow Dog*, however, Easy finds a way away from the pull of the streets and describes himself as "an astronaut who had completed his orbit of the earth and now . . . was pulled by some new gravity into a cold clean darkness" (300). In a sense, his movement is a transcendence of the double consciousness that has plagued him; his ability to pull out of the orbit of that double conscious life indicates new possibilities for him in his process of identity formation.

Mosley adds to the significance of this death of double consciousness by having Mouse's death occur on November 22, 1963, the same day that John F. Kennedy was assassinated. By linking Mouse's apparent demise and Easy's mental liberation with this landmark day in the development of the American national consciousness, Mosley expands the significance of his statement. In many ways, Kennedy's death marked a shift in the tenor and momentum of the Civil Rights struggle, as it coincided with African Americans' growing resistance to the double-consciousness-producing marginalization of the social order. The convergence of Easy's personal history and the national history indicate his symbolic significance as a representative of the new black consciousness that emerged in the 1960s stage of the Civil Rights struggle. In the fiction, as in the historical record, that shift can come only with the sacrifice of the views of the previous era, in this case double consciousness.

As Stephen Soitos explains in his recent study of the African American mystery novel, *The Blues Detective* (1996), double consciousness is a distinctive feature of the African American mystery story. The liminal position Du Bois describes, and that I refer to in one of the epigraphs to this essay is, in Soitos's vision, a place of advantage for the African American detective, who can use his liminality as a means of gaining access to locations and information that enable him to solve crimes. Soitos's name for this phenomenon is "double consciousness detection." There is much of value in Soitos's work and it is certainly long overdue as a theoretical study of the form itself. In a critical system drawing heavily on Bernard Bell's *The Afro-American Novel and Its Tradition* and Henry Louis Gates, Jr.'s *The Signifying Monkey*, Soitos articulates a theory of the African American detective novel that depends on four tropes: double consciousness detection, the modified detective persona, the use of black vernaculars, and the presence of hoodoo. In his afterword, Soitos identifies Mosley as one of a number of new African American writers who are "continuing" the development of the four tropes of African American detective fiction.

Certainly there is some merit to this assertion; as John Gruesser notes in his "An Un-Easy Relationship," signifyin(g) is a key feature of Mosley's plan for his hero. There is also evidence of an element of double consciousness at work in Easy's approach to obtaining information. Despite these attributes, however, Mosley's project has, with the publication of *A Little Yellow Dog*, taken a new direction that makes it more than the sum of the parts these critics identify. As the author notes, "the genre itself is in flux" (Silet 12), and he participates in that change by articulating a new vision for the African American detective.

One key site of this new creation is the recasting and reformulation of double consciousness. Unlike the potentially beneficial state of mind Soitos describes, double consciousness in Mosley's work more often than not indicates limitation rather than opportunity. Easy's constant struggle against double consciousness causes him much frustration and anxiety throughout the stories, a state which fulfills Mosley's goal of "talk[ing] about him as this incredible, complex psyche . . . with all of these hopes and aspirations and what he can and cannot do for both external and internal reasons" (Silet 12). In *A Little Yellow Dog*, Easy manages to resolve some of those conflicts and to transcend his double consciousness, in effect moving away from definitions by the white value system. As I have suggested, this has implications in terms of the historical situation of the story; it also points towards coming developments in African American literature as well. The death of double consciousness that Easy experiences in the middle 1960s in many ways resonates with the call of the Black Arts Movement. Throughout the saga, Mosley has developed this sense of "twoness" in his hero; now, in *A Little Yellow Dog*, he affects a resolution of sorts that once again casts light on the cultural moment in which he situates the story.

For Mosley, the clearest manifestation of Easy's double consciousness is his relationship with Mouse, his boyhood friend and sometime romantic rival. In describing the evolution of his hero, Mosley reveals the absoluteness of this central relationship in his work.

> I was writing a short story about Mouse but from a first person point of view. It started out: His name was Raymond but we called him Mouse. . . . It goes on and on explaining Mouse, and by page four, Mouse looks up and says, "Hey, Easy, how you doin'?" and he was talking to my narrator and that's where he started. So Easy started from his relationship, his feeling for this guy Mouse. (Silet 11)

Just as Easy began from Mouse, we can see through the novels that his growth is linked to his murderous double as well. As several critics have noted, it is the evolution of their relationship that tracks the development of Easy's sense of self. Appearing together in all of the stories, Easy and Mouse present two different images of the black male. Initially, Easy is a caretaker, a concerned father, and a preserver of the common good; Mouse, whom Thomas Michael Stein refers to as "a violent antithesis to Rawlins" (202), is a dangerously malevolent sociopath whose killer instinct perpetually threatens everyone around him, including his best friend.

This initial dichotomy in many ways reflects conventional uses of the trope of doubling in detective literature. As Claire Rosenfeld explains, the double in detective fiction often manifests itself in the "juxtapos[ition of] two characters; the one representing the socially acceptable or conventional personality; the other externalizing the free, uninhibited, often criminal self" (314). In the early stages of the saga, as Thomas Michael Stein notes, this characterization works for Easy and Mouse. Stein sees Easy as driven by desire for economic success that makes him an advocate of integration; he understands Mouse, on the other hand, as "an advocate of racial segregation and black solidarity" (202). In this configuration and the cultural moments of the early novels, Easy represents the "socially acceptable" alternative Stein describes. As Mosley develops these characters throughout his novels, however, the lines between them that Stein sees so clearly in the early stages of the saga begin to blur. Originally willing to consider the possibilities of integration, Easy ends up in *A Little Yellow Dog* in a "cold clean darkness" (300) that indicates an attitude of separatism. In this new formation, freed from the binary by the death of his double, Easy represents a new consciousness, one that clearly resonates in its separatist bent with the ideas of the Black Arts Movement.

In the novel, as in the cultural historical record, with that separatism comes a revolutionary rage. Easy's increasing ambivalence and racial anger draw him closer and closer to the murderous violence that is Mouse's stock in trade until *A Little Yellow Dog*. In *Black Betty*, Easy goes so far as to say that Mouse is "darkness on the other side of the moon" (64), a statement that draws a sharp contrast between Mouse's malevolence and Easy's attempt at nonviolence. Nevertheless, throughout that novel the dark side of the moon calls out to Easy and he moves toward it. Still, at this point. the boundary holds; as drawn as he is to Mouse's rage, Easy cannot surrender to it. By the end of *Black Betty*, scarred by the ultimate threat of Mouse's murdering him, he stands ready to give up the street life forever, "definitely sure that [he'd] never enter work that didn't have a paycheck and benefits involved" and "through with the streets" (253). And yet, as *A Little Yellow Dog* opens, Easy has fully entered into that conventional world and now chafes under it, torn by his conflicting desires for the thrill of the streets and the stability of his new life. In many ways, his consciousness is more fragmented than ever before, and the shift in Mouse emphasizes the severity of that fragmentation.

As *A Little Yellow Dog* begins, Easy works as "supervising senior head custodian" at Sojourner Truth Junior High School (1). In charge of a multicultural janitorial staff, Easy must strike a balance between the demands of his management position and the frustration and anger that fills him in response to school principal Hiram Newgate's racism. His rage at the mistreatment and distrust he encounters from Newgate's office in many ways resonates with the frustration that he felt in *Devil In a Blue Dress* in response to the racist assumptions of Benny Giacomo, his boss at Champion Aircraft. Stein notes that this episode represents the victimization of one minority by another and emphasizes its importance to Easy's becoming a detective (200). Unlike that earlier situation, however, where Easy "does not imagine himself inclined to reinstall the racial understandings of the 1930s in 1948" (Mason, 179), and sacrifices his economic security for the ability to speak his piece, Easy now elects to hold his tongue and to maintain his position in the hierarchy at Sojourner Truth.

Determined to resist the street and to provide a decent life for his adopted children, Jesus and Feather, Easy must repress his rage and accept a certain amount of verbal abuse from his superior. Although he asserts his power within the hierarchy, Easy clearly feels a division in his consciousness because of the position. When Newgate accuses Easy of a series of crimes at the school, Easy suggests they call the police immediately, apparently indicating his feeling of security. As he makes the statement, however, he silently acknowledges that "bluff [is] all [he has] left" (24) and reflects on his history with the Los Angeles Police that he does not want revealed. His division between his new and old lives demonstrates the severity of his double consciousness limitations.

One other point in this passage contributes to Mosley's larger agenda in the novel: the description of Easy's clothes. In the midst of interrogating Easy, Newgate comments on his subordinate's appearance. In response, Easy reflects on the impetus behind his new wardrobe.

> Ever since I wangled my job at the Board of Ed I decided that I was going to dress like a supervisor. I'd had enough years of shabby jeans and work shirts. That day I was wearing a buff, tending toward brown, jacket that had trails of slender green and red threads wending through it. My fine cotton shirt was open at the neck. The wool of my pants was deep brown. (23)

In addition to their inappropriateness for Easy's custodial position—we will soon see him doing particularly filthy cleaning jobs dressed this way—Easy's clothes present a marked contrast from his appearance in the earlier novels. Throughout the saga, simplicity has been his watchword; indeed, more often than not, Easy dresses as the working man that he is. The fineness of his clothes in *A Little Yellow Dog* evokes the earlier presence of Mouse, a man who has long been known in both the intra- and extra-textual world for his attention to fashion and appearance. The initial incongruity of this description intensifies when we see Mouse, whom Easy is on the way to get immediately after his interview with Newgate. He appears "wearing a soft gray workshirt and matching pants" and holding a position as a member of Easy's janitorial crew at the school (32). The role reversal is obvious from this first description, which resonates with a description of Easy from *A Red Death*, where he holds a janitorial position; this figure in the gray work outfit is, after all, the same man whom we have seen consistently gravitating towards finery much more like Easy's outfit described above. A description of Mouse from an early encounter illustrates the point:

> He wore a cream double-breasted suit with a felt brown derby and brown, round-toed shoes. His white shirt looked to be satin. His teeth were all aglitter with gold edgings, silver caps, and one lustrous blue jewel. He didn't wear rings or bracelets, because they got in the way of weapons handling. (*A Red Death*, 56)

Mouse, who has always been the street hero, the "bad man" of the African American folk tradition, and the sharp dresser, now consciously attempts to make a place for himself within what has formerly been Easy's world. Furthermore, as we see from his comfortable manner with Easy on the way to Sojourner Truth, he does so without the apparent self-torture and dividedness that currently torments Easy.

The changes in appearance, while significant in their own right, actually point to a much greater evolution in Mouse's self-understanding. The first view of him in work clothes gives way to a conversation with Easy about going to church, an action that seems completely out of character for the "old" Mouse. Furthermore, he takes up new roles that indicate his shift in consciousness. Near the end of the novel, Mosley characterizes Mouse as "gesturing at Puddin' and Hannah like a schoolteacher, or a cop" (258), two roles that he could and would never have filled earlier in the saga, before the mental and emotional change that marks the development of his more conventional self. Perhaps most significantly, this "new" Mouse is working to learn to read. This struggle to gain control of the word, an emblem of the African American attempt to escape the mastery of societally defined oppression, is the clearest indication we have of the shift in Mouse's perspective toward the world view that Easy, an avid and thoughtful reader in many of the novels, has long lived by.

Easy's reading has been a medium for Mosley to convey his foundational ideas from *Devil in a Blue Dress* through *Black Betty*. In the latter, for instance, as Easy begins to feel his equanimity fragment as his racial rage grows, he refers to W. E. B. Du Bois's *Souls of Black Folk*, which he read in the course of events in *A Red Death* at the suggestion of his friend Jackson Blue. The insertion of this detail, as Easy takes the advice of "the smartest guy in that world" (Silet 14) and reads this landmark text which exactly reflects his state of mind, allows Mosley to convey his message about double consciousness. Mosley further emphasizes the importance of Easy's literacy with his description in *Gone Fishing* of the young, illiterate Easy's recognition of his need to master the word in order to gain control of his own life—and the novel ends with a statement of the opportunities that learning to read has provided him in the lapse of time between the events of the text and his retrospective narration of them. The idea of control of the word as a means of liberation ties Mosley into a literary tradition in the African American canon that extends back to the slave narrative, where, as we see clearly in the archetypal *Narrative of the Life of Frederick Douglass, An American Slave, Written by Himself*, learning to read is the first step towards both mental and physical liberation for the bondsman. However, in Mosley's text, the liberation that Mouse gains is qualified, a temporary freedom from the death-affirming world of the streets that is now simultaneously drawing Easy deeper and deeper in.

The qualification of Mouse's transcendence points toward a reinforcement of my earlier assertion about the relationship between this text and the sensibilities of the Black Arts Movement. One might infer from Mouse's gaining the word and losing his street skills that Mosley is, on some level, including a subtle commentary about the potential harmful side effects of mastering the word. The word, emblematic of the Western literary tradition, has long been the object of attempts at mastery within the black literary tradition. In the era of the

Black Arts Movement, however, a counter commentary arose that warned pointedly of the danger of being controlled by the word, the destruction of a sense of selfhood that comes from internalization of the values of the dominant culture. One of the strongest examples of this trend is Toni Morrison's first novel, *The Bluest Eye* (1970). Although I do not mean to imply that Mosley consciously engages in a critique of this severity, the connection between Mouse's new life and his ultimate end does suggest perhaps a reinforcement of the sensibilities the text presents as arising in the wake of its particular cultural moment.

Before his new life can do Mouse harm, though, it appears to significantly benefit him. As he gains access to the stories of others, he also begins to revise his own stories. In one of his late night conversations with Easy, Mouse retells the story of his encounter with Agnes Varel, in which he and she are interrupted during intercourse by Agnes's boyfriend, Cecil; Mouse responds by hitting him with a bottle and then continuing with Agnes. A version of this story appears also in *A Red Death*, where Mouse tells it to amuse a crowd in the barroom where he and Easy are reunited. Initially, Mouse presents this story humorously, as an indication of his malevolence and his sexual prowess, and Easy notes in the telling of it Mouse's absolute amorality and his response to it: "My heart thrilled and quailed at the same time. Mouse was the truest friend I ever had. And if there is such a thing as true evil, he was that too" (57).

In the new version, however, Mouse tells the story only to Easy, and he clearly feels sympathy for Cecil, whose name, incidentally, never appears in the first account of these events. Although he claims that the event is "water off [his] back," a continuation of his pose of amorality, he precedes the telling by remarking "'You know, Easy. . . . I done some terrible things'" (*Yellow* 63-64). This self-representation is much more in line with the torment that Easy feels over every morally questionable act he has performed throughout his life, and it solidifies our understanding of how much Mouse has changed and how similar he is to who Easy has always been.

In that same conversation, Mouse also makes the statement from which I take the title for this essay: "'maybe I killed my own blood'" (65). An expression of regret for his slaying of Sweet William Doakes, an event which Easy has already described in the course of his reflections on what motivated Mouse to take a conventional job, the statement points toward Mosley's larger purpose in terms of his modifications of Easy's character and the connections between his work and Edgar Allan Poe's. Although Mosley is clearly indebted to Poe, through the filters of many layers of modification by intervening writers such as Raymond Chandler, Dashiell Hammett, and Chester Himes, for the development of the detective form, their major connection in this instance is Mosley's use of the device of killing the double/destroying the self that resolves Poe's story of the doppelgänger, "William Wilson."

As Easy notes, Sweet William Doakes represents the same set of values that has long driven Mouse. A "dapper man who had taught Mouse everything about good dress and conduct with the ladies" (*Yellow* 28), Sweet William becomes Mouse's drinking buddy, roommate, and confidant upon arriving in Los Angeles. Feeding each other's criminal impulses, Sweet William and Mouse coexist peacefully and fortify their collective identity until their final falling out. The disagreement arises in the wake of Mouse's crisis of sexual confidence and Sweet William's success with the same woman. Moved to strike his double, Mouse must ultimately kill him or be killed—and he chooses the former, though the decision subsequently causes him the first remorse he has ever known and begins the process of his "go[ing] straight" and coming to work for Easy (32).

Mouse's murder of Sweet William works on two important levels in the story. Sweet William is apparently Mouse's biological father, a suggestion supported by the description in *Gone Fishing* of Sweet William's relationship to Momma Jo, Mouse's "swampland voodoo godmother" and biological mother as well (*Yellow* 61). The killing of the father traditionally frees the son to develop on his own; certainly Sweet William's death marks a turning point in Mouse's development. More importantly, however, in a text full of doubles—Easy and Mouse, the Gasteau brothers, and Mouse and Sallie Monroe—Mouse and Sweet William's relationship in these terms is much more clearly articulated and much more significant. It is as doubles that Mouse and Sweet William have primarily existed, and it is in this capacity that Mosley most clearly connects their relationship to "William Wilson," a suggestion of which might be inscribed in Sweet William's name.

In Poe's tale, the destruction of the double leads to the death of the narrator's selfhood, as the passage cited in the epigraph indicates: "*Yet, henceforward art thou also dead—dead to the world and to its hopes. In me didst thou exist—and, in my death, see by this image, how utterly thou has murdered thyself*" (Poe 283). Although Mouse is not literally dead at this point, his reaction to murdering Sweet William certainly leaves him "dead to the world" that he has known throughout the saga of his and Easy's adventures. By taking up "legitimate" work, changing his appearance, choosing marriage and monogamy over his earlier promiscuity, and attempting to acquire control of the word, Mouse deliberately engages in the murder of his *self*, the set of characteristics and attitudes that has consistently defined him. While one might read this series of changes as positive, since they pull Mouse back from the knife-edge of disaster on which he has lived for so long, they are actually both endanger and harm him, leaving him literally and figuratively unequipped to move in that world when he must. That failure will lead to the other death of the double that moves Easy out of his "orbit" and into a new life free from his double consciousness.

The change in Easy that comes at the end of *A Little Yellow Dog* logically results from the apparent death of his double; however, it also marks the culmination of a long evolutionary process in which Easy becomes more like Mouse has always been. He changes as his double changes, ensuring the perpetuation of the tension in their relationship that has been essential to their pairing throughout the saga. The most striking reversals occur in *A Little Yellow Dog*; however, many of those changes carry significance evident only in the context of the shift toward Mouse's consciousness and worldview that Mosley traces through the preceding books in the saga.

In the early stages of the saga, particularly *Devil in a Blue Dress* and *A Red Death*, Easy's primary reaction to Mouse's violence is fear. Haunted by guilt over his implication in the murder of daddyReese Corn, Easy views Mouse's arrival with a mixture of trepidation and relief. The nature of Easy's obligations and involvements in these early stories makes Mouse's particular skills and world view necessary to get jobs done; however, he resists and on some level regrets that need.[1] His fascination with Etta Mae, Mouse's estranged wife with whom Easy has a brief affair in *A Red Death*, further complicates his fear. Despite that complication, however, the primary reservation Easy has about Mouse is clearly the absolute amorality of his violence.

In the middle works of the saga, Easy's attitude towards Mouse and his violence shifts rather subtly, and he begins to work to harness Mouse's malevolence more fully, using him as a partner in *White Butterfly* and then managing to actually direct Mouse's bloody revenge scheme in *Black Betty* to end a terminally ill friend's suffering, a mercy killing that Easy cannot perform himself. As he gains a measure of ascendancy over Mouse, Easy also finds himself moving towards a personal manifestation of that murderous rage. However, despite the anger that he feels, he manages to keep it mainly in check, seething with a rage that he cannot let boil over while Mouse is on the scene. In *A Little Yellow Dog*, as Mouse removes himself from that oppositional space of violence, Easy's hold over his own rage begins to slip and eventually dissolves. That dissolution is not all negative, however. Theodore Mason notes that in the earlier stages of the saga, Mosley places an emphasis on Easy's "negotiation of racial protocols" (179), a process that depends heavily on his non-Mouse mediation skills. Here, as Easy shifts from away from that place towards the "cold clean darkness" where he ultimately lands, he undergoes a process of transcendence and redefinition that frees him from some of the limitations of his former liminality. In that context, many of the changes in Easy in *A Little Yellow Dog* take on greater importance. I have noted already that Easy's interest in fashion indicates one level of change; even more importantly, he also adopts, in the course of his actions in *A Little Yellow Dog*, the manner and *modus operandi* that has previously been Mouse's exclusive purview.

The change in Easy's actions shows itself both in his reversal of roles with Mouse when the two are together and in his individual actions as his difficulties increase throughout the story. One example of the changes in Easy the individual as he becomes more violent is his thinking about and acting like Mouse as he struggles to survive a bad beating from Rupert and Beam. As Easy lies silent, awaiting the torment to come, "[t]hinking about Mouse and his drive to survive flow[s] through [him] like molten steel" (187) and moves him to stand up and fight his way out of the room. This literal standing up and being counted also resonates with another of Easy's Mouse-style moves, his negotiations with Sallie Monroe, the second toughest gangster in the black community of Los Angeles.

Easy meets Sallie Monroe on his own territory to discuss the exchange of money for a photograph that Sallie is using to blackmail Easy's future employer, Bertrand Stowe. Knowing full well that he is in danger, Easy nevertheless sticks to his position and forces a negotiation with Sallie that gets him the photograph on his terms. Throughout the negotiation, Mouse is figuratively, though not literally, present, and Easy makes it clear to the reader that his connection to Mouse is *part* of what saves him. He also makes it clear to Sallie that he is not hiding behind Mouse but rather standing up for himself. In threatening Sallie's life if he refuses to comply, Easy takes up Mouse's methods to get what he wants. The violent impulse is even more striking because of what brings Easy to it in the first place. He has resorted to this confrontation as a means of securing employment for himself, the life off the streets that he is living when *A Little Yellow Dog* opens. He comments that he "could have gotten a job as a dishwasher or stone buster" but that he "was like Sallie when it came to the disrespect shown to blacks by white men" and therefore he needs "a job with responsibility and, at least, some pride" (93). In essence, then, the double conscious desire to make a place for himself within the system even as he recognizes the limitations that system places on him motivates this violence. Chronologically, these events occur not long after the point of conclusion to *Black Betty*, where we see Easy slowly consumed by feelings of dividedness and rage. Ironically, as he attempts to forsake the streets for good, he must give vent to that anger in this "street" fashion, acting out his desires for respect with a malevolence and calculation that has previously been exclusively Mouse's realm.

Even more telling than Easy's encounter with Sallie Monroe, however, are his actions with Mouse on the streets and at the Hangar. As Easy and Mouse work frantically to identify Idabell Turner's killer and to solve the mystery of the drug smuggling, Mouse must consistently keep Easy's murderous rage in check. Part of that shift is presented in humorous terms, as Mouse intercedes on behalf of Pharaoh, the "little yellow dog" who makes much trouble for Easy and gives his daughter, Feather, even more pleasure. In a moment of passion, Easy locks Pharaoh in the trunk of his car; Mouse, however, volunteers to hold the animal on his lap and to protect him from the inevitable death of an extended ride in an airless trunk. In many ways, the moment has a lightness to it, a quality that the presence of the dog lends to much of the mystery. Beneath that lightness, however, Easy's rage is a powerful and ominous presence, and Mouse's new powers as mediator are sharply defined.

Those powers appear in more important and potentially dangerous circumstances when Easy and Mouse encounter Puddin' and Tony, Hannah Torres's violent protectors, whom Easy is seeking in relation to the murders he is investigating. Puddin' and Tony advance on Mouse and Easy intending to harm them; they are held in check only by their recognition of Mouse and their knowledge of his malevolent reputation. Significantly, however, there is no hint of violence in Mouse's approach to the negotiation. Formerly an advocate of the bullet as a bargaining tool, Mouse now seems willing to try simple discussion instead, saying to Easy "[a]in't no need to be all mad and surly. All you got to do is talk. People will listen" (255). Although Mouse attempts to maintain this uneasy peace, it is only a few moments before Easy is lunging over the table, grabbing Tony and shouting "'[m]ove your ass or I'll do it for you,'" a threat that resonates much more strongly with the old Mouse than with the Easy that we have known throughout the saga. In order to make the importance of that incongruity clear, Mosley calls attention to it through Easy's narration: "It was almost funny. Me the one threatening violence and Mouse calmly trying to find solutions" (257).

Even as Easy resorts to this violence, he feels a certain kind of moral pang, a symptom of his double consciousness, that does not trouble Mouse. Knowing that what they are doing involves delivering drugs to a gangster, Easy asks Mouse how he feels about participating in an activity that is "wrong"; Mouse replies that the wrong is all Easy's and therefore none of his concern. Indeed, he makes it clear that he is in no position to judge anyone's actions; he merely wants to "'see what it's like to live wit' your family an' work at a job'" and declares that he is "'lookin' for a new way—that's all'" (252). The finality of Mouse's statement and its connection to his subsequent actions indicates the unity of his consciousness around this point. Indeed, throughout all of the novels, the sense of "twoness" that has always plagued Easy has not been Mouse's issue. Now, as Easy moves closer and closer toward the series of events that will change definitions permanently, the tension in his consciousness is sharply and clearly defined. Easy does what he must as a means of self-preservation, but he does it with reservations about the morality of his actions. As he moves farther into the realm that has previously been Mouse's and deeper into his re-immersion in the "streets" that he both desires and wants to flee, that sense of dividedness intensifies. Only the subsequent tragedy of Mouse's apparent death can break him free from that tension.

Part of what makes Mouse's death so tragic for Easy is his implication and involvement in it. Used to relying on Mouse after many years of calling on his friend for backup in all sorts of situations, Easy naturally turns to Mouse for help when the crisis comes in his dealings with the murderers in *A Little Yellow Dog*. In all of the previous novels, Mouse's involvement in the showdown has been Easy's salvation. In this instance, however, it is their mutual downfall. Mouse agrees to go with Easy for the final meeting with the murderers; however, as he tells Easy on the way out the door, "'I ain't totin' no gun, Ease. I won't do that. Not yet'" (277). Although he subsequently shows himself to be armed with a meat cleaver, Mouse enters this confrontation stripped of both his initial psychological identity and the physical manifestation of it, his big .44 caliber pistol.

He also leaves behind some of his characteristic caution, reasoning out that Easy will not be harmed because the transaction is "a business deal" (282). Unfortunately, the killers doing business with Easy are not driven by logic; like the Mouse of the previous novels, they come to the bargaining table prepared to do violence and reluctant or unwilling to let anyone escape them unharmed. If Mouse were still the man that he used to be, he would not have been caught flat-footed by an enemy, as he almost is in this situation. That he brings the cleaver suggests that there is a residual element of his old ways present, but it is significantly less a part of his world than it was previously. In a sense, he has only enough street smarts for one in a situation where he is called on to save two.

Tragically, although Mouse is equipped enough to still save Easy, he cannot fully protect himself and takes two slugs in the chest, further evidence of the change in him and the extent to which he has become like Easy. Throughout the saga, in the numerous confrontations that Easy and Mouse have weathered, Mouse has never received a scratch, while Easy has been near-mortally wounded on several occasions. The implication throughout the saga is that Mouse's violent nature has in some ways acted as a suit of armor for him; equipped with his cool malevolence, Mouse has suffered no injuries. Simultaneously, Easy has occupied an ambivalent position with regard to violence, engaging in it only as it is necessary and often suffering both physically and psychologically for his participation. Mouse claims no psychological remorse as a consequence of his violence, but he apparently pays the ultimate price for his activity. Significantly, he is in position to be wounded because he has pushed Easy out of the way, thereby literally and figuratively taking his place in the path of harm's way.

Easy's initial response to Mouse's injury is guilt over having taken his friend into this dangerous situation; that guilt pulls him out of his self-absorption and helps him see the mourning in his community that he first thinks is for Mouse. When he gets home that day, November 22, 1963, and realizes that Kennedy has been killed, his grief deepens. As he reacts to Mouse's absence, however, he internalizes even more of the murderous violence that was his double's trademark for so long. The rage crystallizes into a vengefulness that takes Easy even farther down the path towards destruction; he finds that he has "gone way over to the deep end of the pool," but he "d[oes]n't care" (290). At this point, Easy is the most divided he has ever been, torn between remorse and murder. So long as he is aware of Mouse's broken body lying in the hospital, that rage drives him. Only Etta Mae's taking her comatose and dying husband out of the hospital by standing off the nurses and orderlies with Mouse's .44[2] breaks Easy out of the grip of this double consciousness.

Easy's movement outside the limitations of his position and his rejection of both street and schoolhouse values parallels the shift in Mouse subsequent to the death of Sweet William Doakes. In each case, the loss of the double figure functions as an antidote to the poisonous influence of the street life; the death of the double also pulls each individual back, at least temporarily, from the brink of self-destruction. Although Mouse ultimately cannot save himself from the streets because of his loyalty to Easy, a devotion that will finally put him in unavoidable danger, his sacrifice enables Easy to "complete his orbit of the earth," a reference to his process of negotiating the street landscape once again, and move into new, uncharted territory. He finds a new place for himself, a position in the "cold clean darkness" that represents a space beyond both the streets and the power structure that has held him so tightly (300).

In addition to Mouse's physical sacrifice, Easy also benefits from a pair of factors that help him resolve the conflicts of his double consciousness, at least for the time being. In the process of clearing up his affairs with the gangster Philly Stetz, Easy takes payment of "sixty-seven hundred and thirty-five dollars," the equivalent of a year's salary for him and the foundation of a nest egg that will pay for his children's education (292). This money gives him a sense of freedom because of the liberation it represents to him; having this to fall back on, Easy need not feel bound and limited by the petty prejudices of Hiram Newgate at Sojourner Truth Junior High. Throughout the saga, economic security has been a hallmark of Easy's sense of self and his ability to resist societal oppression; here the degree of security gives him the ability to be, in the words of Stetz, "a man that stands up" (292). In some senses, this brings Easy full circle, as he once again is in a position to assert himself, as he did in *Devil in a Blue Dress* when he refused to grovel to Benny Giacomo. This standing up further indicates his rejection of the dehumanizing standards that have long limited and divided his consciousness.

The other element of Easy's liberation is his rejection of the conventional values challenging and restricting his ability to participate in the street community life that we have seen him yearning for throughout this novel. He finds release from this value system by accepting his attachment to Bonnie Shay, a woman he knows he could judge harshly if he were either more hypocritical or more unforgiving. However, he finally realizes that his love and need for Bonnie are more important to him than anything that she might have done. Like Mouse, who recognizes that things that are not "his wrong" are not his problems, Easy comes to see that he need neither judge Bonnie nor deny himself access to her. He has transcended the "shoulds" of conventional morality to a system based on personal need and the integrity of service to that need. That new understanding frees him from the limiting orbit that has held him to explore a life outside the boundaries of other's definitions.

This, then, is the ultimate death of double consciousness for Easy. Moved to change by the death of his double and free from the limits society would place on his consciousness, Easy can transcend the cycle of death, removal from the streets, and eventual return that has been his lot throughout the saga. As Mosley makes clear in the story of Mouse and Sweet William, such a liberation cannot take place so long as one is locked into a relationship with one's double/opposite; only when he is free of Mouse can Easy break loose. On the one hand, this can be read negatively as the loss of one of his primary moorings. On a more positive note, however, this death also represents the transcendence of the limitations of a double conscious state. That reading translates to a larger social message for Mosley's work, where the white community represents a double/opposite for the African American consciousness. With Mouse gone, Easy no longer feels the "twoness" that he has in his dealings with Mouse. On a larger symbolic level, he has also found a way to transcend that sense of "twoness" in his dealings with American society in general.

One might well argue that this has been the direction of Mosley's project from its inception. Stein notes that "Mosley obviously thinks it possible to transfer Du Bois's 'double vision' of black and white into a trans-ethnic concept of American culture" (211) and suggests that the transcendence of double consciousness occurs as early as *A White Butterfly*, where, he notes, "Mosley, in making Rawlins leave the world of his beloved privacy, newly emphasizes that non-involvement, a withdrawal into the security of black individuality, is out of the question" (206). Although I agree with the spirit of Stein's assertion, the trajectory of the saga clearly indicates that the full transcendence of double consciousness cannot have occurred in *White Butterfly*. In both *Black Betty* and *A Little Yellow Dog*, Easy turns increasingly toward "black individuality" as a means of self-preservation and protection. He breaks this cycle only after Mouse dies, when the pull of his double has diminished enough to let him break free, out of the "orbit" of this mindset.

The idea of the societal level of liberation ties also to the historical element of the plot, the coincidence of Mouse's injury and Kennedy's assassination. Mosley's use of history is one of the more important and interesting characteristics of his fiction, and his practice of incorporating and revising historical events and situations has drawn notice from many critics. He consistently works with and modifies the American historical record to articulate an alternative image and understanding of both our heritage and our understanding of history as a discipline. This endeavor places him firmly within a long tradition of African American writers engaged in this signifyin(g) historical correction project. Within the mystery tradition, he shares this interest and practice with a variety of writers, including Pauline Hopkins (*Hagar's Daughter)*, Rudolph Fisher (*The Conjure-Man Dies*), Chester Himes (the Harlem domestic series), and Ishmael Reed (*Mumbo Jumbo* and *The Last Days of Louisiana Red*).

Throughout the saga, Mosley has linked the events in the novels to specific events in the history of African Americans, moving from the period in the wake of World War II through the ferment of the Civil Rights movement. Mosley notes the importance to him of "all these important events since WW II, contemporary, historical events which Black people have been edited out of" (Silet 11). In each case, the events of the novel or Easy's state of mind around those events provides insight into/commentary on the events in question and given some sense of their significance to the development of African American identity. In *A Little Yellow Dog* the death of Kennedy and the concomitant demise of Easy's double consciousness represent a significant shift in the tenor of the Civil Rights Movement in the middle 1960's.

Despite the significant advances that were made in the struggle for racial equality during his term, Kennedy's presidency was marked by his ambivalence over real commitment to the Civil Rights struggle. Many historians suggest that the important contributions his administration made to this struggle are properly credited to *Robert* Kennedy, who was then Attorney General. Nevertheless, as historian John Hope Franklin notes, nothing "filled blacks with such despair as the murder of the young president in Dallas" (507). That despair ultimately gave way to hope as the aftermath of Kennedy's death saw some real advances in the fight for racial justice. One result of those changes was a partial dissolution of the sense of "twoness" that had marked race relations in the pre-reform era.

As I have noted, this death of double consciousness also resonates with a chronologically relevant development, the Black Arts Movement. In this mid- and late-1960's era of artistic production, African American artists such as Larry Neal would, in his landmark essay, "The Black Arts Movement," call for "a cultural revolution in art and ideas" and the creation of art useful in the "destruction of white ideas, and white ways of looking at the world" (799). Implicit in this call is a vision of cultural production that resolved the tensions embodied in Du Bois's double consciousness model.[3] Read in this context, Mosley's novel takes on even greater significance. The death of Easy's double consciousness that begins with Mouse's demise functions as an individualized metaphor for a collective process of transcendence. In telling the story within this time frame and resolving as he does, Mosley points towards the larger liberation to come. On this level, the novel resonates with Theodore Mason's comment about *Devil In a Blue Dress*: "The mystery here is finally not about money or murder. Rather the mystery concerns the shifting nature of racial 'being' and cultural knowing" (182). In breaking Easy out into the "cold, clean darkness" he inhabits at story's end, Mosley presents a new answer to that mystery, one that goes farther than anything he has written up to this point.

That interpretation of the novel, while useful, might bear one qualification; it risks an overstatement of positive resolution, as much of the later 1960s saw new versions of the double consciousness tension arising. However, the ambivalence of Mosley's ending and the enigmatic suggestion that Mouse *might* be dead, coupled with the fact that Etta has taken up Mouse's pistol and his ways at least temporarily, suggests that Mosley is guardedly optimistic rather than unrealistic. He points out the hope arising from despair in this particular historical moment and suggests what could come of it; at the same time, though, he does not make a definitive or limiting statement of everything that will be. If Mouse is not dead and returns in *Bad Boy Bobby Brown*, which Mosley has suggested will be his "homage to Malcolm X" (Silet 16), then there might well be the possibility for treatment of the frustration and rage associated with the era around Malcolm X's assassination. For the moment, however, we see the resolution of this conflict in personal terms that suggest a larger picture as well.

As Easy himself notes, the events in *A Little Yellow Dog* enable him to complete an orbit that he began in *Devil in a Blue Dress.* Thrown in that earlier novel into the world of the streets and divided internally about his liminal position between the street and a "respectable" world, Easy begins a journey in and out of that underworld that is marked by his increasing feelings of rage and isolation. Through all of his changes, Mouse is a constant presence, the figure who helps him balance on a knife edge and avoid falling to his destruction. With Mouse gone in *A Little Yellow Dog*, Easy does indeed fall off that knife edge. However, because of the turn in the development process that the death of Mouse's double has caused, Easy falls to potential salvation and [at least temporary] freedom from the bondage of body and mind that his double consciousness has held him to throughout the other novels. Free of the physical manifestation of his divided consciousness, Easy can break free from his cycle. In showing that liberation, Mosley also comments on the potential for transcendence yet to come for the African American community and points the way towards that freedom, suggesting in Easy's lesson that love and liberation from judgment can lift one to a new, "clean darkness," a positive self-understanding and an affirmation of one's blackness that counters the destruction of the streets that both beckon and threaten.

NOTES

1. As I noted earlier, *Gone Fishing* offers further insight into the daddyReese affair; however, in many ways the "resolution" of that mystery does not match the guilt that Easy has borne in relation to it for the intervening years. He literally stumbles on Mouse in the process of committing the murder, but that is the extent of his involvement prior to taking the money that Mouse offers him, money that Easy must take in order to save his own life. Although that plot outline matches the bare bones of the story that Easy recounts in *Devil in a Blue Dress*, in the first of the mystery stories Easy appears to feel that he bears guilt for taking "blood money" ; the actual chain of events suggests a

level of self-preservation that at least partially exonerates Easy for his participation.

2. Etta Mae's adoption of Mouse's favorite weapon and his approach to the world is an interesting and important twist to the events of the saga. Formerly a woman who feared her husband's rage, Etta Mae has found a source of similar emotion in herself and harnesses it here to protect her family from harm. Whether or not Mouse is actually dead, a point that one can debate at the end of the novel, his presence and power in Easy's life seems certain to resurface, through Etta Mae if not directly from Mouse himself.

3. See also Addison Gayle, *The Black Aesthetic* (1972).

WORKS CITED

Du Bois, William Edward Burghardt. *The Souls of Black Folk.* New York: Penguin Books, 1969.

Franklin, John Hope, and Alfred A. Moss, Jr. *From Slavery to Freedom.* 7th ed. New York: McGraw-Hill, 1994.

Gayle, Addison, ed. *The Black Aesthetic.* New York: Doubleday, 1972.

Mason, Theodore O., Jr. "Walter Mosley's Easy Rawlins: The Detective and Afro-American Fiction." *Kenyon Review,* XIV(4): 173-183.

Mosley, Walter. *Black Betty*. New York: W. W. Norton, 1994.

———. *Devil in a Blue Dress.* New York: W. W. Norton, 1990.

———. *Gone Fishing.* Baltimore, MD: Black Classics Press, 1997.

———. *A Little Yellow Dog*. New York: W. W. Norton, 1996.

———. *A Red Death.* New York: W. W. Norton, 1991.

———. *White Butterfly*. New York: W. W. Norton, 1992.

Neal, Larry. "The Black Arts Movement." In *Cavalcade: Negro American Writing From 1760 to the Present.* Arthur P. Davis and Saunders Redding, eds. Boston: Houghton Mifflin, 1971. 797-810.

Poe, Edgar Allan. "William Wilson: A Tale." In *The Short Fiction of Edgar Allan Poe*. Stuart Levine and Susan Levine, eds. Urbana, Illinois: U of Chicago P, 1990. 271-283.

Rosenfeld, Claire. "The Conscious and Unconscious Use of the Double." In *Stories of the Double*. Albert J. Guerard, ed. New York: J. B. Lippincott Company, 1967. 311-330.

Silet, Charles P. "On the Other Side of those Mean Streets: An Interview with Walter Mosley." *The Armchair Detective*, 26(4): 8-19.

Soitos, Stephen F. *The Blues Detective: A Study of African American Detective Fiction*. Amherst, MA: University of Massachusetts, 1996.

Stein, Thomas M. "Ethnic Vision in Walter Mosley's Crime Fiction." *Amerikastudien*, 39(2): 197-212.

thought and rhetorically-based approaches to African American literary criticism in that they both share what Peterson calls "language-oriented modes of cultural interrogation" (91). As I argue here, it is Peterson's "genuinely dialogic" relationship that forms what Caryl Emerson refers to as the dialogic angle in Bakhtinian thought, the point at which one linguistic consciousness is juxtaposed to another (11). I locate the dialogic angle between Bakhtin and African American literature in the Bakhtinian notion of *čužoj* as it occurs in Rudolph Fisher's *The Conjure-Man Dies* (1932), written at the conclusion of the "very specific sociohistorical condition" known as the Harlem Renaissance. As the first detective novel set in an all-black environment, Fisher's text is the first to infuse the (Eurocentric) genre of detective fiction with what Bakhtin refers to as "alien" (in this case Afrocentric) discourse and so is the first to challenge the "hegemony of [the] single and unitary language" inscribed in the formula of origin. The result does indeed qualify as a "fundamental liberation of cultural-semantic and emotional intentions," as Fisher infuses the detective formula with his concerns as a black American modernist writer. As such, *The Conjure-Man Dies* becomes a site for Bakhtin's "radical revolution," challenging the genre's "absolute form of thought" and marking the beginning of multicultural detective fiction, whose literary and linguistic consciousness will in turn launch—not a subgenre—but a second line of stylistic development in the genre as a whole.

The plot of *The Conjure-Man Dies* centers on the alleged murder, "resurrection," and finally real murder of N'Gana Frimbo, no ordinary Harlem conjure-man, but an African king, graduate of Harvard, amateur scientist, and student of Western philosophy. The murderer is Stanley Crouch, Frimbo's landlord, who kills the conjure-man for having an affair with his wife, but not before mistakenly killing N'Ogo Frimbo, N'Gana Frimbo's servant and fellow countryman, who, disguised as the conjure-man, customarily sits with clients in a darkened room while N'Gana communicates through a television lens located in a room nearby. After the murder is discovered, the investigation conforms to the rules of the genre: the police are called in, too many clues are discovered, too many people have motives, and all could, or could not, be telling the truth. The twist in the narrative occurs when the conjure-man seemingly "does a Lazarus" (170), making a dramatic reappearance seated in the very chair on which he was presumed to have been murdered. It is in the second investigation to solve the servant's murder that Fisher "fleshes out the mystification structure" (Cawelti 110) with issues characteristic of black modernist texts.

While Fisher's portrait of the black community includes sketches of Africa and African ritual as well as rituals of Harlem night life, including drugs and numbers racketeering, he avoids the decadent exotica that emblemize black characters in white modernist texts, the most obvious of which are found in Carl Van Vechten's *Nigger Heaven*, a work that "sold almost 100,000 copies immediately" (Huggins 114). Van Vechten's success was not an isolated phenomenon:between 1920 and 1926, nine works by "major" (white) American authors focused on the topic of "Negro life," including Eugene O'Neil's *Emperor Jones* (1920), e.e. cummings's *The Enormous Room* (1922), Sherwood Anderson's *Dark Laughter* (1925), and DuBose Heyward's *Porgy* (1922). However, as Nathan Huggins points out, it was Van Vechten who proved to what extent there was a "market . . . for the author—white or black—who could treat the subject properly" (116). For white writers, "properly" meant portraying blacks in terms of the (white) modernist cult of primitivism[3]: for Fisher and other black modernist writers, "properly" meant contextualizing black experience from an autonomous black perspective; and it is the difference in (cultural) definition that provides the dialogic angle where Bakhtin's notion of *čužoj* intersects black modernist texts.

ČUŽOJ AND THE VOICE OF NOBODY'S OTHER

While most Bakhtinian analyses turn on the Bakhtinian utterance, this analysis turns on Bakhtin's notion of *čužoj*, the position from which utterance is engaged. As defined by Emerson and Michael Holquist in the glossary of *The Dialogic Imagination*:

> *Čužoj* is the opposite of svoj [one's own] and implies otherness—of place, point of view, possession or person. It does not (as does "alien" in English) imply any necessary estrangement or exoticism. . . . In Bakhtin's system, we are all *čužoj* to one another by definition; each of us has his or her own [*svoj*] language, point of view, conceptual system that to all others is *čužoj*. Being *čužoj* makes dialogue possible. (423)

Although the formal definition situates *čužoj* in Bakhtin's discourse, the notion of "other" in itself has been appropriated by a number of critical views. Therefore, because "[e]very reader seems to make his own Bakhtin" (Morson 14), and because Bakhtin's basic writings "occupy a strategic and distinct position within the contemporary discourse on discourse" (Peterson 90), it is necessary at this point to clarify my use of the term. To begin, the *čužoj* notion of "other" differs from that engaged by feminist Bakhtinian analyses that assume the woman's structural place as the "excluded other" (Herndl 8). Neither is *čužoj* the communal voice to which Mary O'Connor refers in her application of Bakhtin to Alice Walker's *The Color Purple*, wherein all differences are "dispersed in a fairy-tale ending" and move beyond Bakhtin's world of dialogism into a world of ideal community, a social state where the "'aggressive intercutting of discourse' is no longer necessary" (O'Connor 209). Nor is the voice of *čužoj* that of "indentured discourse," which Peterson describes as the "plain protest of 'humans like us' . . . subjecting itself to an imposed definition of universal sameness" (92). In terms of "contemporary discourse on discourse," the African American *čužoj* is not the "other" of minority discourse, "consigned to play the role of the ontological, political, economic, and cultural Other according to the schema of a Manechian allegory" (JanMohamed 2).

I use the term as the voice of nobody's "other," aligning the notion with that of Barbara Christian, who, addressing the critical role of subject position, points out simply that "many of us have never conceived of ourselves only as somebody's other" (40). My use assumes *čužoj* not as altering "self" to accommodate "other," but rather altering the notion of "other" to one that retains the subject of "self." It is as the voice of nobody's "other" that black modernist writers such as Fisher, Langston Hughes, Nella Larsen, and Marita Bonner intersect my reading of Bakhtin's notion of *čužoj* in their task of redefining the "other" of black culture as equal to the rest of the world, and it is this voice that Fisher introduces to the traditional stylistics of detective fiction.

For Bakhtin, stylistic development is possible only when we become "sensitive to the 'internal form' . . . of an internal language, and to the 'internal form' of one's own language as an alien form" (367). What is necessary for this to occur is an "intersecting of language" within a "single consciousness, one that participates equally in several languages," a consciousness that is sensitive toward how the world is perceived in ways that are "organically part and parcel" with the language that expresses them (367-368). While Bakhtin continues his discussion in terms of the verbal-ideological world of the novel, his notion of a single consciousness that participates equally in several languages is significant in terms of Fisher himself. Indeed, as Joseph McCluskey points out, Fisher is a "case study" of how a formally trained intellect expands to integrate the culture of his training with that of his experience as a black man in urban America (xii).[5]

It is as a single consciousness participating equally in the languages of different cultures that Fisher is able to manipulate what Bakhtin terms artistic reformation, the intention on the part of the author that both recognizes and intensifies the potential dialectic behind the isolated utterance. Such reformulation requires two linguistic consciousnesses—the one that represents and the one that is represented; interaction between the two consequences produces in the utterance a dialogized, or double-languaged, overtone. Bakhtin reduces devices for such artistic reformulation into three main categories: hybridization, the dialogized interrelation of language, and pure dialogue (358). Hybridization, the collision of two social languages within the limits of a single utterance, is most easy recognized in Fisher's first novel, *The Walls of Jericho* (1928), where Harlemese, the black vernacular of the 1920s, figures prominently in the text. Here, Fisher infuses the language with "the adroit irony and clever banter" of "one at home with his subject" (Botkin 346) and supplies the reader with an eleven-page glossary as a guide to the "alien word." Indeed, it is Fisher's talent for hybridization that has garnered the majority of his critical attention.[6]

While *The Conjure-Man Dies* incorporates Harlemese into its language system, hybridization plays a lesser role here than it does in Fisher's first novel. Rather, *The Conjure-Man Dies* focuses on the second of Bakhtin's devices, the dialogized interrelation of languages, where language systems do not collide but interact in ways that illuminate an awareness of both language systems, a process Bakhtin presents as mutual illumination, or internal dialogue. For Bakhtin, the most characteristic form of mutual illumination is stylization, where the linguistic consciousness that represents is that of the stylizer and the consciousness represented is that of the stylized (362). Unlike hybridization, where only one language is actually present, stylization requires that the stylized language must also be present, which means that the stylizer must be articulate in both language systems.

In *The Conjure-Man Dies*, the voice of the stylizer is that of John Archer, the physician/detective who has a "penchant for dropping into exaggerated pedantic and technical vocabulary" (Davis 320). It is through stylization that Archer, a model of urbane wit and intelligence, emerges as one of Fisher's most unique artistic reformations and manages to comply with Du Bois's lamentation that Fisher allow "his own soul" to appear in his pages.[7] However, in order to appreciate Fisher's success in stylization, it is necessary to first understand Bakhtin's system of language stratification, the often dissimilar stylistic unities into which novelistic discourse generally breaks down (261-262). Bakhtin separates these compositional unities into five basic categories, the fourth of which is "literary but extra-artistic authorial speech," which includes, among others things, scientific statements (262).[8] Through Archer the system of professional language and the system of contemporaneous language interpenetrate and illuminate the other, with the professional jargon of medical statements serving as the language represented and contemporary language serving as the voice that represents. The artistic challenge lies in the second linguistic consciousness—the language represented—which must be stylized in its original form and it is only in this language the stylizer can speak about the stylized subject directly (362). The problem, of course, is that medical terminology doesn't readily lend itself to "everyday" social discourse. Bakhtin comments on this in particular, noting that the "entire methodological apparatus of the . . . natural sciences is directed toward mastery over mute objects . . . that do not reveal themselves in words" (351). Fisher's artistic solution is to subject scientific language to comic style, which demands—as does stylization—a continual shifting in distance between the speaker and the language.

These exchanges occur most notably between Archer and Detective Dart, the plain-spoken policeman who constantly reminds Archer "You're talking to a cop, now, not a college professor" (15). In Bakhtin's analysis, the primary language in the comic novel is a highly specific treatment of common language used by the author as the voice of common view (301). Dart, therefore, as the voice of the common language system, forces the system of medical language to interact with the common view. The result is not only comic but didactic, as Fisher demystifies scientific language by making it accessible to the common view. An example of the comic/didactic nature of these exchanges can be seen in Archer's explanation of the servant's death, coupled with Dart's response:

"Couldn't a man be killed by a blow on the head that didn't fracture
his skull?"

"Well—yes. If it fell just so that its force was concentrated on certain parts of the brain. I've never heard of such a case, but its conceivable. But this blow didn't land in the right place for that. A blow t this point would cause death only by producing intracranial hemorrhage—"

"Couldn't you mange to say it in English, doc?"

"Sure. He'd have to bleed inside his head."

"That's more like it." (16)

Another example is Archer's explication of Frimbo's delusion of grandeur—which is also a parodic satirization of Freud[9]—argued against Dart's diagnosis that Frimbo is a "nut." Archer responds:

"You transform a portrait into a cartoon. Say, rather, that under the influence of certain compulsions, associated with a rather intricate psychosis, he was impelled to dispose of his servant for definite reasons."

"All right. Say it anyhow you like. But to me it's still because he was a nut."(290)

The best example, perhaps, is the one to which Arthur Davis refers in his 1932 review for *Opportunity*: "Rudolph Fisher's medical education again stands him in good stead when he allows Archer to brilliantly interpret [sic] a clue based solely on the division of types in the human blood" (320). The passage is also noteworthy for the comic exchange between Archer and Dart, wherein the scientific process of agglutination is explained, not by Archer, but Dart, who is observing blood cells through a microscope:

[Archer] "Look, look, and keep looking. If you see anything happen, don't keep it a secret."

Dart, squinting one eye shut, gazed with the other down the barrel.

"A lot of little reddish spots," he announced.

"What are they doing?"

"Nothing." Dart grinned. "Must be Negro blood."

> "Jest not, my friend. It is a Sunday. All blood reposes. But keep looking."
>
> "Well, maybe they are moving a little. Hey—sure! They are moving—so slow you can hardly see it, though."
>
> "In what direction?"
>
> "Every direction. Boy, this is good. They can't make up their minds. . . . There things are going into a huddle. No—into a flock of huddles. No kidding—they're slowing collecting in little bunches." (203)

Confirming Dart's observations, comic distance is regained as Archer resumes his roles as the pedantic stylizer. At the same time, however, Fisher uses the strategy for inadvertent learning, telling Dart, "I think I can safely say your observations are correct—though 'agglutination' is a far more elegant term than 'huddle'" (203).

CUZOJ AND THE DETECTIVE FORMULA

As Stephen Soitos notes, Fisher is the first detective writer to apply "detective themes in a completely black environment with an all-black cast of characters" (93). The shift to an Afrocentric perspective is one Bakhtin would describe as a shift in apperceptive background, in this case, a shift toward the African American listener against whose experience and worldview meaning is now understood. As Bakhtin explains:

> The linguistic significance of a given utterance is understood against the background of other concrete utterances on the same theme, a background made up of contradictory opinions, points of view and value judgments. . . . Only now this contradictory environment of alien words is present to the speaker not in the object, but rather in the consciousness of the listener, as his apperceptive background, pregnant with responses and objections. (281)

What is more, Bakhtin continues, the apperceptive background is not linguistic but "rather one composed of specific objects and emotional expressions" (281), one that lends itself to an active understanding that comes to fruition only in the response. As Bakhtin defines it, an active understanding is one that assimilates the word into new conceptual systems, those of the listener who is "striving to understand" (282).

This orientation toward the listener enables "various social languages" to interact with each other but against the listener's—as opposed to the speaker's—apperceptive background. In Bakhtin's words, rather than that of the speaker, "the arena for the encounter" becomes the listener's subjective system (282).

That Fisher intended the novel's orientation to be toward a shared, as well as empowered, *čužoj* audience is evidenced at the novel's beginning, where even the wind, which has given "Battery Park a chill stare and . . . [that] would undoubtedly freeze the Bronx," grows "warmer and friendly" when it passes through Harlem (3). This passage is immediately followed by an exchange between the street smart Bubber Brown and the pedantic Dr. Archer regarding payment for Archer's services for examining what is believed to be the conjure-man's corpse. The exchange demonstrates Fisher's artistic intention to orchestrate Harlem's diverse language systems and to insure that differences in that system impede neither response nor understanding:

> "Questions are forever popping into my head. For example, which of you two gentlemen, if either, stands responsible for the expenses of medical attention in this unfortunate instance?"
>
> "Mean who go'n' pay you?"
>
> "That," smiled the doctor, "makes it a rather bald question."
>
> Bubber grinned understandably.
>
> "Well here's one with hair on it, doc," he said.
>
> "Who got the medical attention?" (10)

Bubber's response is significant in terms of stylistic differences between Fisher as a black modernist writer and the generation of black writers preceding him. For nineteenth-century African American writers, the voice of education presumed hierarchical privilege. Fisher's treatment, however, is characteristic of Bakhtin's active understanding, where understanding and response are so dialectically merged and mutually conditioned. . . that "one is impossible without the other" (282). As if to emphasize the orchestrated interaction, the dynamic is repeated:

> "Now this case . . . even robbed of its material promise, still bids well to feed my native curiosity—if not my cellular protoplasm. You follow me, of course?"
>
> "With my tongue hangin' out," said Bubber. (11)

That the encounter between the traditional utterance of classical detective fiction and the *čužoj* other-as-equal "makes itself felt as a new and unique influence on [the novel's] style" is also reflected in the "distinctive" and "peculiarly racial" phase of the book Davis notes in his review. Here, Davis refers to the language and humor expressed by Bubber Brown and Jinx Jenkins, characters who first appear in *The Walls of Jericho*. As Davis points out, the humor expressed by the language is "peculiar to the Negro," consisting "mainly in the apt use of certain slang phrases and in the constant but ever changing manner of 'slipping'" (320). What Davis refers to specifically is the pair's use of the Dozens, the black folkloric ritual of insult characterized by indirection, allusion, and metaphor in which two or more people insult each other and each other's ancestors (Levine 344-358). The ritual occurs during the first investigation phase, when, waiting their turn for interrogation, Bubber tells Jinx that he has seen Death on the Moon, a sign that, according to black folklore, foretells three deaths to be witnessed by the observer. Jinx initiates the ritual, suggesting "somebody ought to poke [Bubber's] eyes out in self-defense" (32). From there, the dynamic of "asymmetrical joking" (Levine 344) progresses to insults, which in turn encompass looks, color, brains and the lack thereof, and finally, ancestors in Africa. It ends with the following exchange:

> "Don't worry, son. Nobody'll ever know how ugly you is. Yo' ugliness is shrouded in mystery."
>
> "Well yo' dumbness ain't. It's right there for all the world to see. You ought to be back in Africa with the other dumb boogies."
>
> "African boogies ain't dumb," explained Jinx. "They jes' dark. You ain't been away from there long, is you?" (33)

Davis's observes that there is "no other humor quite like [the Dozens]" but also points out that, while it is a humor that registers with "those of the inner circle," it may also "be lost on the uninitiated" (320). I would suggest that Davis's point illustrates the consequences of not distinguishing "difference" in cultural definitions, as demonstrated by critic Helen Lock, who reads the exchange as a denigration of Africanity (46). While the origins of the Dozens are obscure, "there is no question that institutionalized ritual insult was well known and widely practiced in the African cultures from which the slaves came" (Levine 350). And while Fisher refuses in *The Conjure-Man Dies* to "translate" Harlemese to the uninitiated, this particular passage is one of the few followed by authorial intrusion:

> Thus as always, their exchange of compliments flowed toward the level of family history, among other Harlemites a dangerous explosive which a single word might strike into instantaneous violence. It was only because the hostility of these two was actually an elaborate masquerade, where under they concealed the most genuine affection for each other, that they could come so close to blows that were never offered. Yet to the observer this mock antagonism would have appeared alarmingly real. (33)

AFROCENTRIC DETECTIVE FICTION AND THE TROPE OF THE CHANGING SAME

As a member of a "culture within a culture," it is only logical that Fisher "should take an established genre of the dominant culture, designed to privilege certain unique modes of thought, and, working from within, open it up to new possibilities" (Lock 25). Certainly Fisher is not the first African American writer to adapt a literary formula designed to privilege the dominant hierarchy to his own end, as demonstrated by reappraisals of novels by nineteenth-century black authors who appropriate sentimental novels for political agendas (Carby 1987, Tate 1992). Neither is Fisher the first African American to write detective fiction—Pauline Hopkins in *Hagar's Daughter* (1901) and John E. Bruce in *The Black Detective* (1906-07) both employ detective devices in their serialized detective novels (Soitos 1996). Nor is Fisher the first African American to write a nonserialized detective novel, a "first" that belongs to Walter Adolphe Roberts, author of *The Haunting Hand* (1926), whose detective is described as "a spunky young white woman," who solves crimes by intuition (Bailey 53). However, as the first detective writer to write against what Soitos coins a "blackground" (38), Fisher initiates a shift in the epistemology against which the literary formula is understood, and in so doing, becomes the first to engage in what Bakhtin terms an internally persuasive discourse within the genre itself.

Bakhtin frames his most direct definition of internally persuasive discourse in terms of what it is not—externally persuasive discourse. Rather, he explains, it is discourse "tightly interwoven with 'one's own word'" wherein "creativity and productiveness consist precisely in the fact that such a word awakens new and independent words, that it organizes masses of our words from within, and does not remain in an isolated and static condition" (345). That this internal dialogue is "not so much interpreted . . . as . . . applied to new material, new conditions" (345) can be seen in new contexts resulting from Fisher's use of Harlem as the new zone of contact for the literary formula. For example, as George Grella notes, in the formula for classical detective fiction there is always "at least one representative of the squirearchy, one professional man—commonly a doctor, but sometimes a lawyer, professor, or school Master—a clean-cut sporting type, and a military man. . . . [a] Vicar . . . frequently hovers about, providing a link with the Established Church" (39). Fisher's shift in apperceptive background, however, changes not only the traditional stock of characters, but also the composition of heteroglossia—the sociohistorical background—against which such standard characters must be read. As a result, formula begins to "sound in a different way," suggesting new insights and "newer ways to mean" (Bakhtin 346). The squirearchy, for example, is now represented by N'Gana Frimbo, who, although a king, nonetheless suffers discrimination because of American racial politics, while the vicar is replaced by Aramintha Snead, a devoutly religious woman, who, "wonderin' lately if there ain't some things the devil can 'tend to better'n the Lord" (80), turns to the conjure-man for help against her husband's abuse.

The Harlem version of the military man is Spider Webb, a smooth-talking numbers runner involved in a war between Harlem's two racketeering bosses, and the successful clean-cut sporting type is revealed in the end as the murderer. The professional man remains in the character of Dr. Archer, but a doctor who sees only two patients in the course of the novel: "the first pleaded a bad cold and his liquor prescription, the second pleaded hard times and borrowed three dollars" (197). The other doctor in the text is a dentist who keeps showgirls in his waiting room to attract walk-in business. Both testify to Frimbo's assessment of the sacrifices and limited opportunities available to black physicians in America, particularly at that time. Although Dart seems to comply with Grella's description of the typical "baffled" policeman, he is one of only ten black men on the police force in Harlem and the only one to hold the rank of detective. Bubber, on the other hand, has become a private detective only because he has been laid off from his job with the city.

While the trope of the changing same is Amiri Baraka's signification for the interplay between traditional and individual expression in African American music (Jones 118), it also captures Fisher's signifyin(g) relationship with classical detective fiction. In Houston Baker's terms, Fisher's "mastery of form" and "deformation of mastery" produces a "more accurate and culturally enriching interpretation" of the "sound and soundings of Afro-American modernism" (xvi), one that reanimates the formula for classical detective fiction. Like the Sophistic novel that Bakhtin locates as the starting point for the European novel's First Stylistic Line of Development, the primary characteristic of classical detective fiction "is the fact that it knows only a single language and a single style" (Bakhtin 375). And while, like Fisher's experiment, the Second Line incorporates heteroglossia into the novel by "exploiting it in order to orchestrate its own meaning," classical detective novels—like the novels of the First Line—leave heteroglossia outside the novel by stylizing language in a "special" and "novelized way" (Bakhtin 375). Bakhtin describes this treatment as "a sideways glance" in which the word of traditional stylistics acknowledges the word of another as the "word of no one in particular, as simply the potential for speech" (276). Such a philosophy of language fosters a passive understanding, one that acknowledges neutral signification but not actual meaning (281).

Unlike active understanding, which enriches discourse, passive understanding takes into consideration "only those aspects [of style] that are deprived of any internal dialogism, that take the listener for a person who passively understands but not for one who actively answers and reacts" (280). Passive understanding is indigenous to the formula of classical detection, particularly the clue puzzle, or whodunit, whose process of detection is, as Lock notes, a matter of "rejecting misleading signs until the sign is finally united with the signified" (17). Stephen Knight reinforces the idea of the genre's inclination toward passive understanding, as well as Lock's contention that the singular vision inherent in the decoding process of the whodunit assumes a final unity meant to represent an "empirical truth" (17). As Knight explains:

> It is true that many readers could not solve the puzzle, and hardly tried to do so; indeed some novels are not quite fairly open to such solving. But these facts do not remove the crucial ideological force of the clue-puzzle, which marshaled the simple skills of a respectable, leisured, reading public and applied them in their own personalised

> defense system, with an inquiring agent to represent the reader who could only aspire to such observing and ordering powers. (107)"

Lock's observation that this "act of decoding" performed by the classical detective requires the "imposition of a single vision," absorbing everything unfamiliar as "alien but containable" (24), echoes Bakhtin's discussion of the "unitary and singular" language encased in poetic genre, where, "no matter how many contradictions and insoluble conflicts the poet develops within it, [the world of poetry] is always illumined by one unitary and indisputable discourse" (286).

Like First Line novels, poetic genres never presume "alien utterances beyond [their] own boundaries," a characteristic that qualifies classical detective fiction as "poetic in the narrow sense." As Bakhtin explains, the language of poetic genres positions itself as all-encompassing and is sufficient unto itself. And although conflict and doubt can exist as subject matter, the language "realizes itself as something about which there can be no doubt," even to the point that "discourse about doubts must be cast in a discourse that cannot be doubted" (Bakhtin 286). The point is particularly relevant to classical detective fiction, which—again like works of First Line Development—stylizes language in a way that positions heteroglossia as background without actively engaging the dynamic. Unlike novels of the First Line, however, whose unities are "rooted in nothing" (373), classical detective fiction depends on a singular interpretation of clues designed to insure the moral fantasy embedded in the original formula by assuring "all problems have a clear and rational solution" (Cawelti 43). The result, according to Knight, is that, while the novels of classical detection are constructed in such a way that they appear to deal with real problems, such problems are in fact "both conceived and resolved in terms of the ideology" (4). Therefore, while a text that may not be "simple or single" in meaning and may in fact contain views that seem to perceive conflict in the world, such conflict is "artificially and consolingly" resolved through the formulaic plotting and structure (Knight 5). For example, while Agatha Christie rejects Arthur Conan Doyle's pattern of the authoritarian male as the protecting force, she nonetheless offers her respectable, leisured, middle-class reading public "a dream of collective security," one that promises "respectable people the continued enjoyment of the life-style they or their forbears have personally earned by successful conflict with others" (Knight 128).

Critics of the genre agree that the underlying moral fantasy controls the very nature of mystery in classical detective fiction. Lock, for example, defines mystery as intellectual rather than existential (5), while John Cawelti finds mystery a structural element, an intellectual activity pursued as an end in itself (43). However, Fisher's Afrocentric/*čužoj* reamination of the detective formula not only subjects the monologic voice of classical detective fiction to "alien discourse," but also reconceptualizes the nature of mystery by replacing the mythological model on which the ur-formula is based from the myth of Oedipus, whose story depends on the correct reading of the word, to the myth of Osiris, the Egyptian god/man whose story represents cycles of death and rebirth. And while the story of Oedipus turns on a "fundamental logocentrism" (Lock 17), the story of Osiris resists fixity of signification, celebrates mystery as indeterminate, and valorizes its potential for "the possibilities it suggests" (Lock 33).[10]

Frimbo is the character most readily identified with Osiris, not only because of his "resurrection," but because his powers defy the logic of science. For example, while Archer and Dart prove the impossibility of Frimbo's "resurrection" through the test of agglutination, neither can account for his effectiveness as a metaphysician. Whether or not being a conjure-man is a "racket," as Dart declares, a young man under Frimbo's spell does survive an otherwise fatal knife wound to the head. Neither is the reader meant to simply dismiss as coincidence Frimbo's prediction that Jinx Jenkins—falsely arrested for the servant's murder—will find "physical security" sooner than he thinks. Certainly Frimbo is correct in his observation that Stanley Crouch, disguised as Easely Jones, has murder in his heart. Most haunting of all is Frimbo's premonition of his own death. Lock's observation that "[w]hen emphasis is laid on the value and endurance of mystery, the role played by the criminal becomes comparatively unimportant" (34) is reflected in Bubber's statement at the novel's conclusion. For Bubber, Crouch's motives for killing Frimbo are understandable: "He jes' didn't mean to lose his wife and life both. Couldn't blame him for that. Jes' ordinary common sense" (316).

As a reanimation of the the literary formula for classical detective fiction, *The Conjure-Man Dies* succeeds in Todorov's definition of a "major work [that] creates, in a sense, a new genre and at the same time transgresses the previously valid rules of the genre" (Todorov 43). Yet at the same time, such narrative innovation cannot apply to detective fiction, since "to develop the norms [controlling the genre] is also to disappoint them; to 'improve upon' detective fiction is to write 'literature,' not detective fiction" (Todorov 43). Fisher, however, manages to accomplish both by subjecting the classical detective formula to the *both/and* logic shared by black American modernists,[11] conforming to the rules of the genre even as he transgresses them. Like First Line novels, whose rules concerning style are "more or less rigorously consistent" (Bakhtin 375), the rules shaping classical detective fiction are so "rigidly uniform" as to be "familiar to every reader in the English speaking world" (Grella 30). However, like novels of the Second Line, *The Conjure-Man Dies* exploits the "valid rules of the genre" even as the shift in apperceptive background reaccentuates these same rules.

Nor are the rules of any less importance to critics than to writers of classical detective fiction. Todorov's discussion of detective fiction, for example, consults S.S. Van Dine's "Twenty Rules" (1928), which were themselves published the same year as Monsignor Ronald Knox's "A Detective Story Decalogue," a treatise referred to by Howard Haycraft as the "Ten Commandments of Detection" (194). In "Aristotle on Detective Fiction" (1946), Dorothy L. Sayers subjects the rules of the genre to Aristotelian analysis, while John Cawelti contends that to not comply with the rules of the genre is to write "something other" than classical detective fiction (81). Fisher's success in complying with the rules of classical detection is evidenced by favorable reviews, not only in *Crisis* and *Opportunity*, but mainstream publications, including *Time* (Bailey 54). Until recently, the little attention paid the novel in African American literary criticism focused on the work solely in terms of compliance with genre conventions, ignoring completely its racial commentary (Soitos 93). Even Davis, who notes many of the novel's "firsts," ultimately concludes that while such "firsts" are indeed important, of more importance "is the fact that this first adventure in this new field is a thoroughly standard one" (320).

BEYOND TRANSGRESSION

Todorov's paradox of rules enables insight into three ways Fisher's re-accentuation of the literary pattern both complies with and trangresses the classical detective formula. According to Todorov's construct, the detective story is based on two murders. The first, which is committed by the murderer, become the occasion for the second, "unpunishable" murder—the murder and/or apprehension of the murderer by the detective (Todorov 44). In *The Conjure-Man Dies*, the first murder does indeed become the occasion for the second, but the second murder does not go unpunished. Here, Fisher capitalizes on a strategy often employed in the classical detective formula, in that Frimbo deliberately exposes himself to a second attack in order to catch the killer. However, the consequence, that of Frimbo's own murder, is more characteristic of the thriller, or *série noire*, a genre in which "everything is possible, and the detective risks his health, if not his life," a form, as Todorov notes, exploited by Chester Himes in *For Love of Imabelle* (47).

Fisher also reformulates Van Dine's edict that "[t]he novel must have at most one detective" (49). *The Conjure-Man Dies* is the first in the genre to use multiple detectives,[12] each reflecting aspects of Harlem's diverse community and each of which reflects different levels of Bakhtin's stylistic unities. Bubber's Harlemese encompasses *skaz*, the stylization of "oral everyday levels of narration,"while Dart incorporates "speech individualized according to characters" (Bakhtin 262), in this case, the plain-spoken flatfoot. Frimbo, as well as Archer, represents forms of "literary but extra-artistic authorial speech" (Bakhtin 262). Archer is grounded in scientific statement and Frimbo—particularly in light of his stories of African ritual—grounded in philosophical and ethnographic description.

While Soitos identifies the novel's four detectives (93), critics tend to focus exclusively on Archer, no doubt because Archer is the novel's controlling consciousness. As a character, John Archer is fashioned after the gentleman detective introduced in E.C. Bentley's *Trent's Last Case* (1913), whose protagonist Grella describes as the "progenitor of all the insouciant dilettantes who breeze gracefully through detective fiction for the next thirty years" (36). As the gentleman amateur, Trent reflects a detective who understands the world he investigates and whose social mobility ranges from "the ability to interrogate the French maid in her native tongue" to "those indecipherable things that characterize the Oxford man" (Grella 37). In Archer's case, social mobility includes his interactions with Harlem's diverse population, while his erudite vocabulary prompts Dart's chiding, "Gosh, doc, it would be so much easier in French" (184).

Trent is described as an "obvious gentleman—immediately apparent by his whimsical speech and shaggy tweeds" (Grella 37); Archer is described as a "bemused anthropologist" who drinks cream sherry while "chuckling and frowning" over the plots of classical literature (McCluskey xxxv). As Grella notes, after Bentley, the detective story turned away from the "atmosphere of gloom and menace—a heritage of the Poe tradition" toward the comic milieu of the English novel (37). Moreover, he notes, the only successful American versions were Ellery Queen and Van Dine's Philo Vance, the latter of whose influence has been noted in *The Conjure-Man Dies.* (Ellin 1971, Lewis 274, Bell 140). Yet, even after accumulating clues that seem to lead to the solution, Archer admits to Dart, "I have a curious feeling that smart as we think we are, we're both guessing wrong" (294). In reality, however, Frimbo is the ratiocinative detective, sharing characteristics with Doyle's Sherlock Holmes;[13] nor does he waver in his conviction that the solution is "calculable." As Archer points out when the servant's killer is revealed, "It was Frimbo . . . who caught him" (312).

In his explication of the duality at the base of the whodunit, Todorov explains that the form contains two stories—the story of the crime and the story of the investigation. The first is over before the second begins, while the second is the story of the first; moreover, the second story "is a story which has no importance in itself," serving "only as a mediator between the reader and the story of the crime" (Todorov 46). However, the second story in *The Conjure-Man Dies* is that of the black *čužoj* and demonstrates concerns Fisher shares with other black modernists, a core of younger black intellegensia whose "single unifying concept" was to "gain authority in [the] portrayal of black life" (Kent 17).[14] For Fisher, the second story is the story of the Harlem community and, as such, has significance in itself. And while in Todorov's duality, the second story is the story of the first, eventually explaining the murder, the first story of *The Conjure-Man Dies* is the story of Africa and African ritual, told by Frimbo in manner that refutes the decadent exotica and "noble savagery" of the modernist cult of white primitivism.

Fisher's third transgression involves a cardinal rule of the genre—that the victim be a character who "cannot really be mourned" (Cawelti 81). The first murder conforms, in the sense of Western tradition, that no one mourns the servant's death. At the same time, it is through N'Ogo Frimbo's death that the readers—and the characters—learn a new definition of mourning in terms of African custom. While Frimbo doesn't mourn the death in a way recognizable to Euro-American culture, as N'Ogo Frimbo's king and fellow countryman, he goes to great lengths to perform the purification ritual. As he explains to Dart, "If I can not complete my duty to this member of my clan, I do not deserve to have been his king. The greatest humiliation I could suffer would be death at the hands of strange people. That is no more than he has suffered" (305). The explanation lends further impact to Fisher's transgression, for Frimbo is himself is killed by Stanley Crouch in the effort to bring the servant's killer to justice and, as a consequence, does suffer "the greatest humiliation": as king he performs the ritual for his countryman, while there are no longer countrymen to perform the ritual for the king.

Whether or not *The Conjure-Man Dies* is a work of "literature" rather than "genre" seems of less importance than the fact that, like Second Line novels, the work succeeds in reformulating the stylistics of the detective genre. Like Second Line novels, Fisher's reaccentuation "further create[s] out of itself" (Bakhtin 421), and its influence on subsequent works can be seen in the reaccentuation of images Fisher's introduces. One of the ways this occurs is in the evolution of the detective figure that survives, not only in the novel, but in black detective fiction—not Frimbo, the ratiocinative detective, or the erudite Dr. Archer, or even the plain-spoken Dart, but that of the street-smart Bubber Brown, who is drawn into the case because his partner has been framed. As Bakhtin observes, new images often evolve through reaccentuation of old ones and a basic method for this transformation is to represent the character in terms of misfortune and suffering, since, according to Aristotle's poetics, suffering translates comic characters into the "higher register" of the tragic (Bakhtin 421). From this perspective, Bubber reappears nearly sixty years later in the image of Walter Mosley's Easy Rawlings, who in the first of the series (*Devil in a Blue Dress*, 1990), becomes a private detective after he is laid off from his job at Champion Aircraft and has a mortgage to meet.

In Houston Baker's words, the task of black modernist writers was to bring representations of black culture "into the twentieth century" (71), a task that, according to Baker, required a "shrewd combination of formal mastery and deformative creativity" (74), or what Bakhtin would call the process of reaccentuation. Both concepts turn on the notion of new possibilities, of causing a monologic tradition to "sound" in a new way. In terms of detective fiction, it would be a mistake to relegate such soundings to the category of subgenre, for Fisher's *čužoj* shift in apperceptive background introduces deep structural transformations that, in turn, affect other subgenres, such as the hard-boiled tradition. As the novel initiating multicultural detective fiction as a second line of stylistic development, in the stylistics of detective fiction, the novelistic images introduced in *The Conjure-Man Dies* continue to grow and develop, producing further reaccentuations as multicultural detective fiction continues to expand the *čužoj* voice of nobody's "other."

NOTES

1. Indeed, as Caryl Emerson points out, Bakhtinian discussions of black literary voices have no "Bakhtinian parallel" in a country with no indigenous black population or whose language and political interaction was shaped on "awful reality"of "race-based slavery," even though the former Soviet Union was itself multiracial (11). What is more, Emerson finds this lack of equivalence consequential in terms of methodology and cites Bakhtin himself on applying Bakhtinian thought to "creole," or dialect, studies:

> One should not confuse mere reified and externalized 'speech characterizations' with a genuine polyphony or individuality of worldview, Bakhtin cautions, for the authenticity and quality of these inner worldviews are measured not by specific words, sounds, syntax, or semantic content—formal matters, which linguists are qualified to assess—but by the dialogic angle at which one consciousness is juxtaposed to another. (11)

Interestingly, Bakhtin's caution is similar to that of Henry Louis Gates, Jr., who, citing Wole Soyinka, cautions that to explicate African American texts in the framework of Eurocentric supposition can be, if one is not careful, "dangerous to [one's] racial self-esteem" (1990, 82). Yet it is precisely at such a "dialogic angle" that Bakhtin intersects African American literature and where the Bakhtinian hypothesis that the "central problem in prose theory is the problem of the double-voiced, internally dialogized word, in all its diverse types and variants" (330) finds resonance in theories of African American literary criticism.

2. See Houston Baker, Jr., *Blues, Ideology, and Afro-American Literature: A Vernacular Theory* and Henry Louis Gates, *The Signifying Monkey: A Theory of Afro-American Literary Criticism.* For background on the shift in the way black texts were read by black critic, see Gates's *Figures in Black: Words, Signs, and the "Racial" Self.* Also see Michael Awkward. "Race, Gender, and the Politics of Reading." *Black American Literature Forum.*

3. I discuss these issues in detail in "The World Would Do Better To Ask Why Is Frimbo Sherlock Holmes: Investigating Liminality in Rudolph Fisher's The Conjure-Man Dies" in *African American Review.*

4. For an interesting account of *Nigger Heaven* and the white modernist cult of white primitivism, see Robert Worth, "*Nigger Heaven* and the Harlem Renaissance." *African American Review.* Volume 39, Number 3, Fall 1995, 461-474.

5. Fisher was by vocation a prominent physician in New York in the late 1920s and early 1930s. Summarizing Fisher's years at Brown University as an undergraduate and student, McCluskey notes that Fisher won the Caesar Misch Prize in German, the Carpenter Prize in public speaking, and the Dunn Premium for the student with the highest standing in courses in rhetoric, English composition, and public speaking, and was awarded keys to Phi Beta Kappa, Delta Sigma Rho and Sigma Xi honor fraternities (xiii). Leaving Brown, Fisher attended Howard University Medical School, taking courses in roentgenology, the study of x-rays in connection with the diagnosis and treatment of disease. In 1925, he was awarded a research fellowship at Columbia which led to position at the Bronx and Mt. Sinai Hospitals in New York. In 1930, by then a physician in private practice, he was elected Chair of the department of roentgenology at International Hospital in Jaimaca, New York. Throughout, in addition to medical treatises, he wrote fourteen short stories, a novella, two novels, and a play.

6. In 1934, for example, John Chamberlain, a reviewer for *The Bookman,* judged Fisher to be the "most able craftsman among the Negro novelists" whose "ear is remarkable" and a "peer of Ring Lardner as a manipulator of native idiom" (606).

7. The comment reflects Du Bois's preoccupation with "high" and "low" culture in the representation of blacks in literature and makes this comment in his review of *The Walls of Jericho.* Although Du Bois found Fisher's novel a step upward from Van Vechten (*Nigger Heaven*) and McKay (*Home to Harlem*), he nonetheless expresses concern that Fisher "does not yet venture to write of himself and his own people; of Negroes like his mother, his sister and his wife. His real Harlem friends and his own soul nowhere yet appear in his pages." See "The Browsing Reader," *Crisis* 35 (1928), 374.

8. The other stylistic unities Bakhtin lists are: direct authorial narration; skaz, or stylizations in "oral everyday narration"; stylization of written everyday narration, i.e. personal letters; and speech individualized according to characters. Also listed as "literary but extra-artistic authorial speech" are moral, oratory, ethnographic descriptions, and memoranda (Discourse 262).

9. Fisher's parody of Freud is part of a larger response to notions of primitivism by white modernists. See "The World Would Do Better To Ask "Why Is Frimbo Sherlock Holmes?"

10. Not only does the shift in world view alter the mythological model, but guilt is eliminated as a structural element in the formula for detection. I discuss the formal ramifications of these transgressions in a forthcoming paper, "When the English Country House Is Harlem."

11. I discuss the "both/and" *Zeitgeist* of American Modernism in "Beyond the Harlem Renaissance: The Case for Black Modernist Writers" in *Modern Languages Studies.*

12. Cawelti notes that *The Moonstone* by Wilkie Collins exhibits characteristics of detective fiction and is told from a multiple perspective, but concludes the work to be "at some point on the line of development between the nineteenth-century novel of sensation and the twentieth-century classical detective story" (135).

13. See "The World Would Do Better To Ask "Why Is Frimbo Sherlock Holmes?"

14. For a detailed analysis of dominant ideologies in the African American community at the turn of the century, see Kevin Gaines, *Uplifting the Race* (1996).

WORKS CITED

Anderson, Sherwood. *Dark Laughter.* New York: Boni and Liveright, 1925.

Awkward, Michael. "Race, Gender, and the Politics of Reading." *Black American Literature Forum.* Volume 22 Number 1 (Spring 1988): 5-28.

Bailey, Frankie Y. *Out of the Woodpile: Black Characters in Crime and Detective Fiction.* New York: Greenwood Press, 1991.

Baker, Houston. *Modernism and the Harlem Renaissance.* Chicago: U of Chicago P, 1987.

———. *Blues, Ideology, and Afro-American Literature: A Vernacular Theory.* U of Chicago P, 1984.

Bakhtin, Mikhail Mikhailovich. "Discourse and the Novel." *The Dialogic Imagination: Four Essays by M.M. Bakhtin.* Ed. Michael Holquist. Trans. Caryl Emerson and Michael Holquist. Austin: U of Texas P, 1981.

Bell, Bernard. *The Afro-American Novel and Its Tradition.* Amherst: U of Massachusetts P, 1987.

Bentley, E.C. *Trent's Last Case.* 1913. Reprint. New York: Grosset and Dunlap, 1930.

Botkin, B.A. "The Lighter Side of Harlem." Opportunity 6 (1928): 346.

Bruce, John E. *The Black Sleuth.* 1907-09. John E. Bruce Collection. Reel 3. Schomburg Center for Research in Black Culture, New York.

Carby, Hazel. *Reconstructing Womanhood: The Emergence of the Afro-American Woman Novelist.* New York: Oxford UP, 1987.

Cawelti, John. *Adventure, Mystery, and Romance: Formula Stories as Art and Popular Culture.* Chicago: U of Chicago P, 1976.

Chamberlain, John. "The Negro as Writer," *The Bookman*, 70. 1930. 603-609.

Christian, Barbara. "The Race for Theory." *The Nature and Context of Minority Discourse.* Eds. Abdul R. JanMohamen and David Lloyd. New York: Oxford UP, 1990. 37-49.

cummings, e.e. *The Enormous Room.* New York: Boni and Liveright, 1922.

Davis, Arthur. "Harlem Mysterious." *Opportunity.* October 1932, 320.

Du Bois, W.E.B. "The Browsing Reader." *Crisis* 35, 1928. 374.

Ellin, Stanley . Introduction. *The Conjure-Man Dies.* New York: Arno Press, 1971.

Emerson, Caryl. "Introduction: Dialogue on Every Corner, Bakhtin in Every Class." *Bakhtin in Contexts: Across the Disciplines.* Evanston, IL: Northwestern UP, 1995. 1-30.

———, and Michael Holquist. "Glossary." *The Dialogic Imagination: Four Essays by M.M. Bakhtin.* Ed. Michael Holquist. Trans. Caryl Emerson and Michael Holquist.

Fisher, Rudolph. *The Conjure Man-Dies.* (New York: Knopf, 1932; Ann Arbor: U of Michigan P, 1992).

———. *The Walls of Jericho.* (New York: Knopf, 1928; Ann Arbor: U of Michigan P, 1994).

Gaines, Kevin. *Uplifting the Race: Black Leadership, Politics, and Culture in the Twentieth-Century.* Chapel Hill: U of North Carolina P, 1996.

Gates, Henry Louis, Jr. "Authority, (White) Power, and the (Black) Critic; It's All Greek to Me." The *Nature and Context of Minority Discourse.* Eds. Abdul JanMohamed and David Lloyd. New York: Oxford UP, 1990. 72-101.

———. *Figures in Black: Words, Signs, and the "Racial" Self.* 1987. New York: Oxford UP, 1989.

———. *The Signifying Monkey: A Theory of Afro-American Literary Criticism.* New York: Oxford UP, 1988.

Gosselin, Adrienne Johnson. "Beyond the Harlem Renaissance: The Case for Black Modernist Writers." *Modern Language Studies* 26.4 (Fall 1996):

———. "The World Would Do Better To Ask `Why Is Frimbo Sherlock Holmes'?": Investigating Liminality in Rudolph Fisher's *The Conjure-Man Dies. African American Review* 32.4 (Winter 1998).

Grella, George. "Murder and Manners: The Formal Detective Novel." *Novel* 4 (1970): 30-48.

Haycraft, Howard. "Introduction." *The Art of the Mystery Story: A Collection of Critical Essays*. Ed. Howard Haycraft. New York: Grossett & Dunlap, 1947.

Herndl, Diane Price. "The Dilemmas of a Feminine Dialogic." *Feminism, Bakhtin, and the Dialogic*. Eds. Dale M. Bauer and S. Jaret McKinstry. Albany: State University of New York P. 1991. 7-24.

Himes, Chester. *For Love of Imabelle*. Greenwich, CT: Fawcett, 1957.

Hopkins, Pauline. *Hagar's Daughter: A Story of Southern Caste Prejudice*. 1901-02. Reprint. *The Magazine Novels of Pauline Hopkins*. The Schomberg Library of Nineteenth-Century Black Women Writers. New York: Oxford UP, 1988.

Huggins, Nathan. *Harlem Renaissance*. New York: Oxford UP, 1971.

JanMohamed, Abdul R. and David Lloyd. "Toward a Theory of Minority Discourse: What Is To Be Done?" *The Nature and Context of Minority Discourse*. Eds. Abdul R.JanMohamen and David Lloyd. New York: Oxford UP, 1990. 1-16.

Jones, Leroi. "The Changing Same (R&B and New Black Music). *The Black Aesthetic*. Ed. Addison Gayle. New York: Doubleday, 1971. 118-131.

Kent, George. *Blackness and the Adventure of Western Culture*. Chicago: Third World Press, 1972.

Knight, Stephen. *Form and Ideology in Detective Fiction*. Bloomington, IN: Indiana UP, 1980.

Knox, Monsignor Ronald. "A Detective Story Decalogue." *The Art of the Mystery Story: A Collection of Critical Essays*. Ed. Howard Haycraft. New York: Grossett & Dunlap, 1947.

Levine, Lawrence. *Black Culture and Black Consciousness: Afro-American Folk Thought from Slavery to Freedom*. New York: Oxford UP, 1977.

Lewis, David Levering. *When Harlem Was In Vogue*. New York: Oxford UP, 1971.

Lock, Helen. *A Case of Mis-Taken Identity: Detective Undercurrents in Recent African- American Fiction*. New York: Peter Lang Publishing. 1994.

McCluskey, Joseph. "Introduction." *The City of Refuge: The Collected Stories of Rudolph Fisher*. Columbia, MO: U of Missouri P, 1987. (xi-xxxix).

Morson, Gary. "Who Speaks for Bakhtin?" *Bakhtin: Essays and Dialogues on His Work*. Ed. Gary Morson. Chicago: U of Chicago P, 1981. 1-19.

Mosley, Walter. *Devil in a Blue Dress*. New York: Pocket. 1991.

O'Connor, Mary. "Subject, Voice, and Women in Some Contemporary Black American Women's Writing." *Feminism, Bakhtin, and the Dialogic*. Eds.

Dale M. Bauer and S.Jaret. McKinstry, New York: State University of New York P, 1991.199- 218.

Peterson, Dale R. "Response and Call: The African American Dialogue with Bakhtin and What it Signifies." *Bakhtin in Contexts: Across the Disciplines*. Eds. Amy Mandelker and Caryl Emerson. Evanston, Illinois: Northwestern UP, 1991. 89-98.

Sayers, Dorothy L. "Aristotle on Detective Fiction." *Detective Fiction: A Collection of Critical Essays*. Ed. Robin Winks. Englewood Cliffs, NJ: Prentice-Hall, 1980. 25-34.

Soitos, Stephen. The *Blues Detective: A Study of African American Detective Fiction*. Amherst, MA: U of Massachusetts P, 1996.

Tate, Claudia. *Domestic Allegories of Political Desire: The Black Heroine's Text at the Turn of the Century*. New York: Oxford UP, 1992.

Todorov, Tzvetan. "The Typology of Detective Fiction." *The Poetics of Prose*. Trans. Richard Howard. Ithaca, NY: Cornell UP, 1977.

Van Dine, S.S. "Twenty Rules for Writing Detective Stories." *The Art of the Mystery Story: A Collection of Critical Essays*. Ed. Howard Haycraft. New York: Grossett & Dunlap, 1947.

Worth, Robert. "*Nigger Heaven* and the Harlem Renaissance." *African American Review* 39.3 (Fall 1995): 461-474.

Index